Vol. 3

Created by
Shoko Conami

HAMBURG // LONDON // LOS ANGELES // TOKYO

7695

GRAPHIC BOOK
CON
V.3

Shinobi Life 3
Created by Shoko Conami

Translation - Lori Riser
English Adaptation - Ysabet Reinhardt MacFarlane
Copy Editor - Daniella Orihuela-Gruber
Retouch and Lettering - Star Print Brokers
Production Artist - Rui Kyo
Graphic Designer - Chelsea Windlinger

Editor - Lillian Diaz-Przybyl
Print Production Manager - Lucas Rivera
Managing Editor - Vy Nguyen
Senior Designer - Louis Csontos
Director of Sales and Manufacturing - Allyson De Simone
Associate Publisher - Marco F. Pavia
President and C.O.O. - John Parker
C.E.O. and Chief Creative Officer - Stu Levy

A **TOKYOPOP**® Manga

TOKYOPOP and 🐸 are trademarks or registered trademarks of TOKYOPOP Inc.

TOKYOPOP Inc.
5900 Wilshire Blvd. Suite 2000
Los Angeles, CA 90036

E-mail: info@TOKYOPOP.com
Come visit us online at www.TOKYOPOP.com

B&T 10.00 12/09

ISBN: 978-1-4278-1162-2

First TOKYOPOP printing: November 2009
10 9 8 7 6 5 4 3 2 1
Printed in the USA

A12005 556063

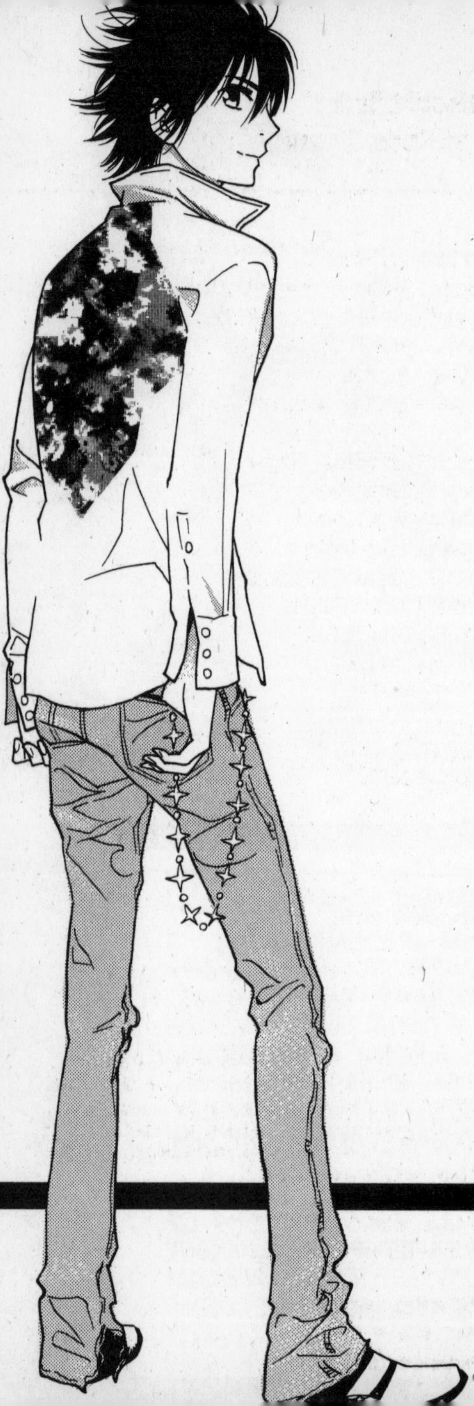

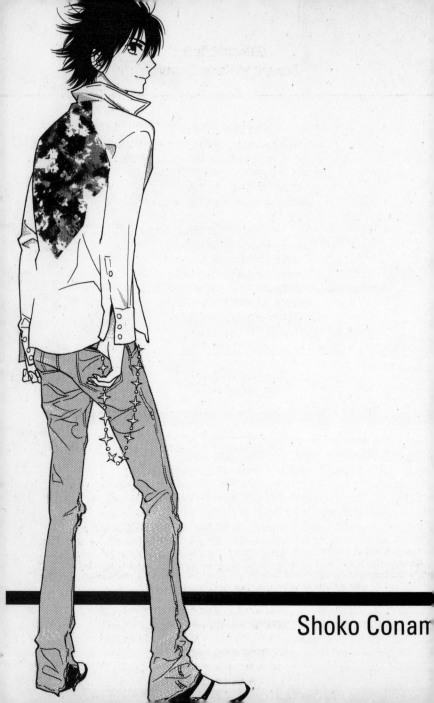

Shoko Conam

Summary & Character Introduction

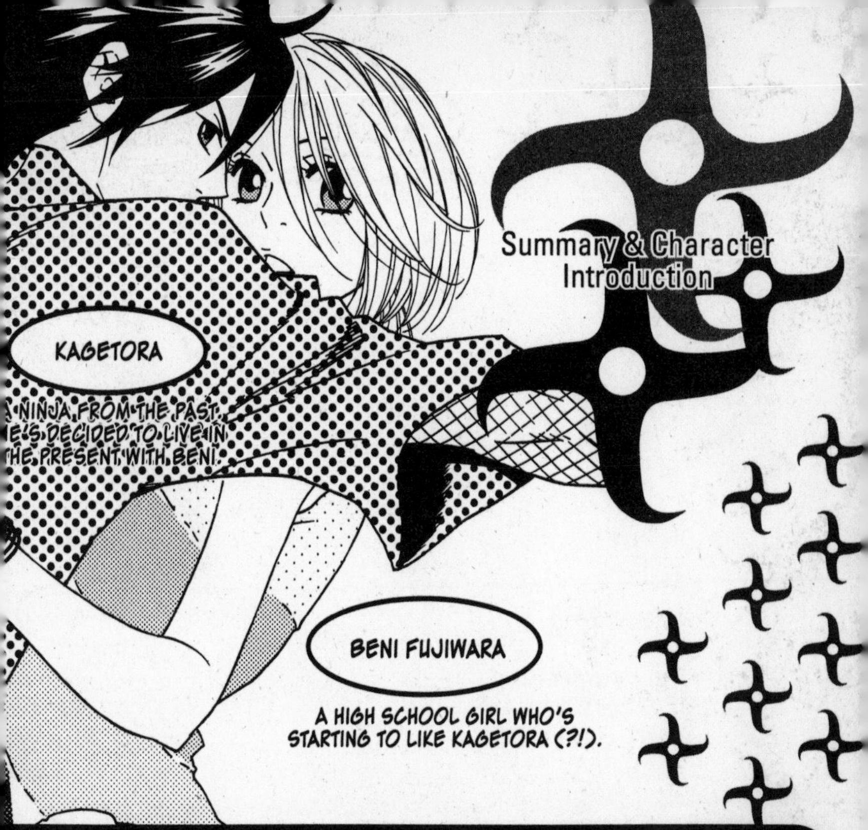
KAGETORA
NINJA FROM THE PAST. E'S DECIDED TO LIVE IN HE PRESENT WITH BENI.
BENI FUJIWARA
A HIGH SCHOOL GIRL WHO'S STARTING TO LIKE KAGETORA (?!).

BENI FUJIWARA, A HIGH SCHOOL GIRL WHO LONGS FOR DEATH AS REVENGE AGAINST HER ARROGANT FATHER, IS UNEXPECTEDLY RESCUED ONE DAY WHEN SHE FALLS OFF A BUILDING. HER SAVIOR? A NINJA NAMED KAGETORA, WHO FALLS FROM THE SKY AT THE RIGHT MOMENT. KAGETORA CALLS BENI "BENI HIME," AND DEVOTES HIMSELF TO PROTECTING HER AT ANY COST...AT FIRST BECAUSE HE MISTAKES HER FOR HER OWN ANCESTOR, WHO LOOKED EXACTLY LIKE HER. YES, KAGETORA IS A NINJA WHO HAS TRAVELED THROUGH TIME FROM THE PAST!

AS TIME PASSES, BENI GRADUALLY BECOMES FOND OF KAGETORA AFTER HE REPEATEDLY SAVES HER FROM DANGER AND PLEDGES HIS ETERNAL LOYALTY. SHE TRIES TO PRETEND TO BE BENI HIME FOR HIM, AND THEY SLOWLY BECOME CLOSER AND CLOSER.

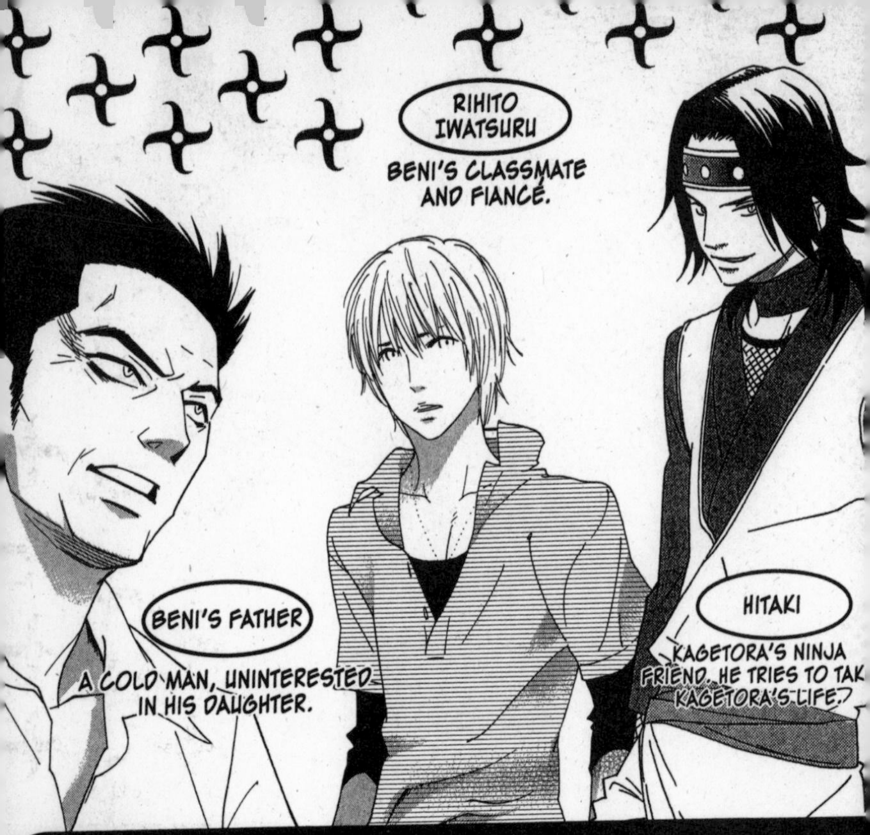
RIHITO IWATSURU
BENI'S CLASSMATE AND FIANCÉ.
HITAKI
KAGETORA'S NINJA FRIEND. HE TRIES TO TAK KAGETORA'S LIFE.
BENI'S FATHER
A COLD MAN, UNINTERESTED IN HIS DAUGHTER.

BUT WHEN THE PAIR UNEXPECTEDLY TRAVELS BACK TO KAGETORA'S TIME, HE RUNS INTO THE REAL BENI HIME AND REALIZES THAT THE TWO WOMEN ARE NOT THE SAME PERSON. AFTER BENI HIME TELLS KAGETORA THAT SHE WANTS TO LIVE AS A NORMAL VILLAGER, HE LOSES HIS PURPOSE IN LIFE. WHEN A FELLOW NINJA, HITAKI, BRANDS HIM A TRAITOR AND TRIES TO KILL HIM, KAGETORA DECIDES TO RETURN TO THE PRESENT WITH BENI AND LIVE WITH HER.

THINGS SEEM TO BE GOING SMOOTHLY FOR BENI AND KAGETORA'S FLEDGLING ROMANCE, BUT THAT COMES TO AN ABRUPT END WHEN BENI'S FATHER REVEALS THAT BENI ALREADY HAS A FIANCÉ--RIHITO IWATSURU! BENI TRIES TO RUIN THE ARRANGED ENGAGEMENT, BUT RIHITO SENDS HITAKI IN TO GET RID OF KAGETORA. HITAKI KIDNAPS KAGETORA, AND...

CONTENTS

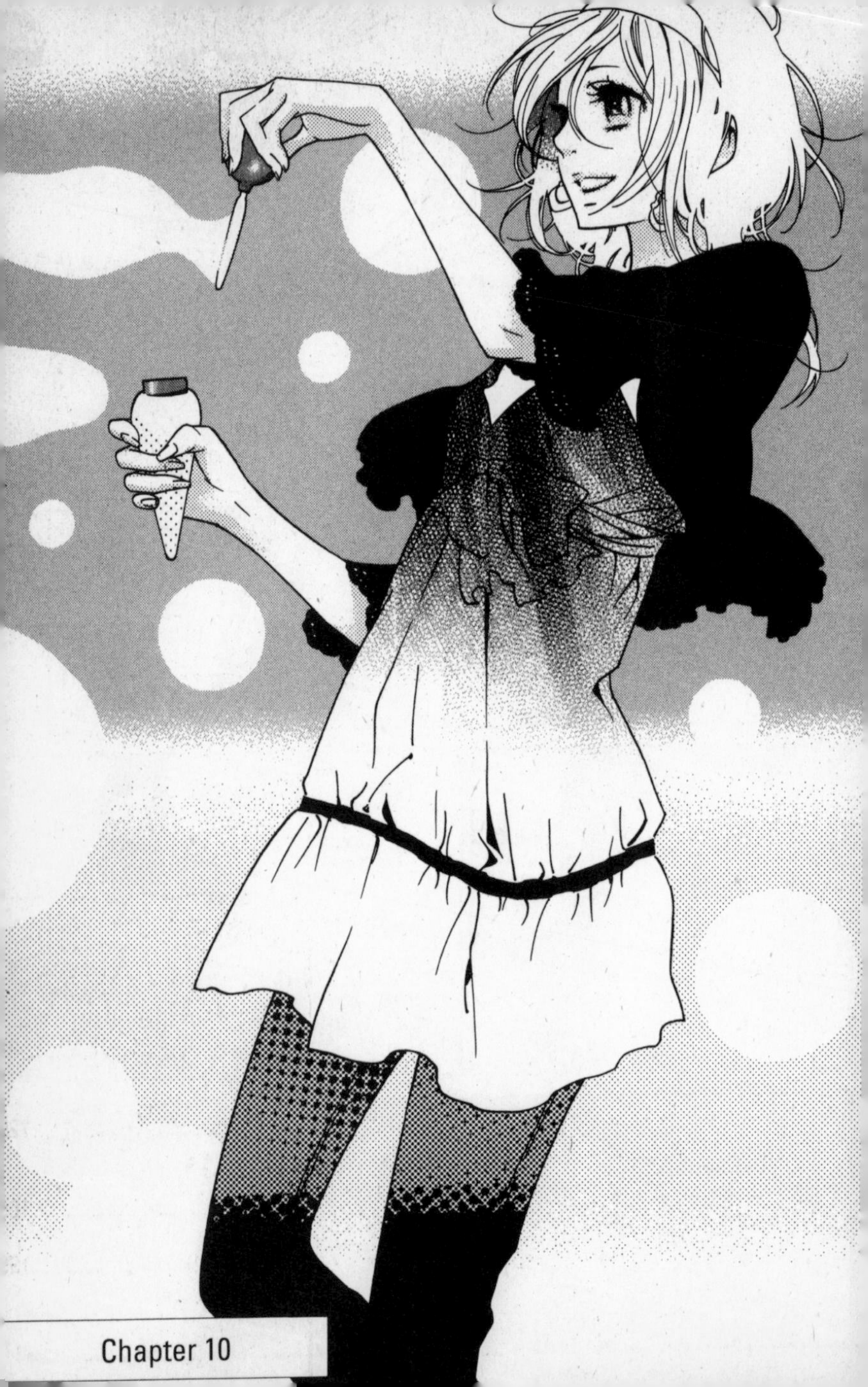

Chapter 10

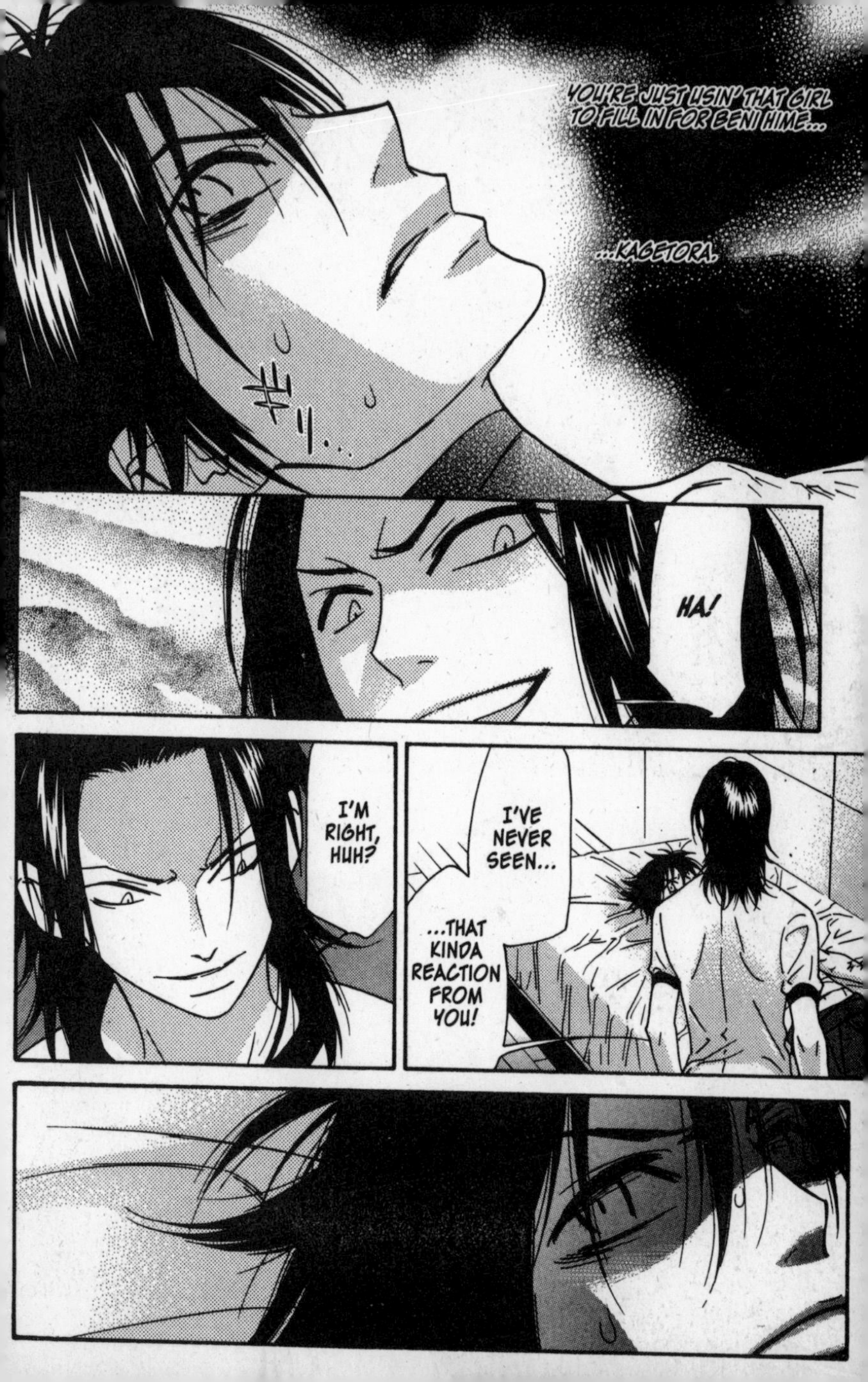
YOU'RE JUST USIN' THAT GIRL TO FILL IN FOR BENI HIME...
...KAGETORA.
HA!
I'VE NEVER SEEN...
...THAT KINDA REACTION FROM YOU!
I'M RIGHT, HUH?

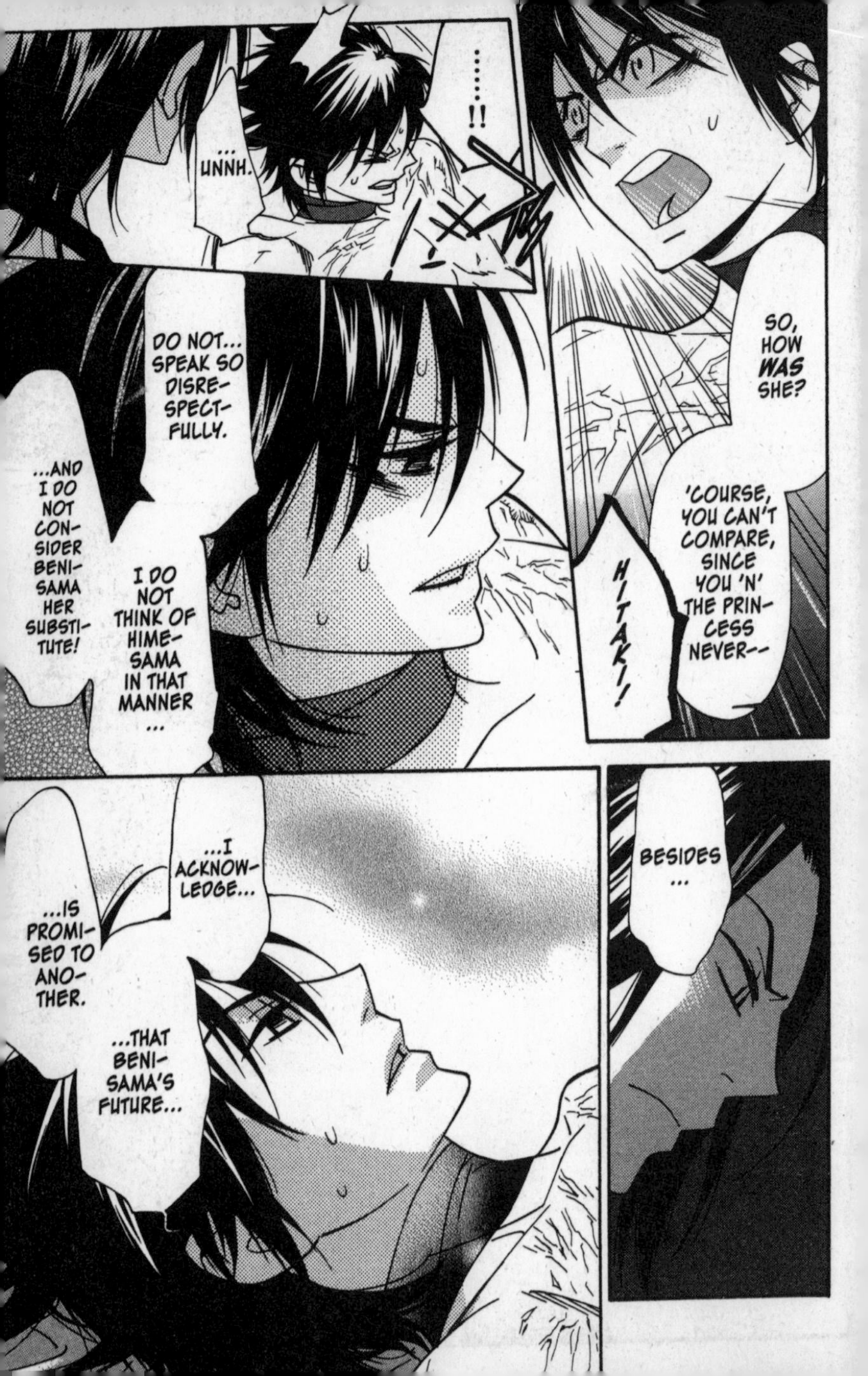
SO, HOW *WAS* SHE?
'COURSE, YOU CAN'T COMPARE, SINCE YOU 'N' THE PRINCESS NEVER--
HITAKI!
......!!
...UNNH.
DO NOT... SPEAK SO DISRESPECTFULLY.
I DO NOT THINK OF HIME-SAMA IN THAT MANNER...
...AND I DO NOT CONSIDER BENI-SAMA HER SUBSTITUTE!
BESIDES...
...I ACKNOWLEDGE...
...THAT BENI-SAMA'S FUTURE...
...IS PROMISED TO ANOTHER.

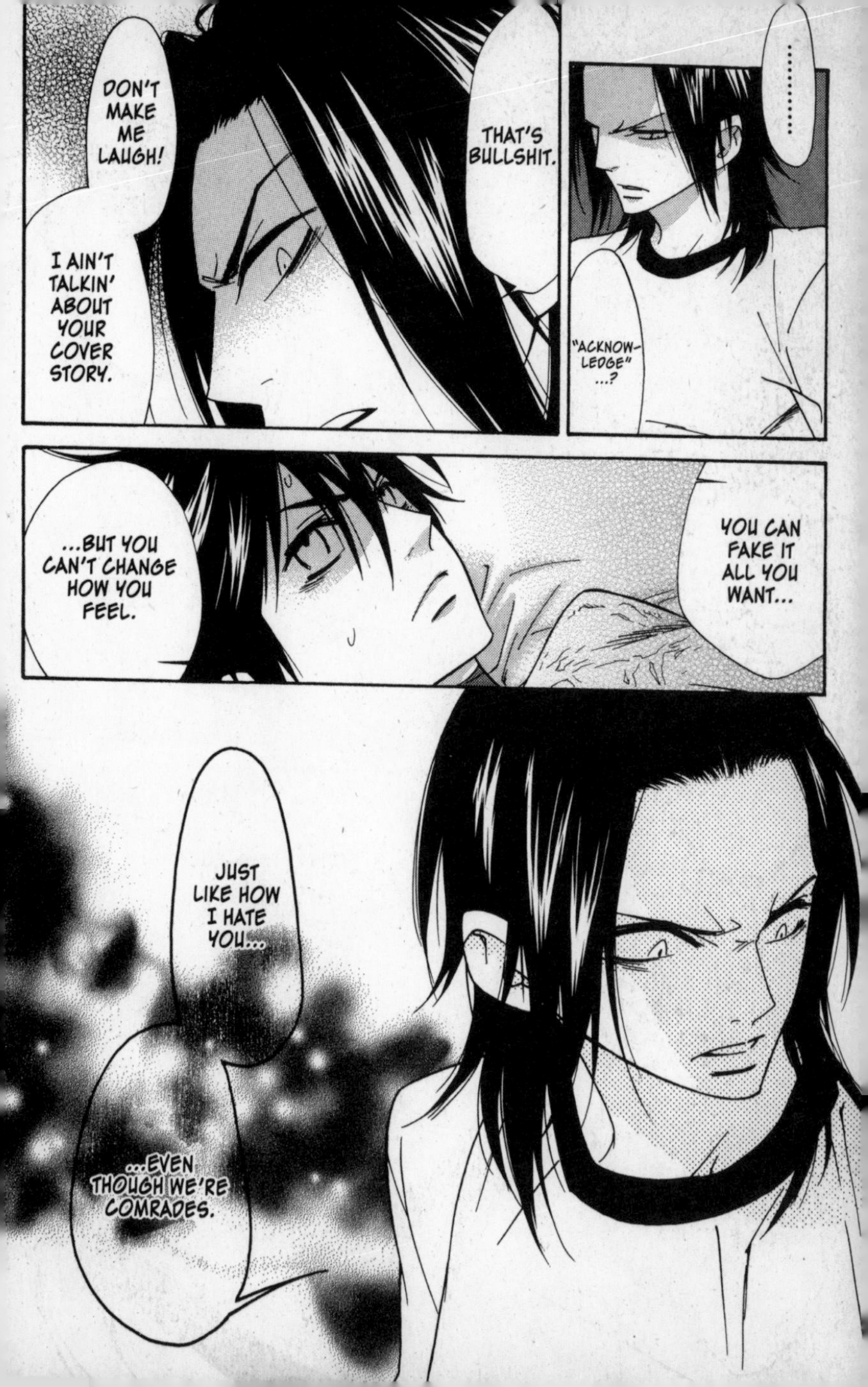
......
"ACKNOWLEDGE" ...?
THAT'S BULLSHIT.
DON'T MAKE ME LAUGH!
I AIN'T TALKIN' ABOUT YOUR COVER STORY.
YOU CAN FAKE IT ALL YOU WANT...
...BUT YOU CAN'T CHANGE HOW YOU FEEL.
JUST LIKE HOW I HATE YOU...
...EVEN THOUGH WE'RE COMRADES.

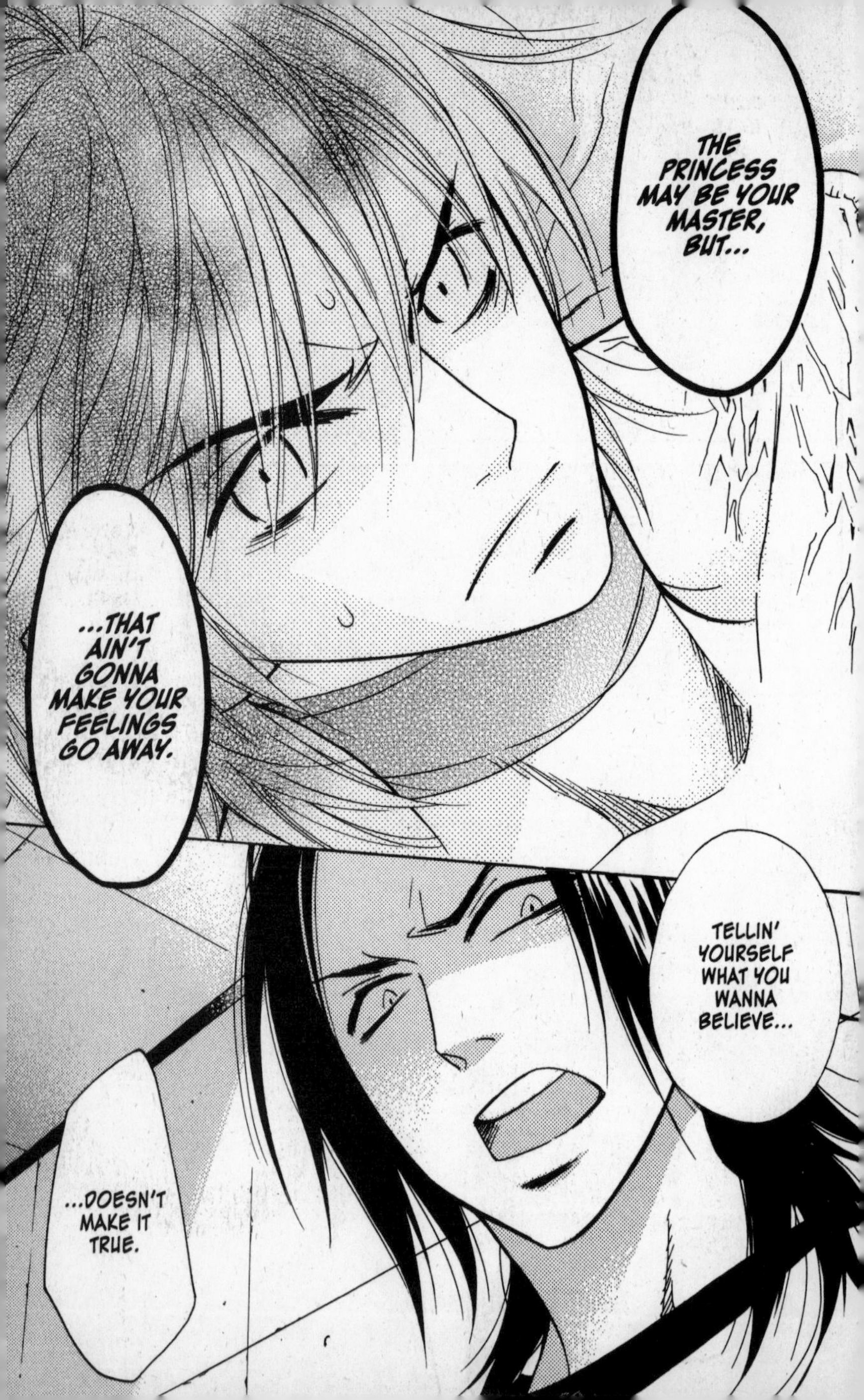
THE PRINCESS MAY BE YOUR MASTER, BUT...
...THAT AIN'T GONNA MAKE YOUR FEELINGS GO AWAY.
TELLIN' YOURSELF WHAT YOU WANNA BELIEVE...
...DOESN'T MAKE IT TRUE.

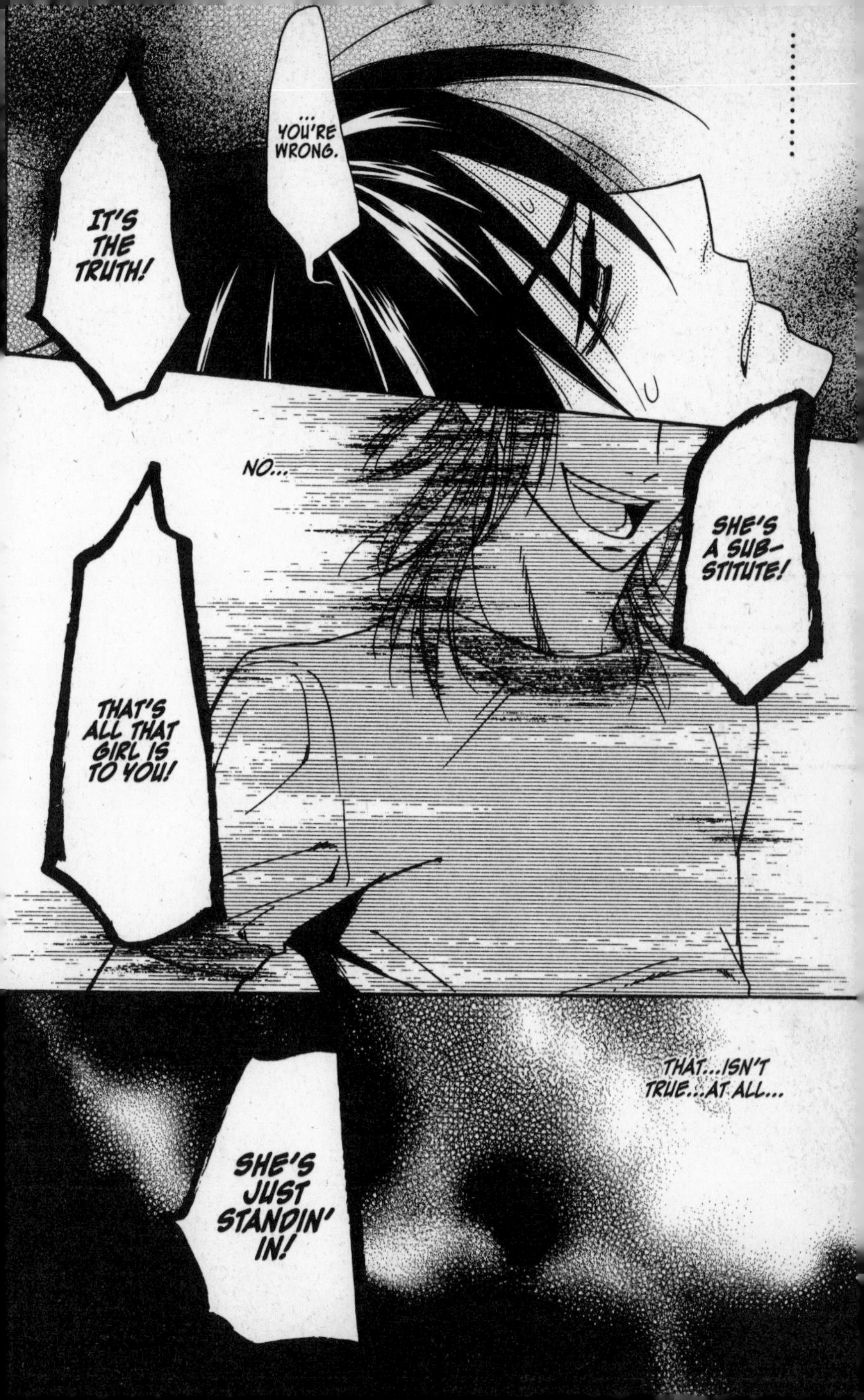
......
...YOU'RE WRONG.
IT'S THE TRUTH!
SHE'S A SUB-STITUTE!
NO...
THAT'S ALL THAT GIRL IS TO YOU!
THAT...ISN'T TRUE...AT ALL...
SHE'S JUST STANDIN' IN!

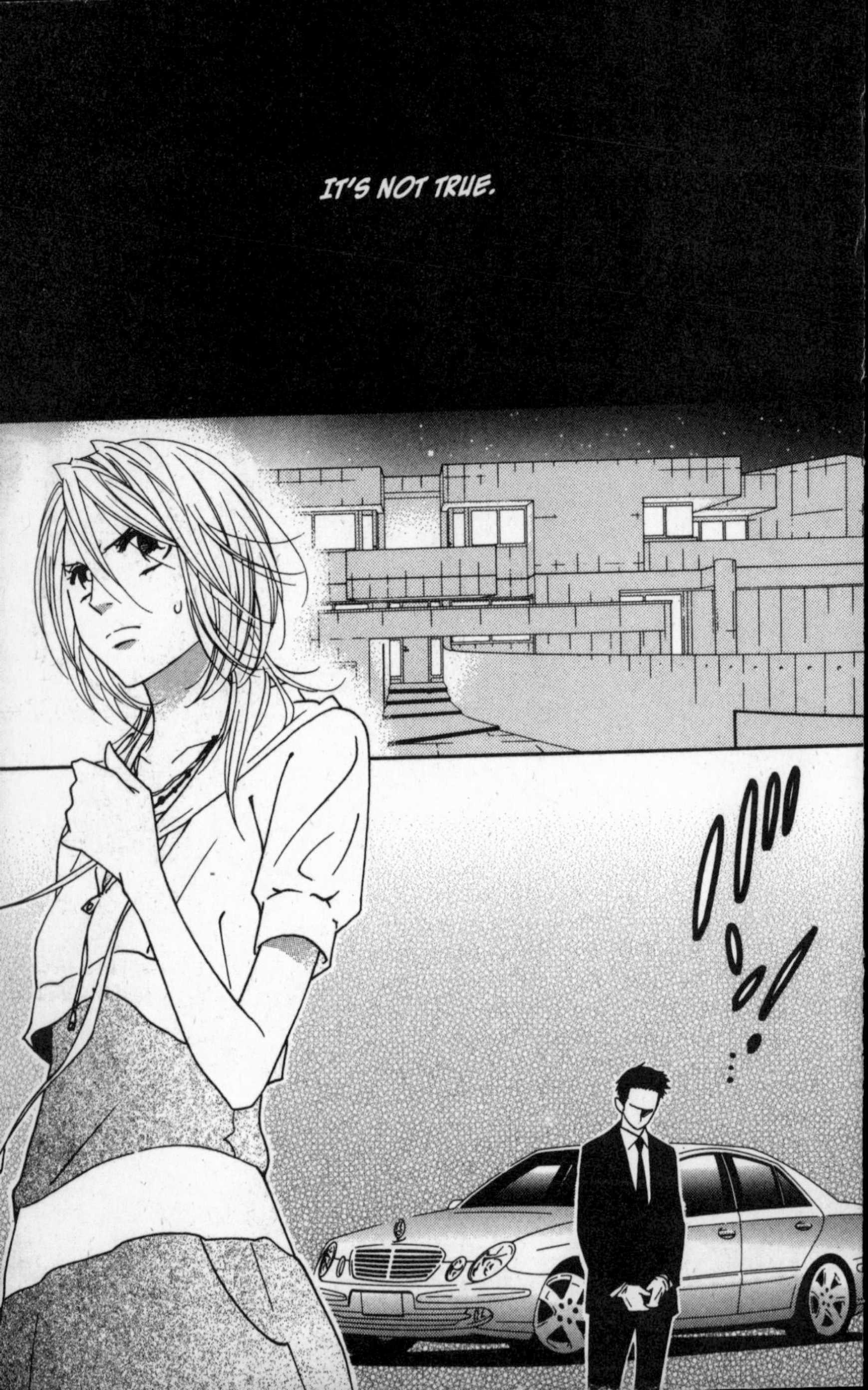
IT'S NOT TRUE.

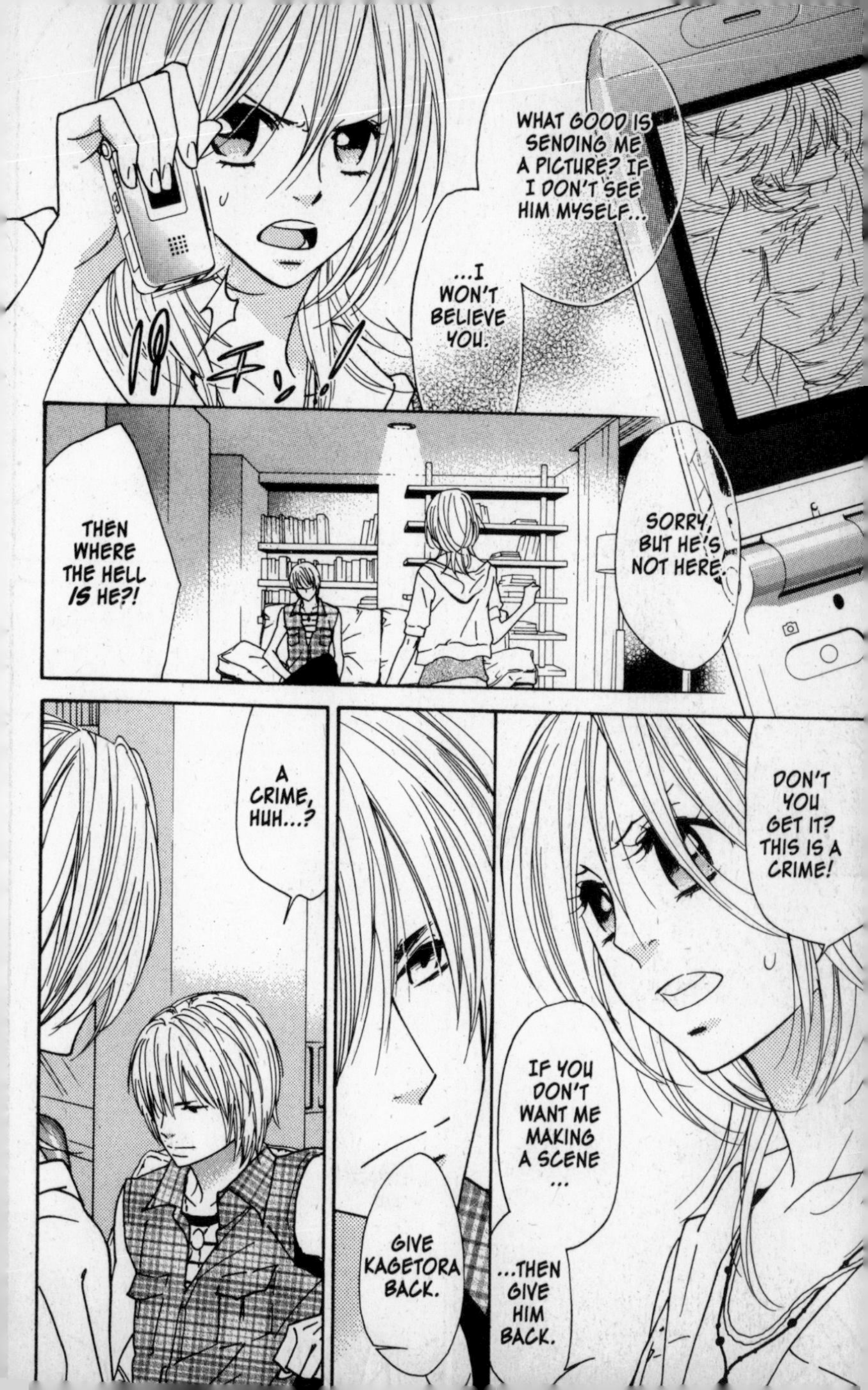
WHAT GOOD IS SENDING ME A PICTURE? IF I DON'T SEE HIM MYSELF...
...I WON'T BELIEVE YOU.
SORRY, BUT HE'S NOT HERE.
THEN WHERE THE HELL *IS* HE?!
DON'T YOU GET IT? THIS IS A CRIME!
IF YOU DON'T WANT ME MAKING A SCENE ...
...THEN GIVE HIM BACK.
GIVE KAGETORA BACK.
A CRIME, HUH...?

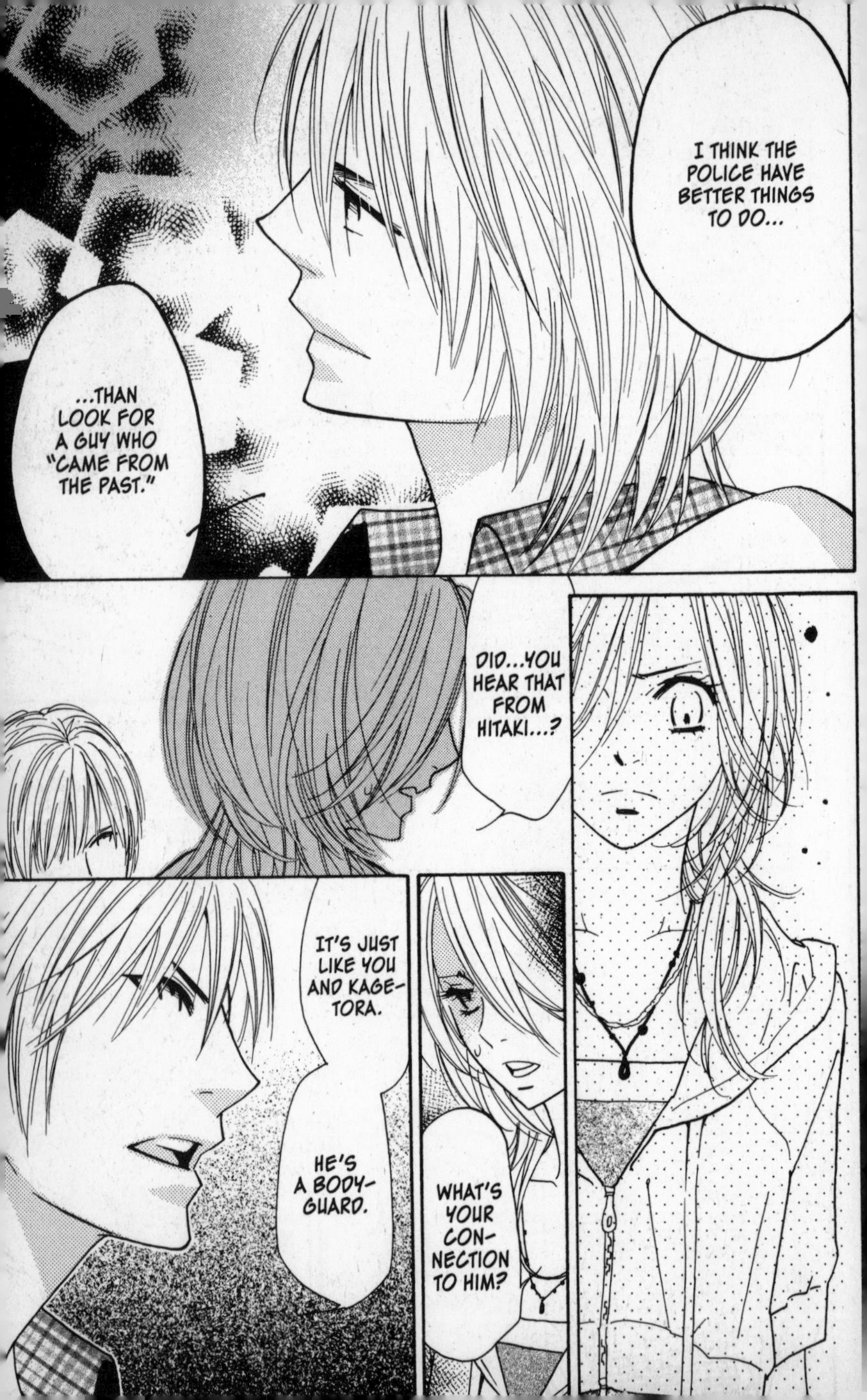
I THINK THE POLICE HAVE BETTER THINGS TO DO...
...THAN LOOK FOR A GUY WHO "CAME FROM THE PAST."
DID...YOU HEAR THAT FROM HITAKI...?
WHAT'S YOUR CON-NECTION TO HIM?
IT'S JUST LIKE YOU AND KAGE-TORA.
HE'S A BODY-GUARD.

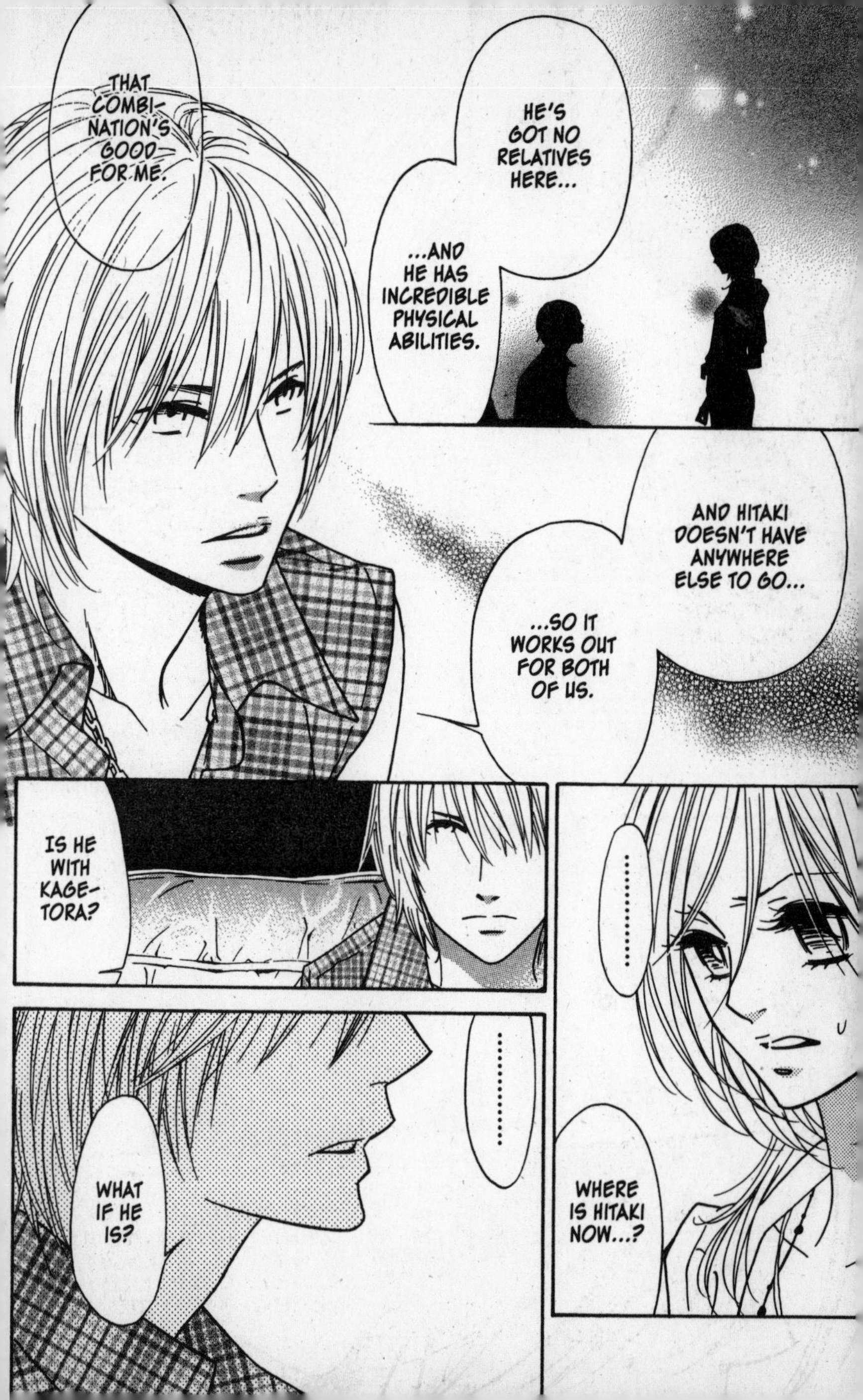
HE'S GOT NO RELATIVES HERE...
...AND HE HAS INCREDIBLE PHYSICAL ABILITIES.
AND HITAKI DOESN'T HAVE ANYWHERE ELSE TO GO...
...SO IT WORKS OUT FOR BOTH OF US.
THAT COMBINATION'S GOOD FOR ME.
......
WHERE IS HITAKI NOW...?
IS HE WITH KAGE-TORA?
......
WHAT IF HE IS?

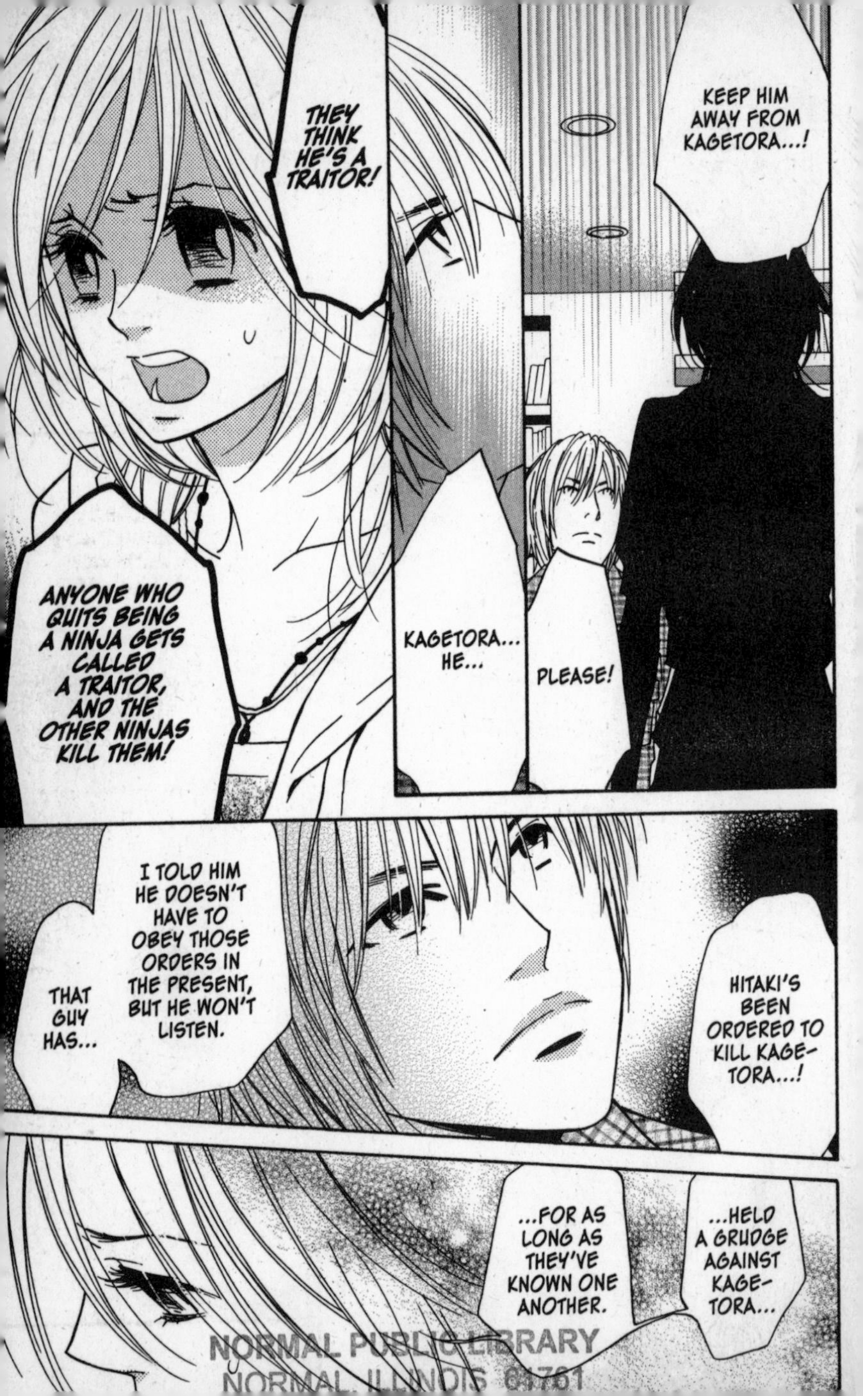
KEEP HIM AWAY FROM KAGETORA...!
PLEASE!
KAGETORA... HE...
THEY THINK HE'S A TRAITOR!
ANYONE WHO QUITS BEING A NINJA GETS CALLED A TRAITOR, AND THE OTHER NINJAS KILL THEM!
HITAKI'S BEEN ORDERED TO KILL KAGE-TORA...!
I TOLD HIM HE DOESN'T HAVE TO OBEY THOSE ORDERS IN THE PRESENT, BUT HE WON'T LISTEN.
THAT GUY HAS...
...HELD A GRUDGE AGAINST KAGE-TORA...
...FOR AS LONG AS THEY'VE KNOWN ONE ANOTHER.

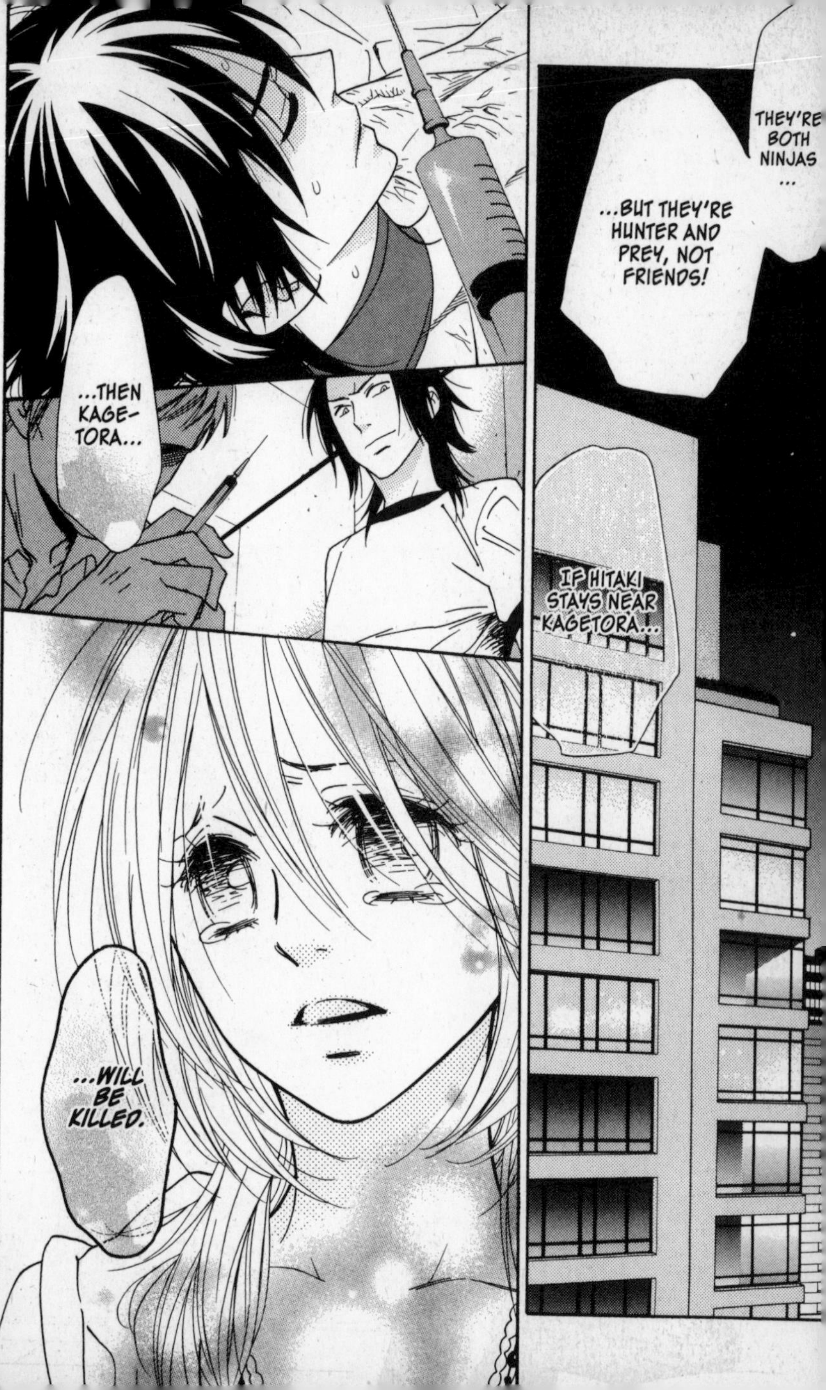
THEY'RE BOTH NINJAS...
...BUT THEY'RE HUNTER AND PREY, NOT FRIENDS!
IF HITAKI STAYS NEAR KAGETORA...
...THEN KAGETORA...
...WILL BE KILLED.

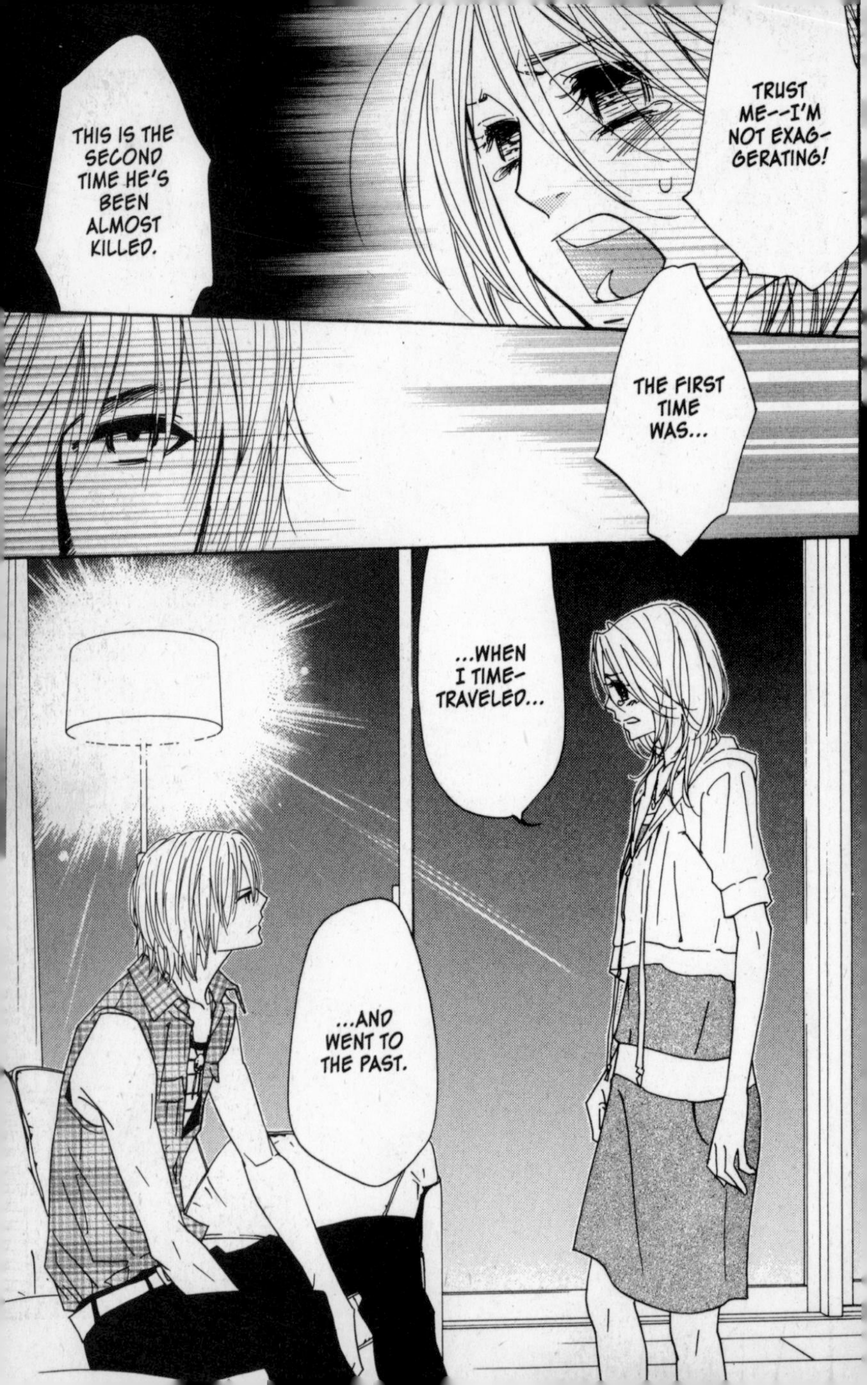
TRUST ME--I'M NOT EXAGGERATING!
THIS IS THE SECOND TIME HE'S BEEN ALMOST KILLED.
THE FIRST TIME WAS...
...WHEN I TIME-TRAVELED...
...AND WENT TO THE PAST.

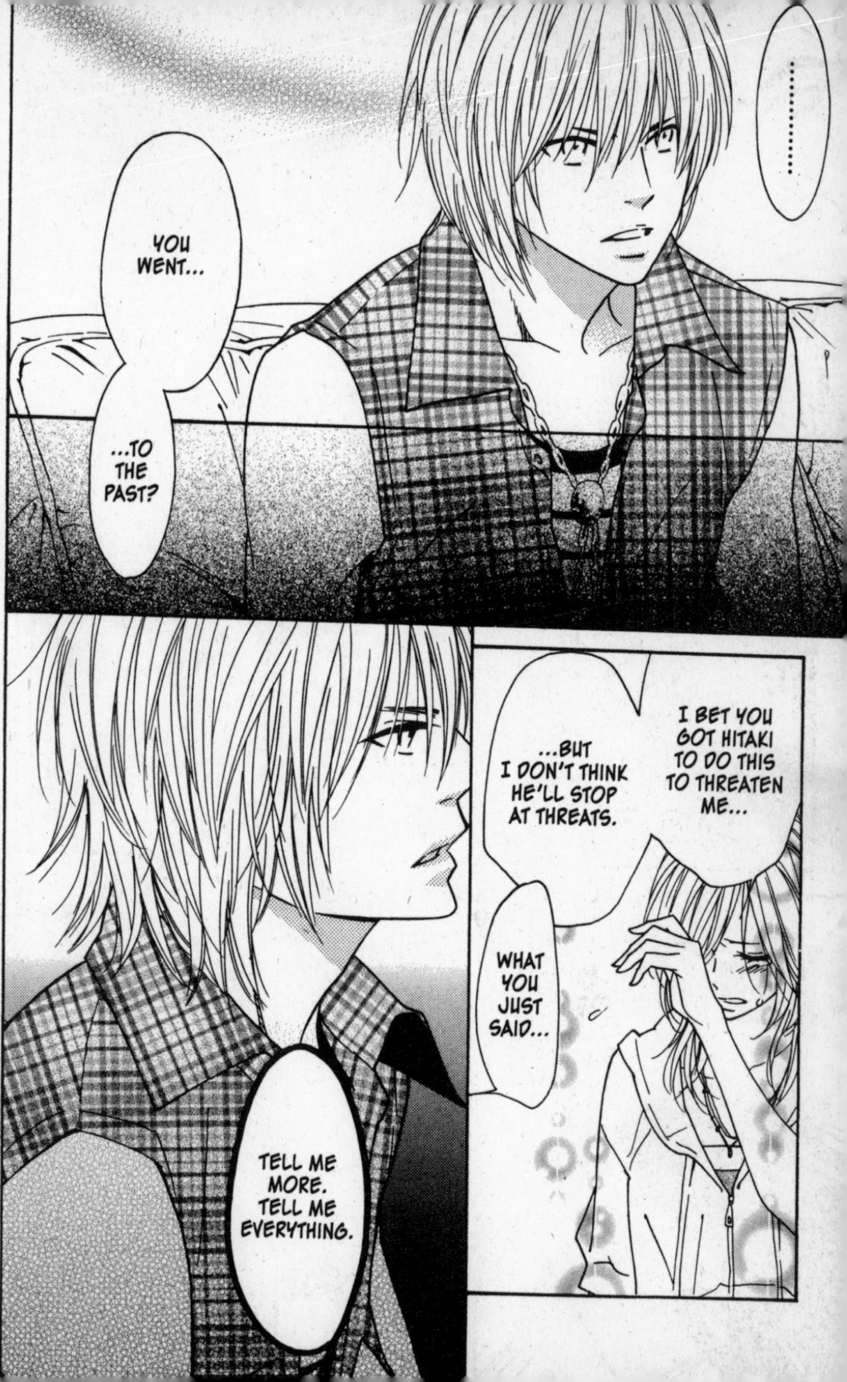
......
YOU WENT...
...TO THE PAST?
I BET YOU GOT HITAKI TO DO THIS TO THREATEN ME...
...BUT I DON'T THINK HE'LL STOP AT THREATS.
WHAT YOU JUST SAID...
TELL ME MORE. TELL ME EVERYTHING.

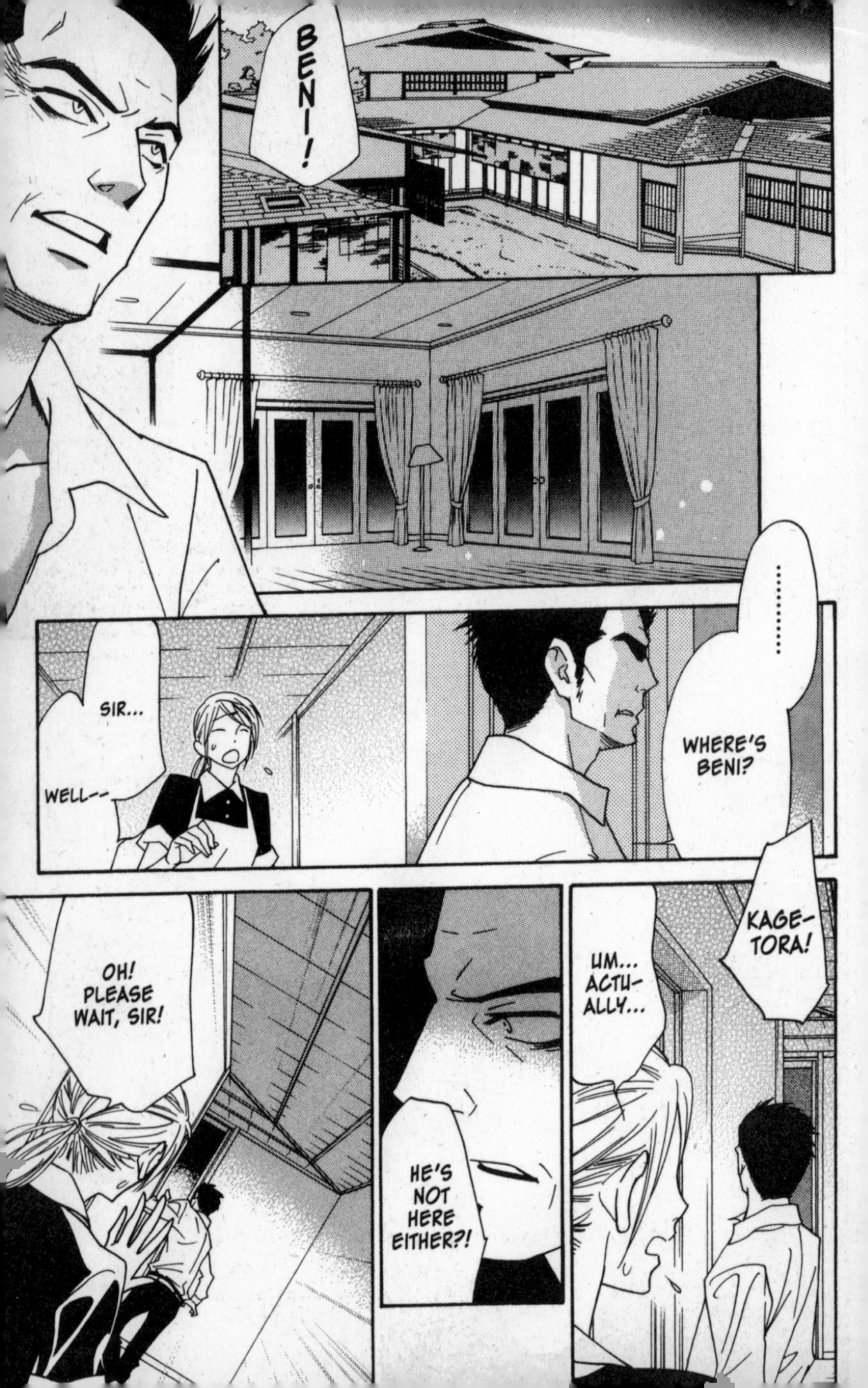
BENI!
......
WHERE'S BENI?
SIR...
WELL--
KAGE-TORA!
UM... ACTU-ALLY...
HE'S NOT HERE EITHER?!
OH! PLEASE WAIT, SIR!

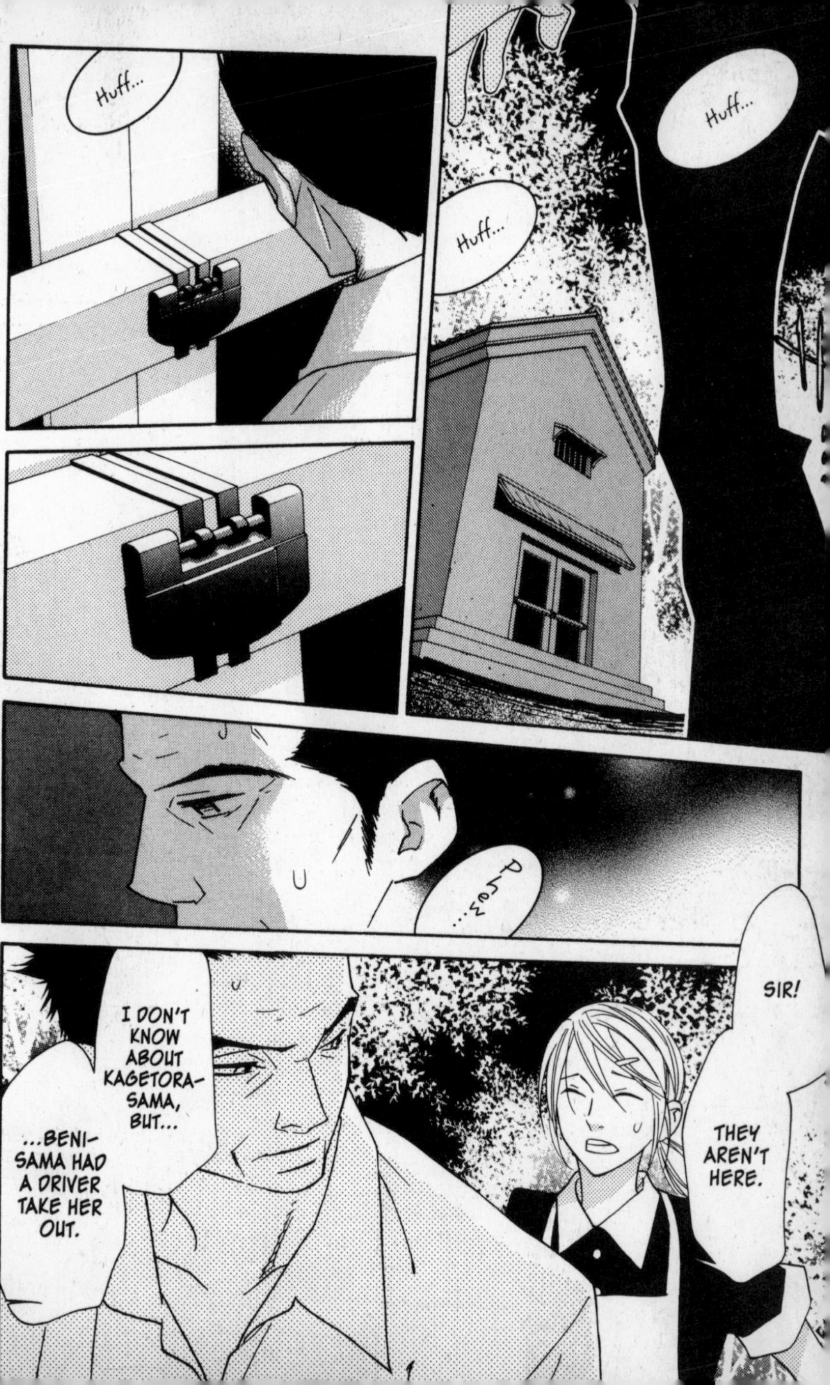
Huff...
Huff...
Huff...
Phew...
SIR!
THEY AREN'T HERE.
I DON'T KNOW ABOUT KAGETORA-SAMA, BUT...
...BENI-SAMA HAD A DRIVER TAKE HER OUT.

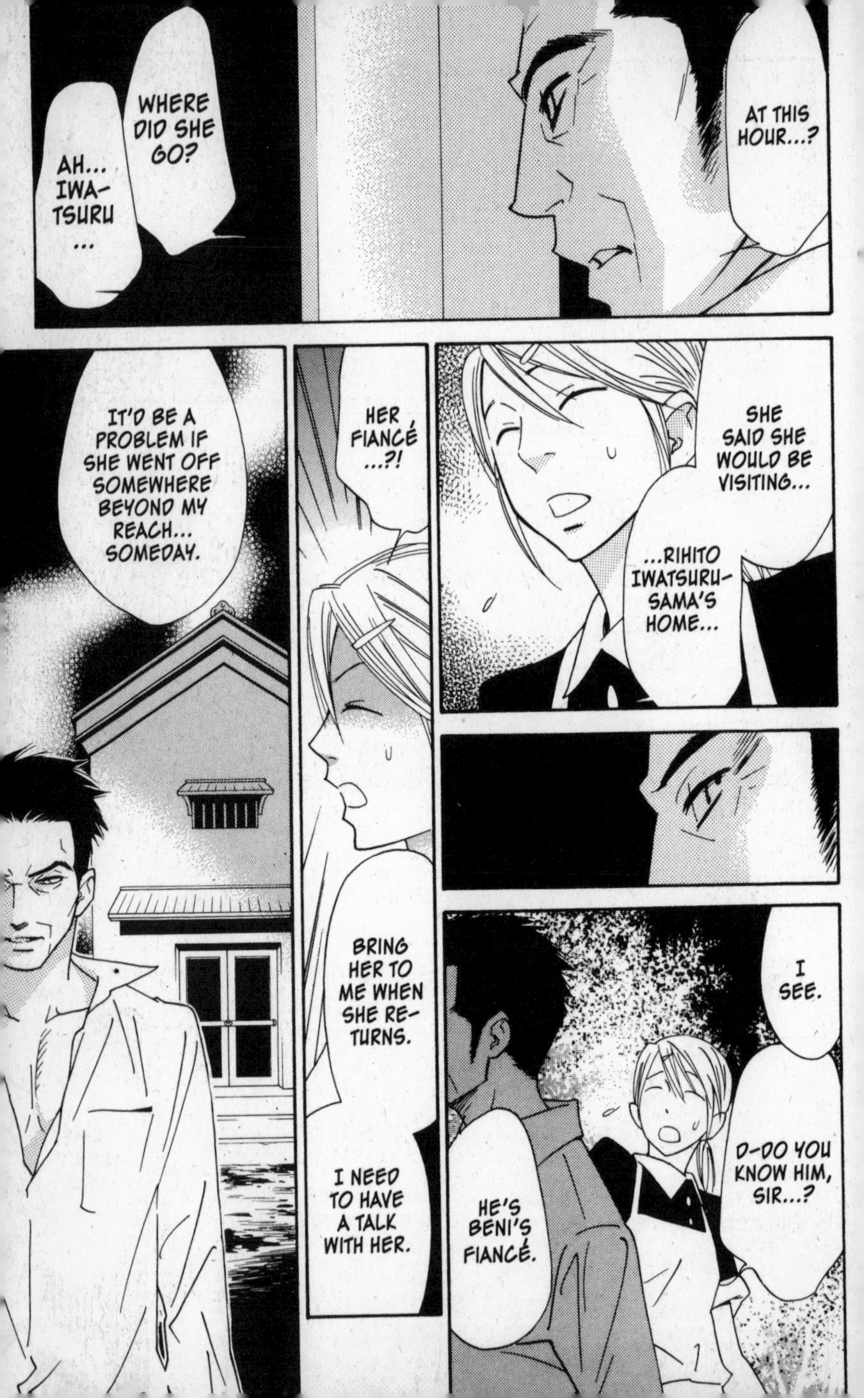
AT THIS HOUR...?
WHERE DID SHE GO?
AH... IWATSURU...
SHE SAID SHE WOULD BE VISITING...
...RIHITO IWATSURU-SAMA'S HOME...
I SEE.
D-DO YOU KNOW HIM, SIR...?
HE'S BENI'S FIANCÉ.
HER FIANCÉ...?!
BRING HER TO ME WHEN SHE RETURNS.
I NEED TO HAVE A TALK WITH HER.
IT'D BE A PROBLEM IF SHE WENT OFF SOMEWHERE BEYOND MY REACH... SOMEDAY.

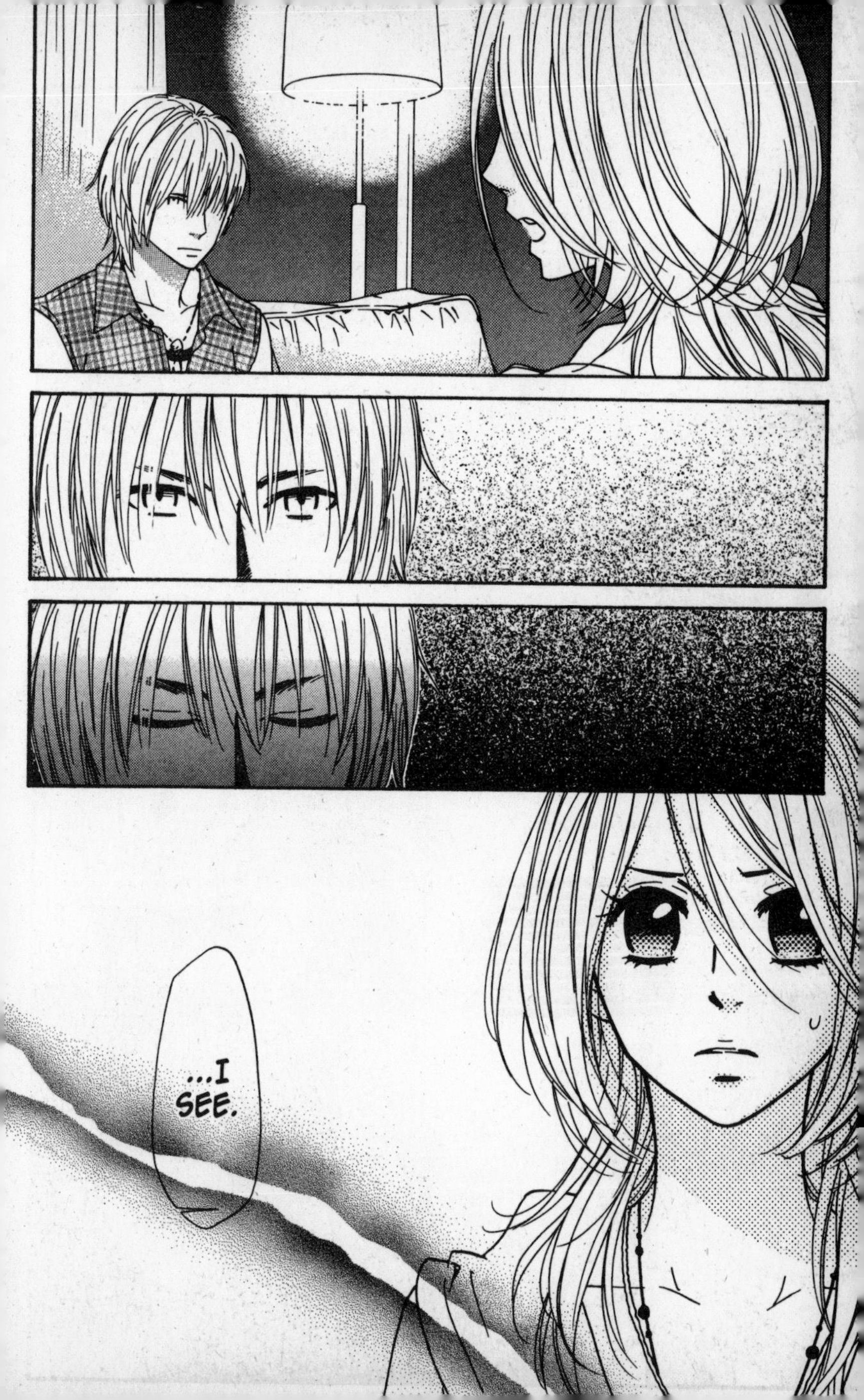
...I SEE.

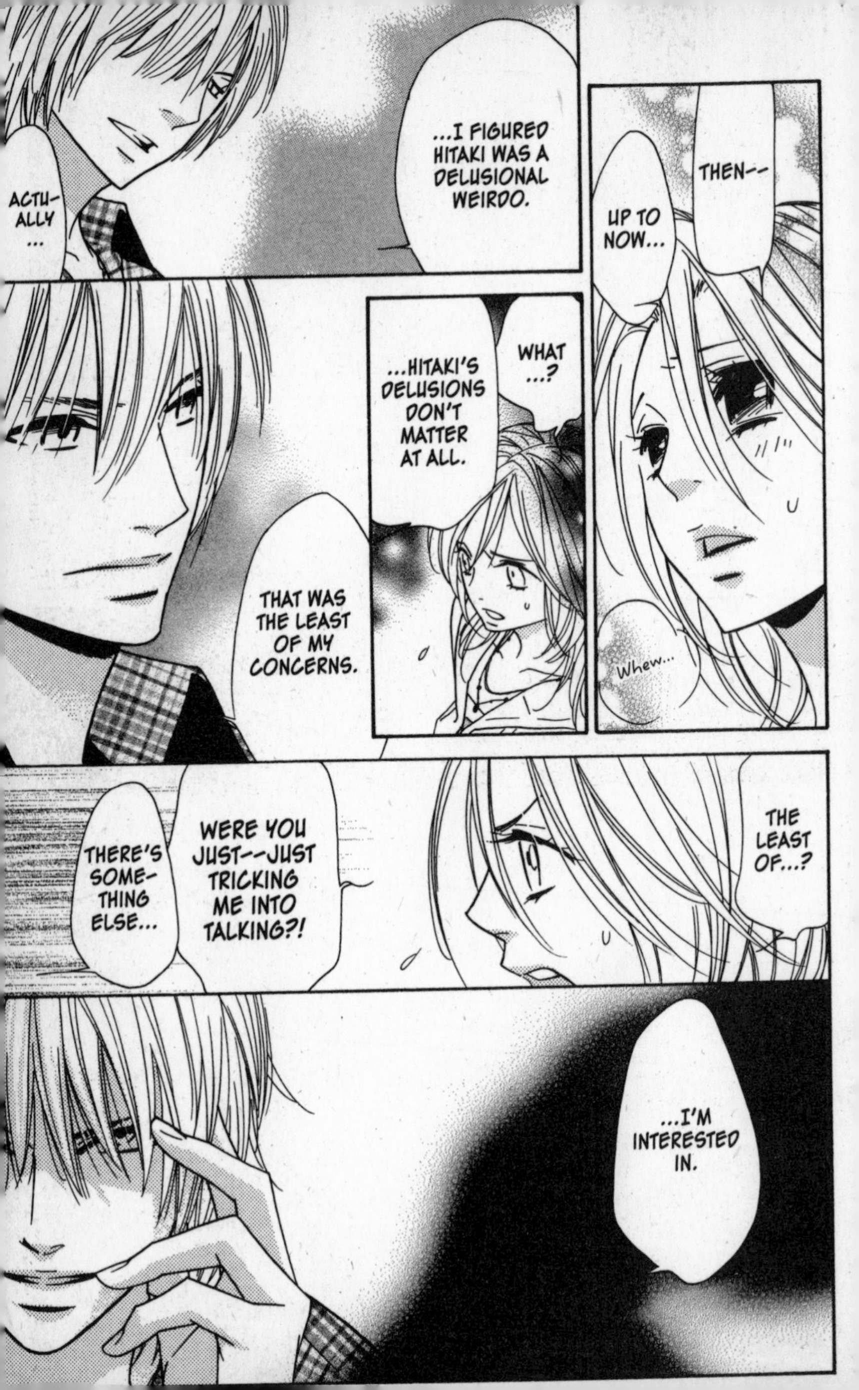

...I FIGURED HITAKI WAS A DELUSIONAL WEIRDO.
ACTU-ALLY ...
THEN--
UP TO NOW...
Whew...
WHAT ...?
...HITAKI'S DELUSIONS DON'T MATTER AT ALL.
THAT WAS THE LEAST OF MY CONCERNS.
THE LEAST OF...?
WERE YOU JUST--JUST TRICKING ME INTO TALKING?!
THERE'S SOME-THING ELSE...
...I'M INTERESTED IN.

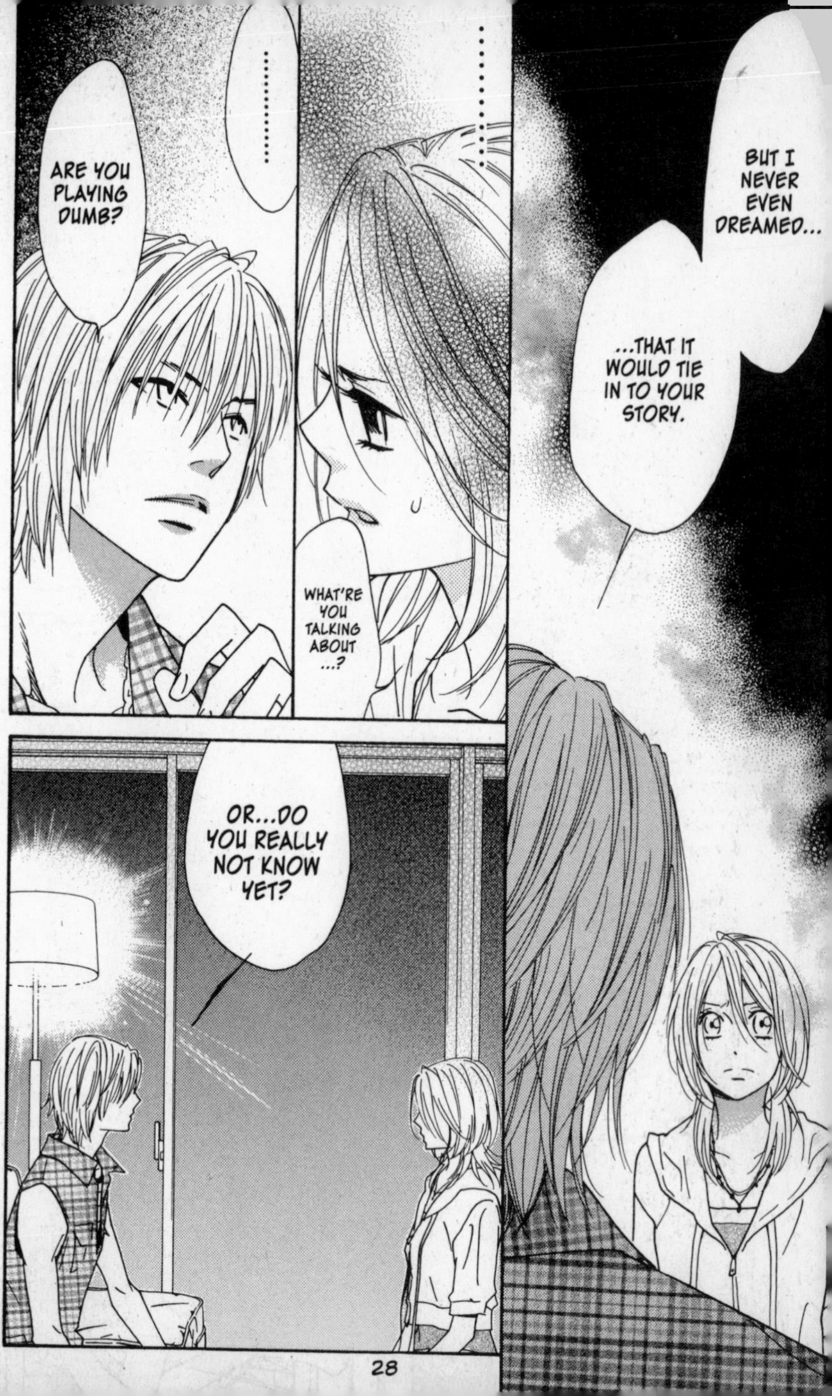
BUT I NEVER EVEN DREAMED...
...THAT IT WOULD TIE IN TO YOUR STORY.
......
WHAT'RE YOU TALKING ABOUT ...?
......
ARE YOU PLAYING DUMB?
OR...DO YOU REALLY NOT KNOW YET?

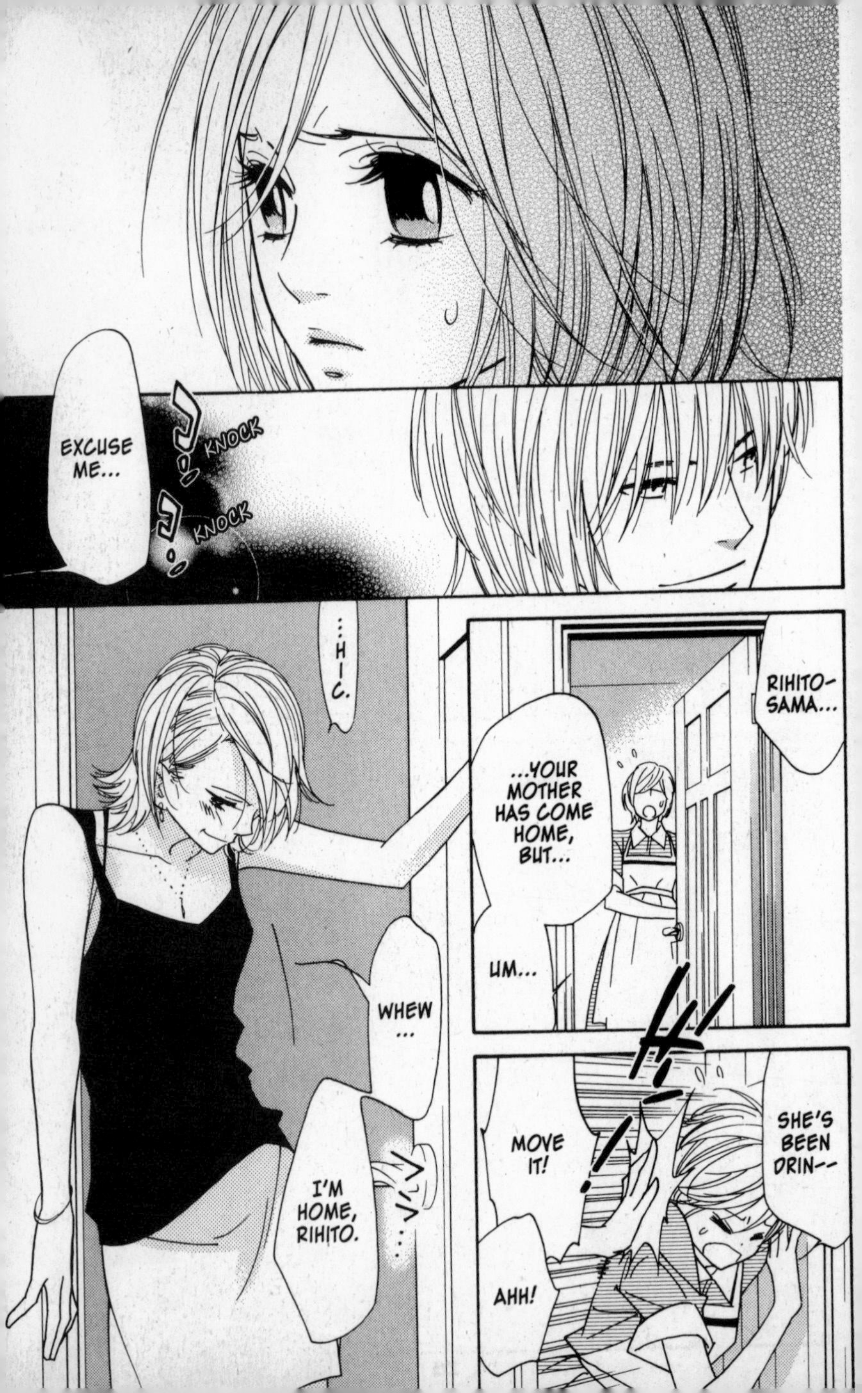
KNOCK
KNOCK
EXCUSE ME...
RIHITO-SAMA...
...YOUR MOTHER HAS COME HOME, BUT...
UM...
SHE'S BEEN DRIN--
MOVE IT!
AHH!
...HIC.
WHEW ...
I'M HOME, RIHITO.

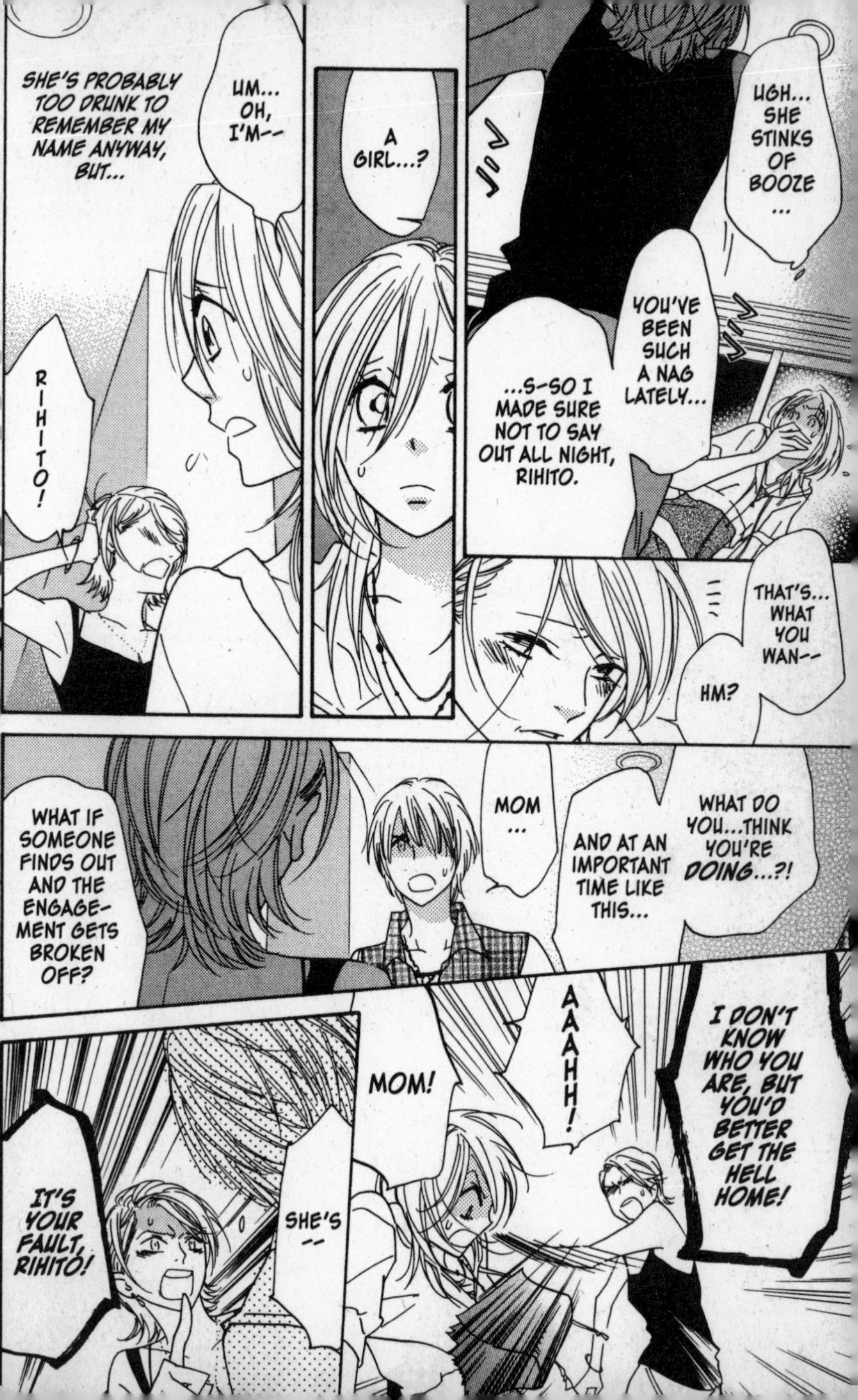
UGH... SHE STINKS OF BOOZE...
YOU'VE BEEN SUCH A NAG LATELY...
...S-SO I MADE SURE NOT TO SAY OUT ALL NIGHT, RIHITO.
THAT'S... WHAT YOU WAN--
HM?
A GIRL...?
UM... OH, I'M--
SHE'S PROBABLY TOO DRUNK TO REMEMBER MY NAME ANYWAY, BUT...
RIHITO!
WHAT DO YOU...THINK YOU'RE DOING...?!
AND AT AN IMPORTANT TIME LIKE THIS...
MOM...
WHAT IF SOMEONE FINDS OUT AND THE ENGAGEMENT GETS BROKEN OFF?
I DON'T KNOW WHO YOU ARE, BUT YOU'D BETTER GET THE HELL HOME!
AAAHH!
MOM!
SHE'S --
IT'S YOUR FAULT, RIHITO!

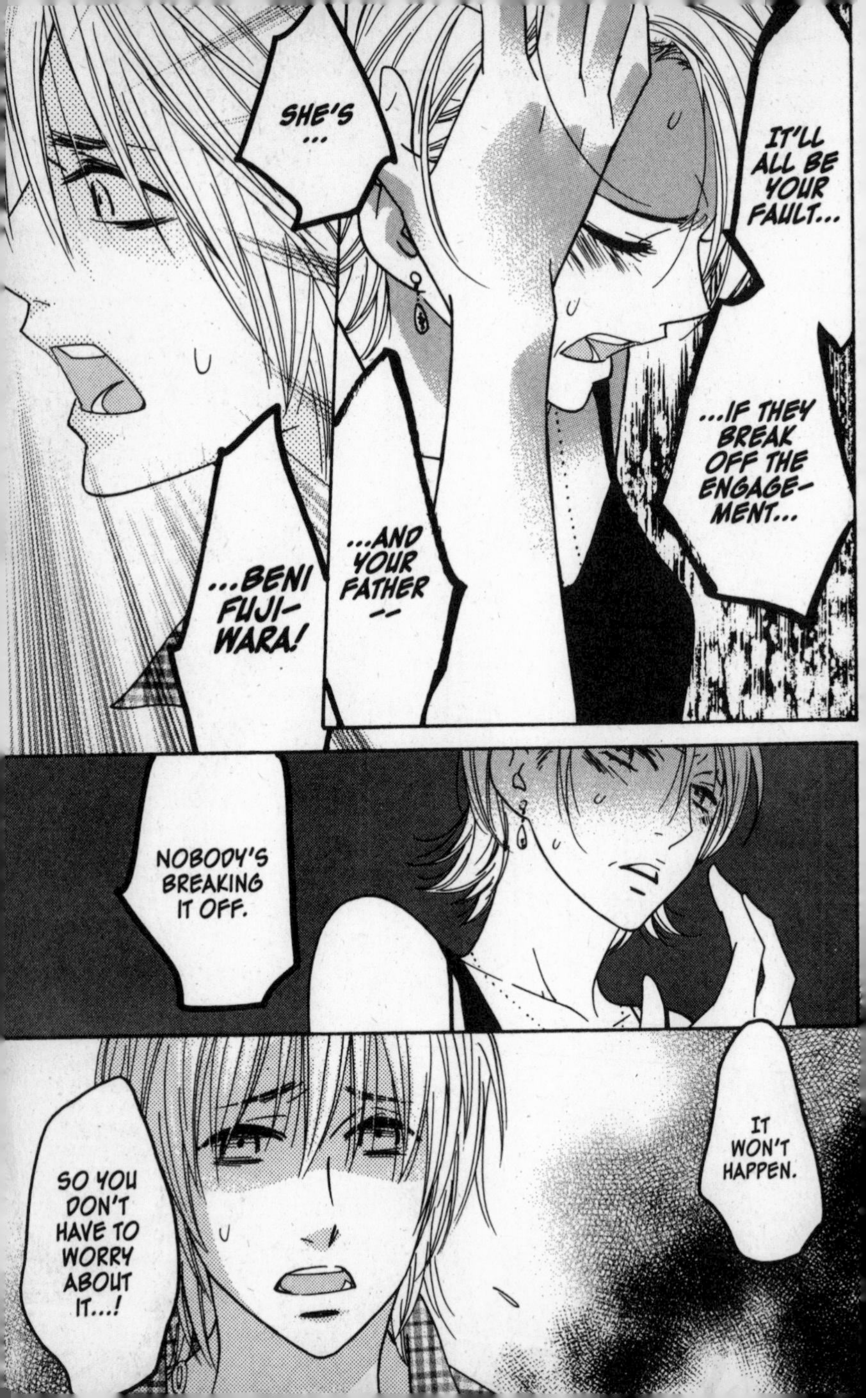
IT'LL ALL BE YOUR FAULT...
...IF THEY BREAK OFF THE ENGAGE-MENT...
...AND YOUR FATHER --
SHE'S ...
...BENI FUJI-WARA!
NOBODY'S BREAKING IT OFF.
IT WON'T HAPPEN.
SO YOU DON'T HAVE TO WORRY ABOUT IT...!

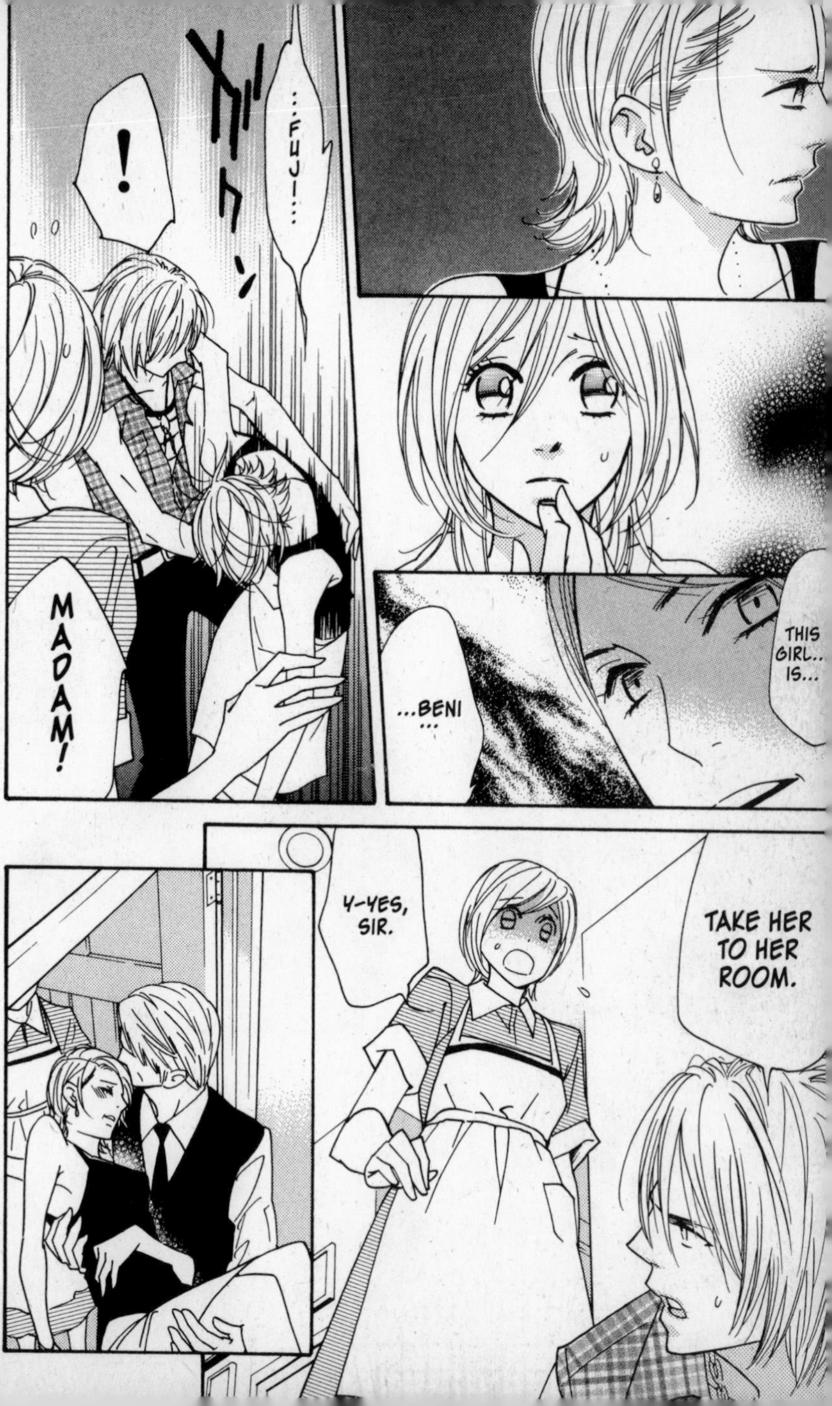

THIS GIRL... IS...
...BENI ...
...FUJI...
!
MADAM!
TAKE HER TO HER ROOM.
Y-YES, SIR.

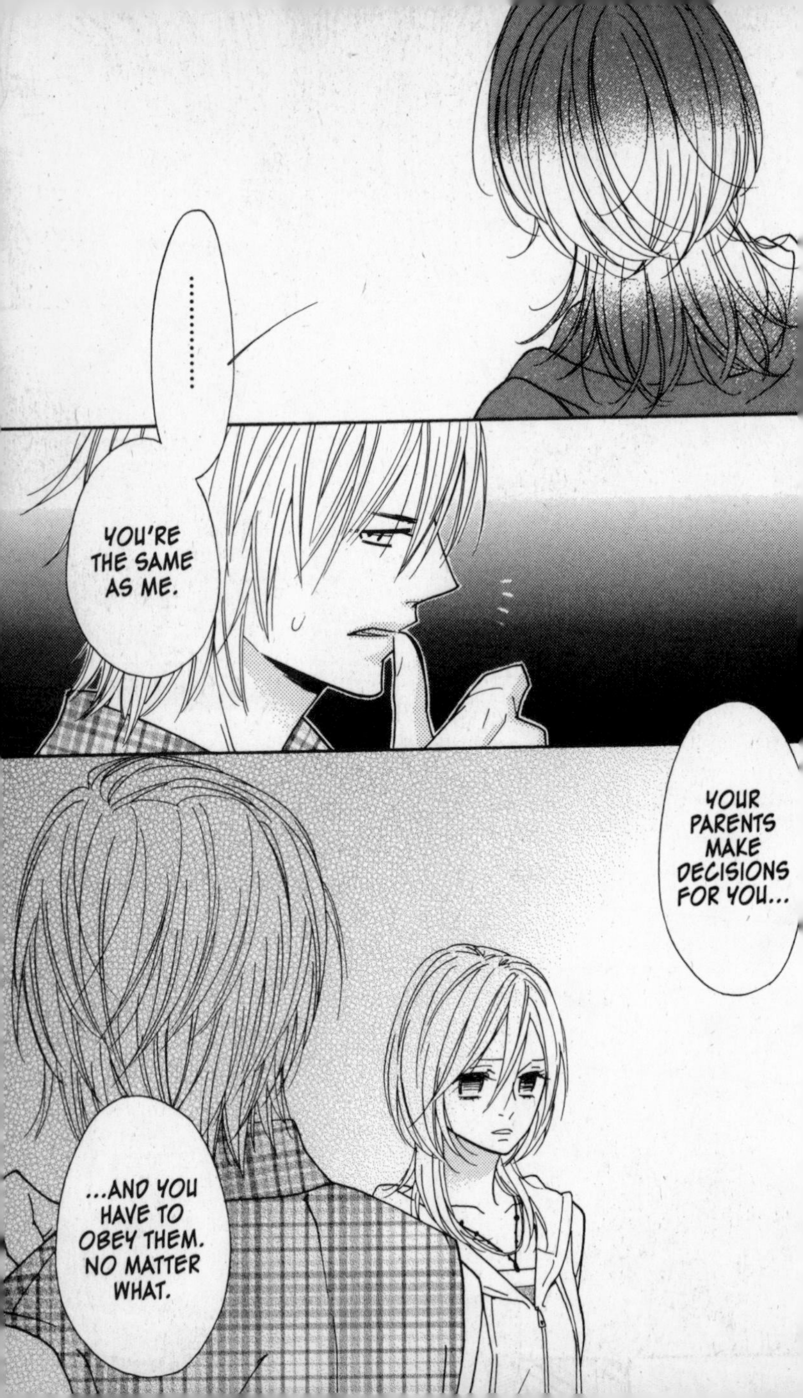
......
YOU'RE THE SAME AS ME.
YOUR PARENTS MAKE DECISIONS FOR YOU...
...AND YOU HAVE TO OBEY THEM. NO MATTER WHAT.

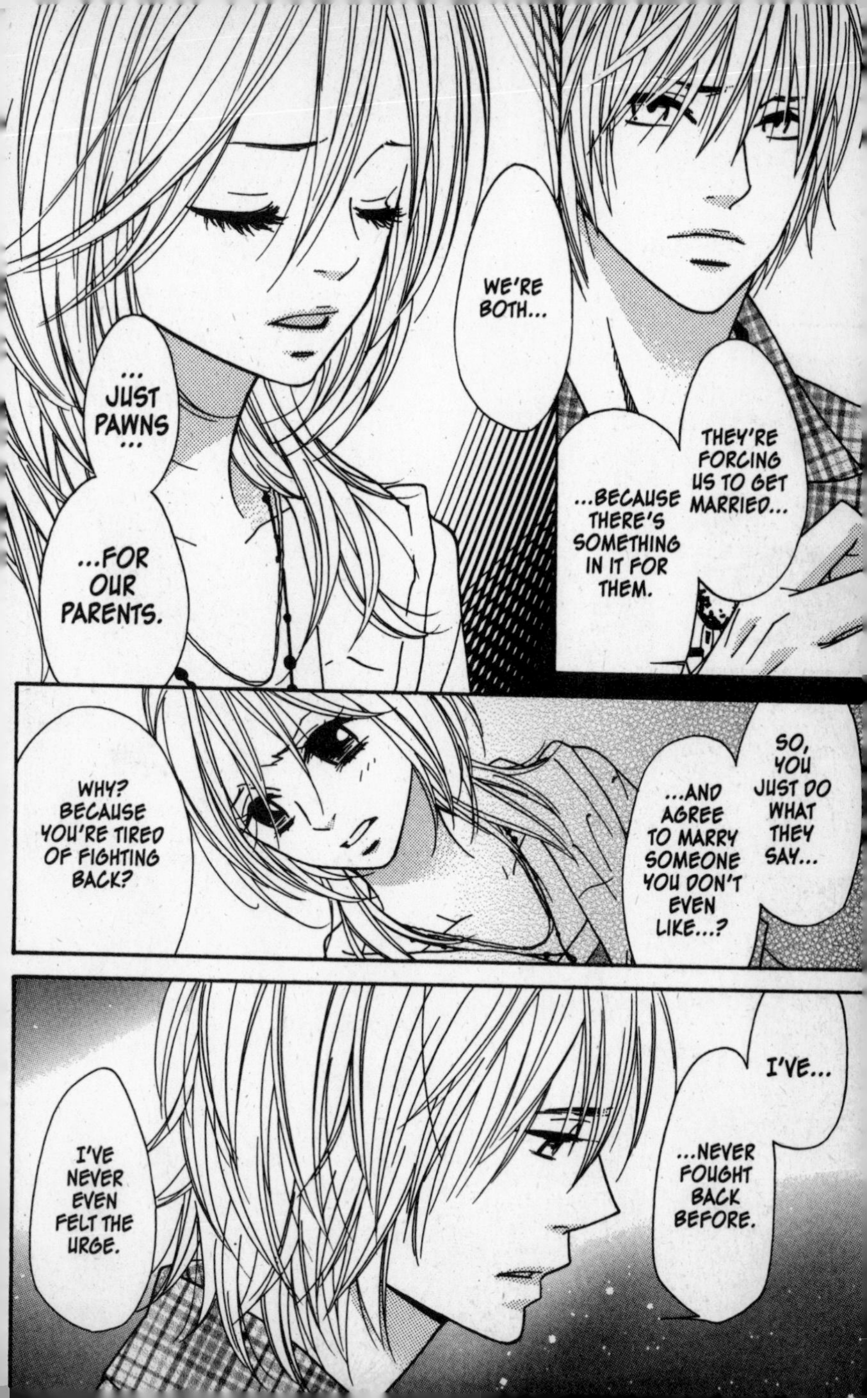
THEY'RE FORCING US TO GET MARRIED...
...BECAUSE THERE'S SOMETHING IN IT FOR THEM.
WE'RE BOTH...
...JUST PAWNS...
...FOR OUR PARENTS.
SO, YOU JUST DO WHAT THEY SAY...
...AND AGREE TO MARRY SOMEONE YOU DON'T EVEN LIKE...?
WHY? BECAUSE YOU'RE TIRED OF FIGHTING BACK?
I'VE...
...NEVER FOUGHT BACK BEFORE.
I'VE NEVER EVEN FELT THE URGE.

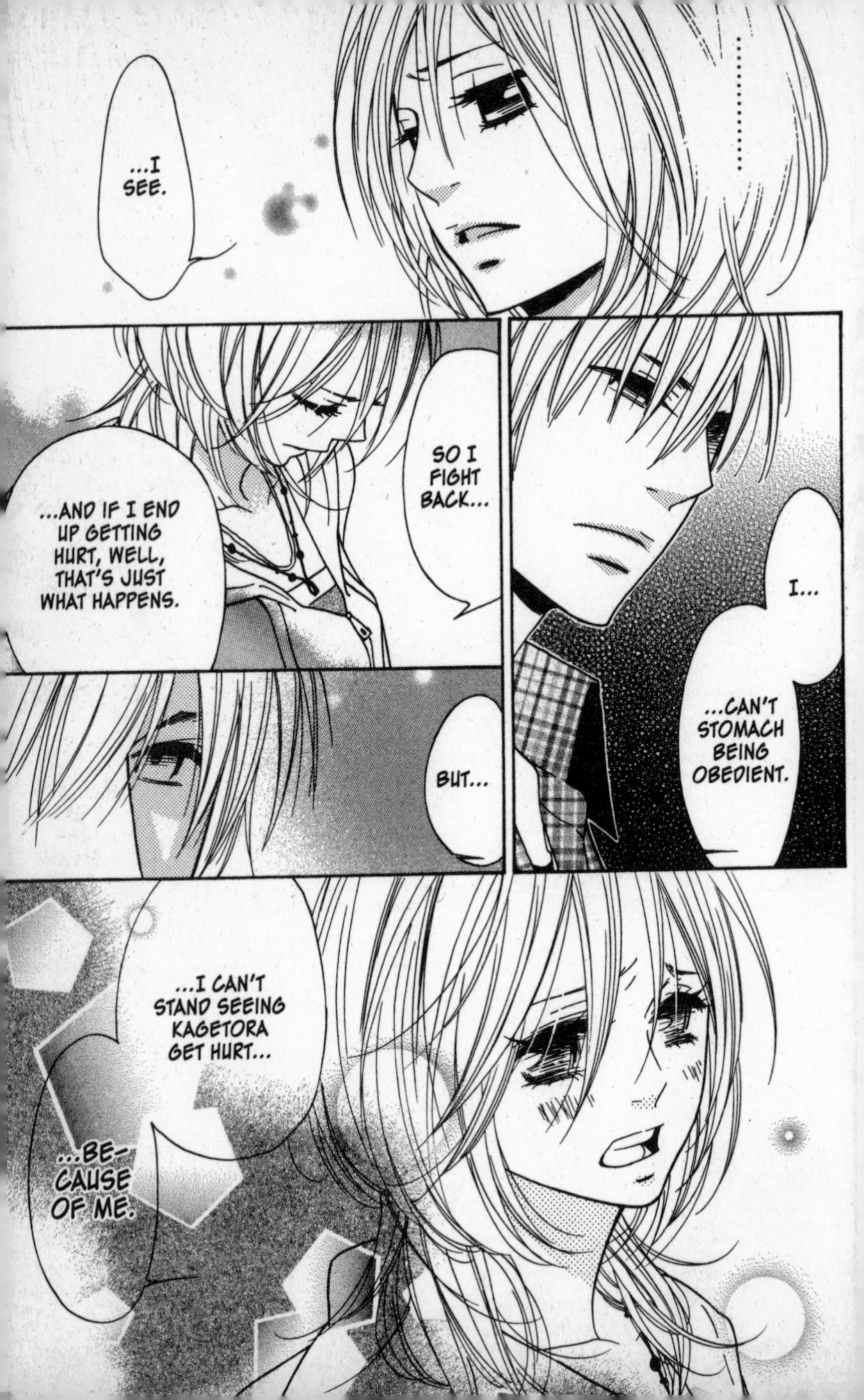
......
...I SEE.
I...
...CAN'T STOMACH BEING OBEDIENT.
SO I FIGHT BACK...
...AND IF I END UP GETTING HURT, WELL, THAT'S JUST WHAT HAPPENS.
BUT...
...I CAN'T STAND SEEING KAGETORA GET HURT...
...BE-CAUSE OF ME.

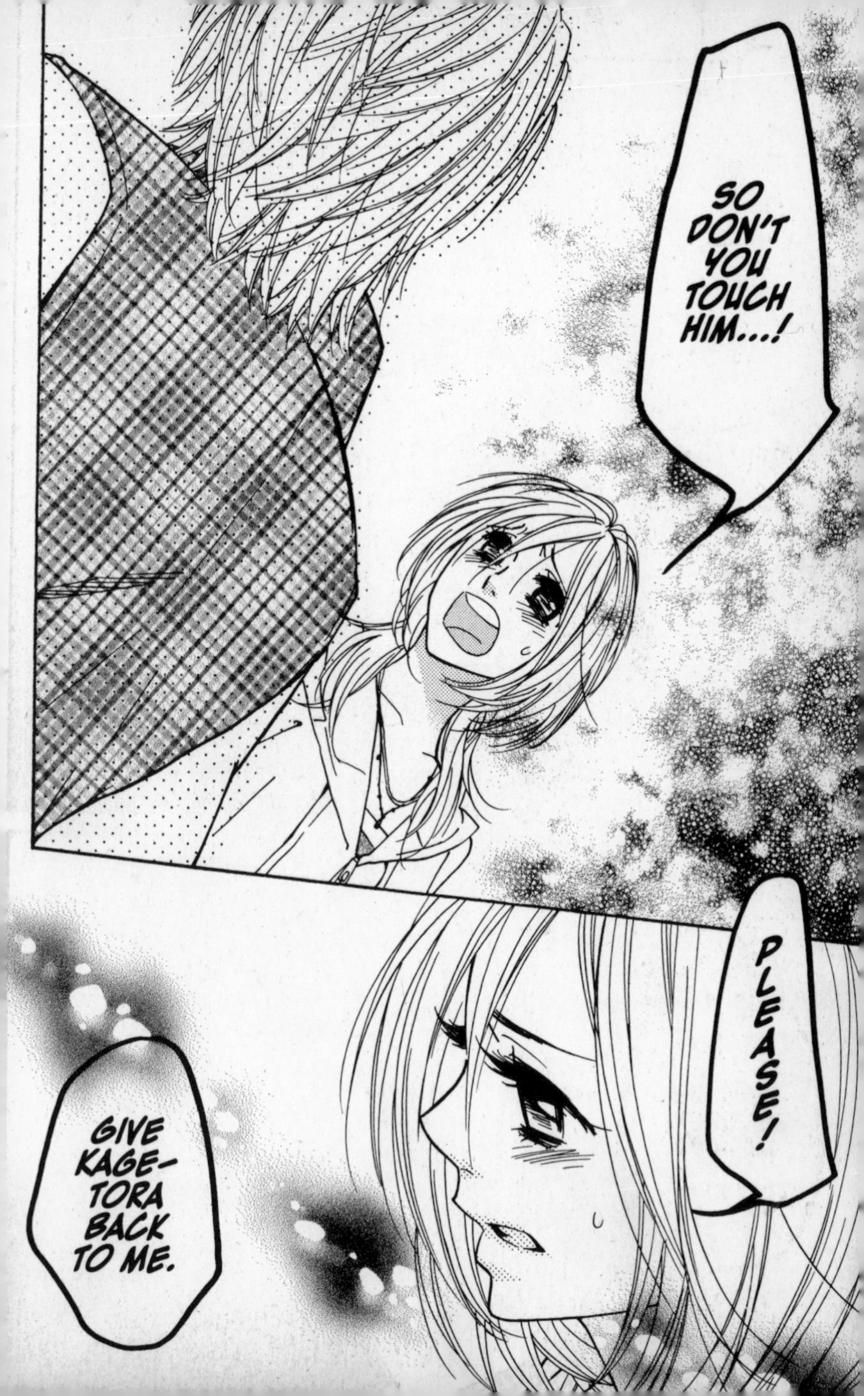
SO DON'T YOU TOUCH HIM...!
PLEASE!
GIVE KAGE-TORA BACK TO ME.

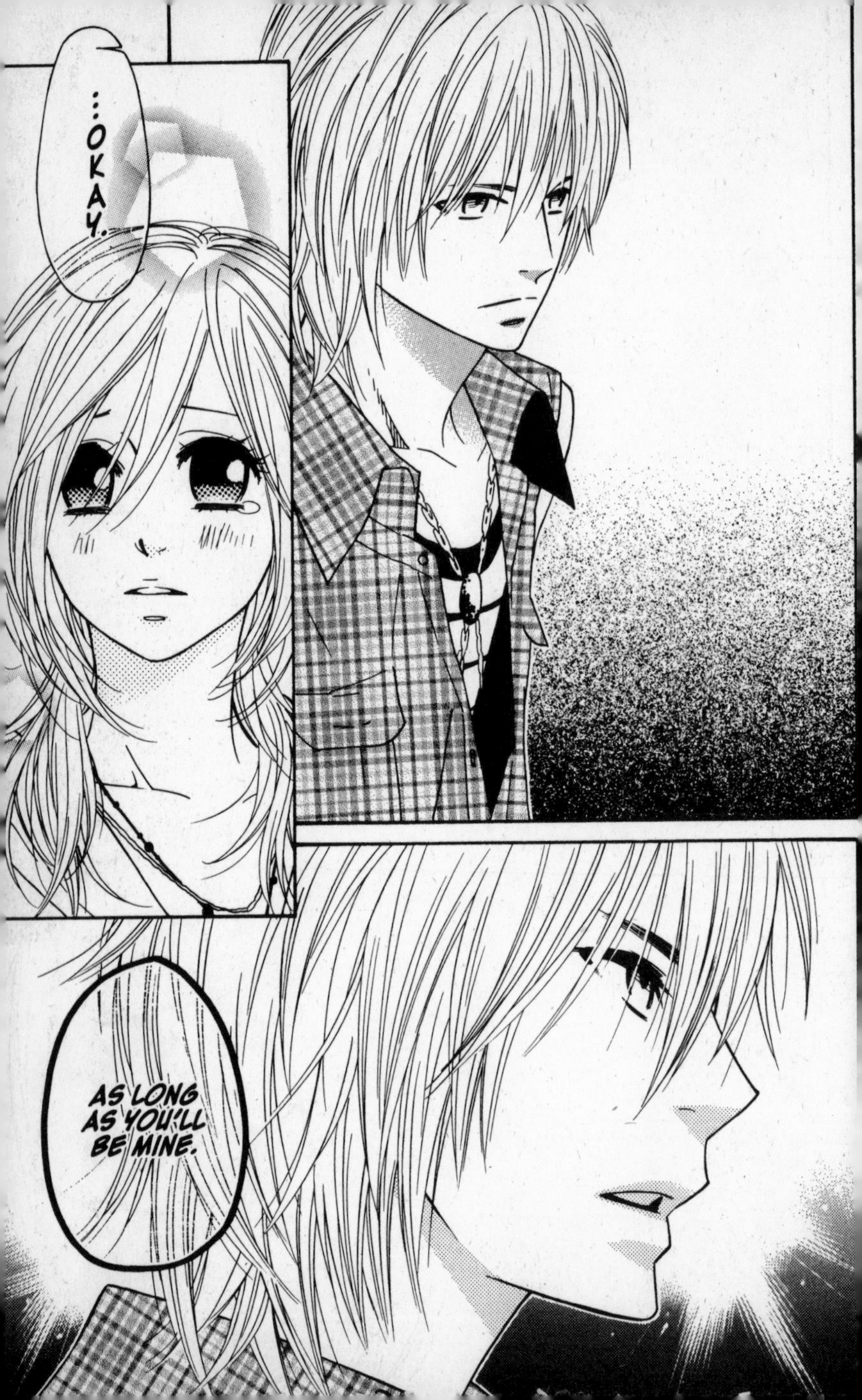
...OKAY.
AS LONG AS YOU'LL BE MINE.

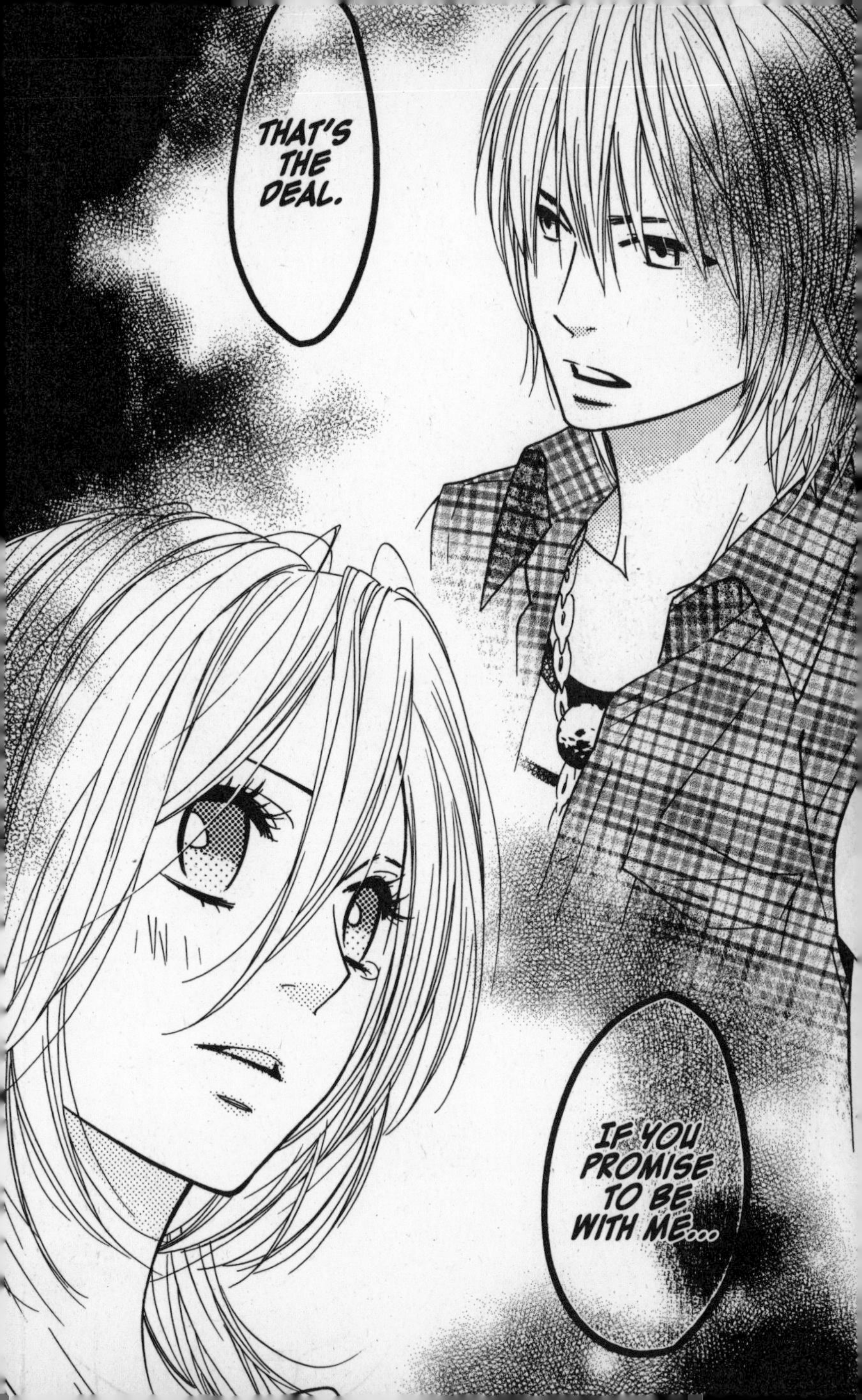
THAT'S THE DEAL.
IF YOU PROMISE TO BE WITH ME...

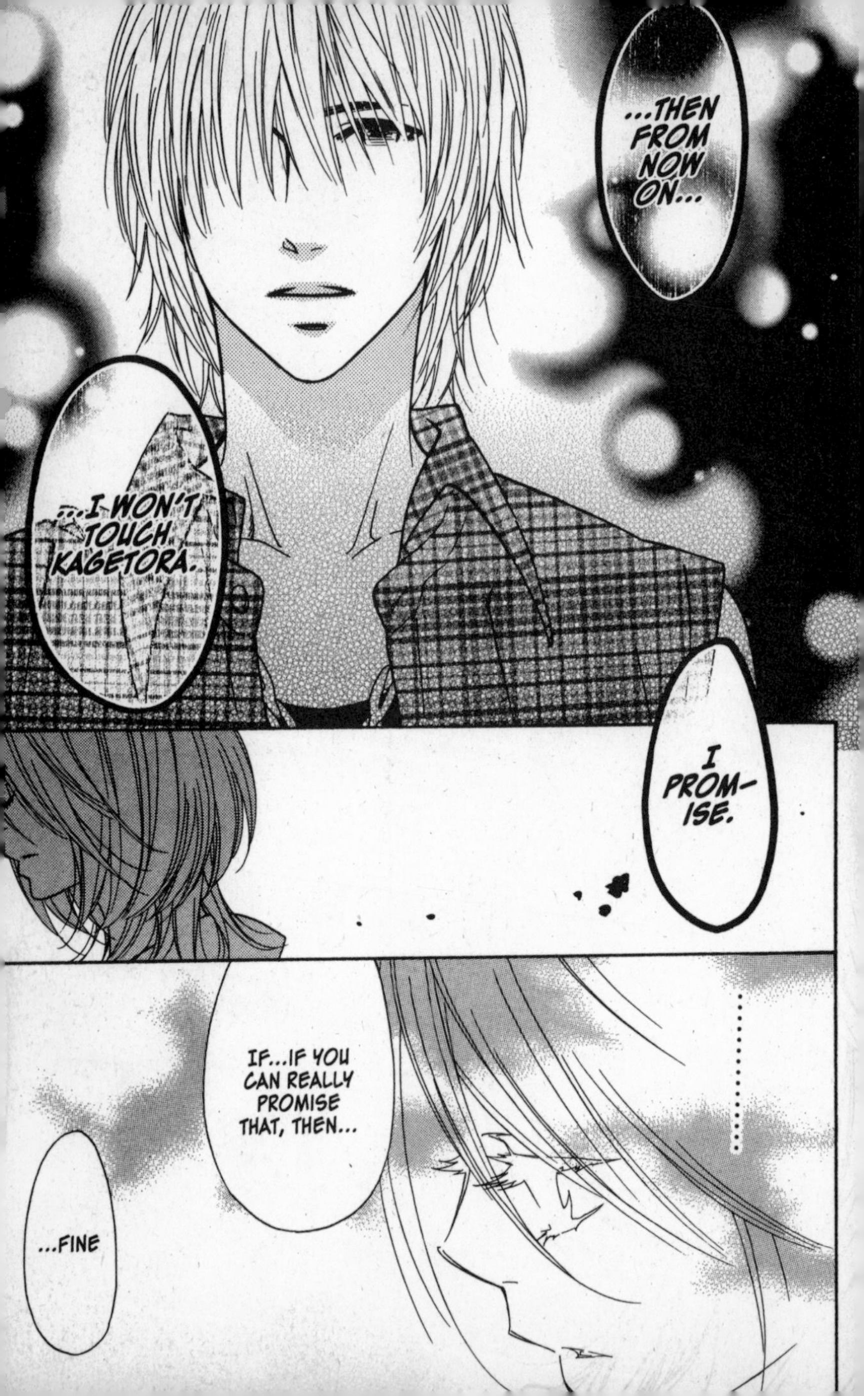
...THEN FROM NOW ON...
...I WON'T TOUCH KAGETORA.
I PROMISE.
....
IF...IF YOU CAN REALLY PROMISE THAT, THEN...
...FINE

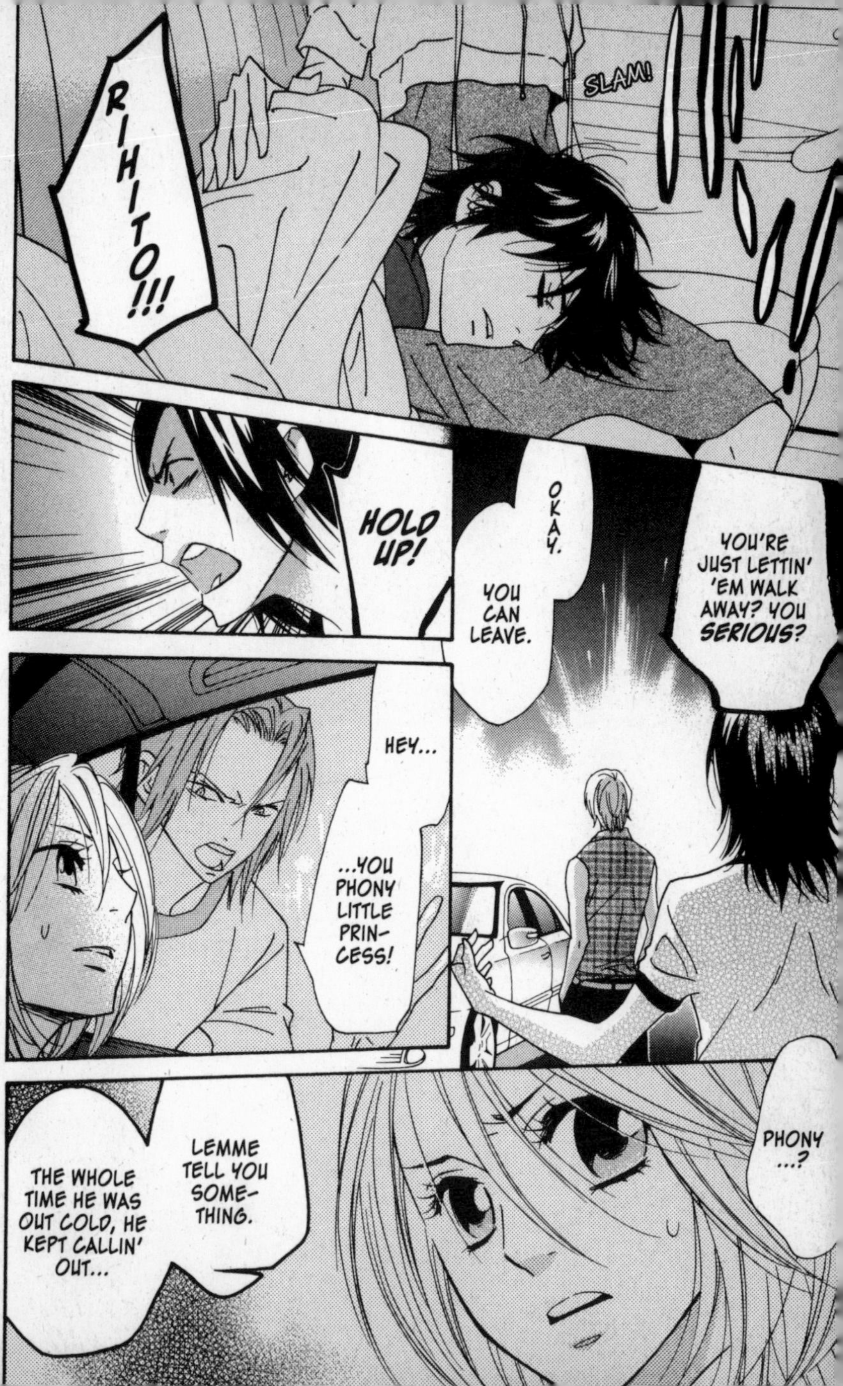
SLAM!
RIHITO!!!
OKAY.
YOU CAN LEAVE.
YOU'RE JUST LETTIN' 'EM WALK AWAY? YOU SERIOUS?
HOLD UP!
HEY...
...YOU PHONY LITTLE PRIN-CESS!
PHONY ...?
LEMME TELL YOU SOME-THING.
THE WHOLE TIME HE WAS OUT COLD, HE KEPT CALLIN' OUT...

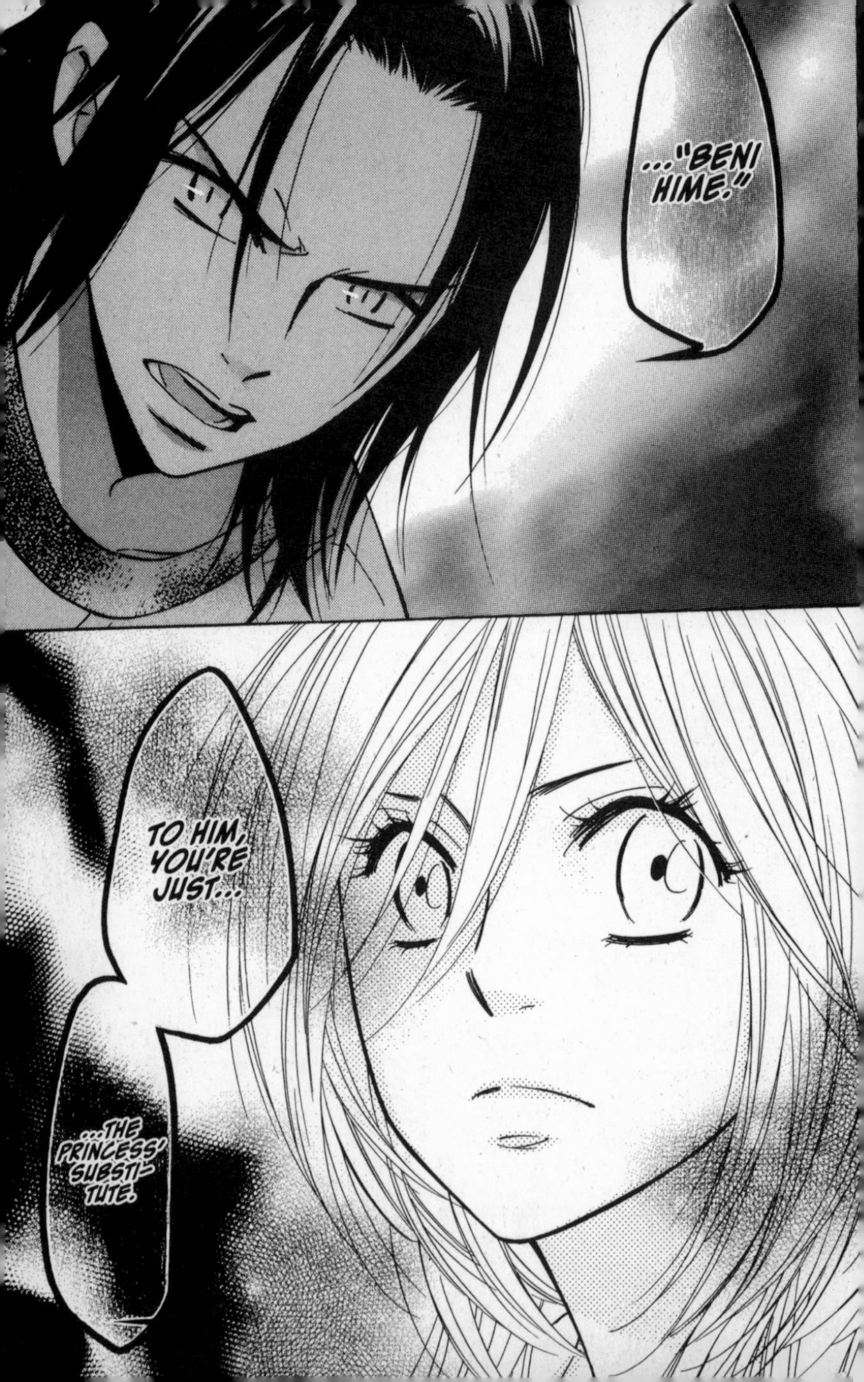
..."BENI HIME."
TO HIM, YOU'RE JUST...
...THE PRINCESS' SUBSTI-TUTE.

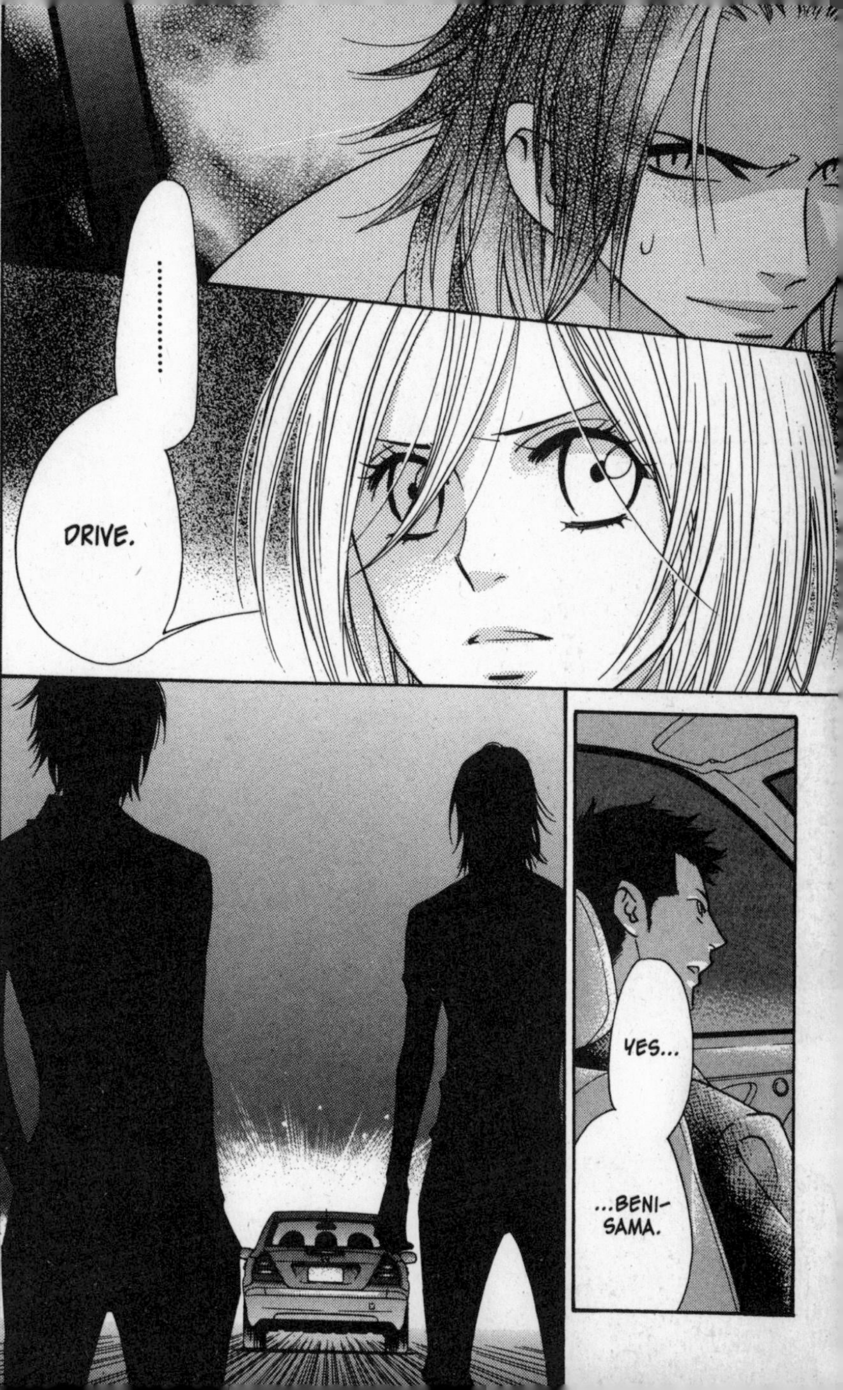
......
DRIVE.
YES...
...BENI-SAMA.

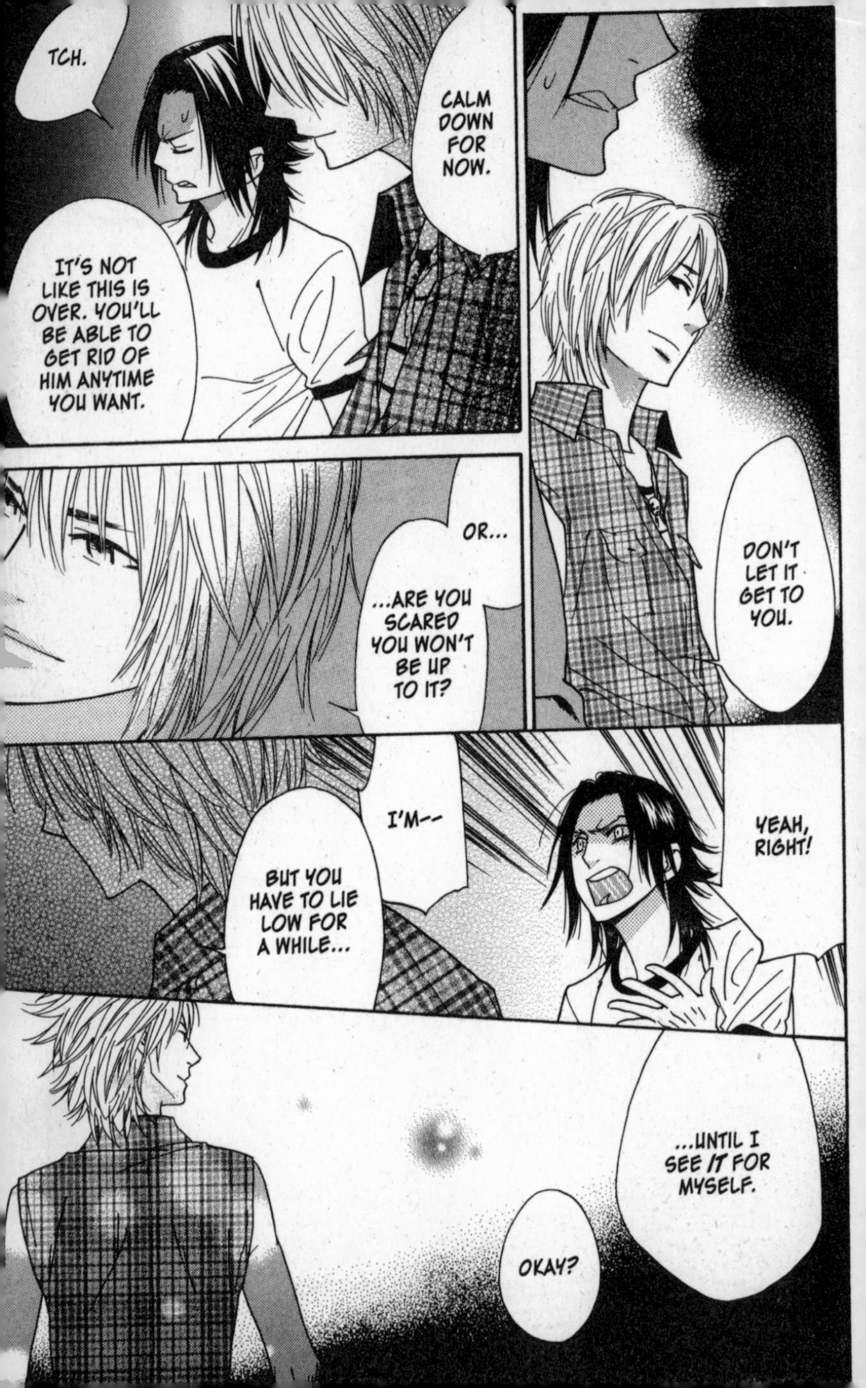
DON'T LET IT GET TO YOU.
CALM DOWN FOR NOW.
TCH.
IT'S NOT LIKE THIS IS OVER. YOU'LL BE ABLE TO GET RID OF HIM ANYTIME YOU WANT.
OR...
...ARE YOU SCARED YOU WON'T BE UP TO IT?
YEAH, RIGHT!
I'M--
BUT YOU HAVE TO LIE LOW FOR A WHILE...
...UNTIL I SEE *IT* FOR MYSELF.
OKAY?

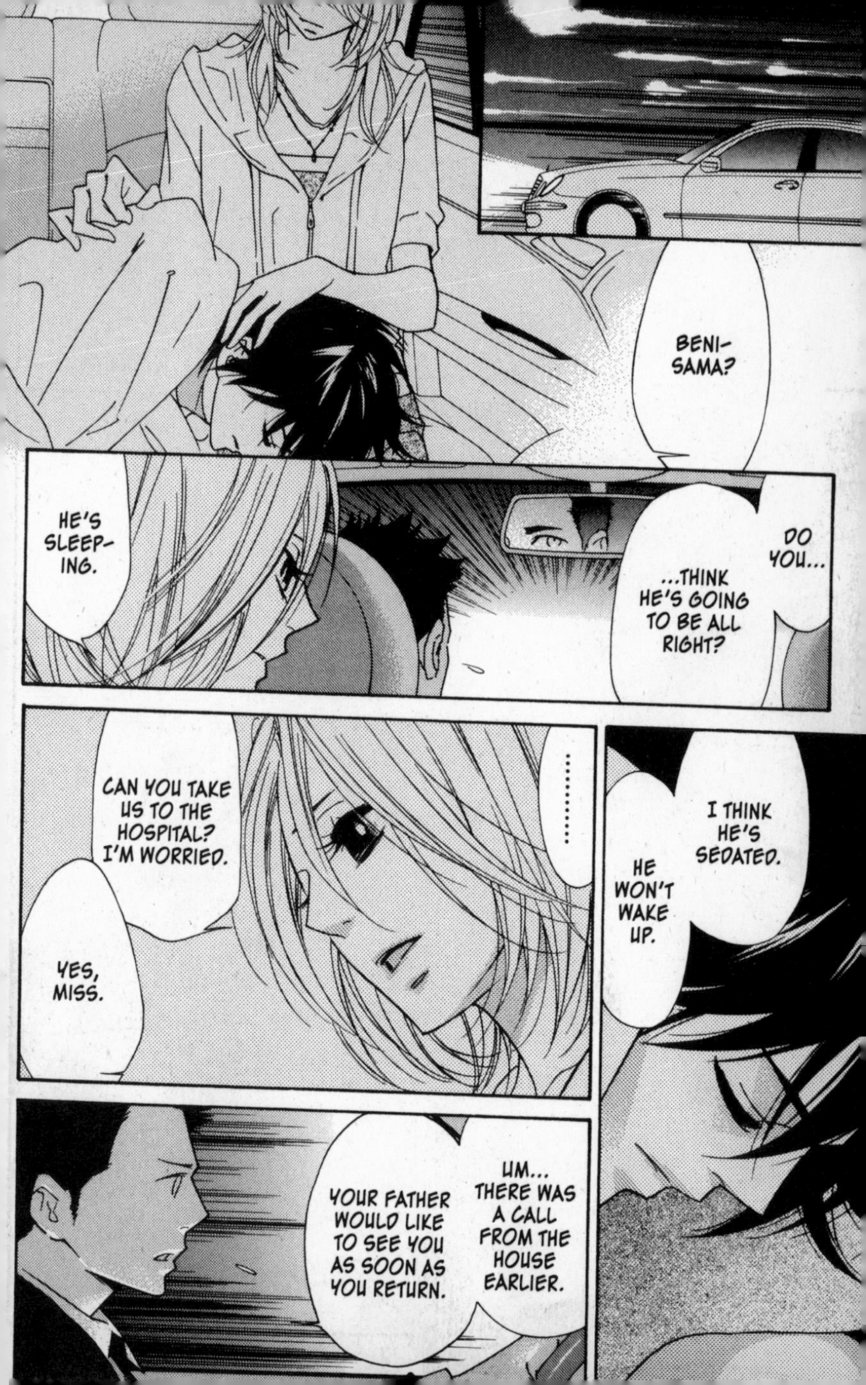
BENI-SAMA?
DO YOU...
...THINK HE'S GOING TO BE ALL RIGHT?
HE'S SLEEPING.
I THINK HE'S SEDATED.
HE WON'T WAKE UP.
......
CAN YOU TAKE US TO THE HOSPITAL? I'M WORRIED.
YES, MISS.
UM... THERE WAS A CALL FROM THE HOUSE EARLIER.
YOUR FATHER WOULD LIKE TO SEE YOU AS SOON AS YOU RETURN.

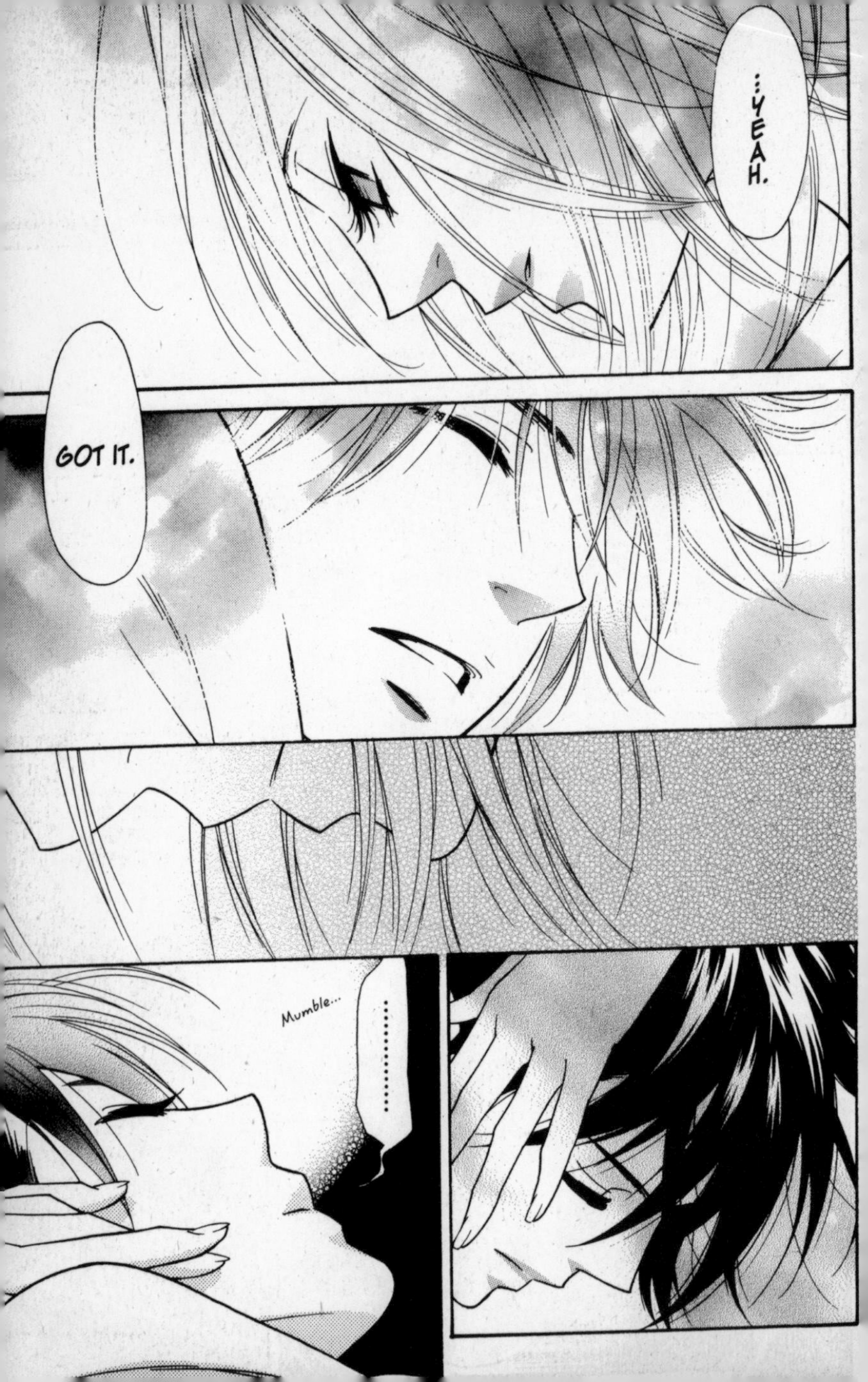
...YEAH.
GOT IT.
Mumble...
....

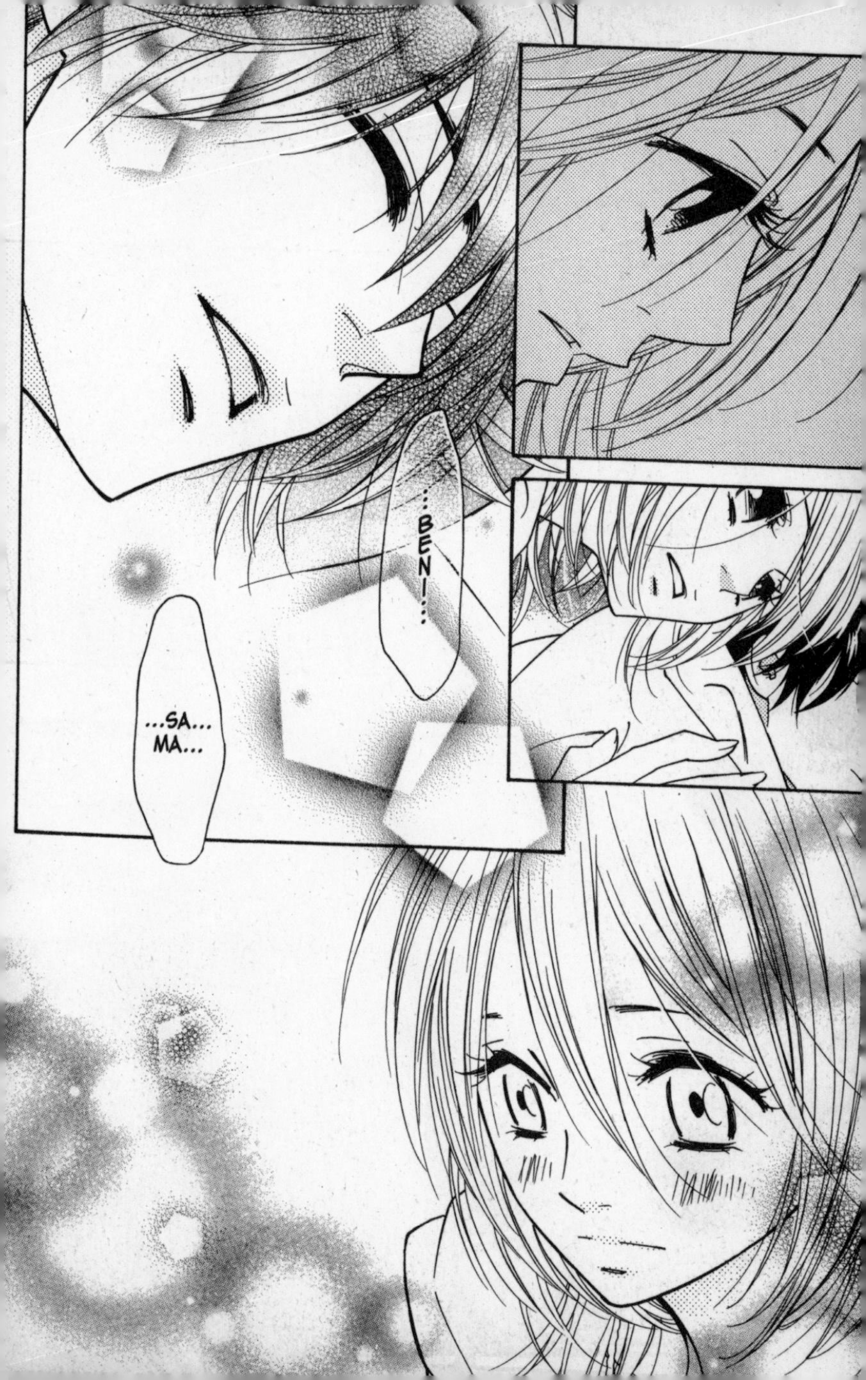
...BENI...
...SA... MA...

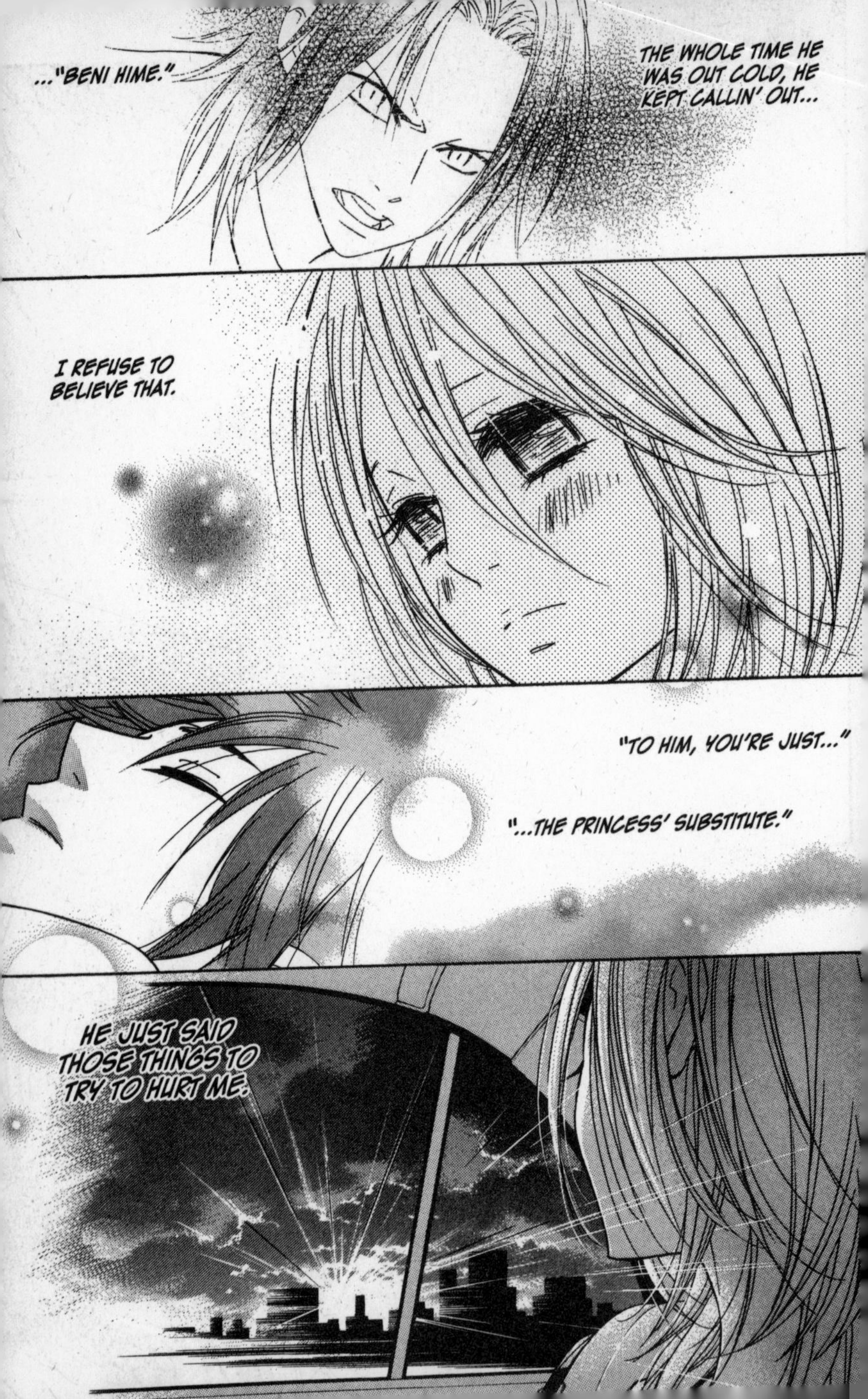
THE WHOLE TIME HE WAS OUT COLD, HE KEPT CALLIN' OUT...
..."BENI HIME."
I REFUSE TO BELIEVE THAT.
"TO HIM, YOU'RE JUST..."
"...THE PRINCESS' SUBSTITUTE."
HE JUST SAID THOSE THINGS TO TRY TO HURT ME.

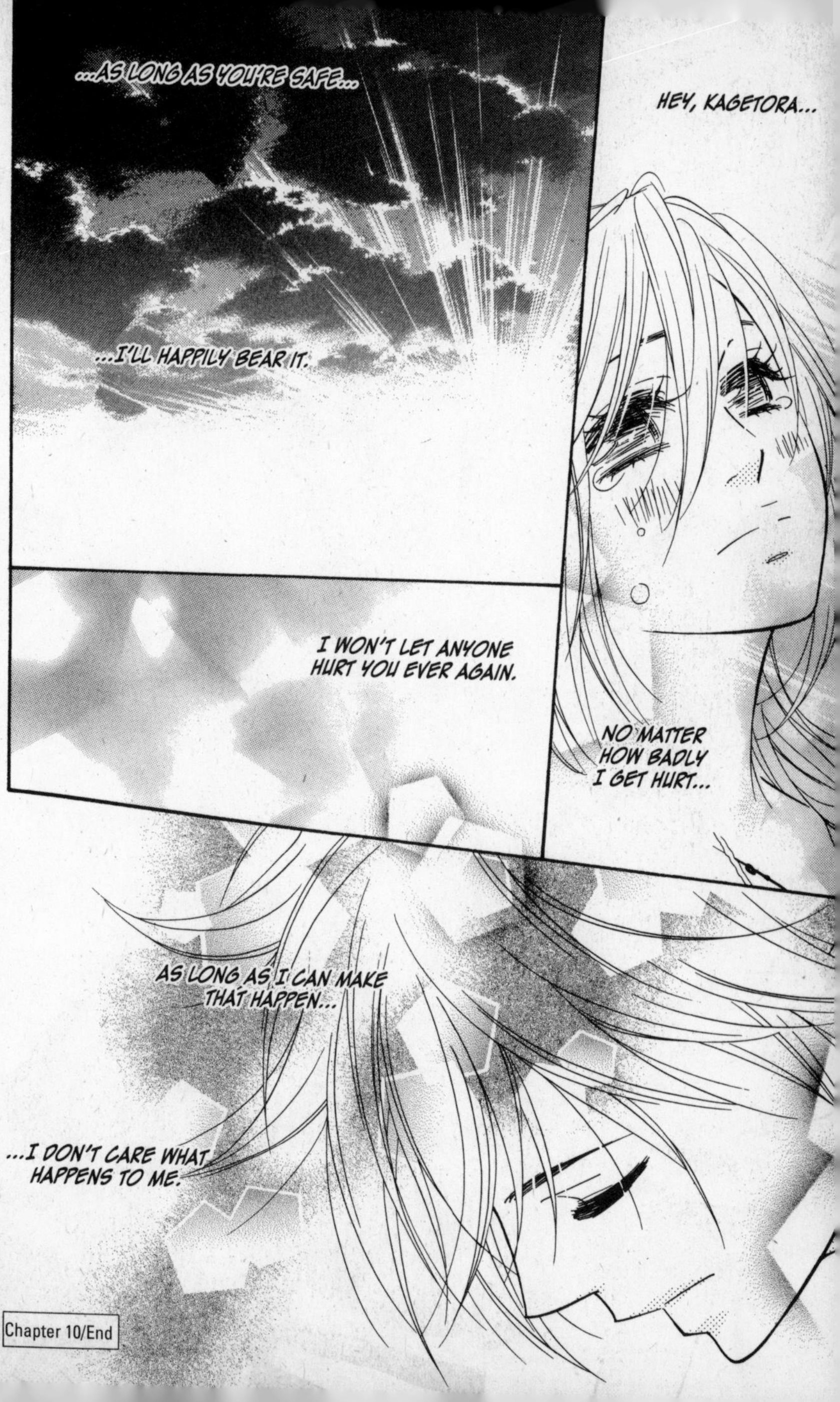
HEY, KAGETORA...
NO MATTER HOW BADLY I GET HURT...
...AS LONG AS YOU'RE SAFE...
...I'LL HAPPILY BEAR IT.
I WON'T LET ANYONE HURT YOU EVER AGAIN.
AS LONG AS I CAN MAKE THAT HAPPEN...
...I DON'T CARE WHAT HAPPENS TO ME.

Chapter 10/End

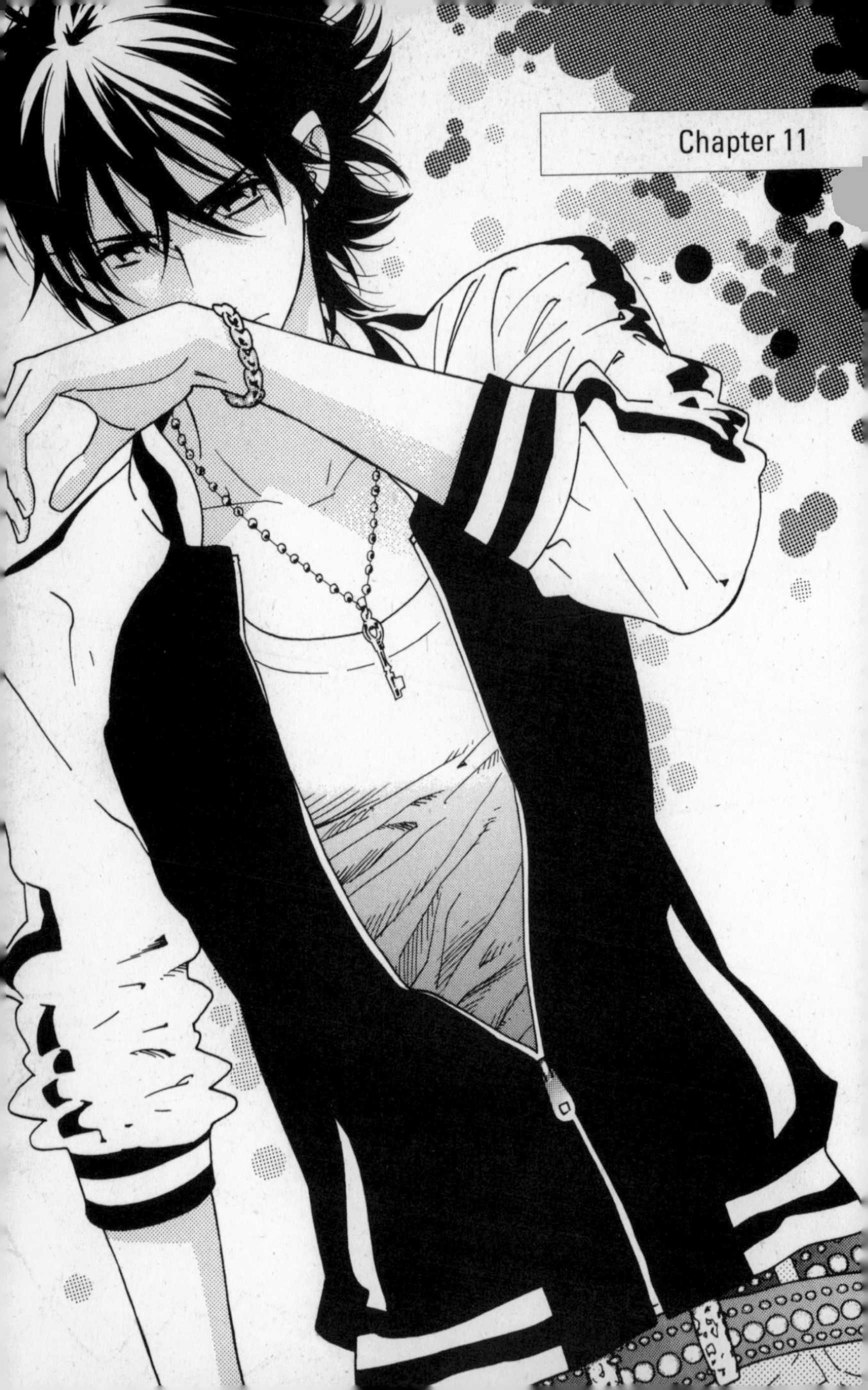
Chapter 11

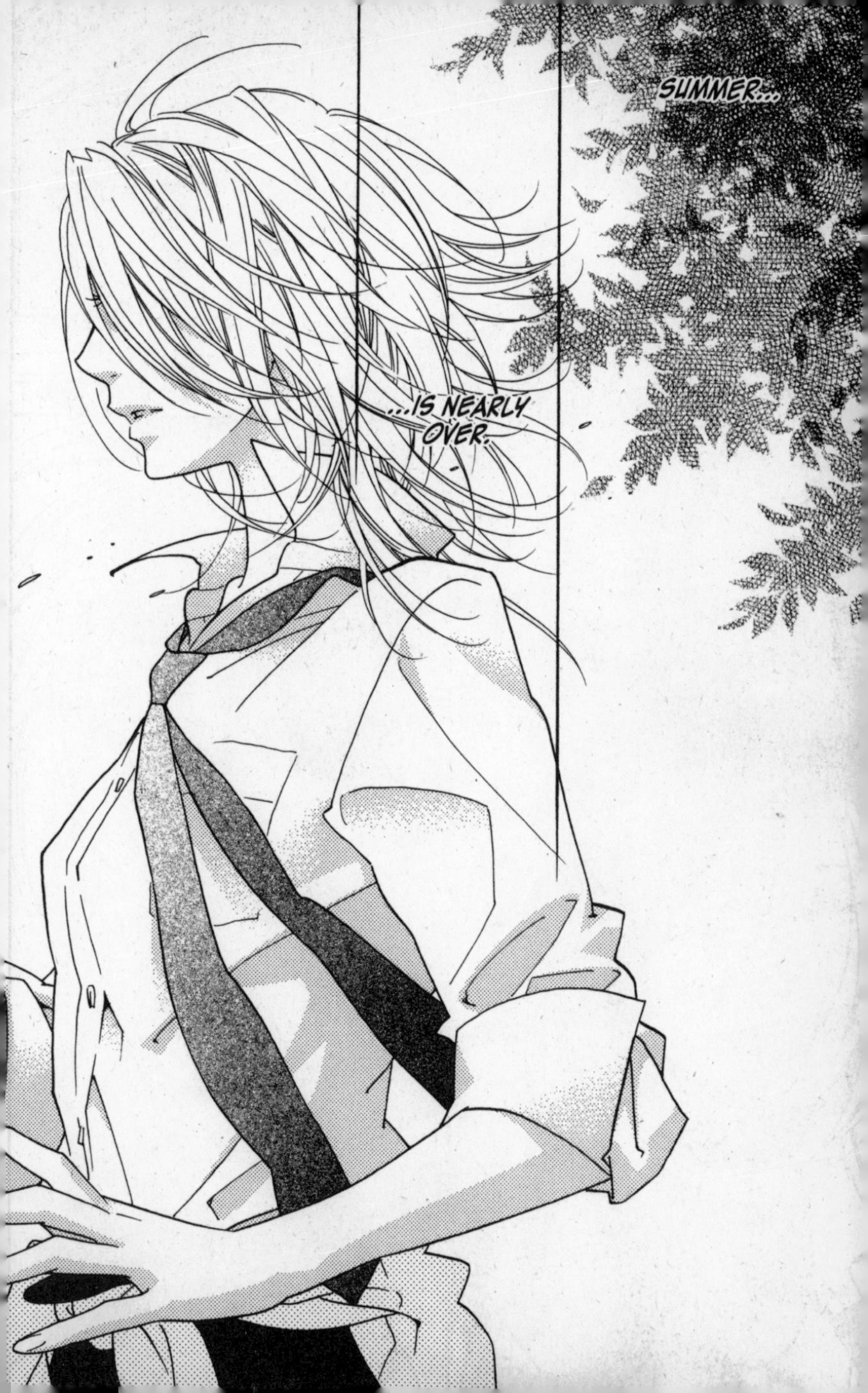
SUMMER...
...IS NEARLY OVER.

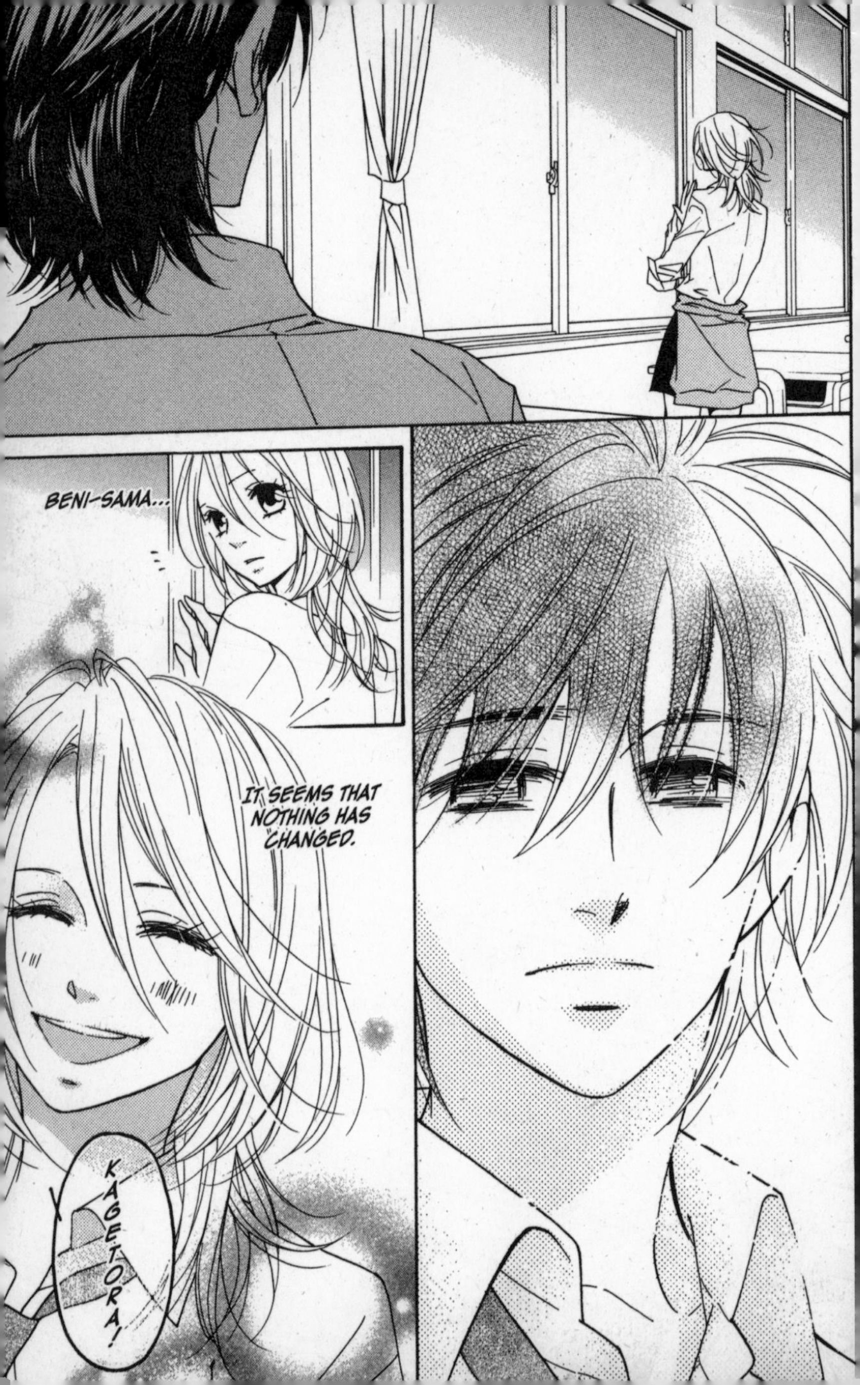
BENI-SAMA...
IT SEEMS THAT NOTHING HAS CHANGED.
KAGETORA!

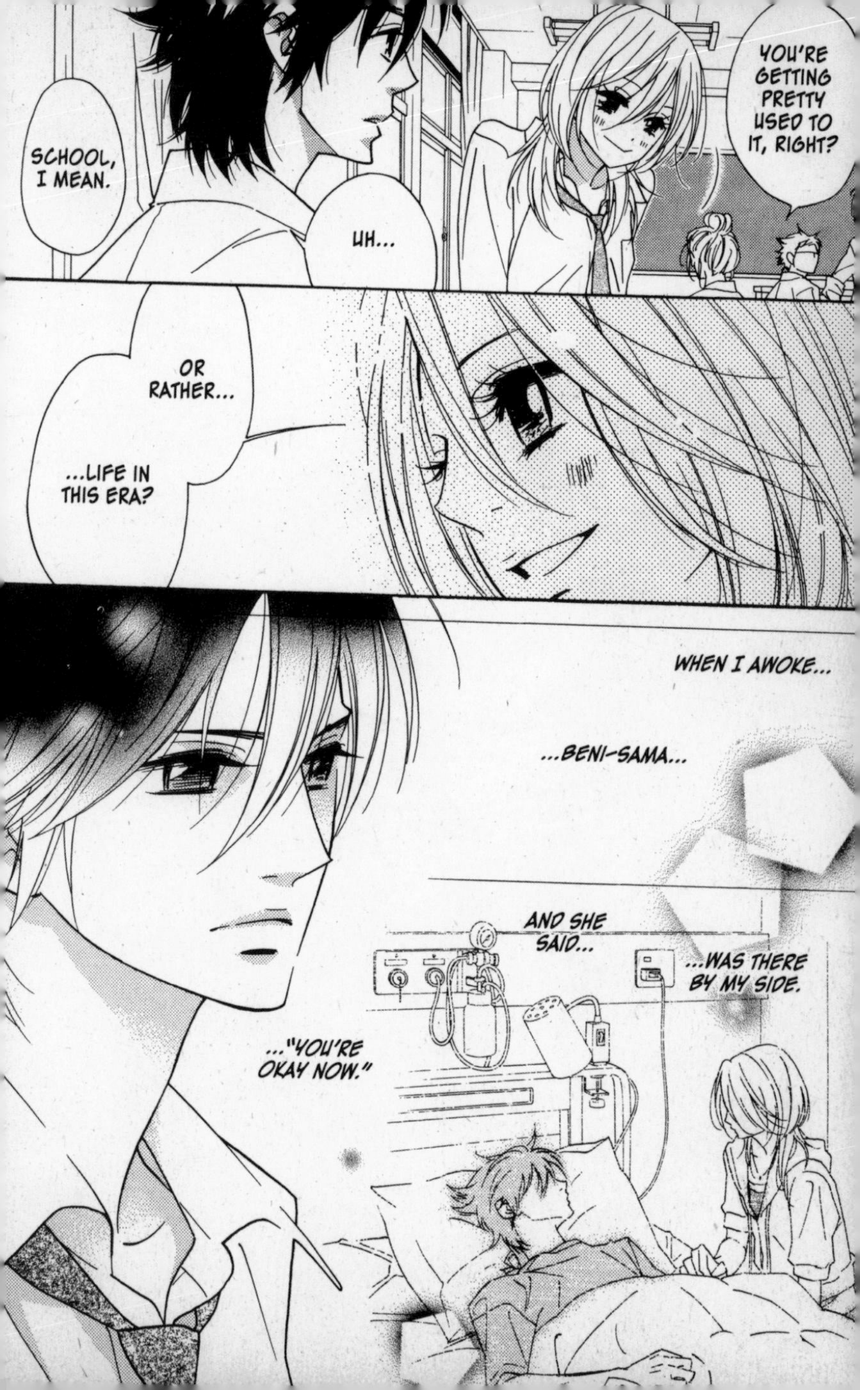
YOU'RE GETTING PRETTY USED TO IT, RIGHT?
UH...
SCHOOL, I MEAN.
OR RATHER...
...LIFE IN THIS ERA?
WHEN I AWOKE...
...BENI-SAMA...
...WAS THERE BY MY SIDE.
AND SHE SAID...
..."YOU'RE OKAY NOW."

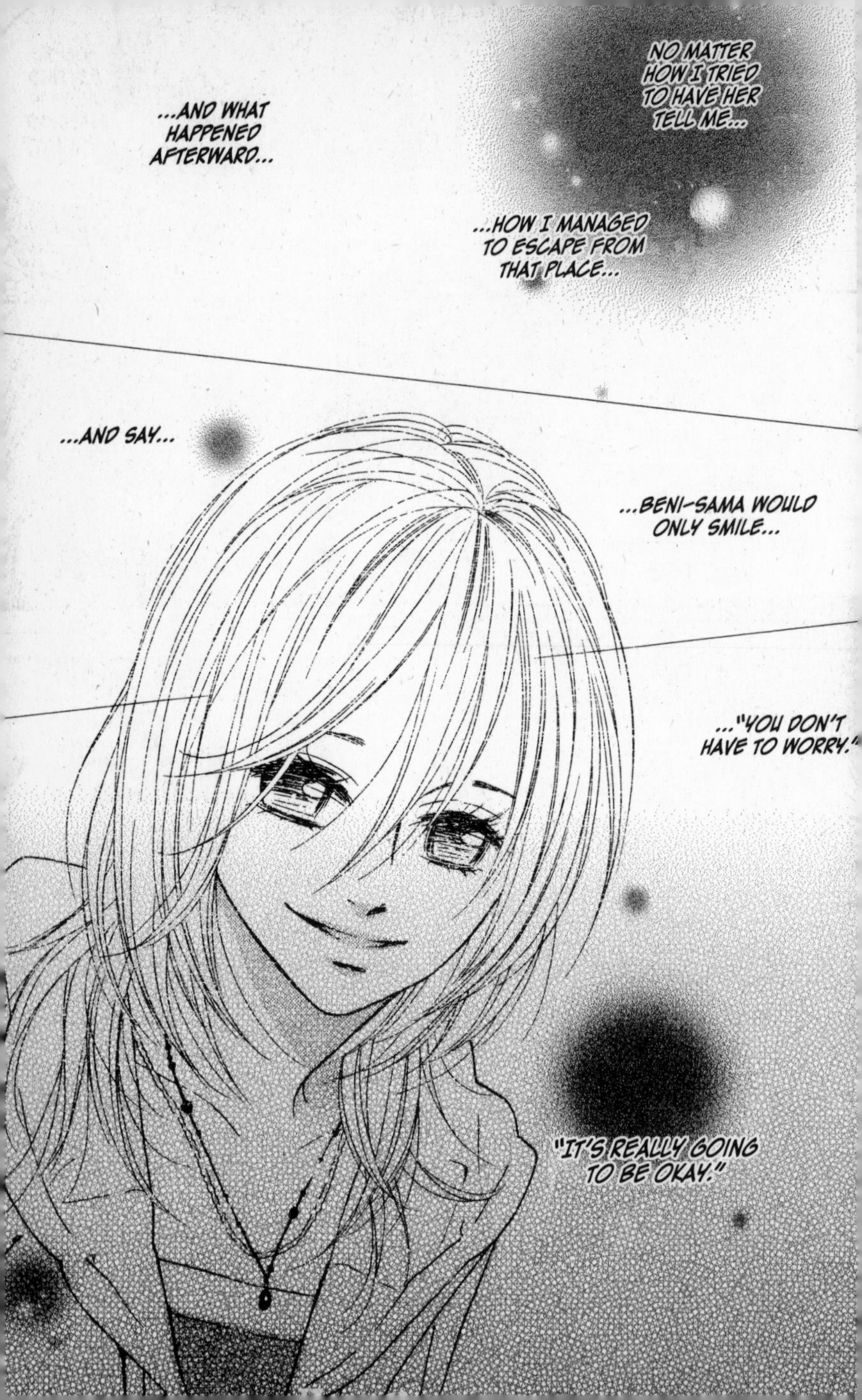
NO MATTER HOW I TRIED TO HAVE HER TELL ME...
...HOW I MANAGED TO ESCAPE FROM THAT PLACE...
...AND WHAT HAPPENED AFTERWARD...
...BENI-SAMA WOULD ONLY SMILE...
...AND SAY...
..."YOU DON'T HAVE TO WORRY."
"IT'S REALLY GOING TO BE OKAY."

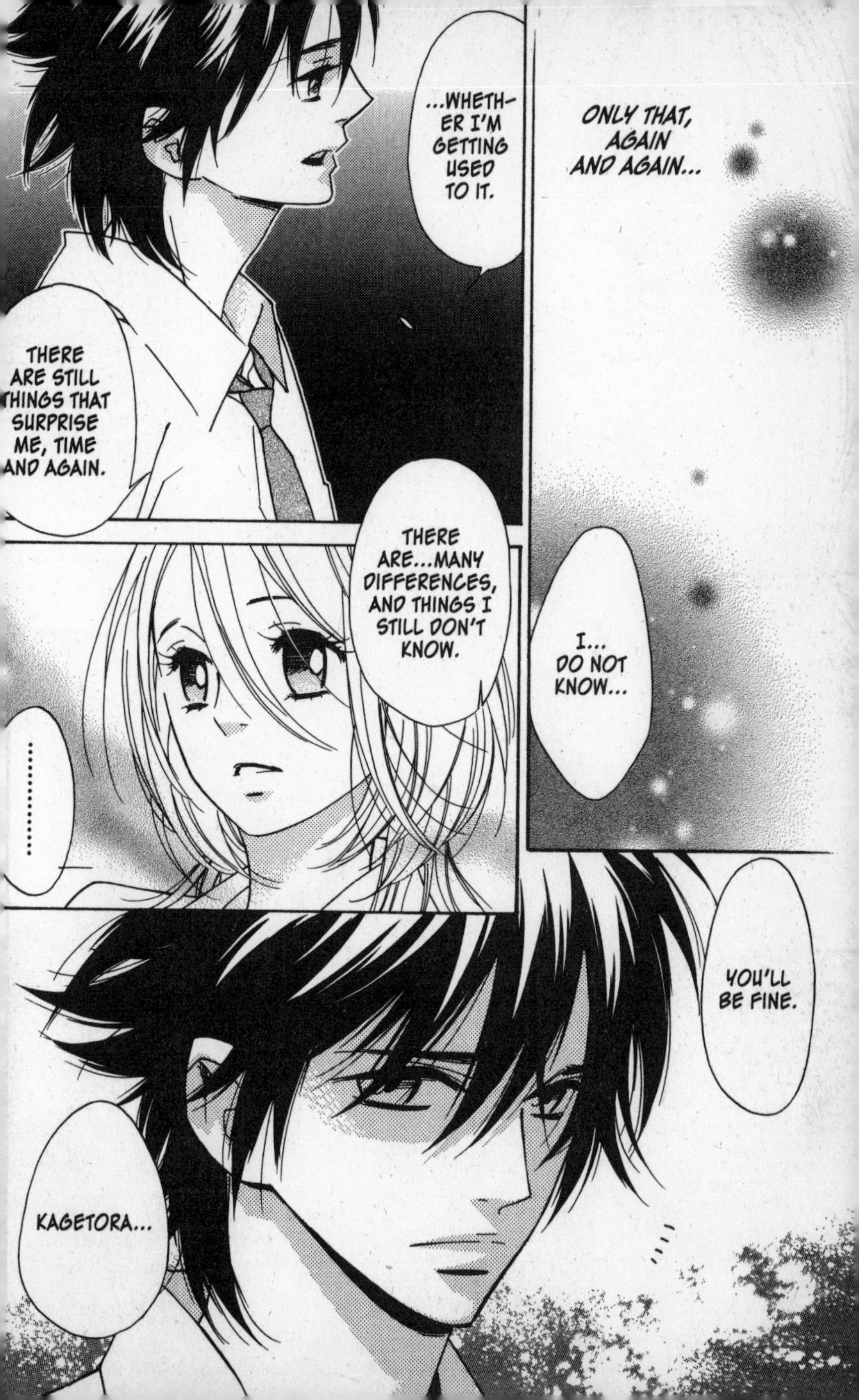
ONLY THAT, AGAIN AND AGAIN...
I... DO NOT KNOW...
...WHETHER I'M GETTING USED TO IT.
THERE ARE STILL THINGS THAT SURPRISE ME, TIME AND AGAIN.
THERE ARE...MANY DIFFERENCES, AND THINGS I STILL DON'T KNOW.
......
YOU'LL BE FINE.
KAGETORA...

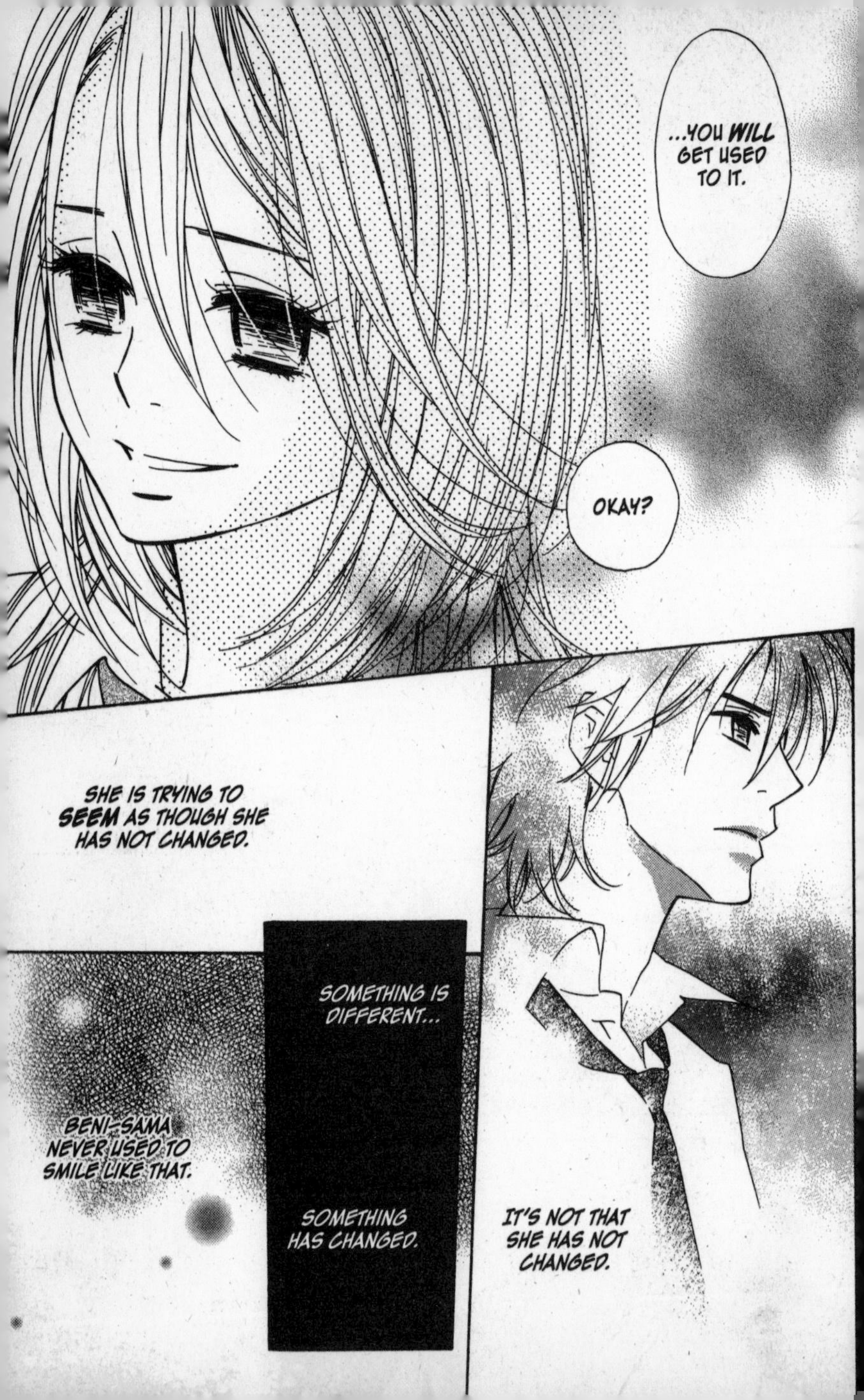
...YOU WILL GET USED TO IT.
OKAY?
IT'S NOT THAT SHE HAS NOT CHANGED.
SHE IS TRYING TO SEEM AS THOUGH SHE HAS NOT CHANGED.
SOMETHING IS DIFFERENT...
BENI-SAMA NEVER USED TO SMILE LIKE THAT.
SOMETHING HAS CHANGED.

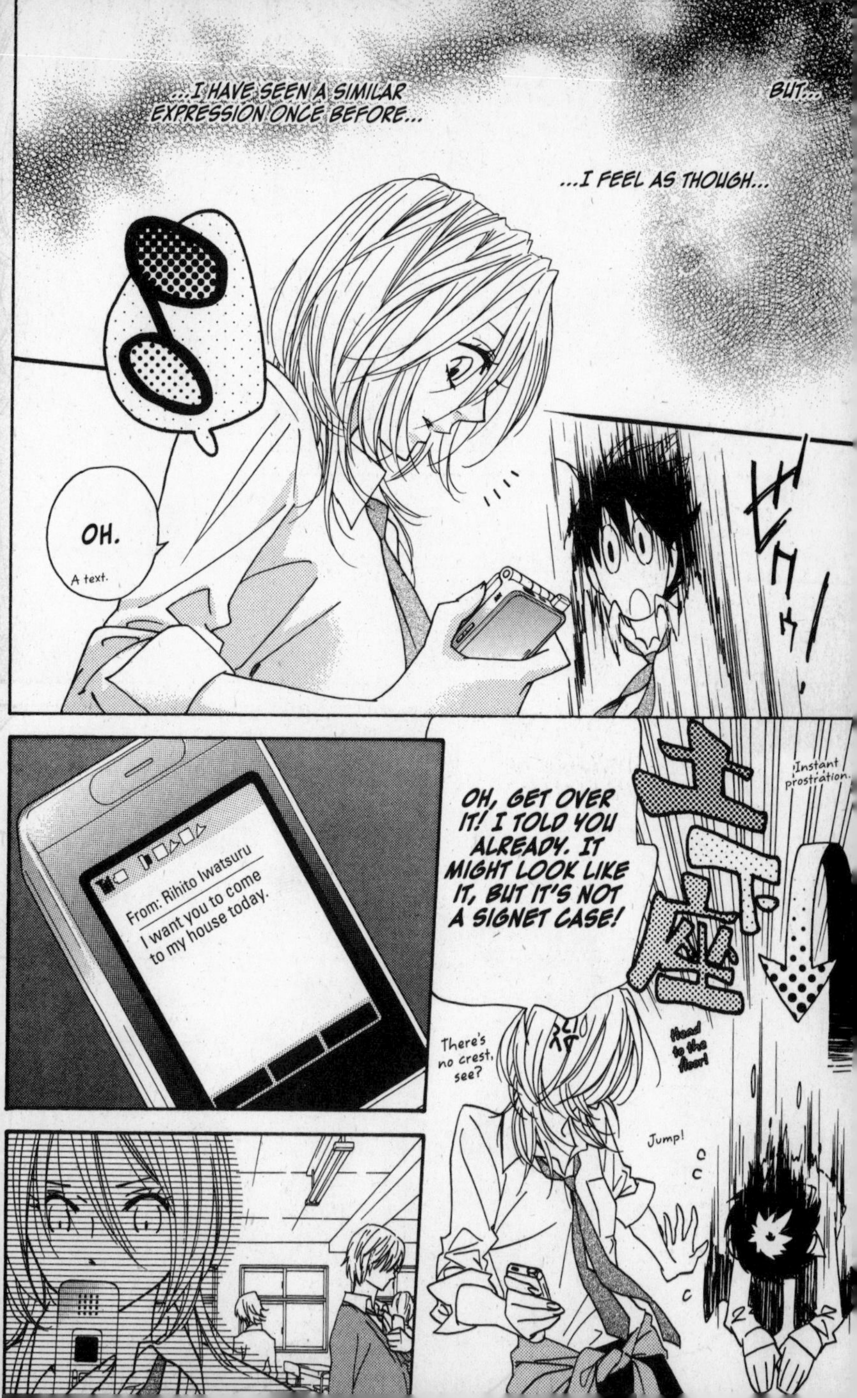
BUT...
...I HAVE SEEN A SIMILAR EXPRESSION ONCE BEFORE...
...I FEEL AS THOUGH...
OH.
A text.
Instant prostration.
OH, GET OVER IT! I TOLD YOU ALREADY. IT MIGHT LOOK LIKE IT, BUT IT'S NOT A SIGNET CASE!
Head to the floor!
There's no crest, see?
Jump!
From: Rihito Iwatsuru
I want you to come to my house today.

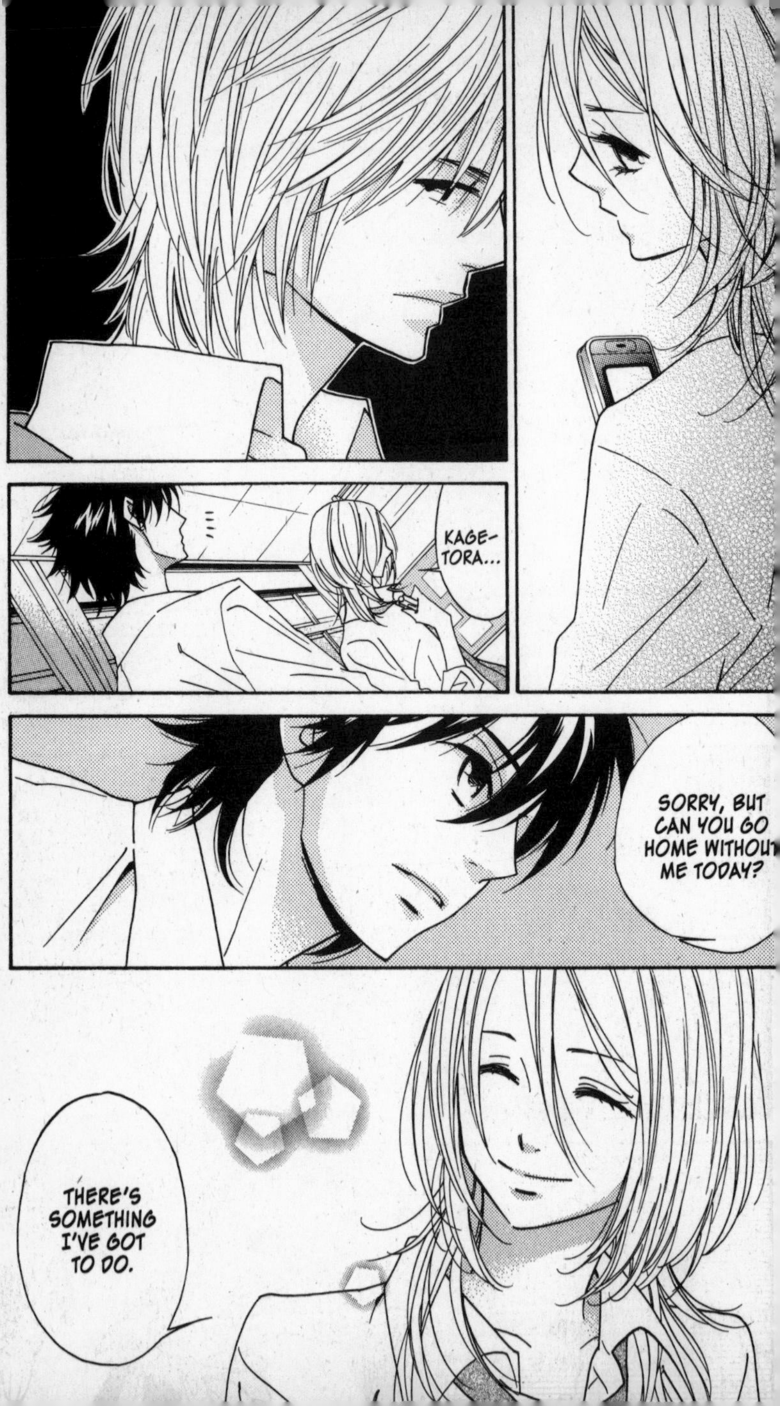
KAGE-TORA...
SORRY, BUT CAN YOU GO HOME WITHOUT ME TODAY?
THERE'S SOMETHING I'VE GOT TO DO.

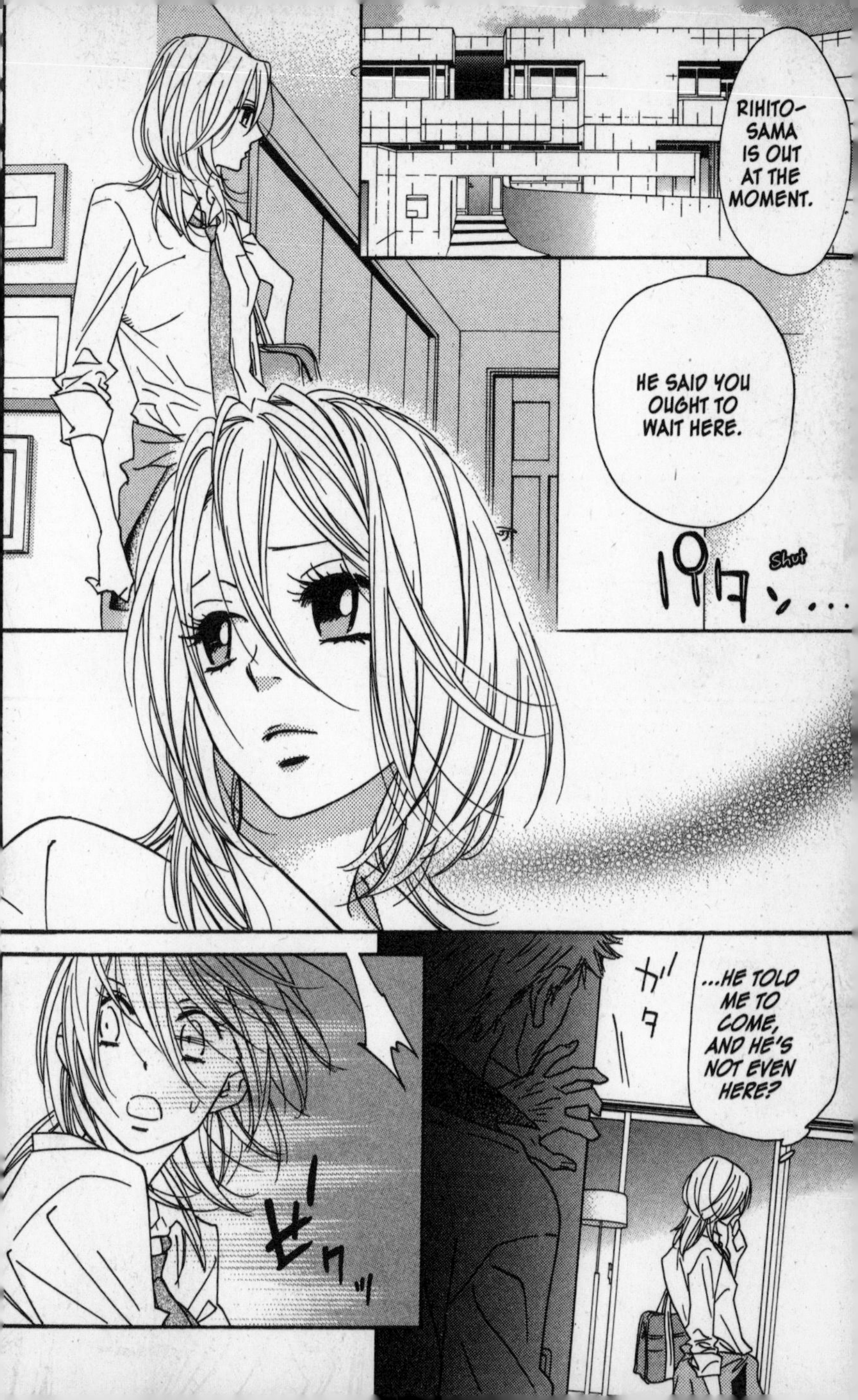
RIHITO-SAMA IS OUT AT THE MOMENT.
HE SAID YOU OUGHT TO WAIT HERE.
Shut
...HE TOLD ME TO COME, AND HE'S NOT EVEN HERE?

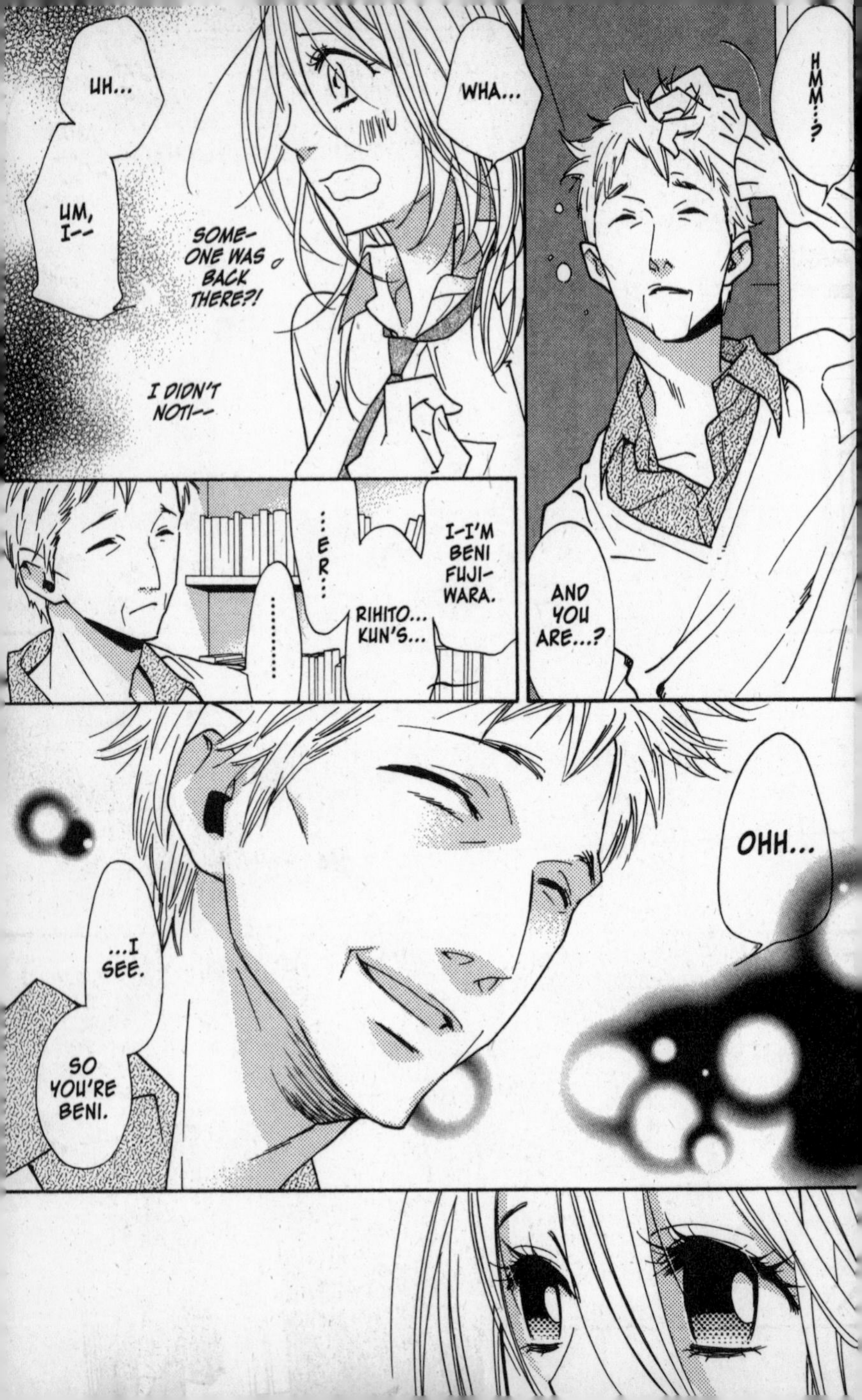
HMM...?
WHA...
SOME-ONE WAS BACK THERE?!
UH...
UM, I--
I DIDN'T NOTI--
AND YOU ARE...?
I-I'M BENI FUJI-WARA.
RIHITO... KUN'S...
...ER...
....
OHH...
...I SEE.
SO YOU'RE BENI.

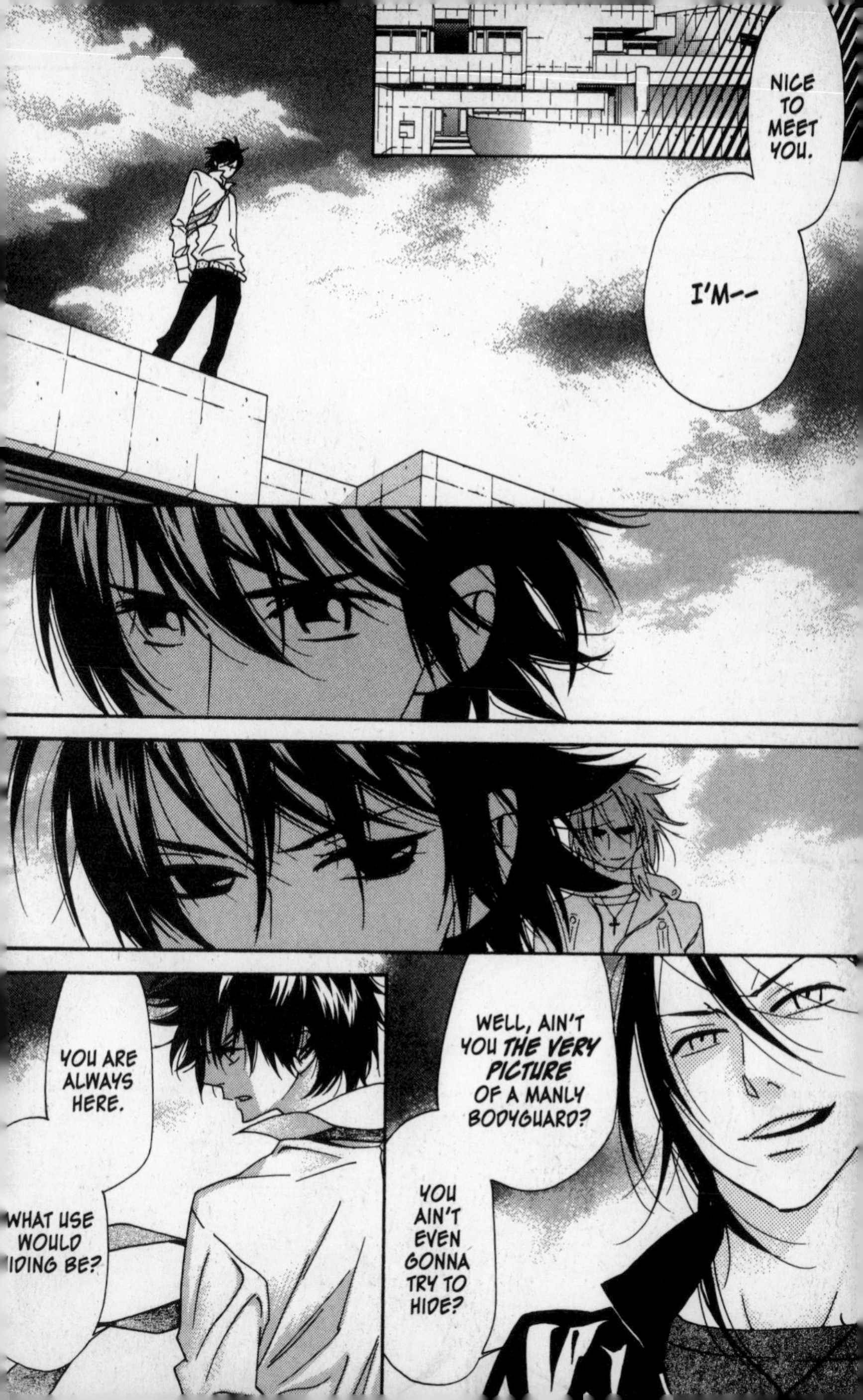
NICE TO MEET YOU.
I'M--
WELL, AIN'T YOU *THE VERY PICTURE* OF A MANLY BODYGUARD?
YOU AIN'T EVEN GONNA TRY TO HIDE?
YOU ARE ALWAYS HERE.
WHAT USE WOULD IDING BE?

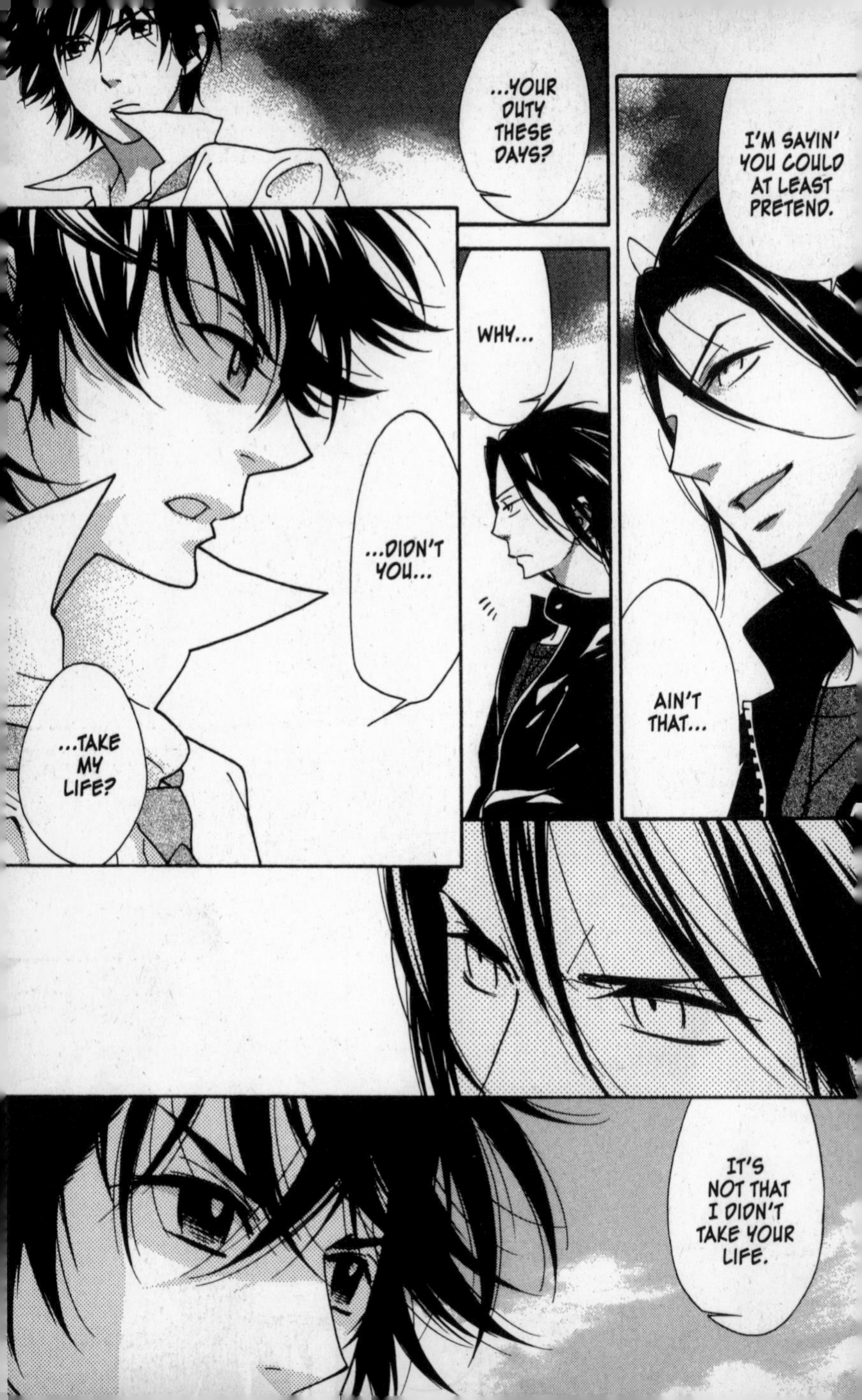
I'M SAYIN' YOU COULD AT LEAST PRETEND.
AIN'T THAT...
...YOUR DUTY THESE DAYS?
WHY...
...DIDN'T YOU...
...TAKE MY LIFE?
IT'S NOT THAT I DIDN'T TAKE YOUR LIFE.

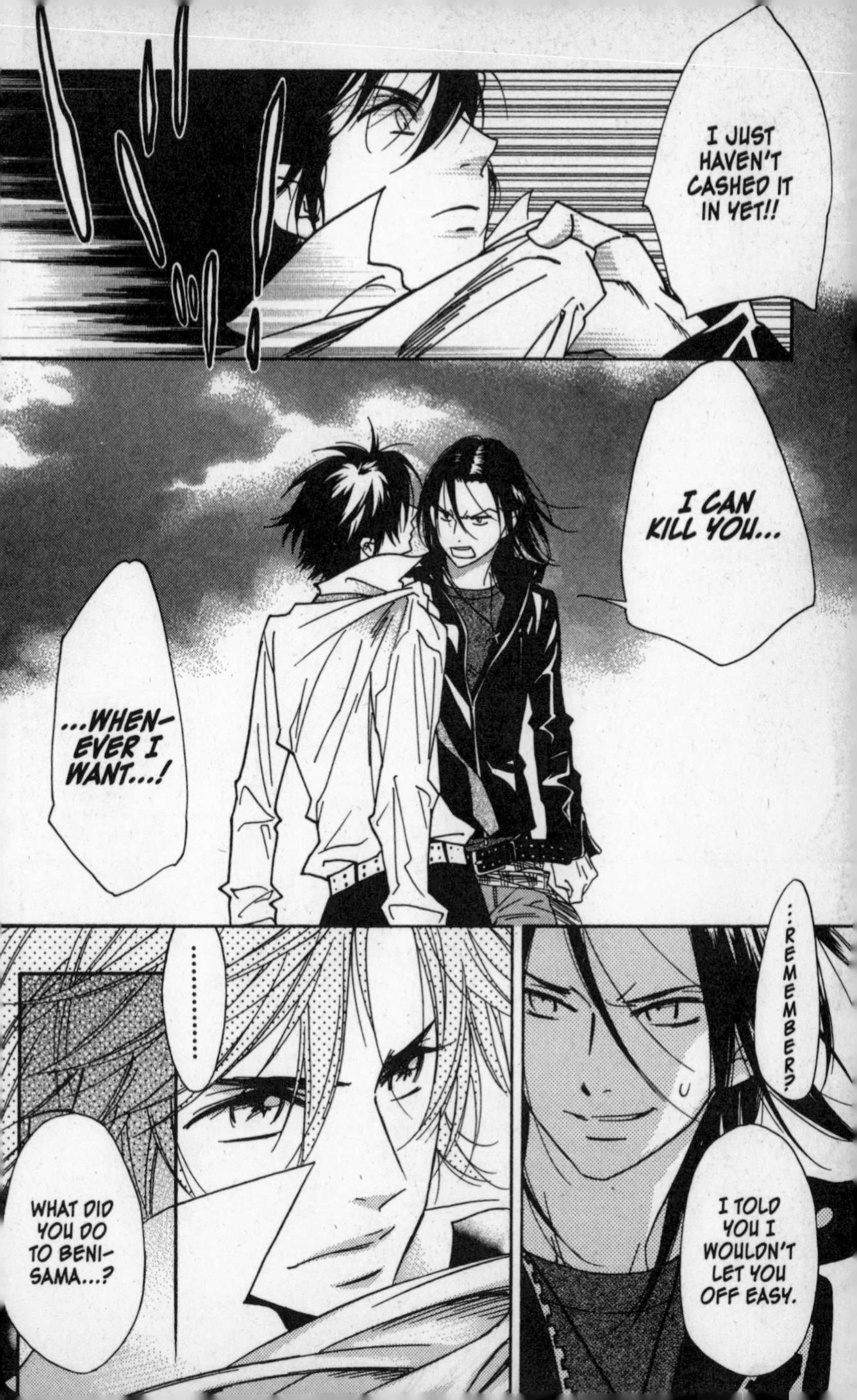
I JUST HAVEN'T CASHED IT IN YET!!
I CAN KILL YOU...
...WHEN-EVER I WANT...!
...REMEMBER?
I TOLD YOU I WOULDN'T LET YOU OFF EASY.
....
WHAT DID YOU DO TO BENI-SAMA...?

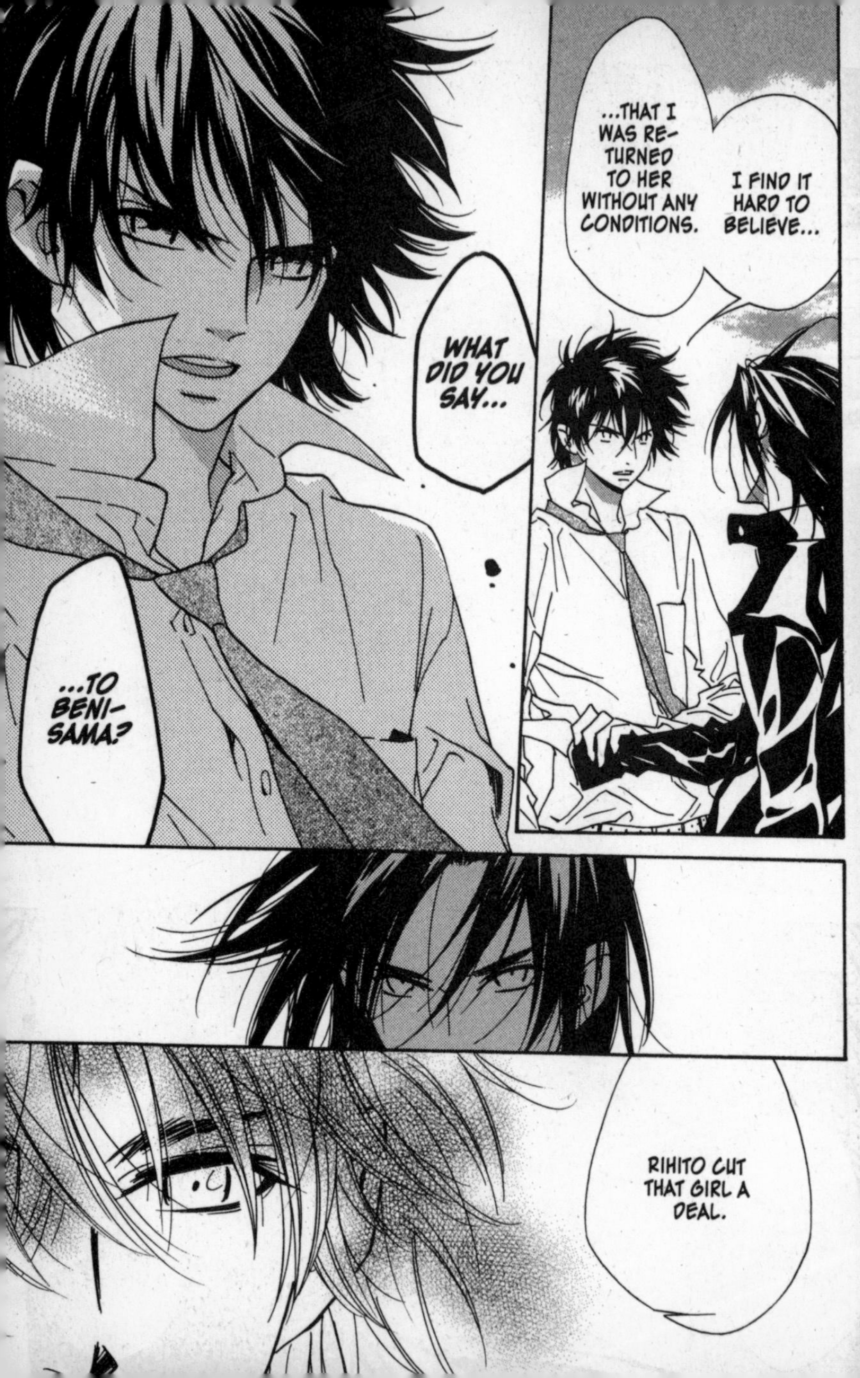
I FIND IT HARD TO BELIEVE...
...THAT I WAS RE-TURNED TO HER WITHOUT ANY CONDITIONS.
WHAT DID YOU SAY...
...TO BENI-SAMA?
RIHITO CUT THAT GIRL A DEAL.

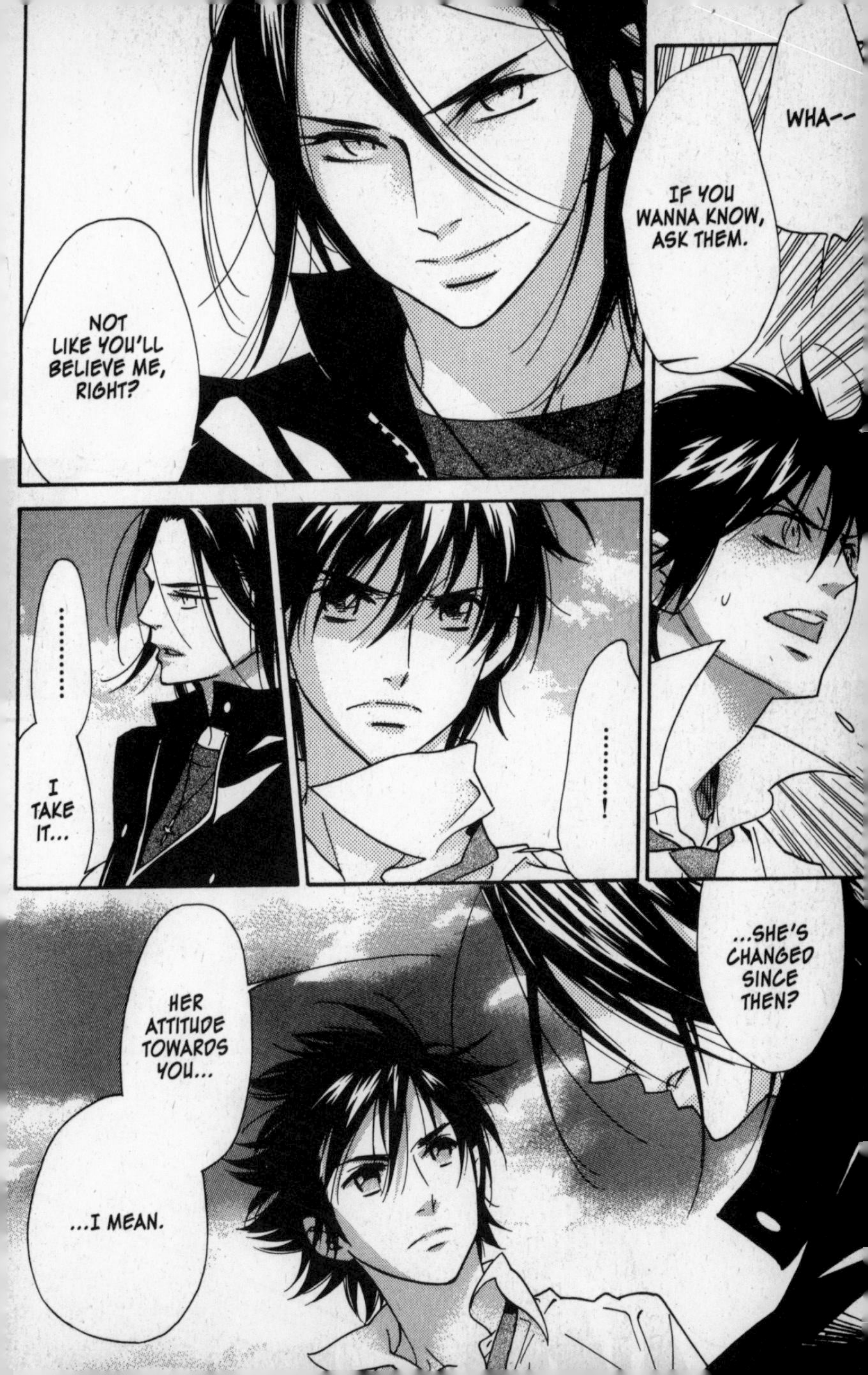
WHA--
IF YOU WANNA KNOW, ASK THEM.
NOT LIKE YOU'LL BELIEVE ME, RIGHT?
......!
......
I TAKE IT...
...SHE'S CHANGED SINCE THEN?
HER ATTITUDE TOWARDS YOU...
...I MEAN.

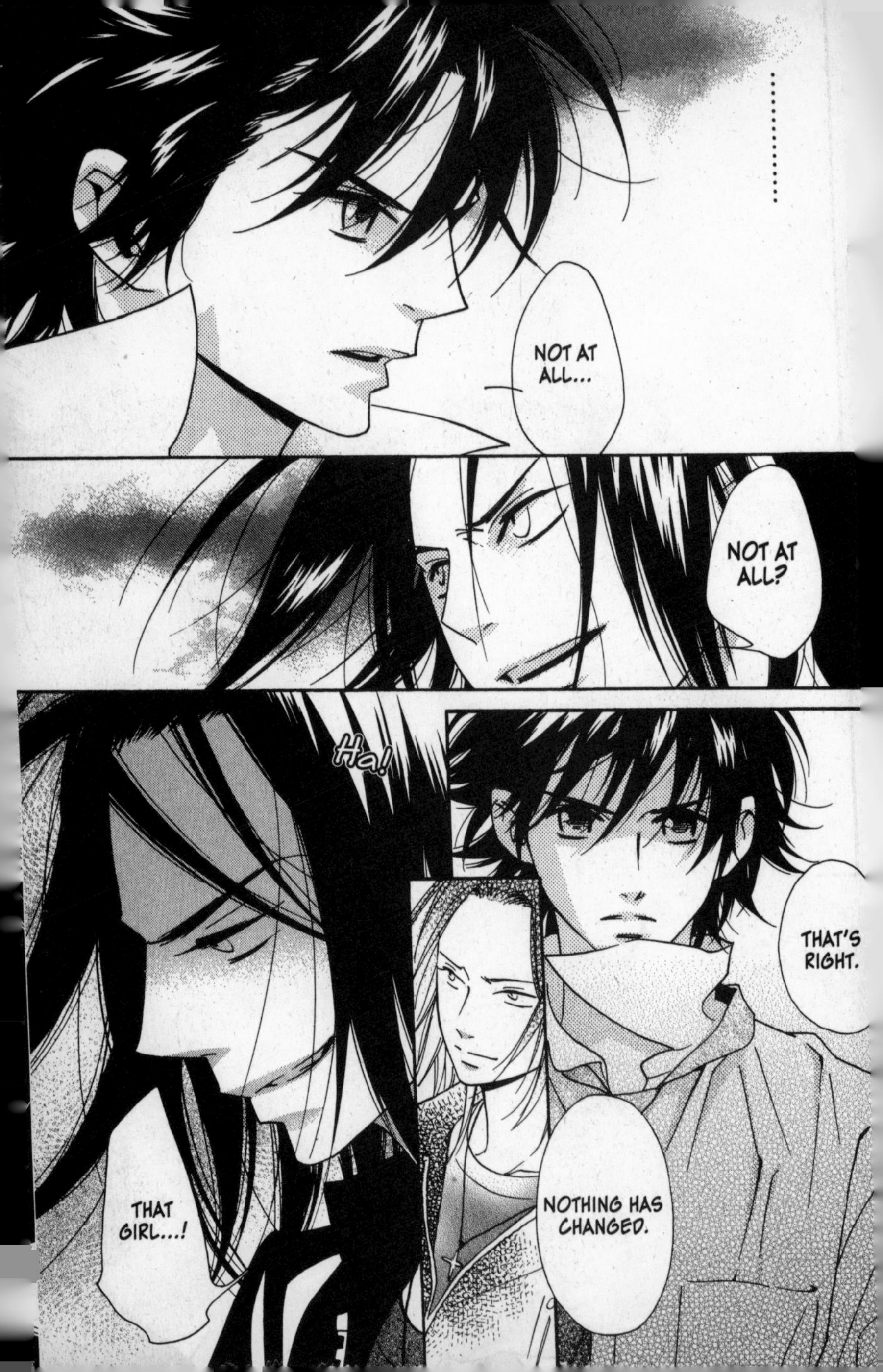
NOT AT ALL...
NOT AT ALL?
THAT'S RIGHT.
NOTHING HAS CHANGED.
Ha!
THAT GIRL...!

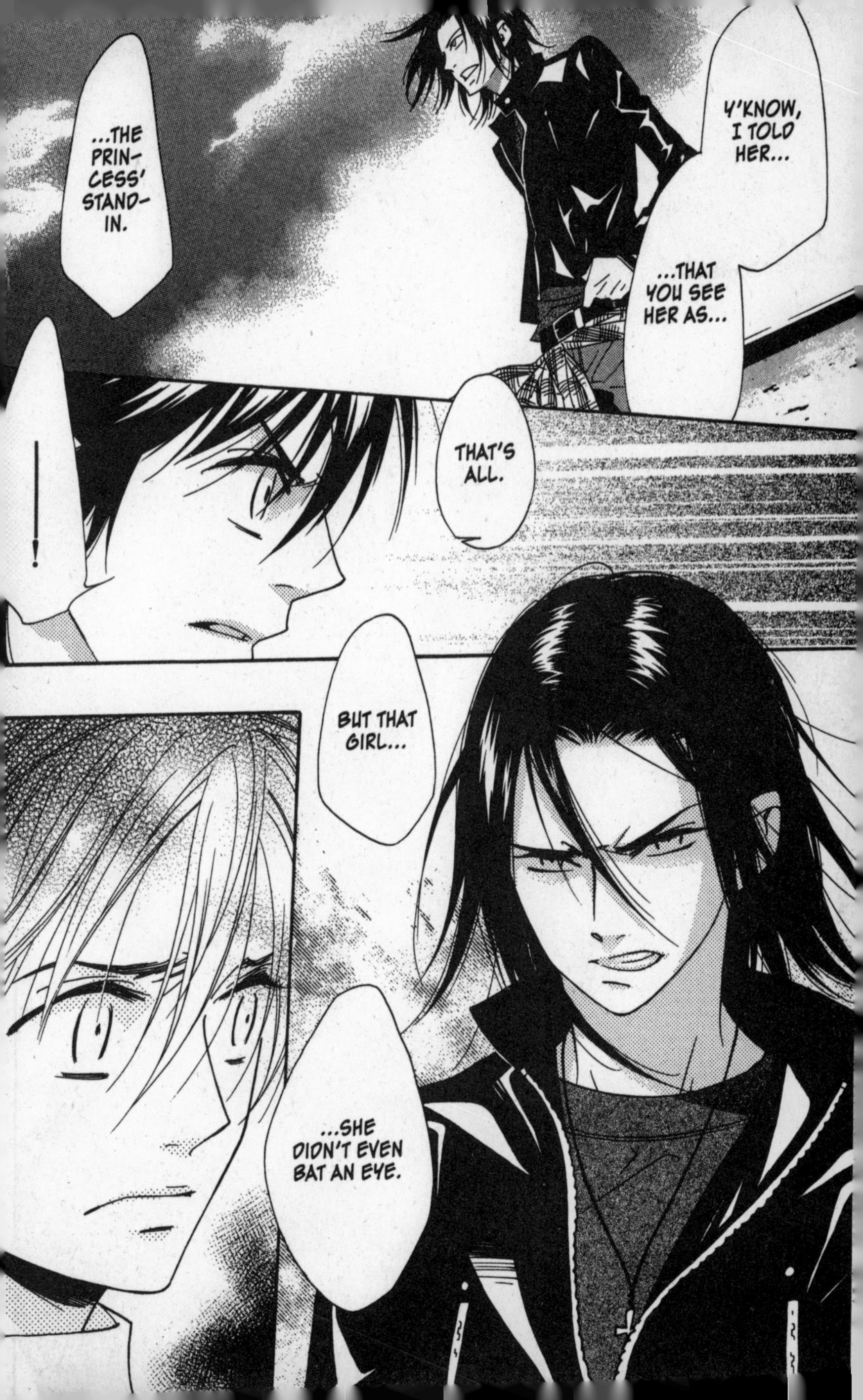
Y'KNOW, I TOLD HER...
...THAT YOU SEE HER AS...
...THE PRINCESS' STAND-IN.
THAT'S ALL.
!
BUT THAT GIRL...
...SHE DIDN'T EVEN BAT AN EYE.

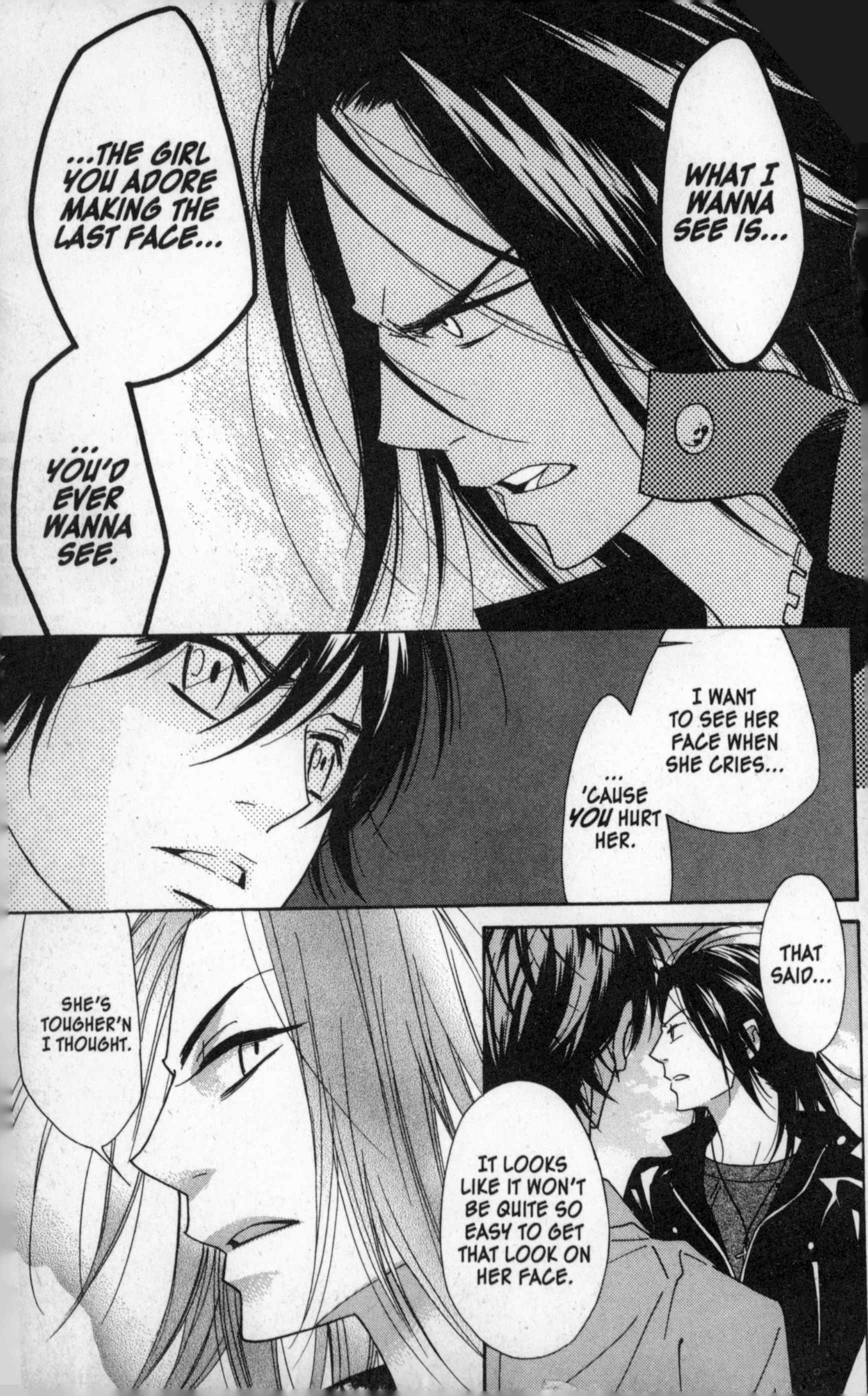
WHAT I WANNA SEE IS...
...THE GIRL YOU ADORE MAKING THE LAST FACE...
...YOU'D EVER WANNA SEE.
I WANT TO SEE HER FACE WHEN SHE CRIES...
...'CAUSE *YOU* HURT HER.
THAT SAID...
IT LOOKS LIKE IT WON'T BE QUITE SO EASY TO GET THAT LOOK ON HER FACE.
SHE'S TOUGHER'N I THOUGHT.

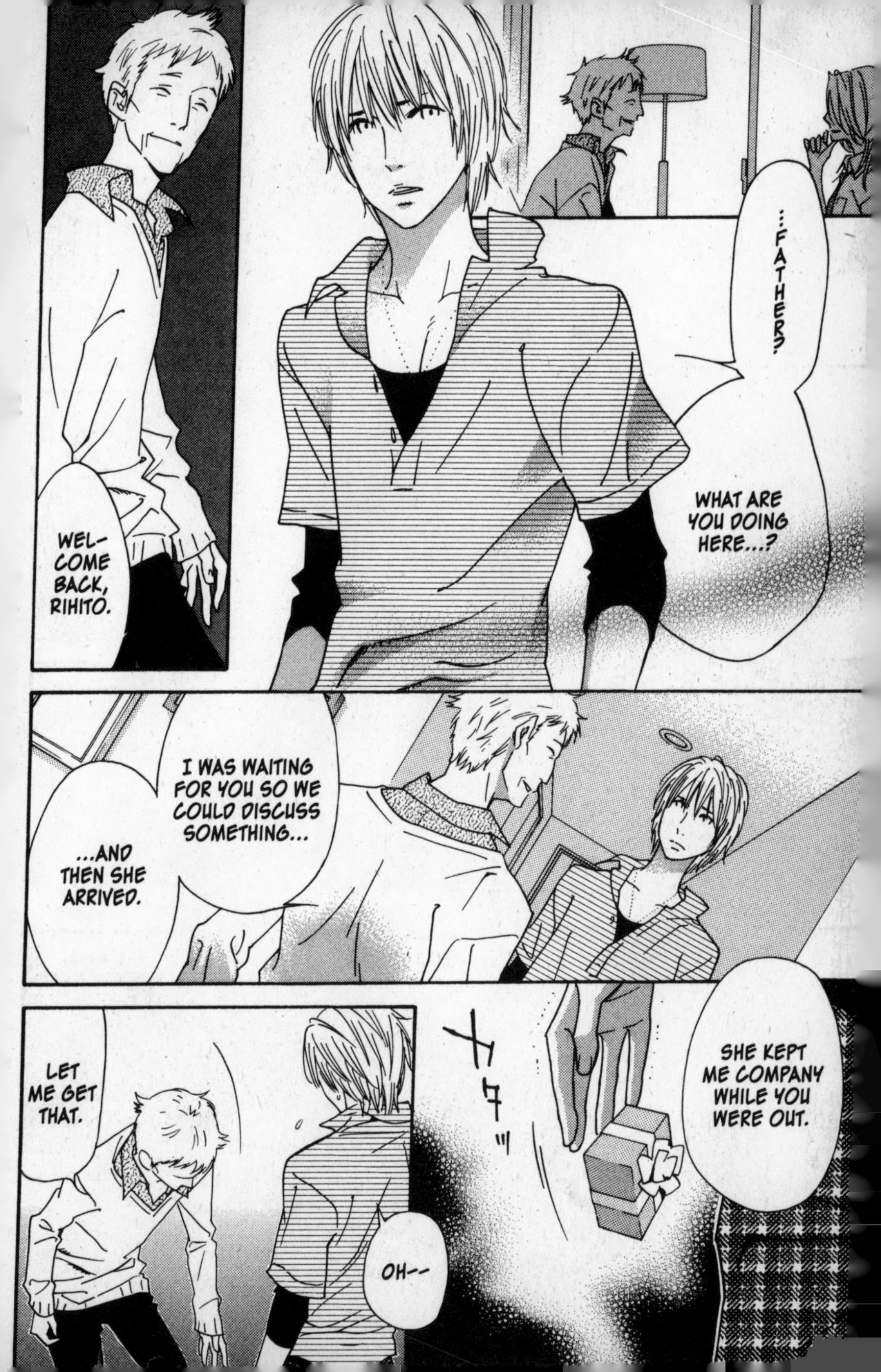
...FATHER?
WHAT ARE YOU DOING HERE...?
WEL-COME BACK, RIHITO.
I WAS WAITING FOR YOU SO WE COULD DISCUSS SOMETHING...
...AND THEN SHE ARRIVED.
SHE KEPT ME COMPANY WHILE YOU WERE OUT.
OH--
LET ME GET THAT.

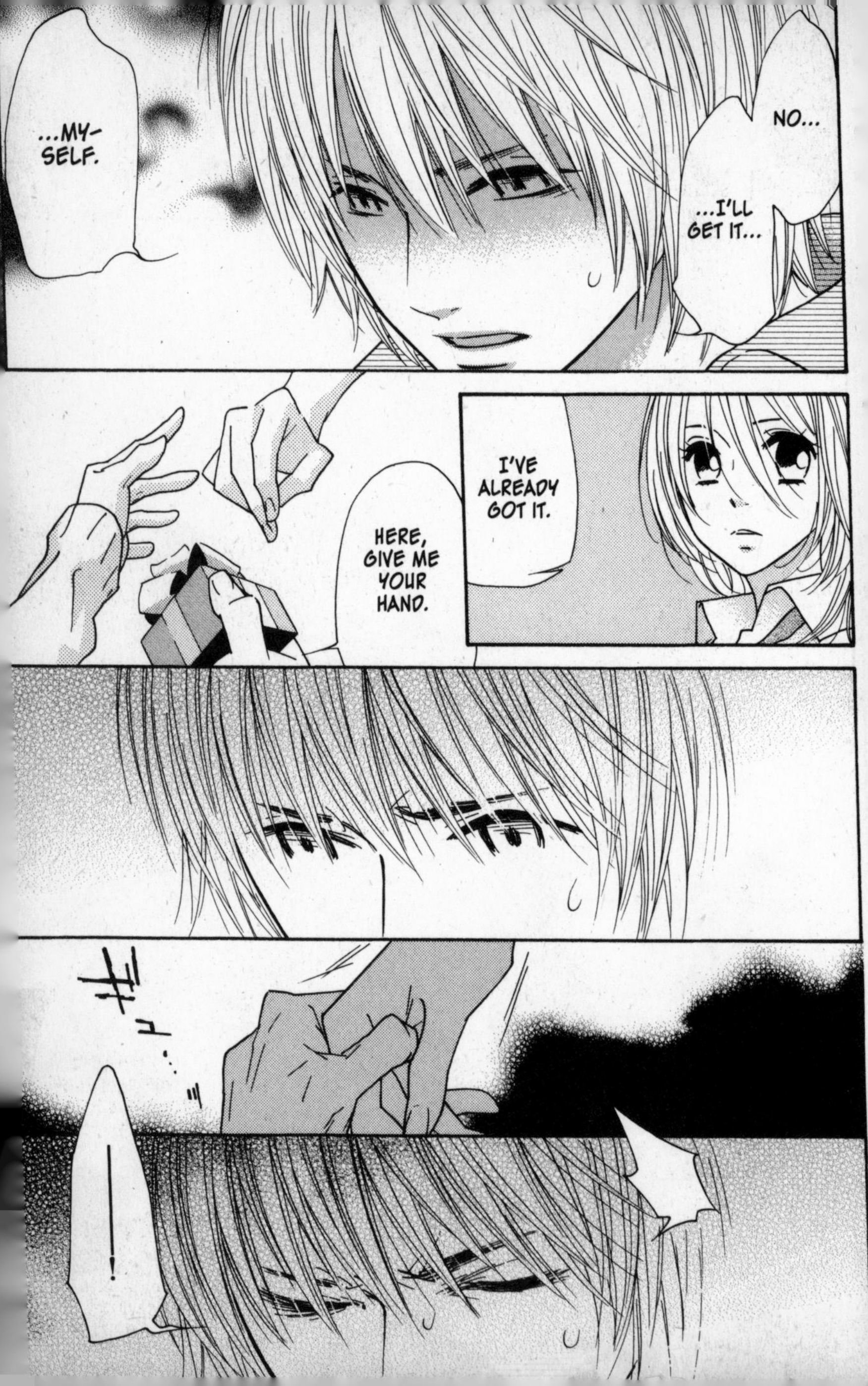
NO...
...I'LL GET IT...
...MY-SELF.
I'VE ALREADY GOT IT.
HERE, GIVE ME YOUR HAND.
ギュ…ッ
—!

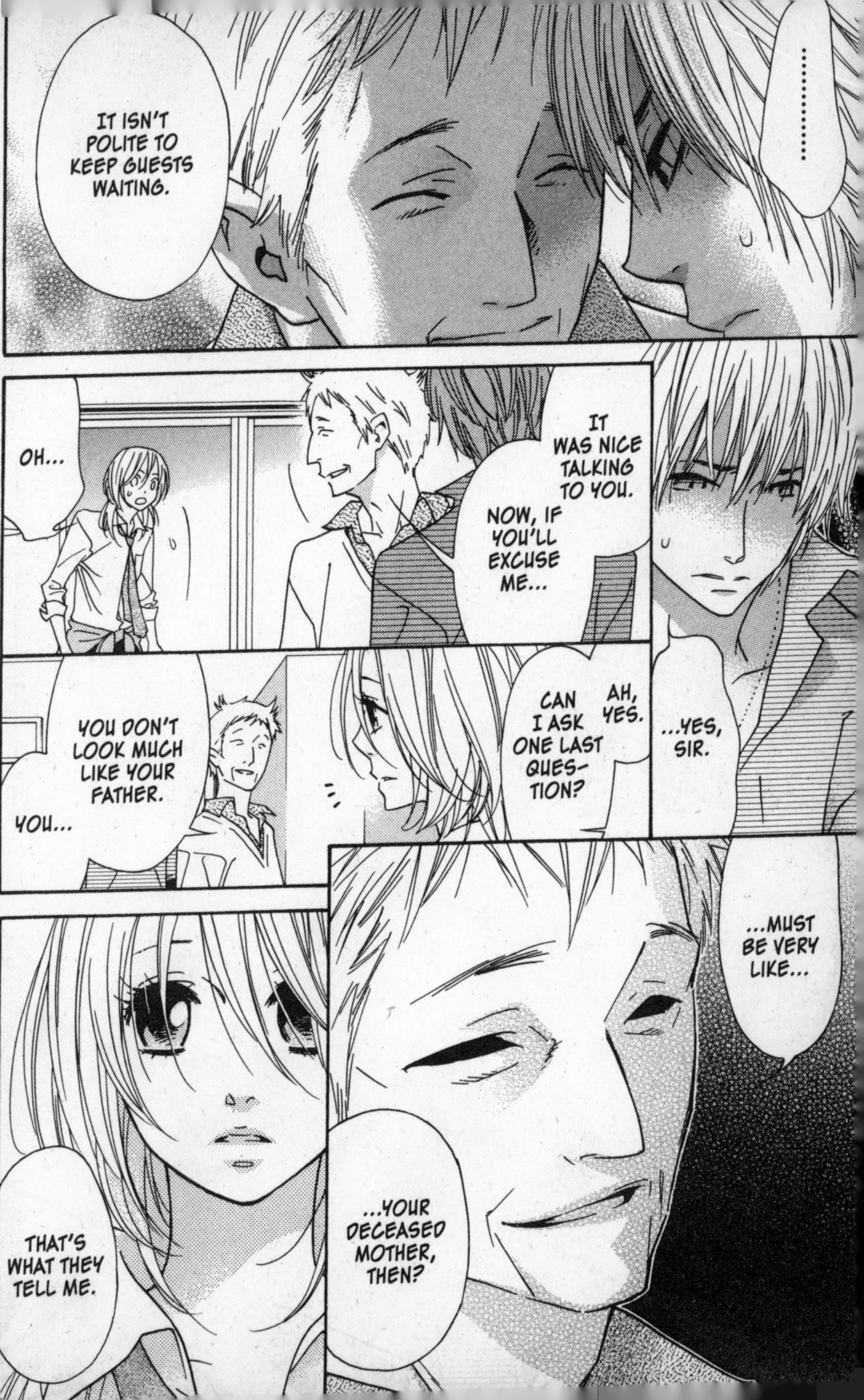
......
IT ISN'T POLITE TO KEEP GUESTS WAITING.
...YES, SIR.
IT WAS NICE TALKING TO YOU.
NOW, IF YOU'LL EXCUSE ME...
OH...
AH, YES.
CAN I ASK ONE LAST QUESTION?
YOU DON'T LOOK MUCH LIKE YOUR FATHER.
YOU...
...MUST BE VERY LIKE...
...YOUR DECEASED MOTHER, THEN?
THAT'S WHAT THEY TELL ME.

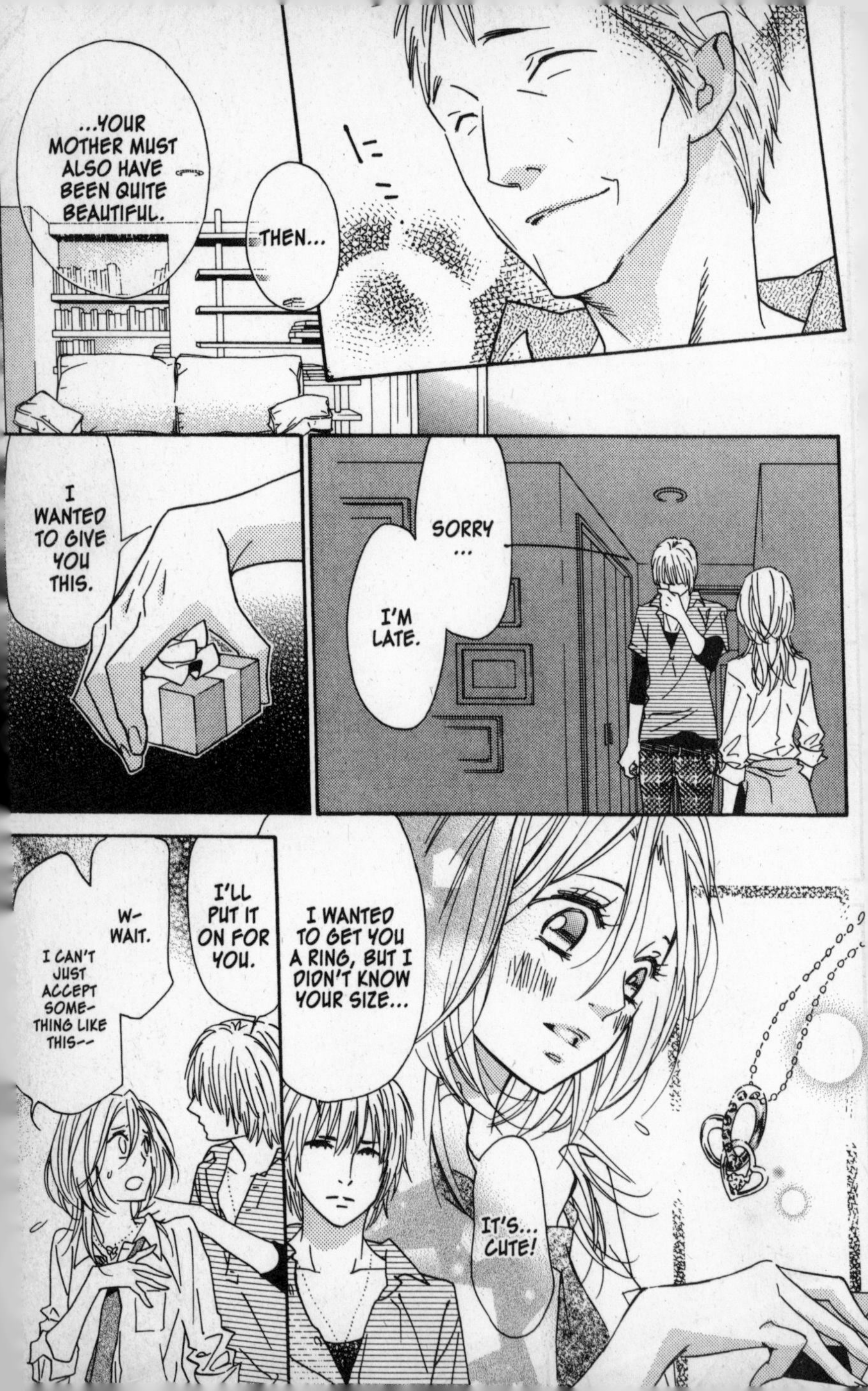
THEN...
...YOUR MOTHER MUST ALSO HAVE BEEN QUITE BEAUTIFUL.
SORRY... I'M LATE.
I WANTED TO GIVE YOU THIS.
IT'S... CUTE!
I WANTED TO GET YOU A RING, BUT I DIDN'T KNOW YOUR SIZE...
I'LL PUT IT ON FOR YOU.
W-WAIT.
I CAN'T JUST ACCEPT SOMETHING LIKE THIS--

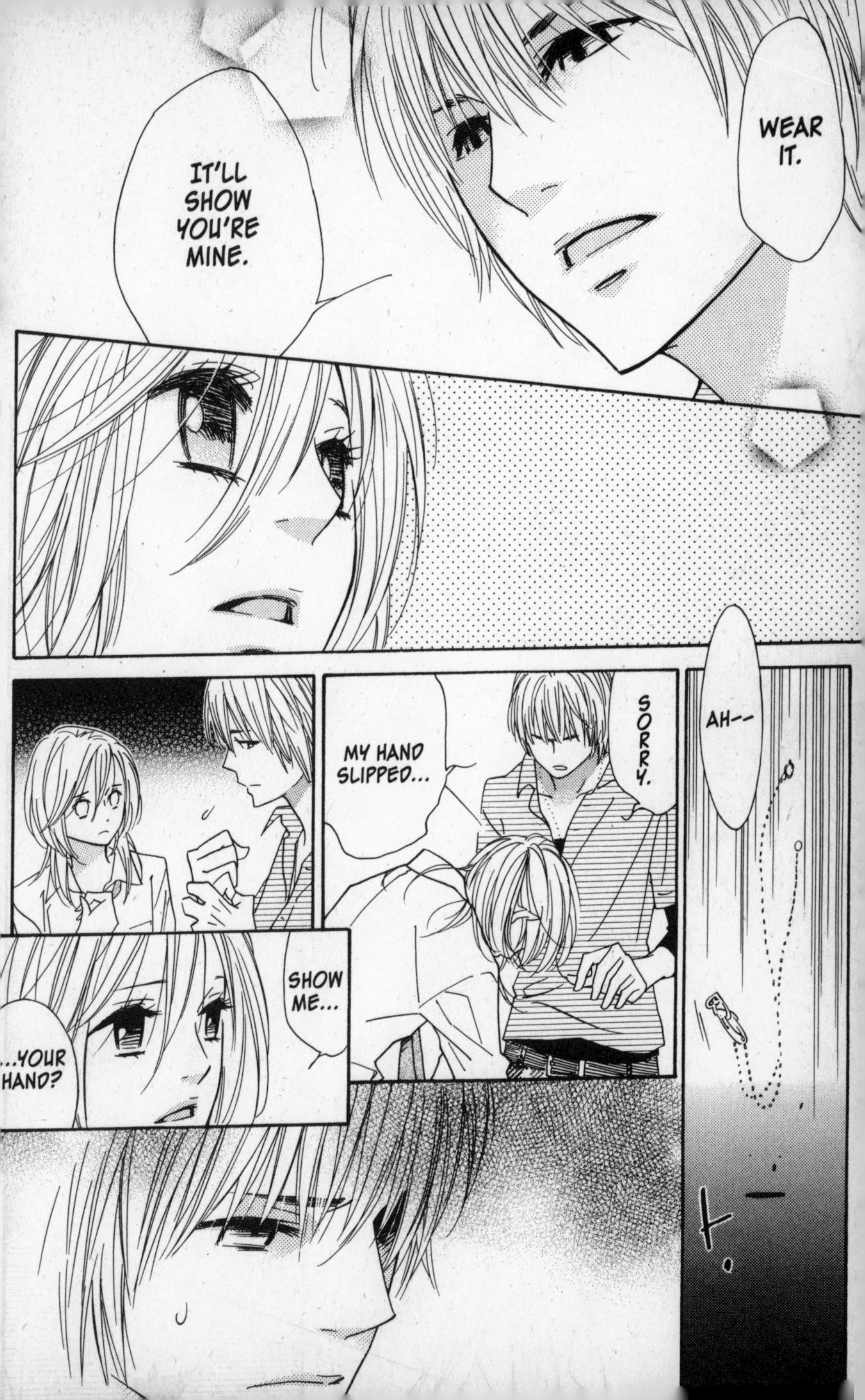
WEAR IT.
IT'LL SHOW YOU'RE MINE.
AH--
SORRY.
MY HAND SLIPPED...
SHOW ME...
...YOUR HAND?

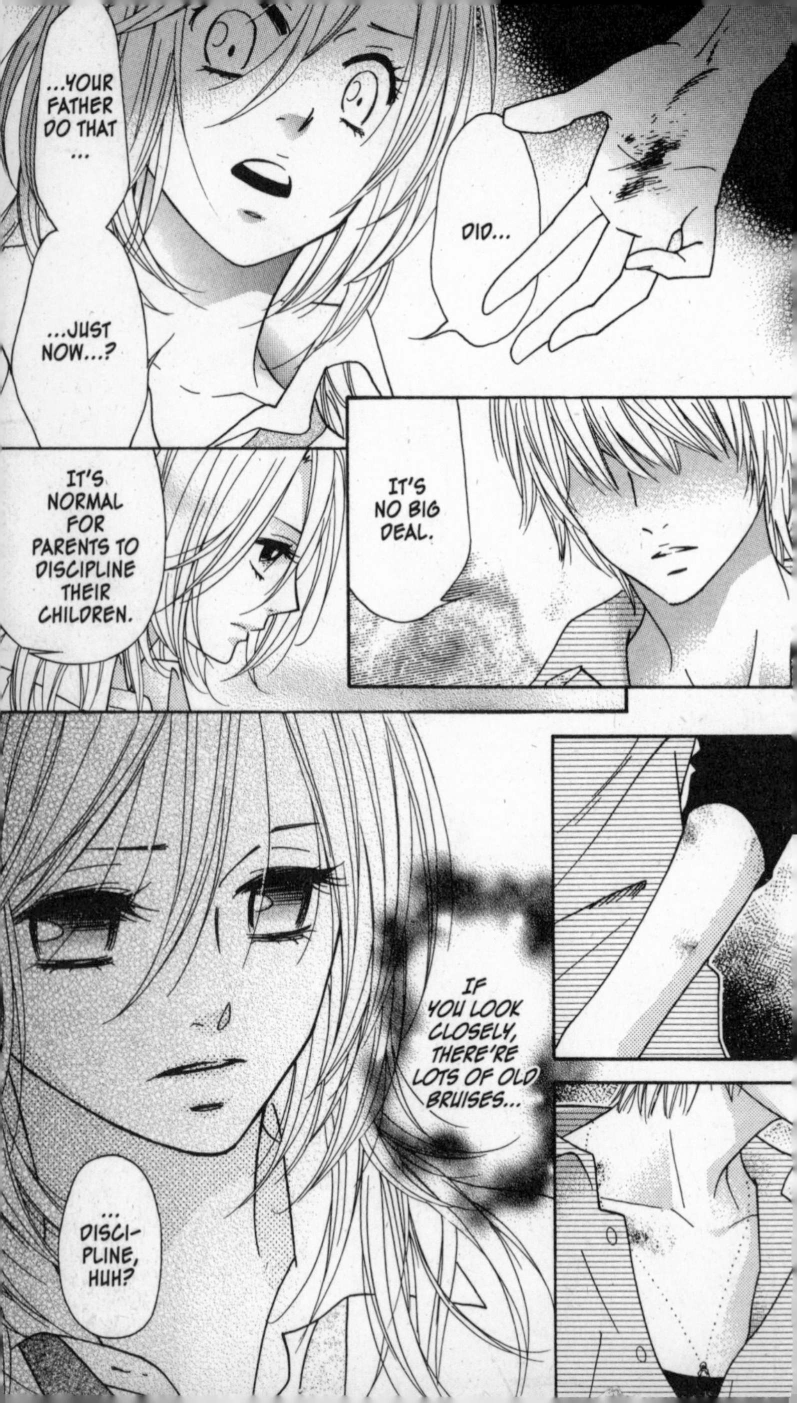
DID...
...YOUR FATHER DO THAT...
...JUST NOW...?
IT'S NO BIG DEAL.
IT'S NORMAL FOR PARENTS TO DISCIPLINE THEIR CHILDREN.
IF YOU LOOK CLOSELY, THERE'RE LOTS OF OLD BRUISES...
...DISCIPLINE, HUH?

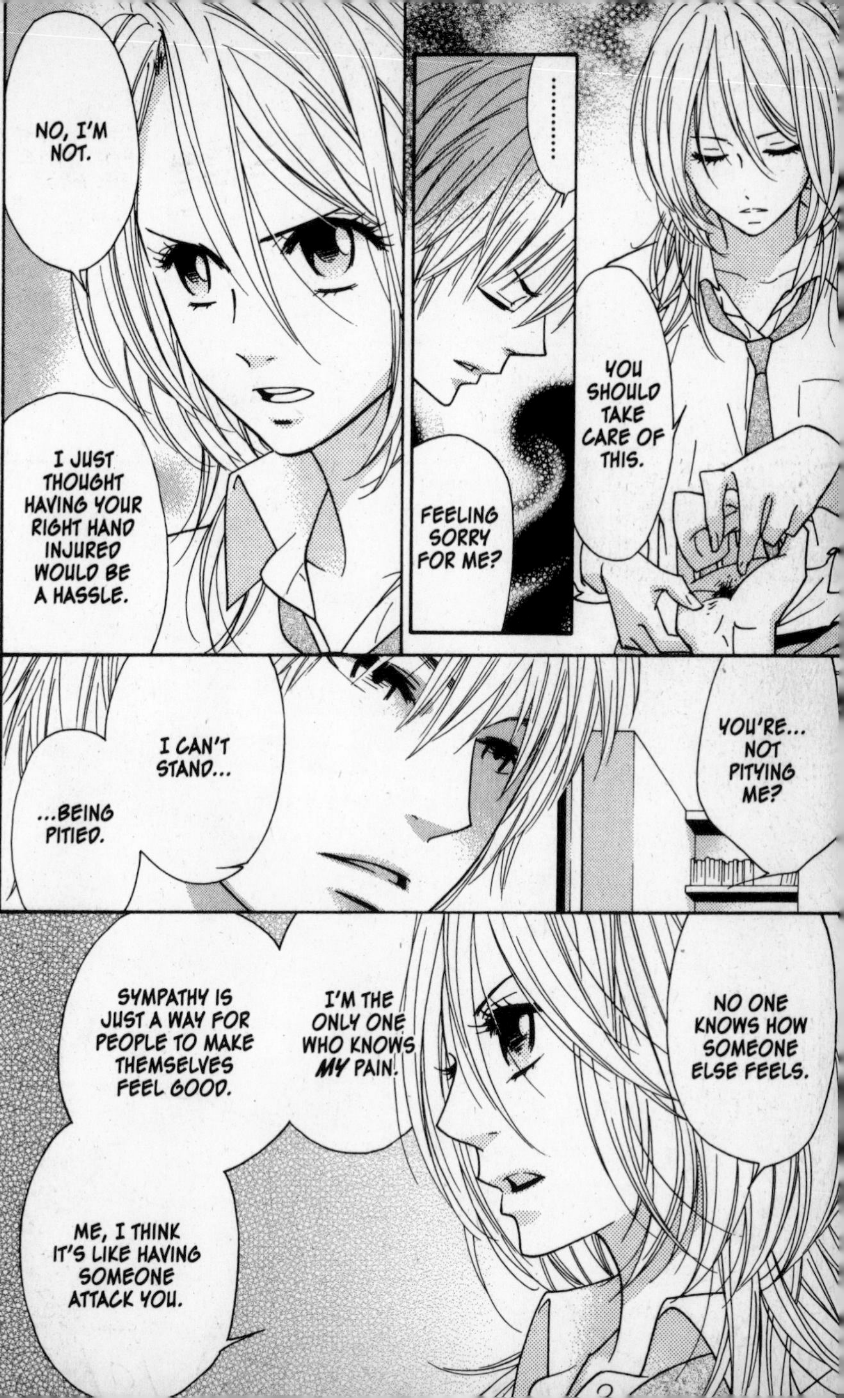
YOU SHOULD TAKE CARE OF THIS.
......
FEELING SORRY FOR ME?
NO, I'M NOT.
I JUST THOUGHT HAVING YOUR RIGHT HAND INJURED WOULD BE A HASSLE.
YOU'RE... NOT PITYING ME?
I CAN'T STAND...
...BEING PITIED.
NO ONE KNOWS HOW SOMEONE ELSE FEELS.
I'M THE ONLY ONE WHO KNOWS *MY* PAIN.
SYMPATHY IS JUST A WAY FOR PEOPLE TO MAKE THEMSELVES FEEL GOOD.
ME, I THINK IT'S LIKE HAVING SOMEONE ATTACK YOU.

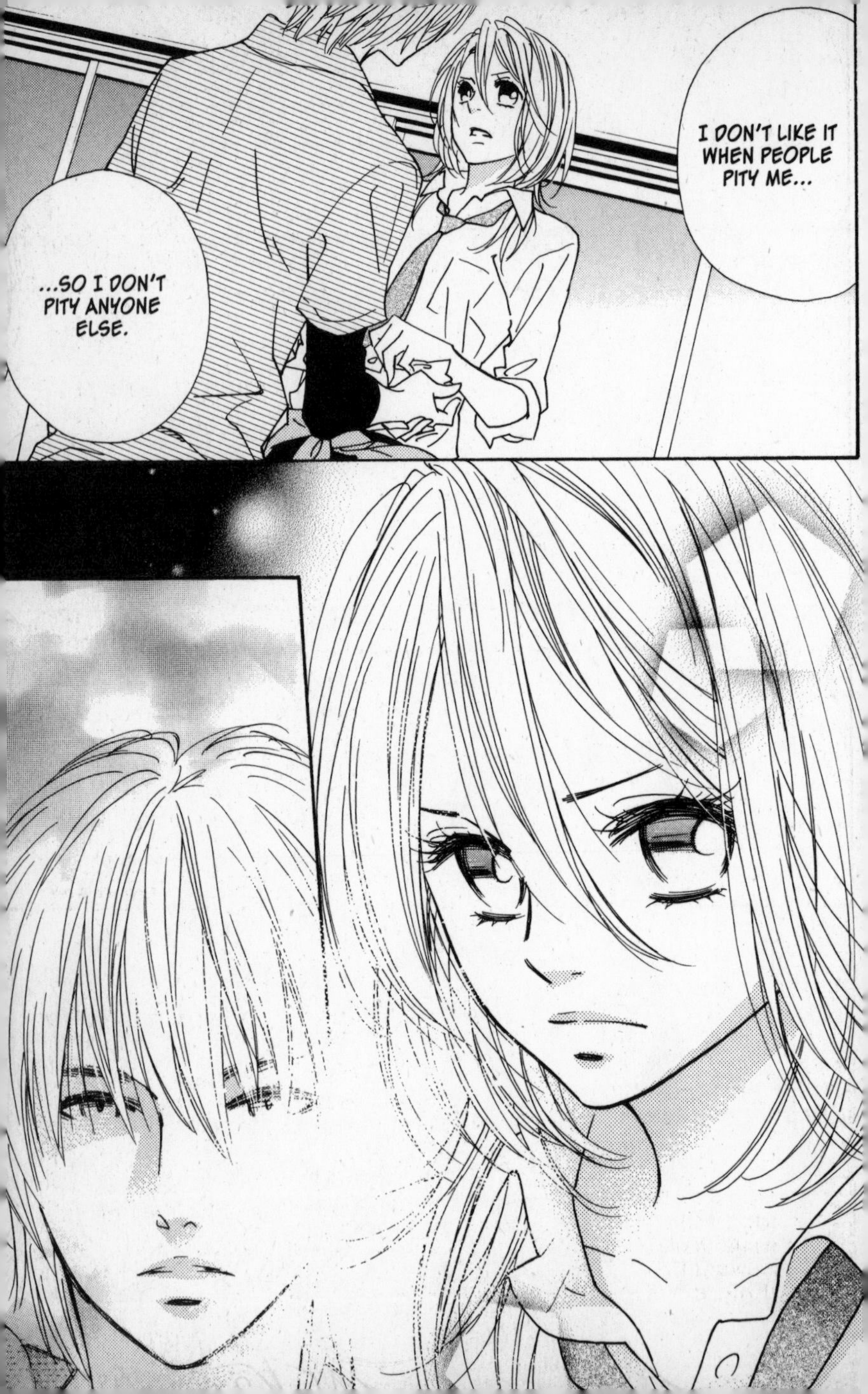
I DON'T LIKE IT WHEN PEOPLE PITY ME...
...SO I DON'T PITY ANYONE ELSE.

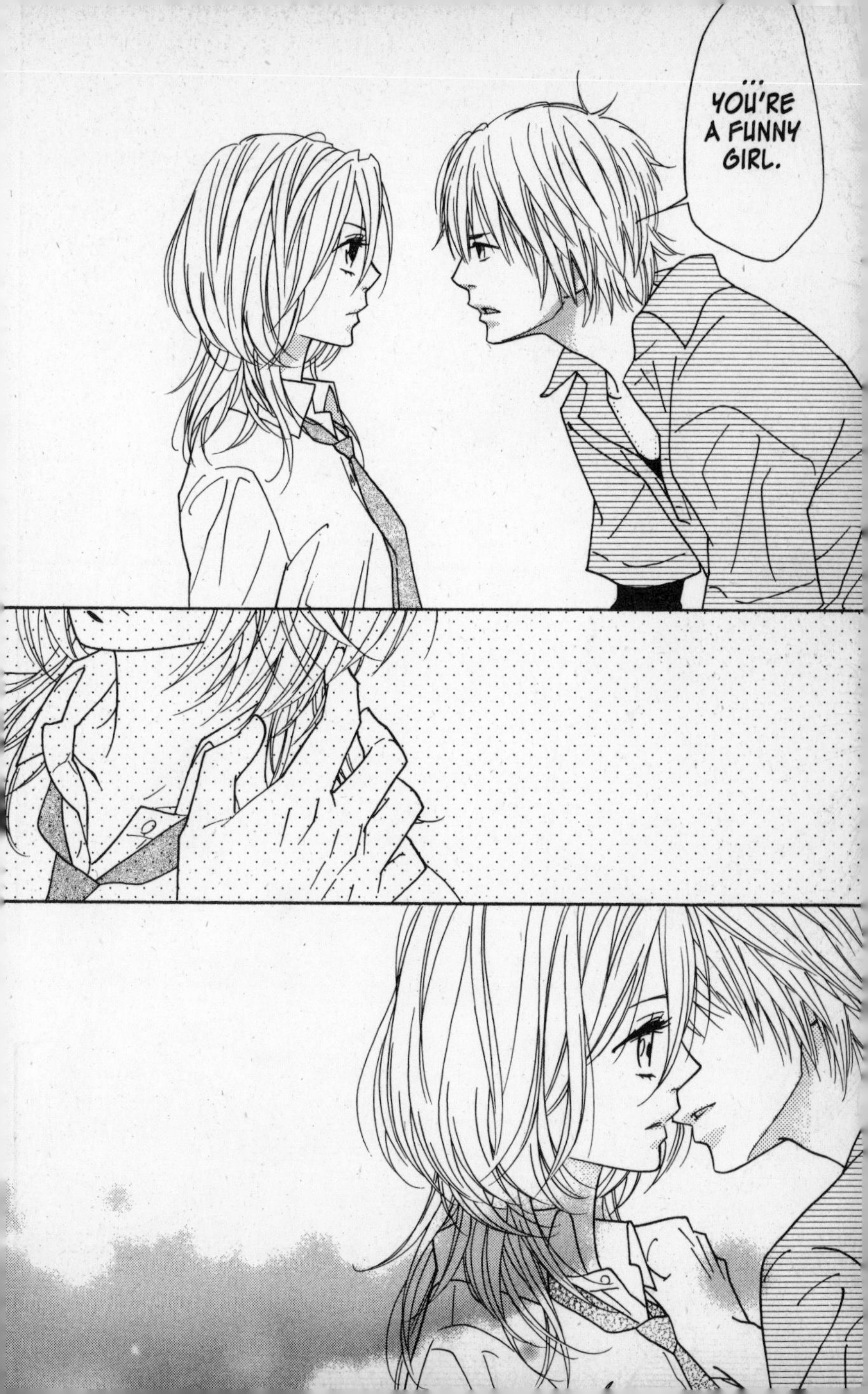
... YOU'RE A FUNNY GIRL.

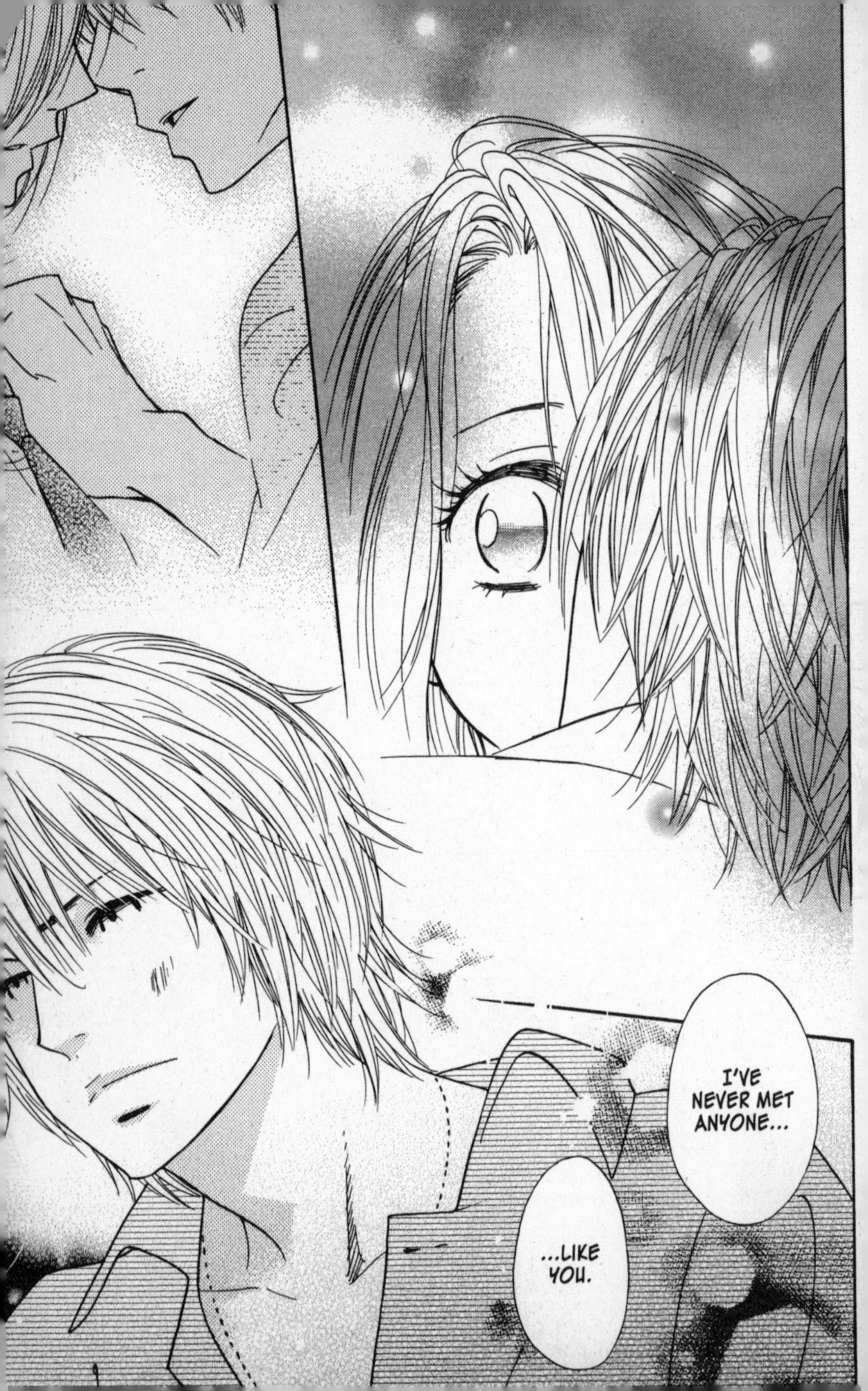
I'VE NEVER MET ANYONE...
...LIKE YOU.

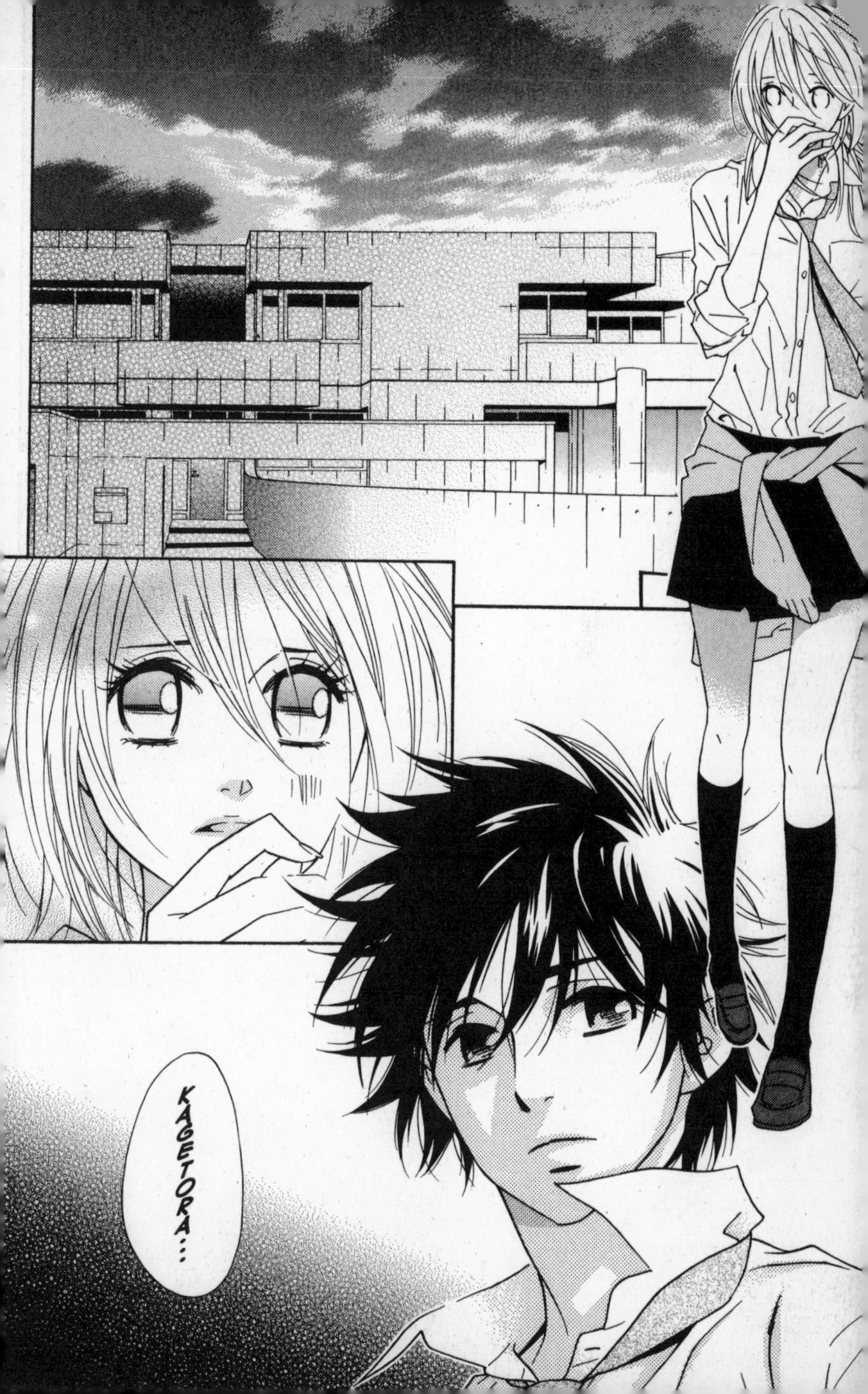
KAGETORA...

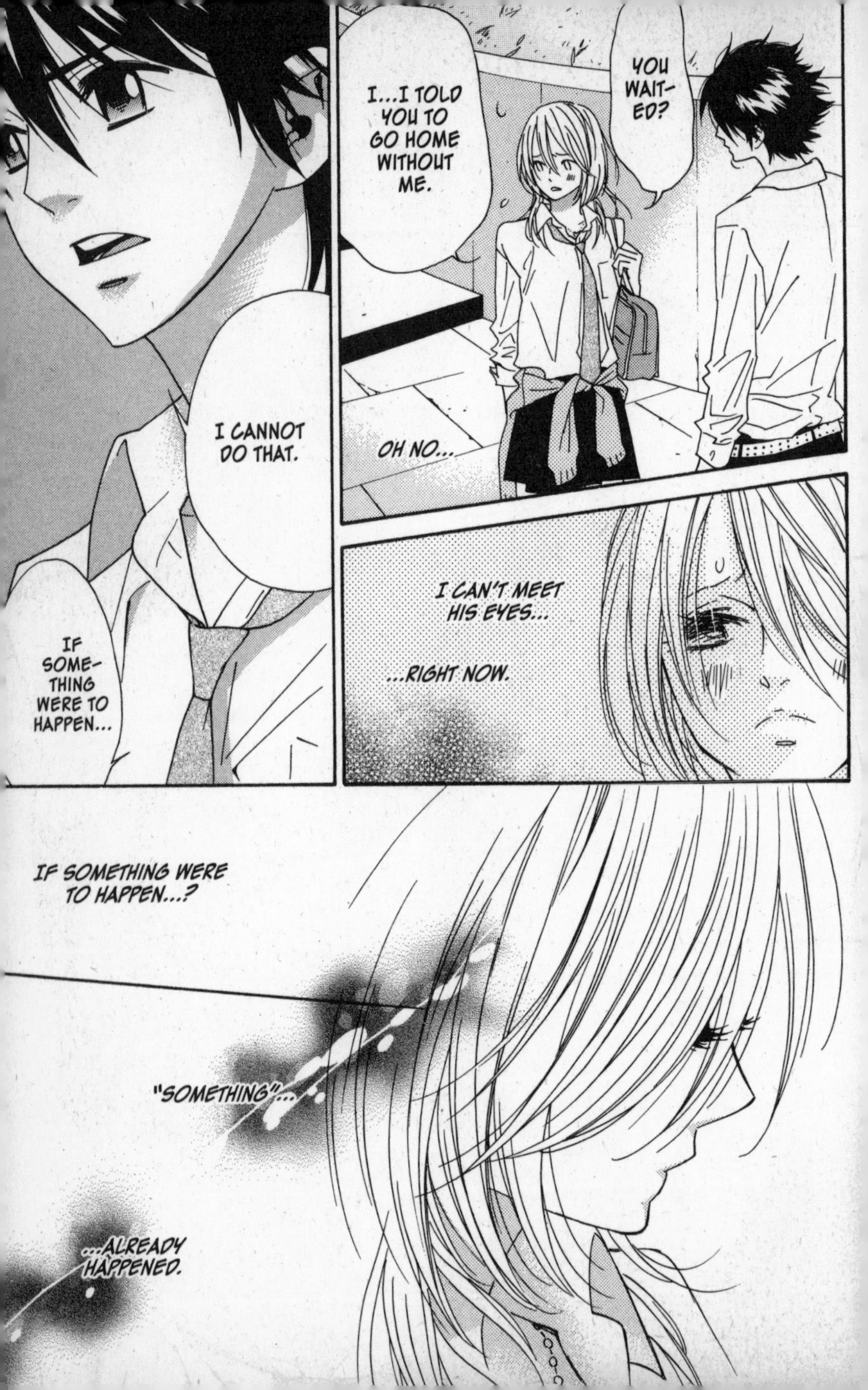
YOU WAIT-ED?
I...I TOLD YOU TO GO HOME WITHOUT ME.
OH NO...
I CAN'T MEET HIS EYES...
...RIGHT NOW.
I CANNOT DO THAT.
IF SOME-THING WERE TO HAPPEN...
IF SOMETHING WERE TO HAPPEN...?
"SOMETHING"...
...ALREADY HAPPENED.

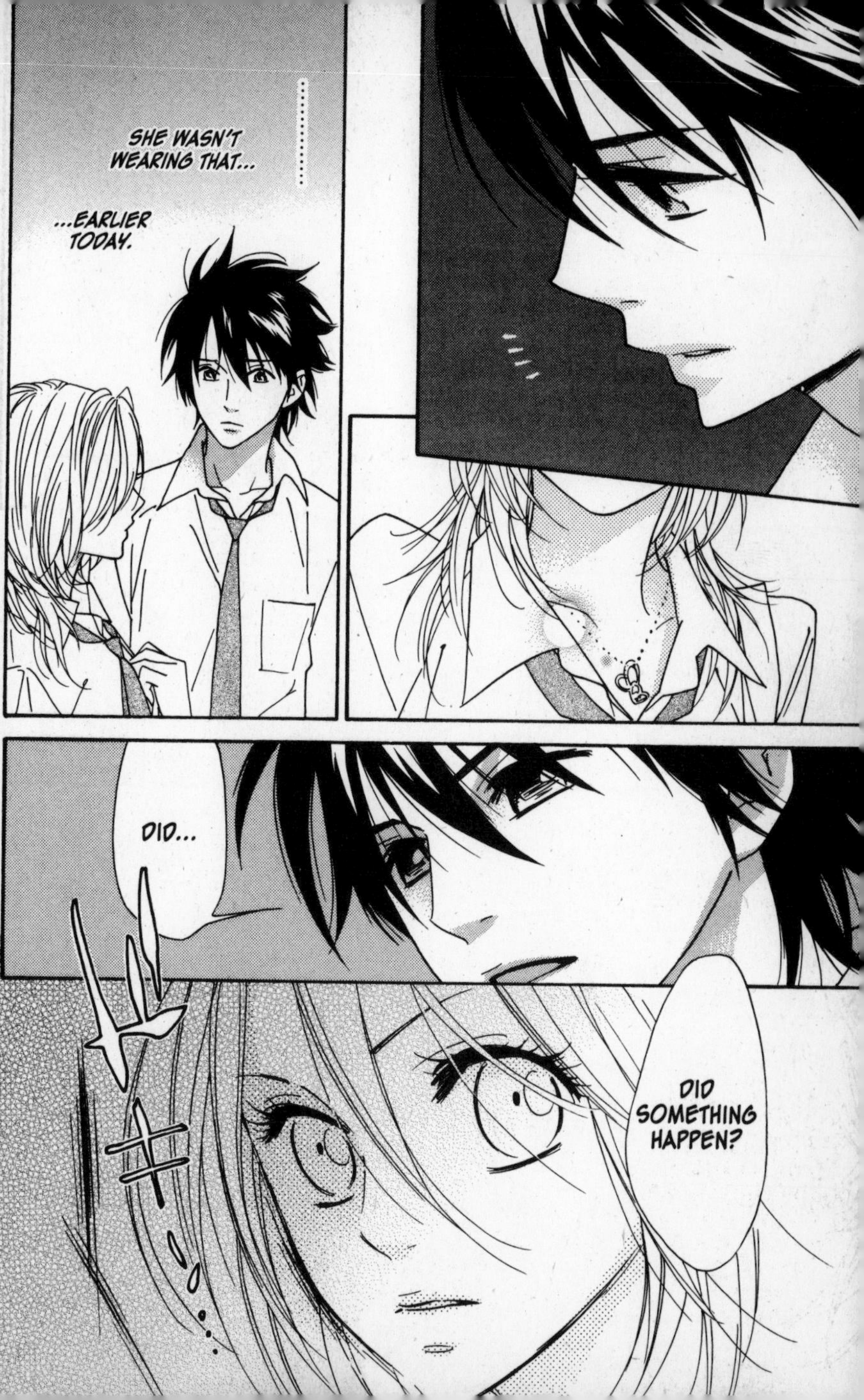
......
SHE WASN'T WEARING THAT...
...EARLIER TODAY.
DID...
DID SOMETHING HAPPEN?

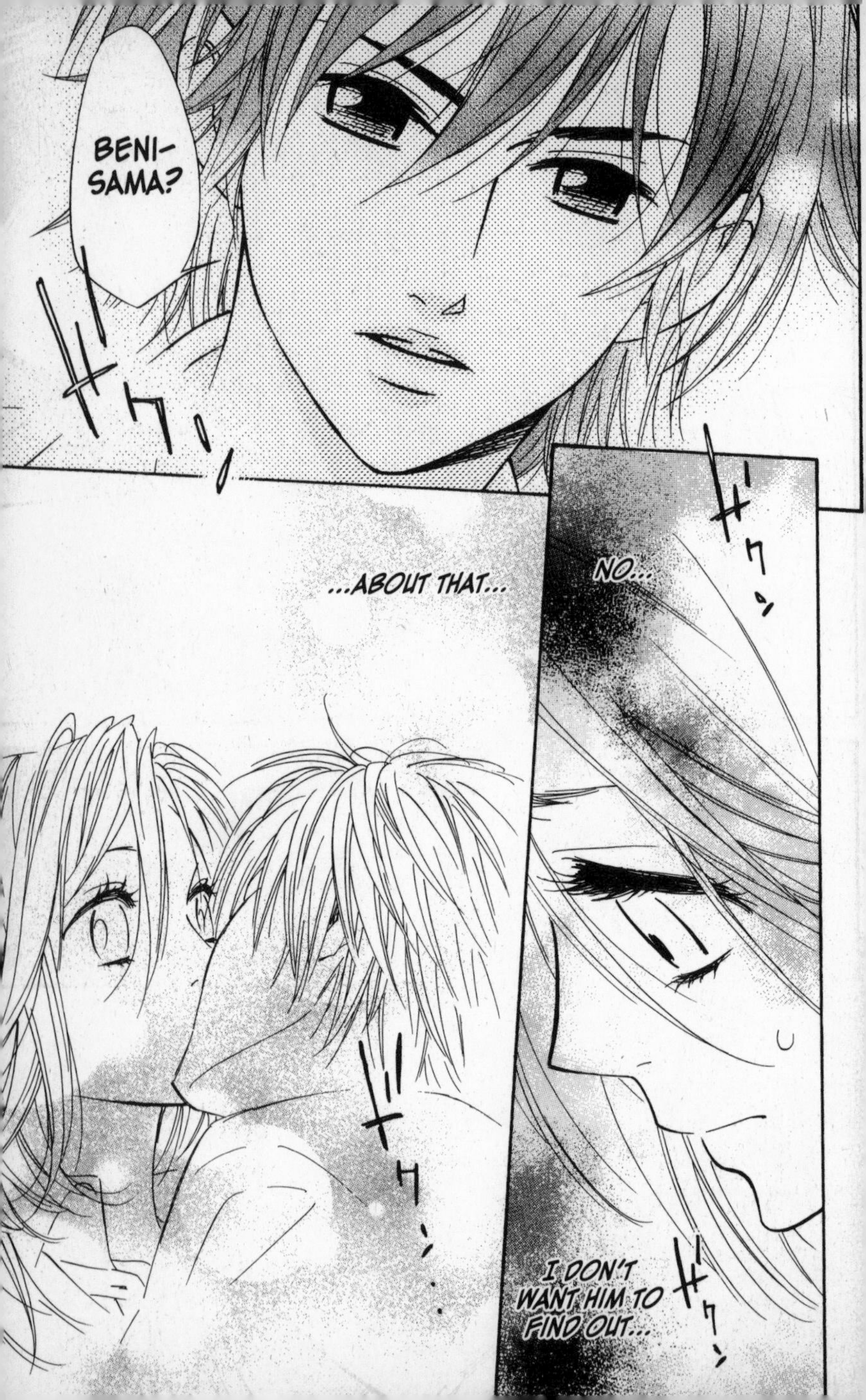
BENI-SAMA?
NO...
I DON'T WANT HIM TO FIND OUT...
...ABOUT THAT...

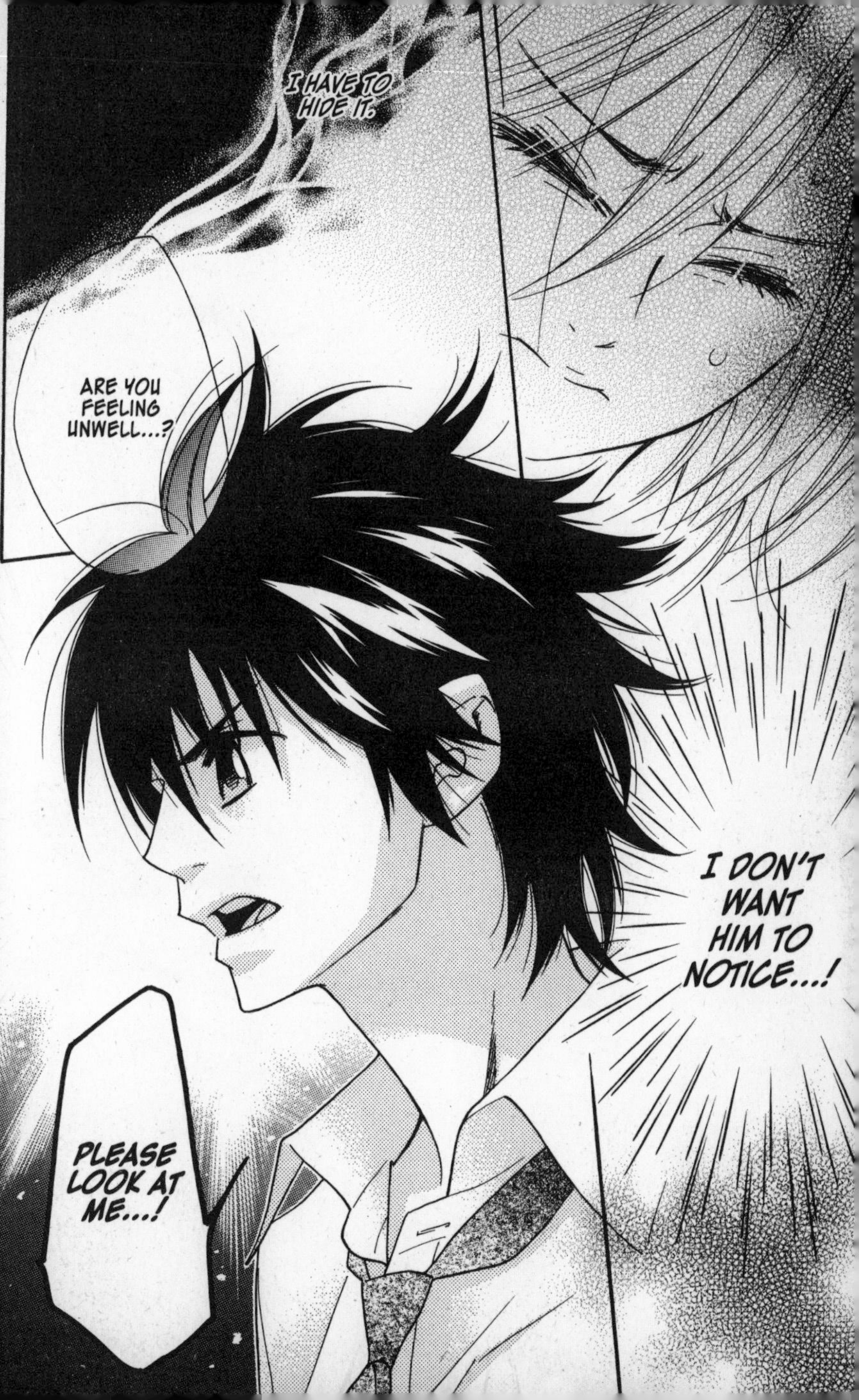
I HAVE TO HIDE IT.
ARE YOU FEELING UNWELL...?
I DON'T WANT HIM TO NOTICE...!
PLEASE LOOK AT ME...!

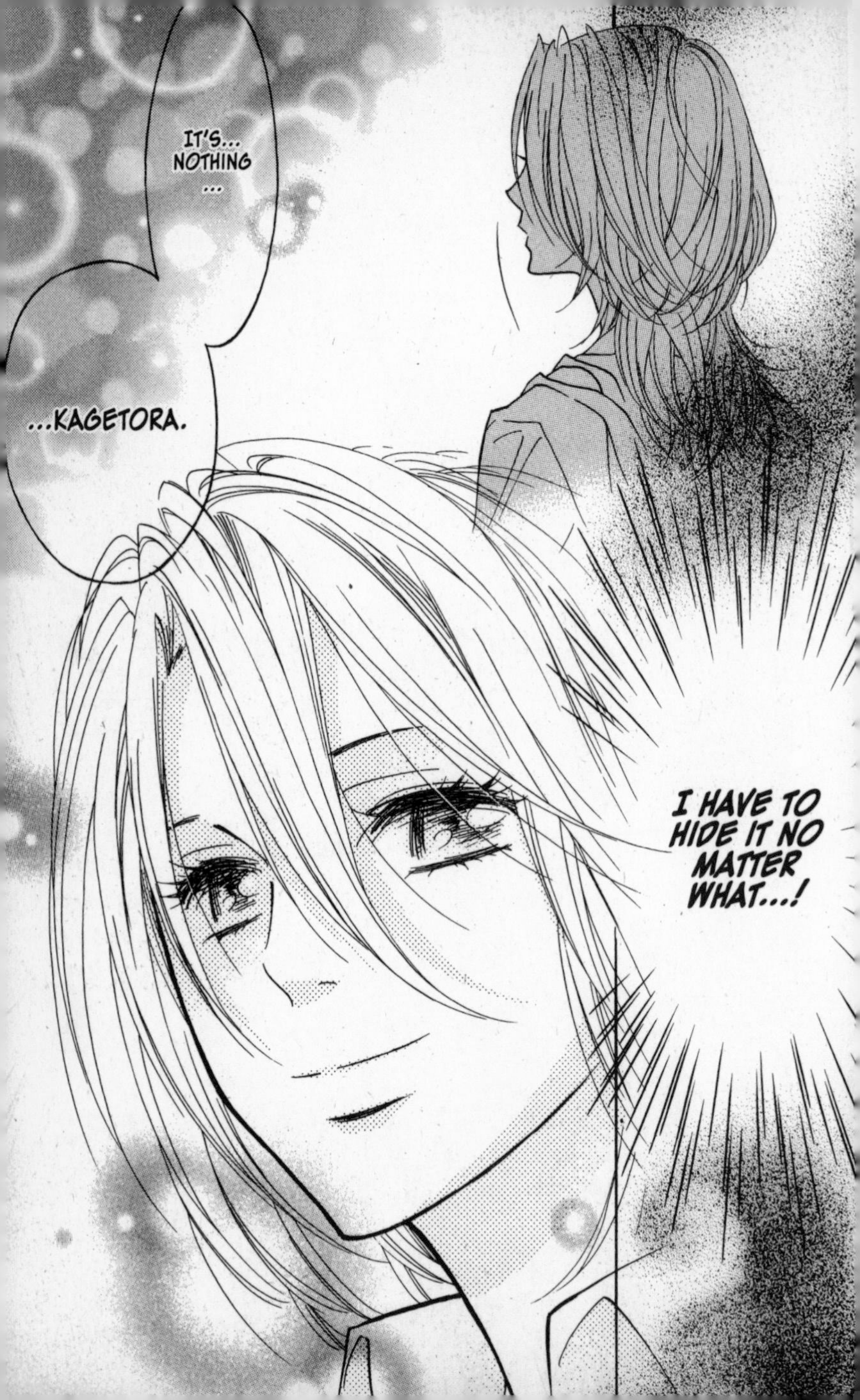
I HAVE TO HIDE IT NO MATTER WHAT...!
IT'S... NOTHING ...
...KAGETORA.

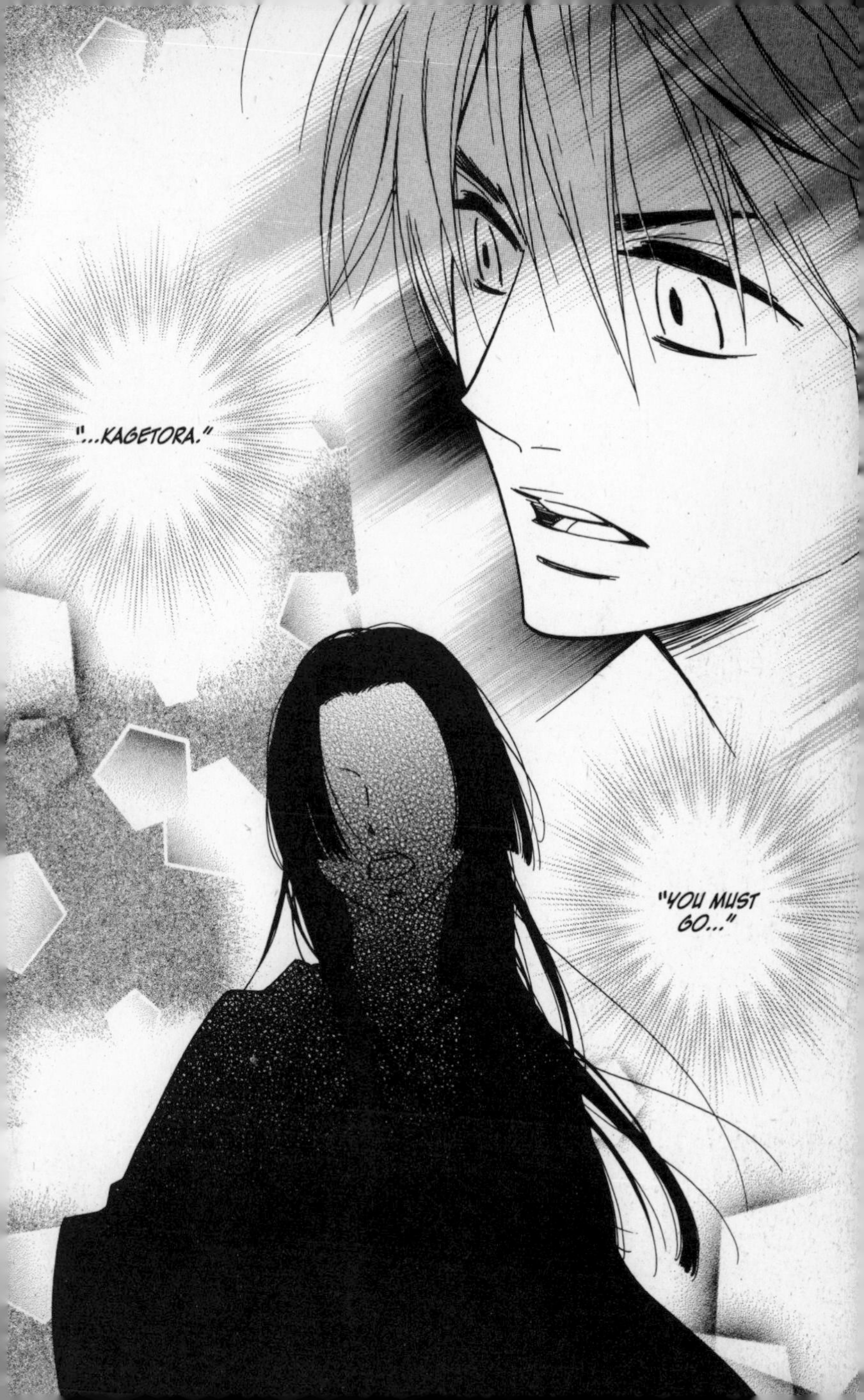
"...KAGETORA."
"YOU MUST GO..."

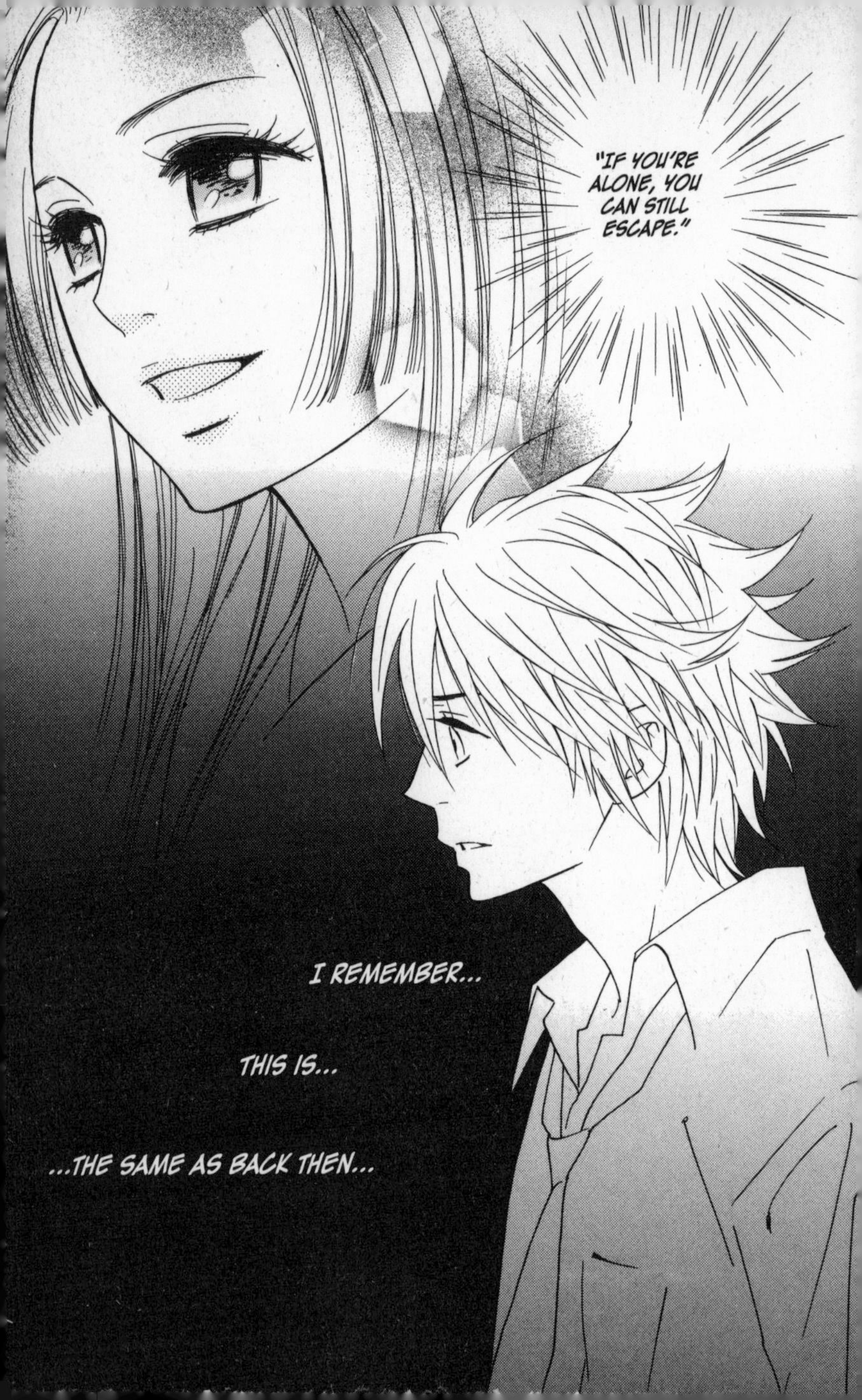
"IF YOU'RE ALONE, YOU CAN STILL ESCAPE."
I REMEMBER...
THIS IS...
...THE SAME AS BACK THEN...

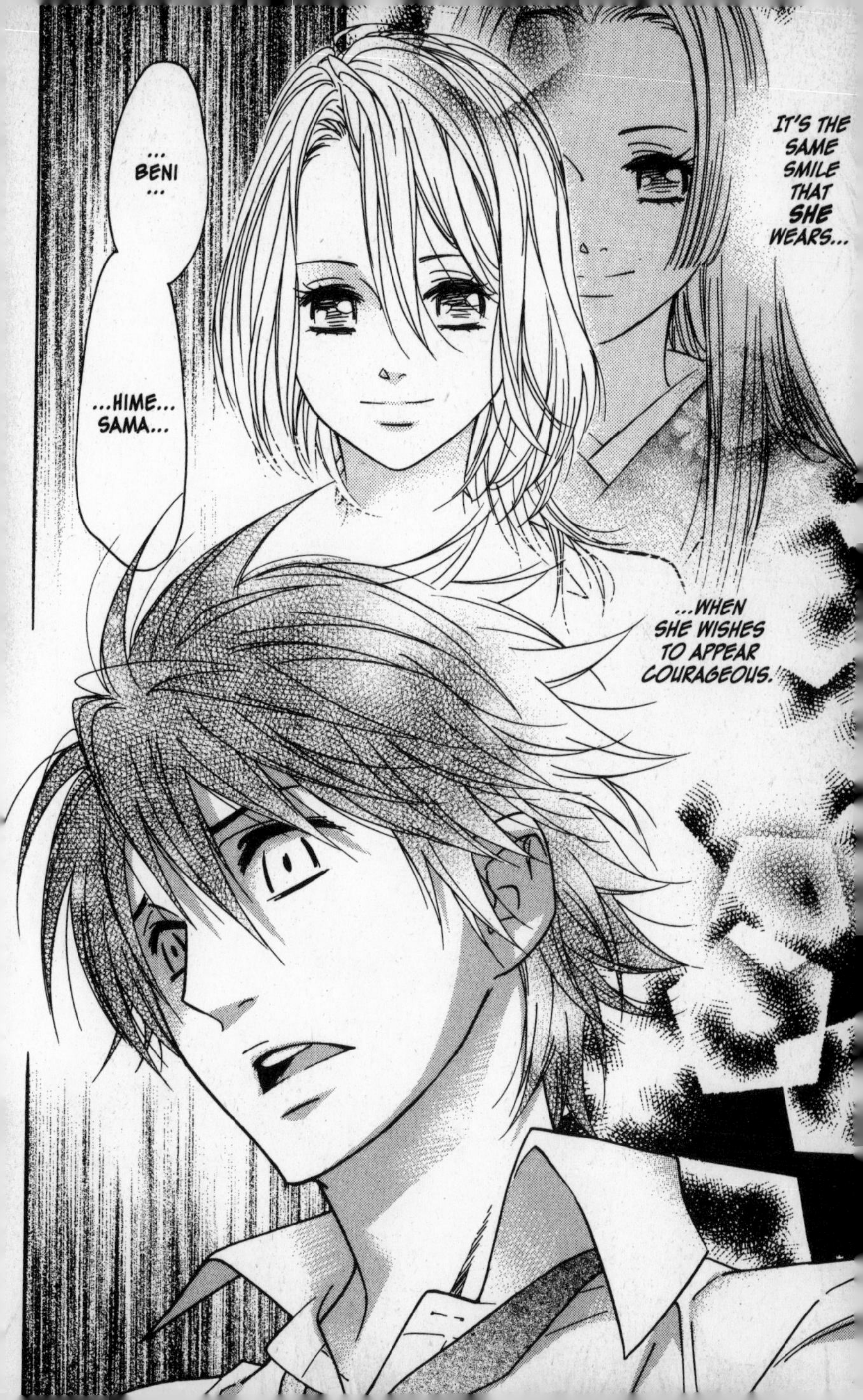
IT'S THE SAME SMILE THAT SHE WEARS...
... BENI ... ...HIME... SAMA...
...WHEN SHE WISHES TO APPEAR COURAGEOUS.

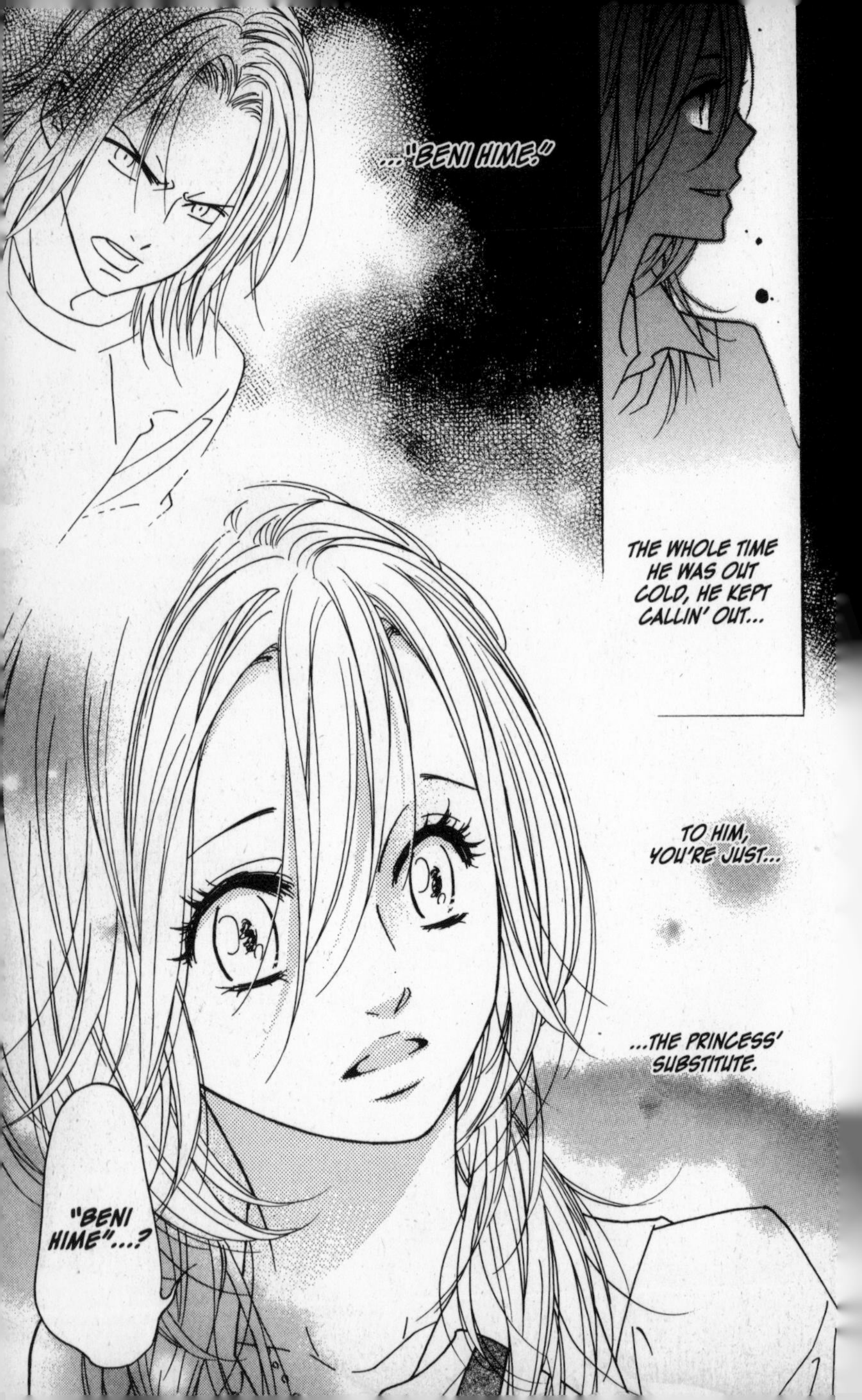
THE WHOLE TIME HE WAS OUT COLD, HE KEPT CALLIN' OUT...
..."BENI HIME."
TO HIM, YOU'RE JUST...
...THE PRINCESS' SUBSTITUTE.
"BENI HIME"...?

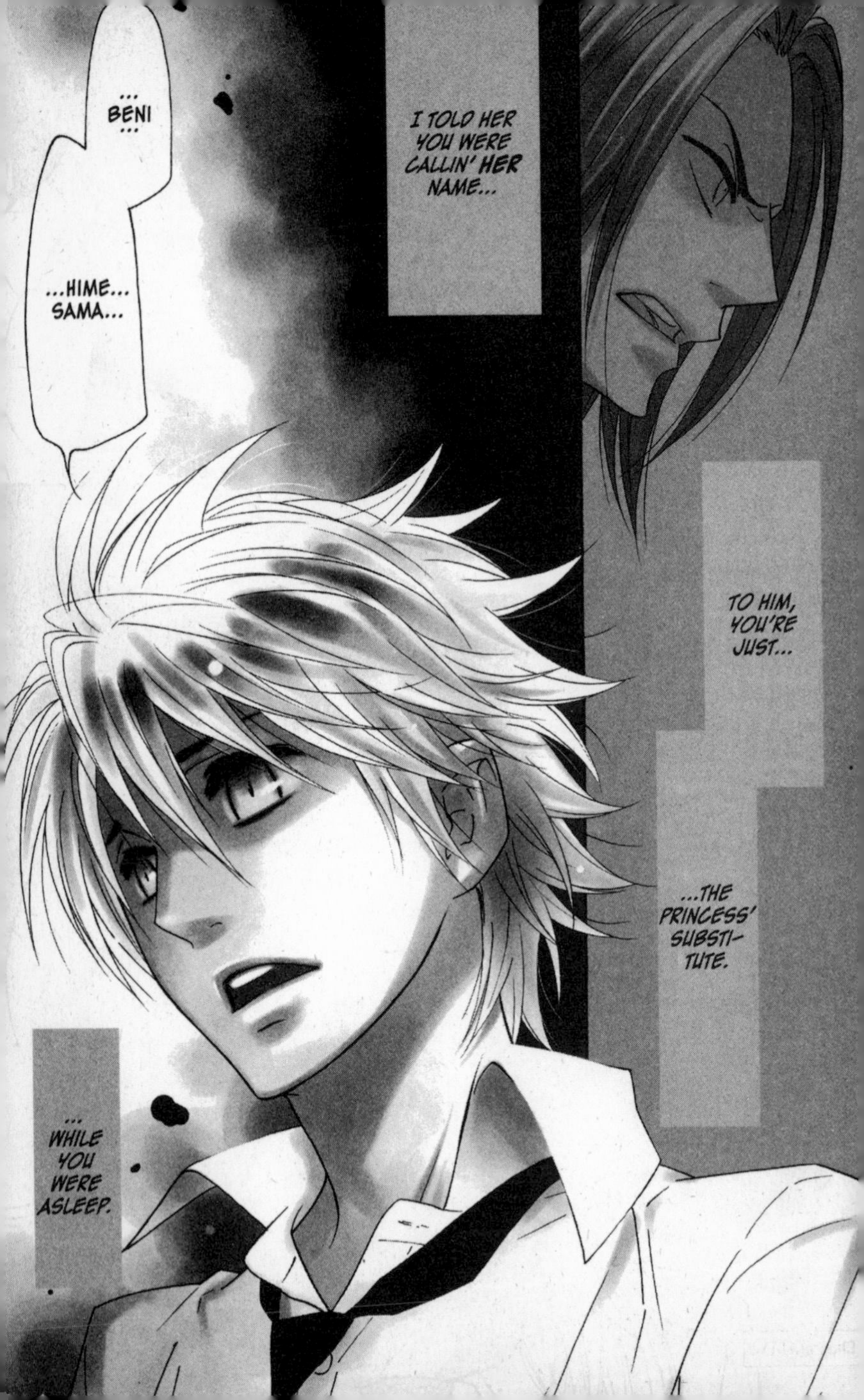
I TOLD HER YOU WERE CALLIN' HER NAME...
...BENI...
...HIME... SAMA...
...WHILE YOU WERE ASLEEP.
TO HIM, YOU'RE JUST...
...THE PRINCESS' SUBSTI-TUTE.

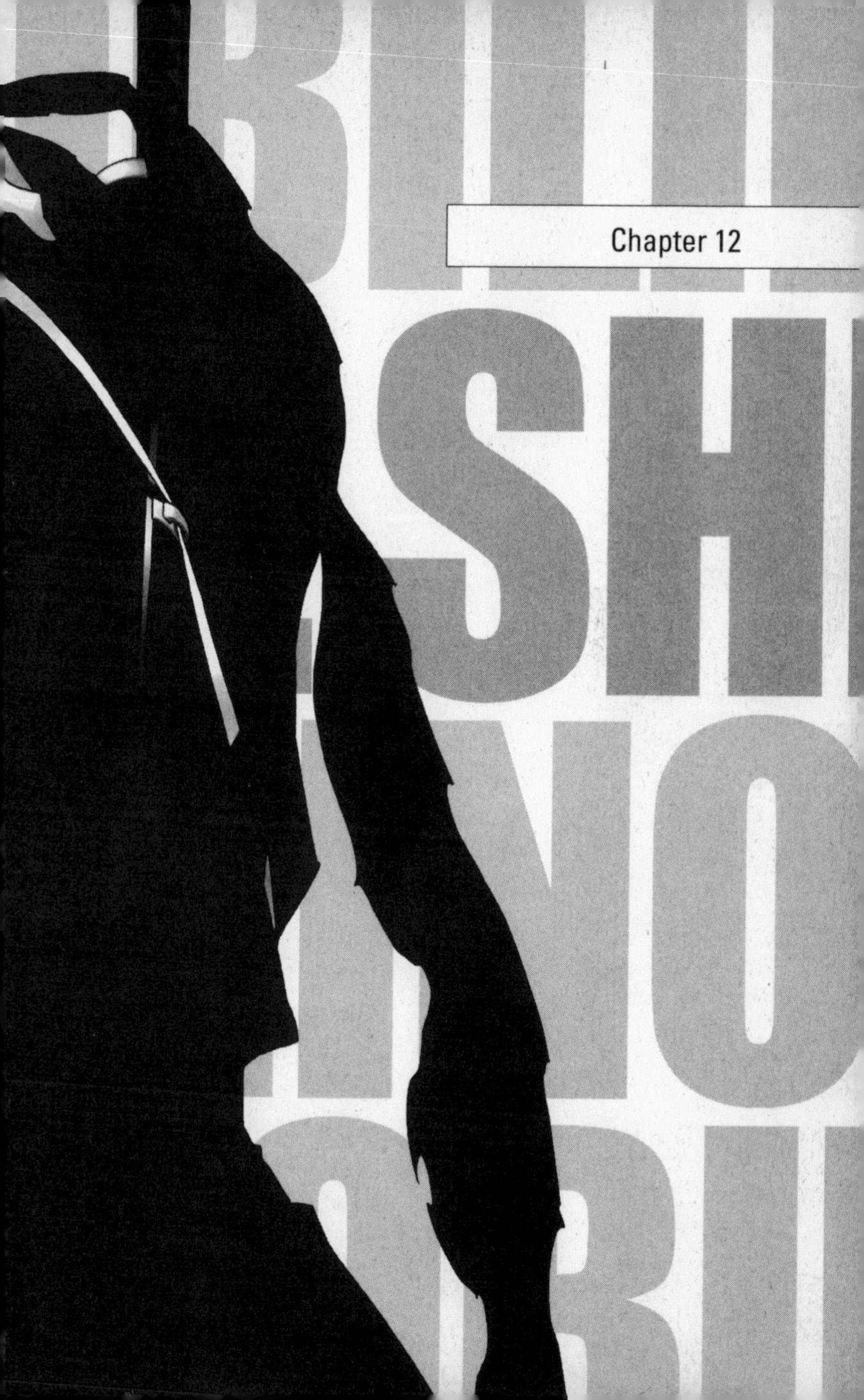
Chapter 12

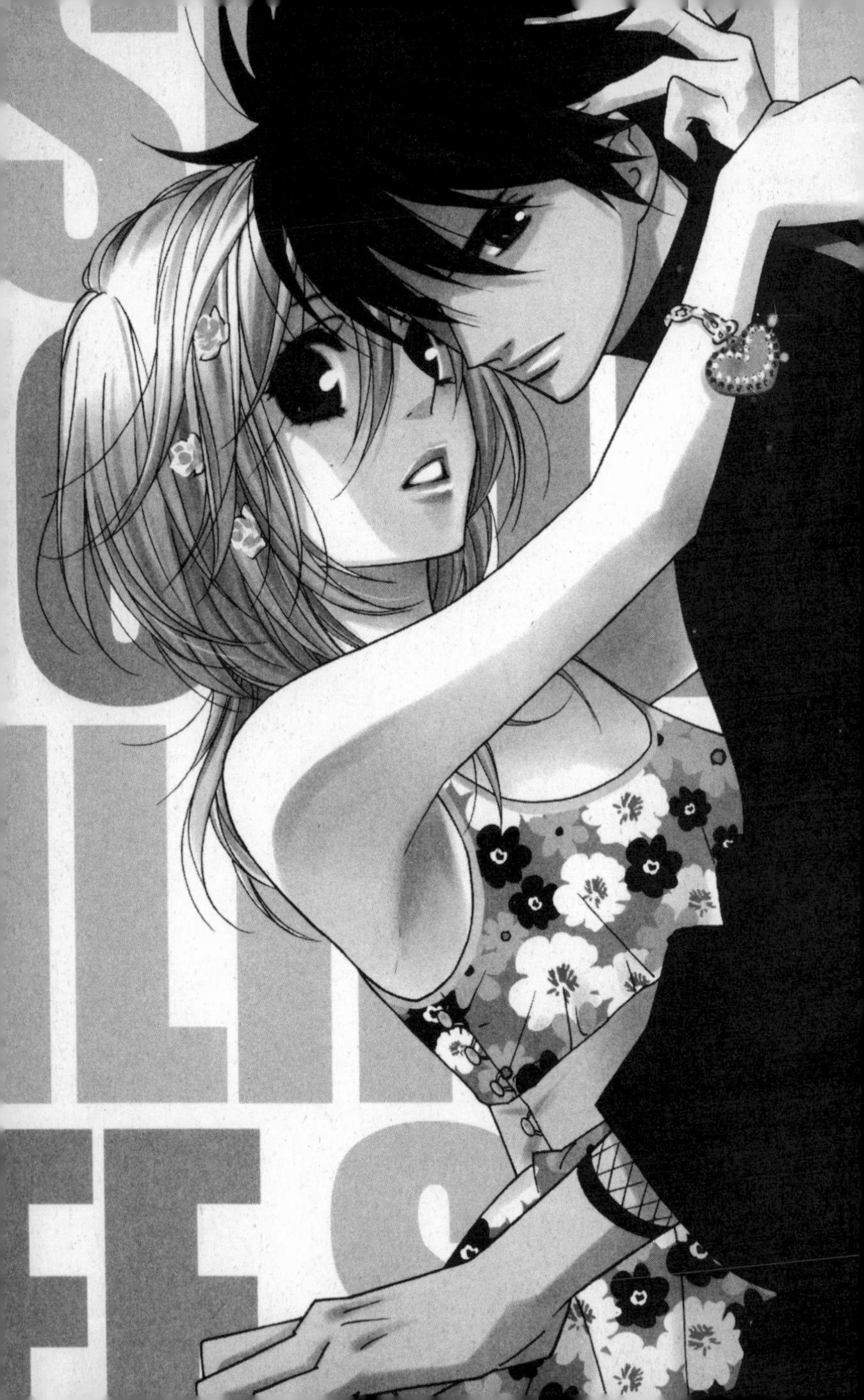

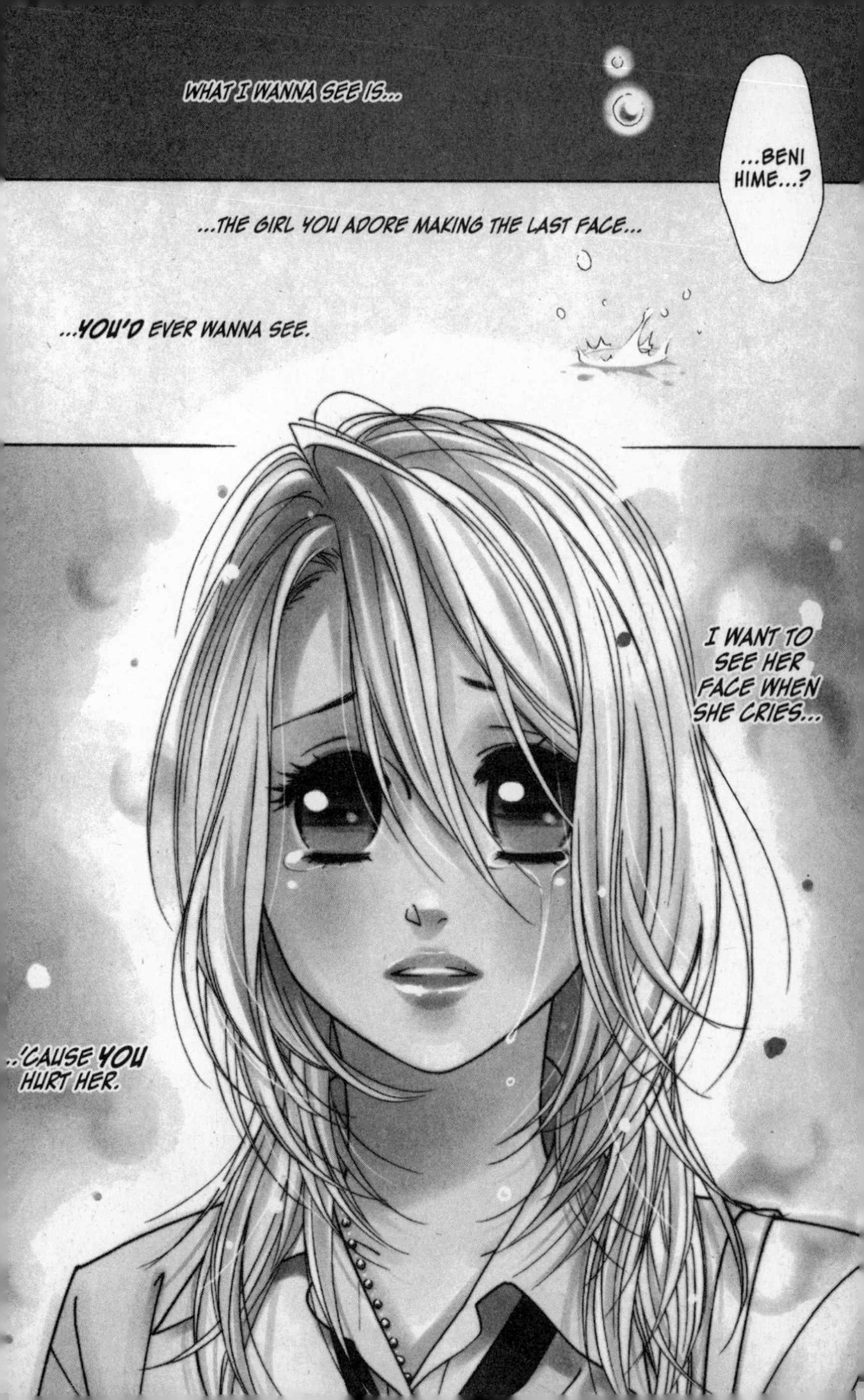
...BENI HIME...?
WHAT I WANNA SEE IS...
...THE GIRL YOU ADORE MAKING THE LAST FACE...
...YOU'D EVER WANNA SEE.
I WANT TO SEE HER FACE WHEN SHE CRIES...
...'CAUSE YOU HURT HER.

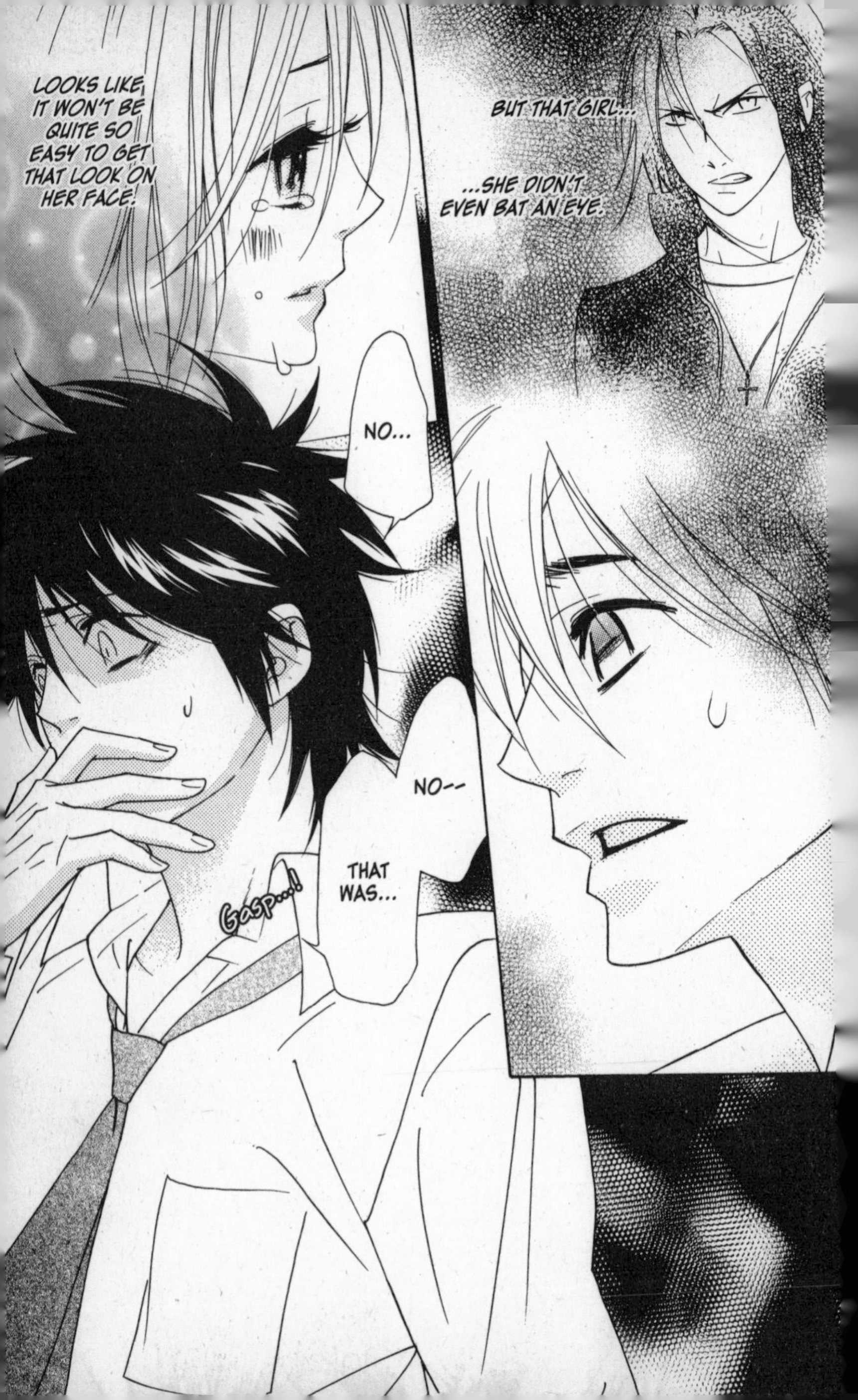
BUT THAT GIRL...
...SHE DIDN'T EVEN BAT AN EYE.
LOOKS LIKE IT WON'T BE QUITE SO EASY TO GET THAT LOOK ON HER FACE.
NO...
NO--
THAT WAS...
Gasp...!

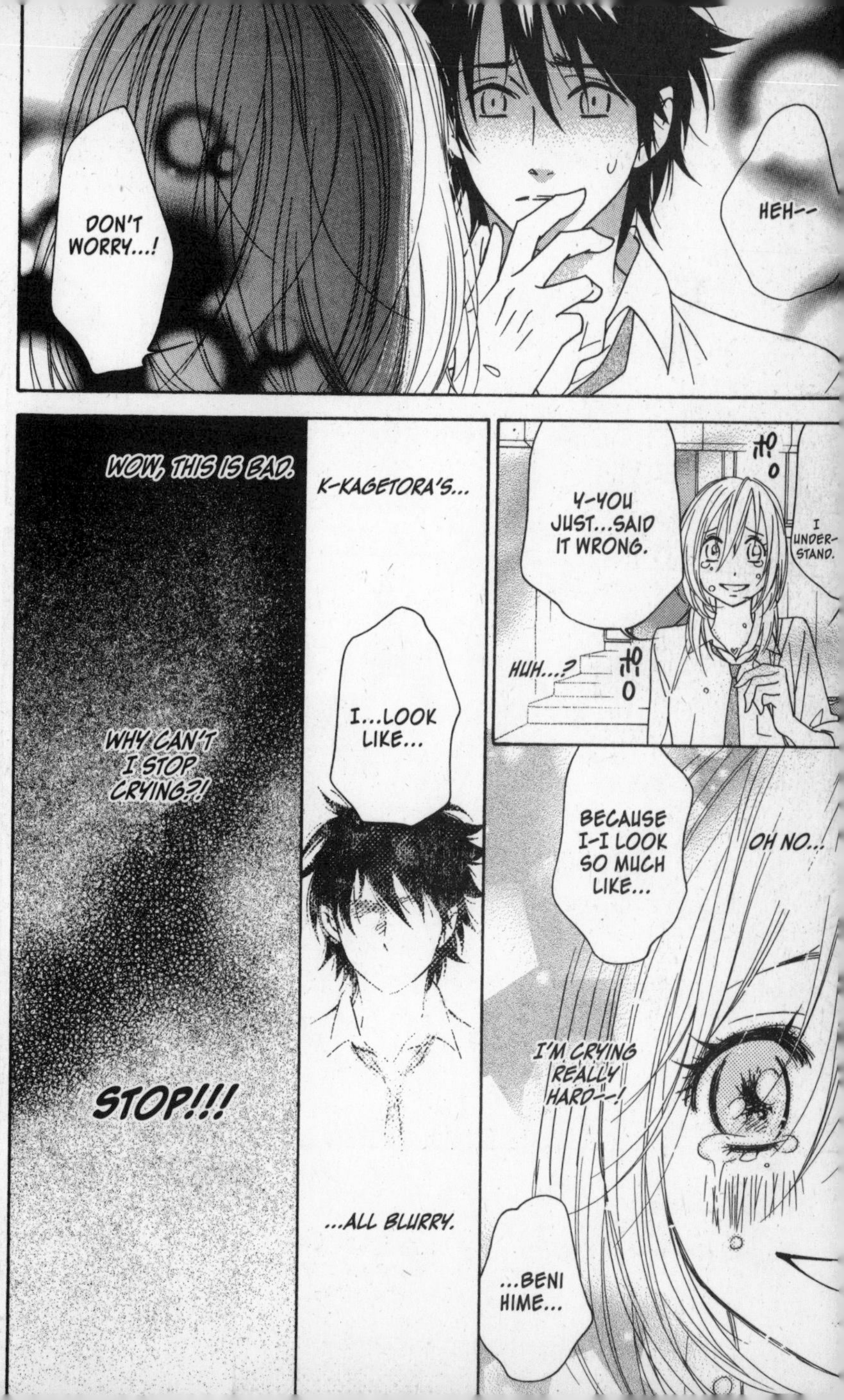
HEH--
DON'T WORRY...!
I UNDER-STAND.
Y-YOU JUST...SAID IT WRONG.
HUH...?
OH NO...
BECAUSE I-I LOOK SO MUCH LIKE...
I'M CRYING REALLY HARD--!
...BENI HIME...
K-KAGETORA'S...
I...LOOK LIKE...
...ALL BLURRY.
WOW, THIS IS BAD.
WHY CAN'T I STOP CRYING?!
STOP!!!

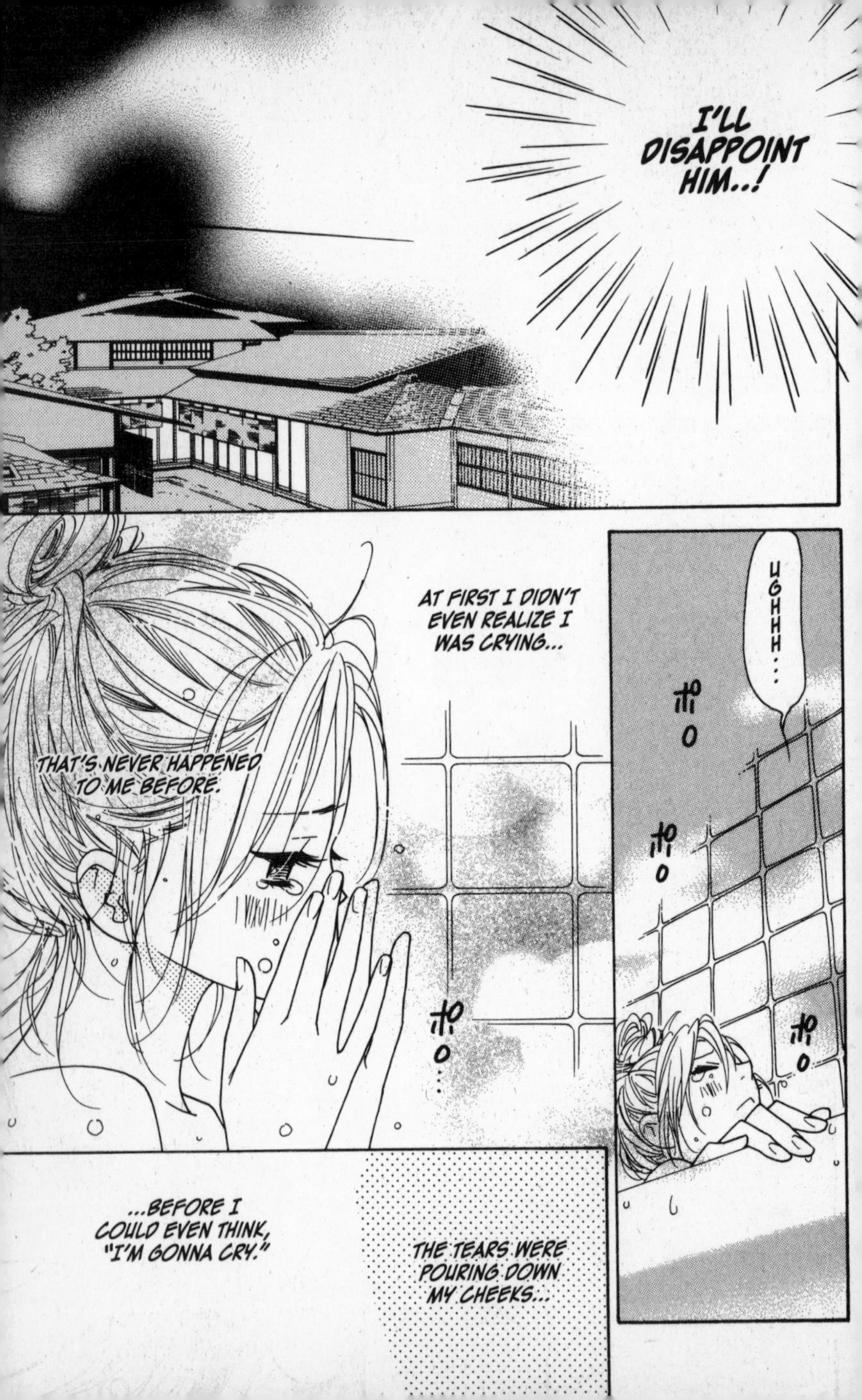
I'LL DISAPPOINT HIM..!
UGHHH...
ポロ
ポロ
ポロ
AT FIRST I DIDN'T EVEN REALIZE I WAS CRYING...
ポロ...
THAT'S NEVER HAPPENED TO ME BEFORE.
THE TEARS WERE POURING DOWN MY CHEEKS...
...BEFORE I COULD EVEN THINK, "I'M GONNA CRY."

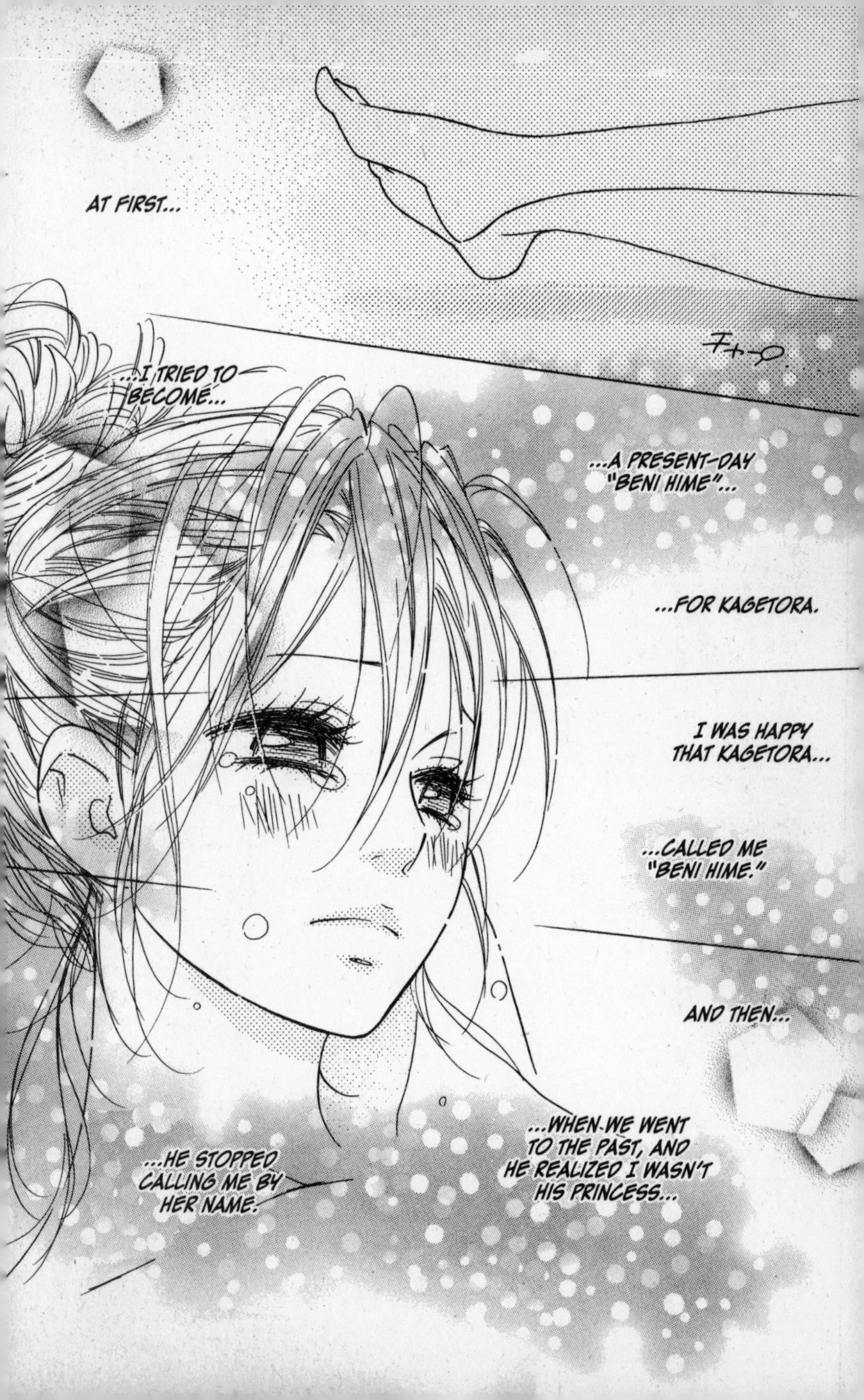
AT FIRST...
...I TRIED TO BECOME...
...A PRESENT-DAY "BENI HIME"...
...FOR KAGETORA.
I WAS HAPPY THAT KAGETORA...
...CALLED ME "BENI HIME."
AND THEN...
...WHEN WE WENT TO THE PAST, AND HE REALIZED I WASN'T HIS PRINCESS...
...HE STOPPED CALLING ME BY HER NAME.

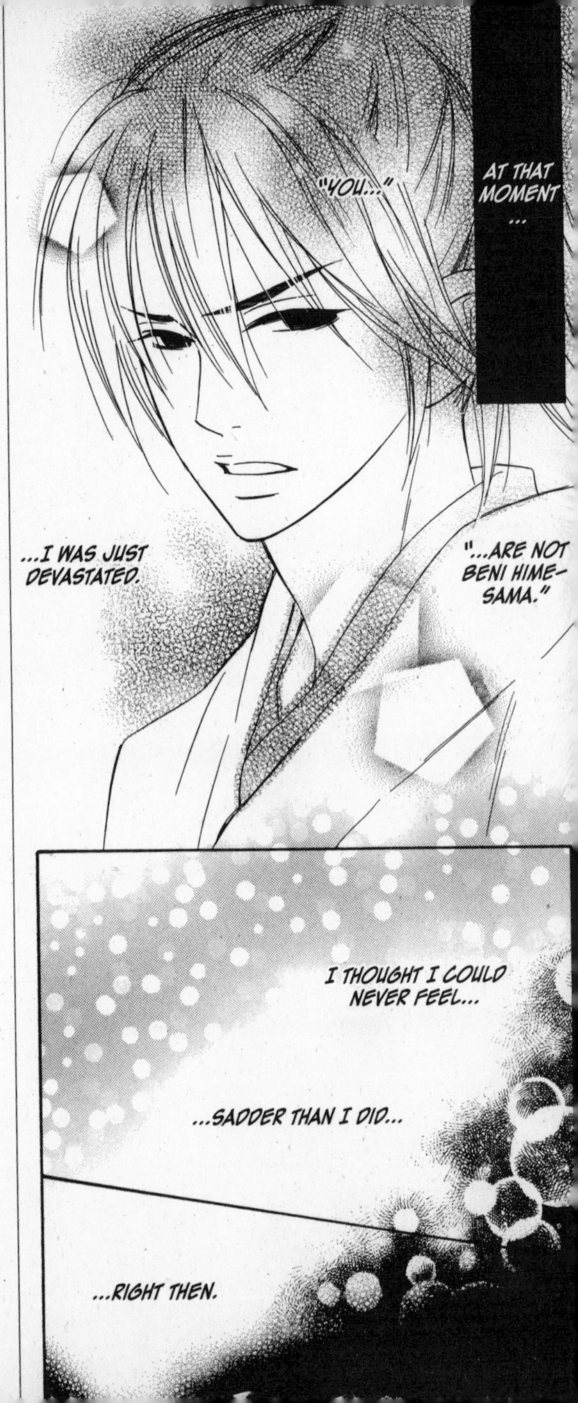
AT THAT MOMENT...
"YOU..."
"...ARE NOT BENI HIME-SAMA."
...I WAS JUST DEVASTATED.
I THOUGHT I COULD NEVER FEEL...
...SADDER THAN I DID...
...RIGHT THEN.

1

Hello! This is Conami! And...this is volume 3. It amazes even me that this series has lasted so long, but I'm able to keep drawing because I'm given so much support by all of you reading this (and also by my editor, assistants and family).

Thank you so much!

I was so surprised by the number of letters I received after I wrote, "I'll be waiting for your comments!" in volumes 1 and 2. I read each and every one of them so carefully. ♥ I might be a little slow to reply, but I'll definitely answer each letter, so please wait for my response!

Some of your letters included questions, so I'll address those in part 2.

So...

To be continued in part 2!

2

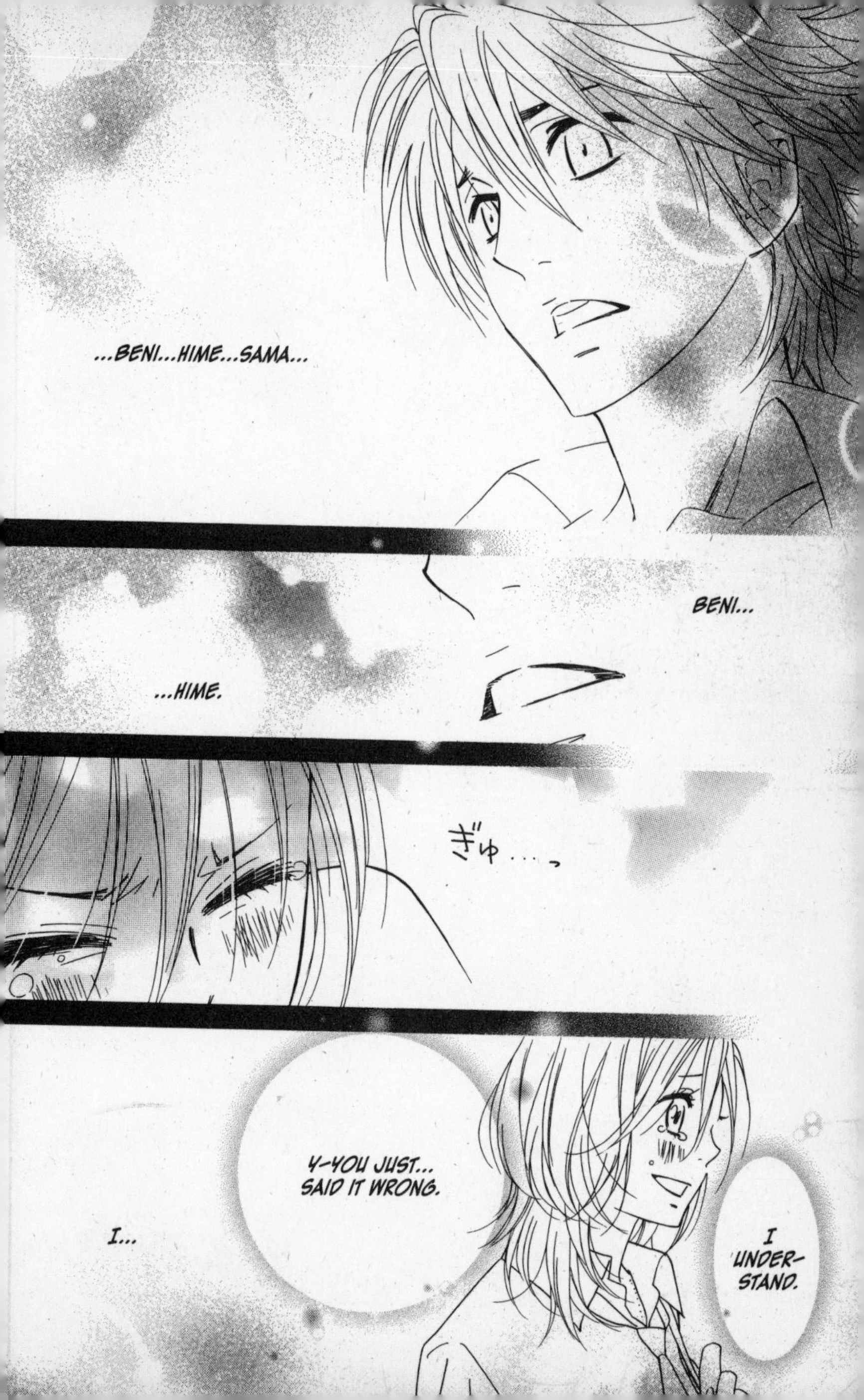
...BENI...HIME...SAMA...
BENI...
...HIME.
ぎゅ…っ
I UNDER-STAND.
Y-YOU JUST... SAID IT WRONG.
I...

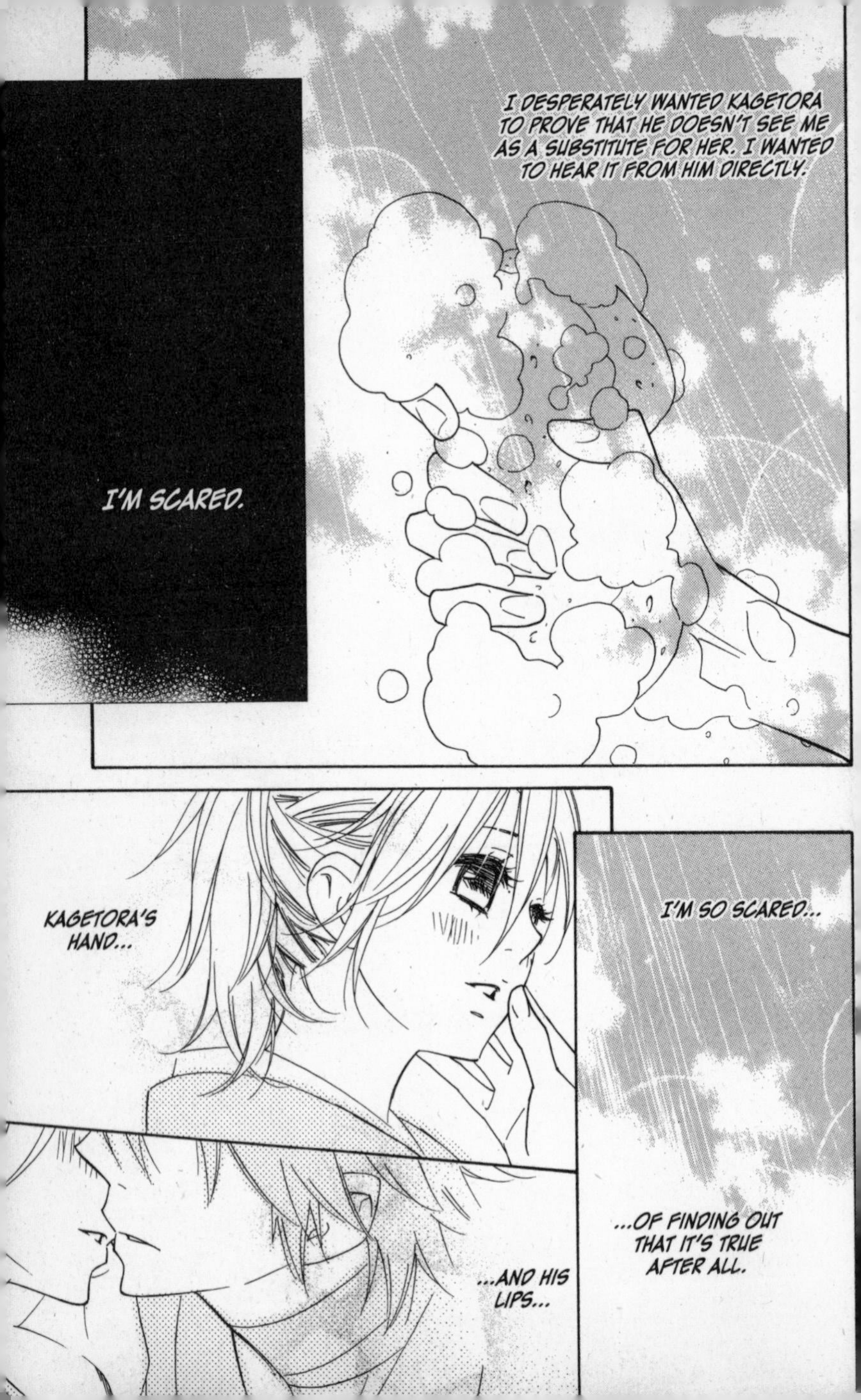
I DESPERATELY WANTED KAGETORA TO PROVE THAT HE DOESN'T SEE ME AS A SUBSTITUTE FOR HER. I WANTED TO HEAR IT FROM HIM DIRECTLY.
I'M SCARED.
I'M SO SCARED...
...OF FINDING OUT THAT IT'S TRUE AFTER ALL.
KAGETORA'S HAND...
...AND HIS LIPS...

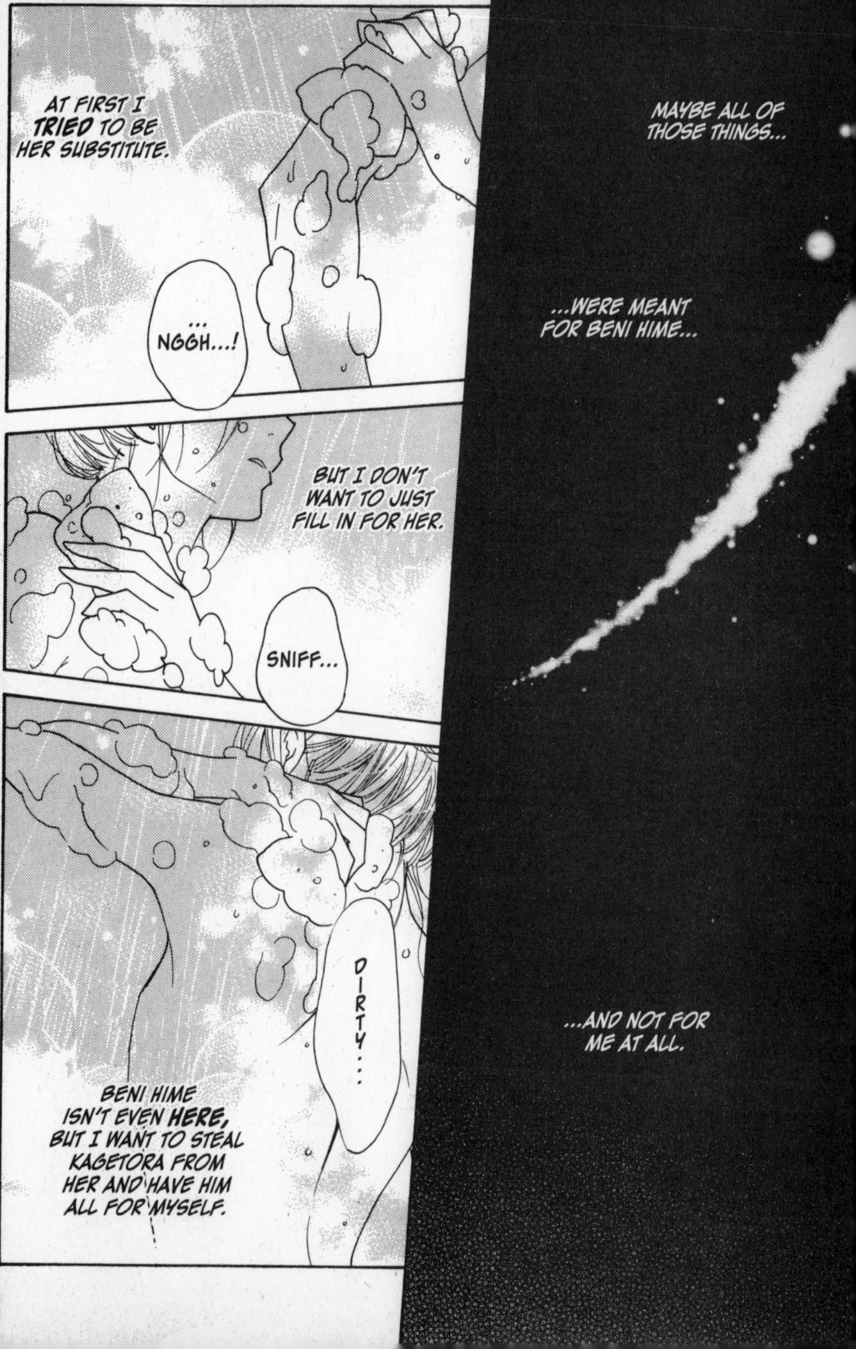
MAYBE ALL OF THOSE THINGS...
...WERE MEANT FOR BENI HIME...
...AND NOT FOR ME AT ALL.
AT FIRST I TRIED TO BE HER SUBSTITUTE.
... NGGH...!
BUT I DON'T WANT TO JUST FILL IN FOR HER.
SNIFF...
DIRTY...
BENI HIME ISN'T EVEN HERE, BUT I WANT TO STEAL KAGETORA FROM HER AND HAVE HIM ALL FOR MYSELF.

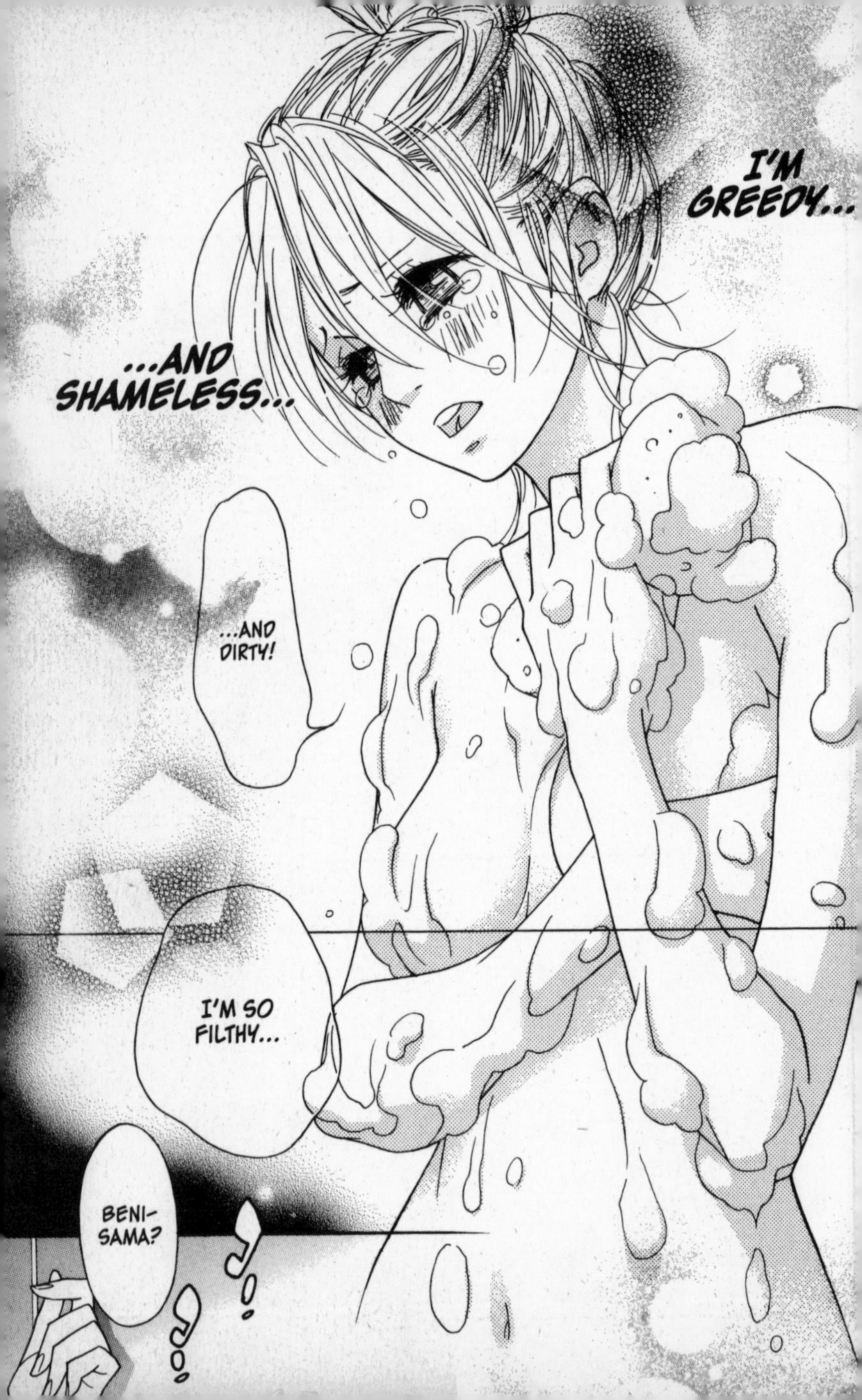
I'M GREEDY...
...AND SHAMELESS...
...AND DIRTY!
I'M SO FILTHY...
BENI-SAMA?

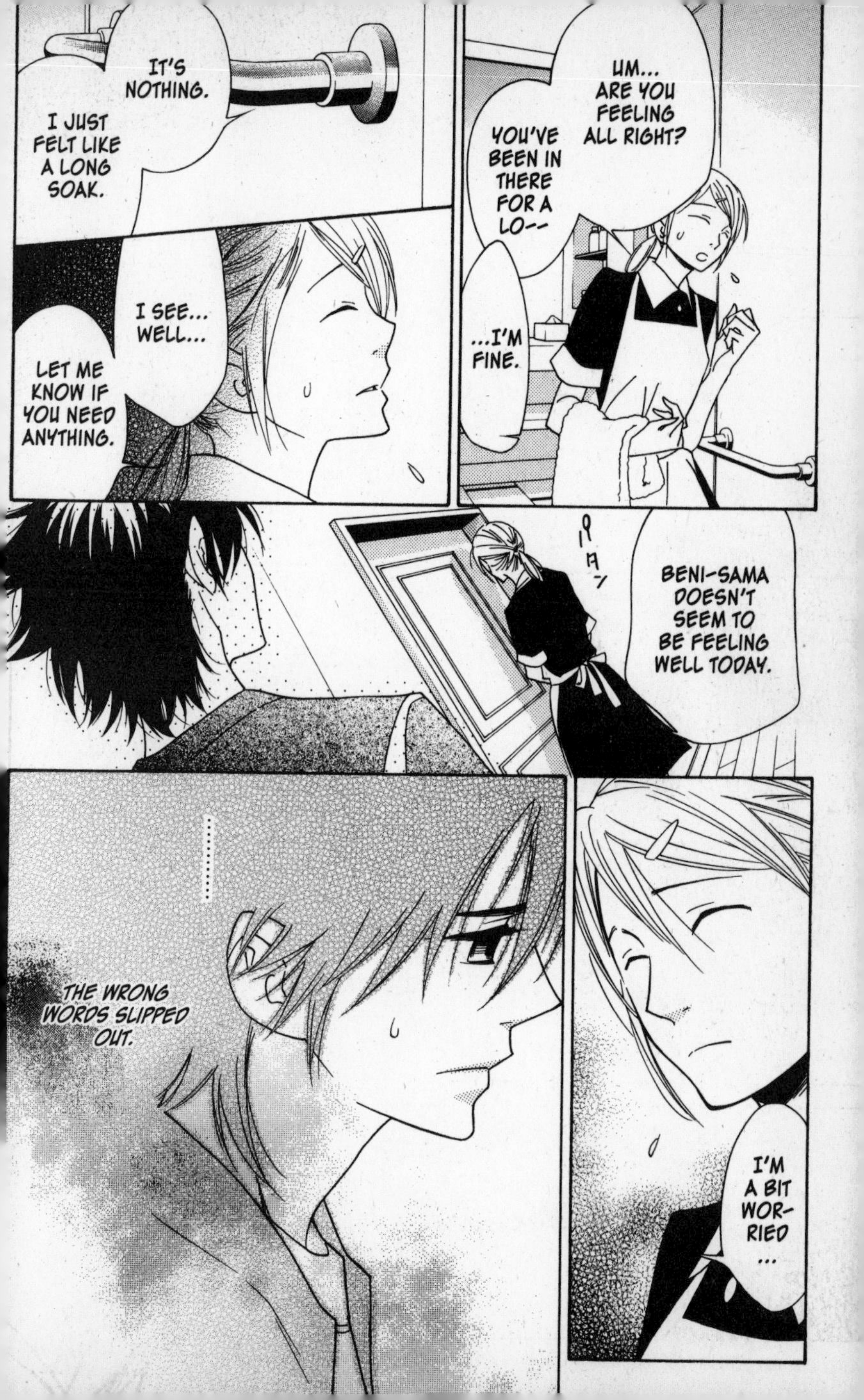
UM... ARE YOU FEELING ALL RIGHT?
YOU'VE BEEN IN THERE FOR A LO--
...I'M FINE.
IT'S NOTHING.
I JUST FELT LIKE A LONG SOAK.
I SEE... WELL...
LET ME KNOW IF YOU NEED ANYTHING.
パタン
BENI-SAMA DOESN'T SEEM TO BE FEELING WELL TODAY.
I'M A BIT WOR-RIED...
......
THE WRONG WORDS SLIPPED OUT.

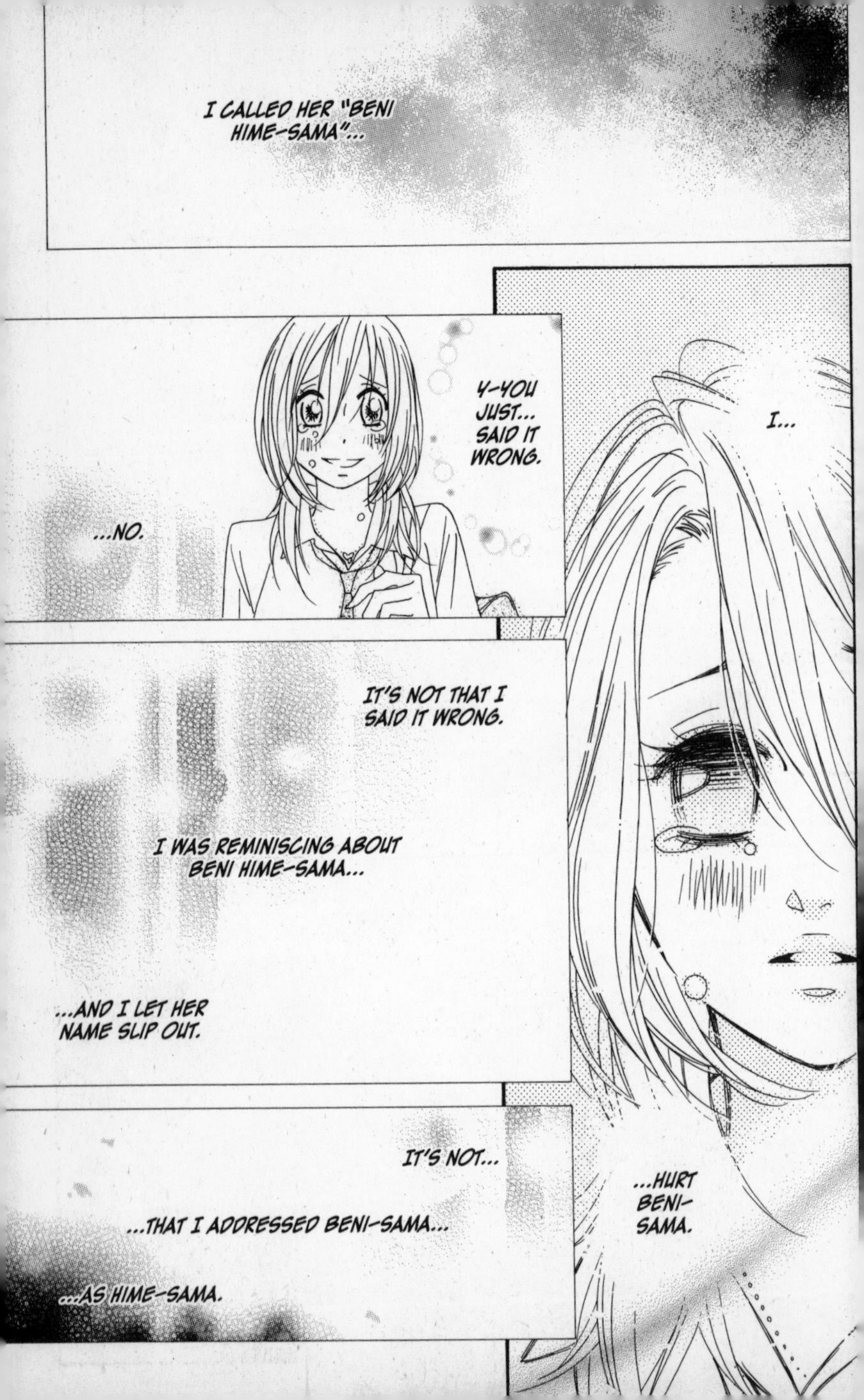
I CALLED HER "BENI HIME-SAMA"...
I...
...HURT BENI-SAMA.
Y-YOU JUST... SAID IT WRONG.
...NO.
IT'S NOT THAT I SAID IT WRONG.
I WAS REMINISCING ABOUT BENI HIME-SAMA...
...AND I LET HER NAME SLIP OUT.
IT'S NOT...
...THAT I ADDRESSED BENI-SAMA...
...AS HIME-SAMA.

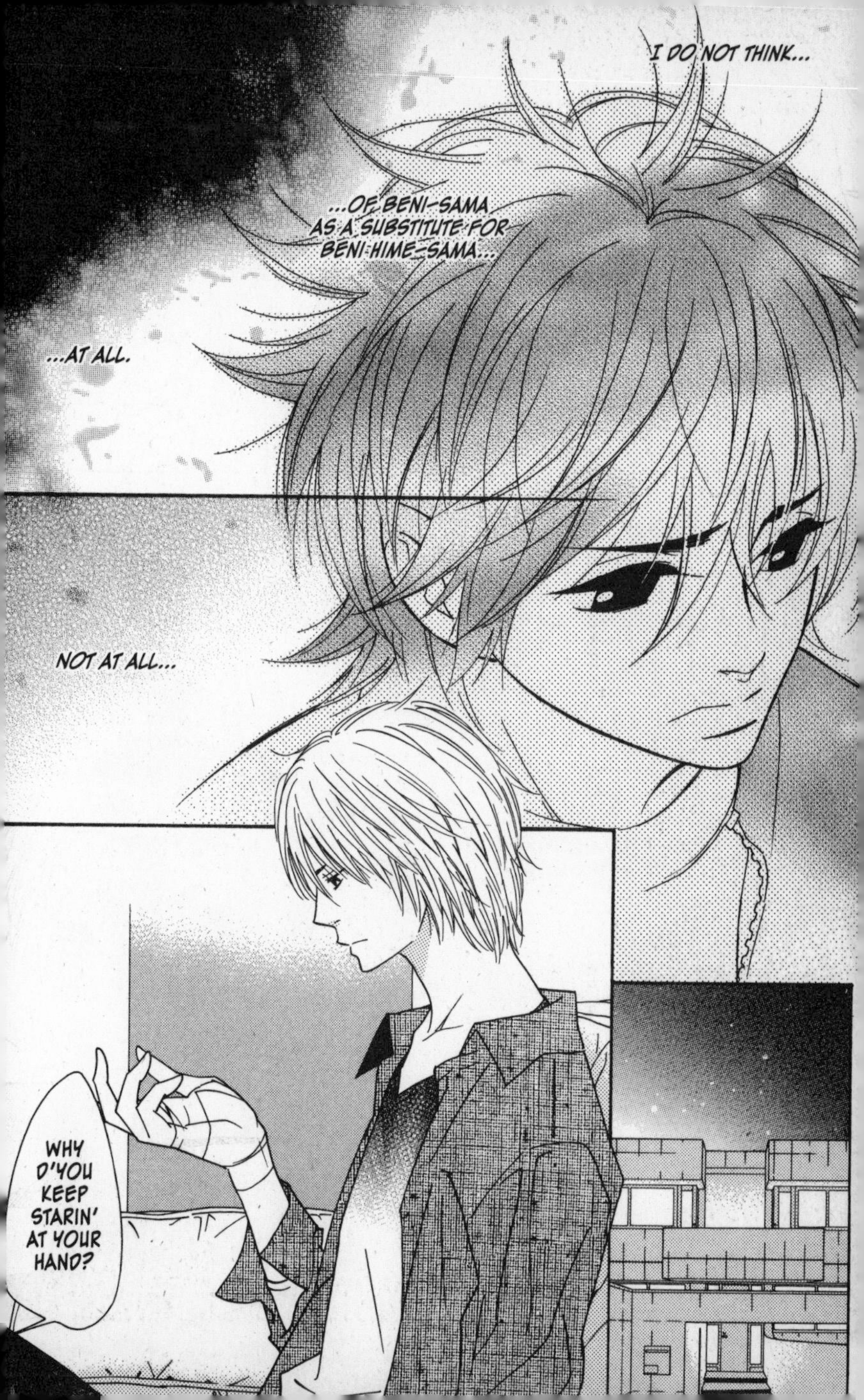
I DO NOT THINK...
...OF BENI-SAMA AS A SUBSTITUTE FOR BENI-HIME-SAMA...
...AT ALL.
NOT AT ALL...
WHY D'YOU KEEP STARIN' AT YOUR HAND?

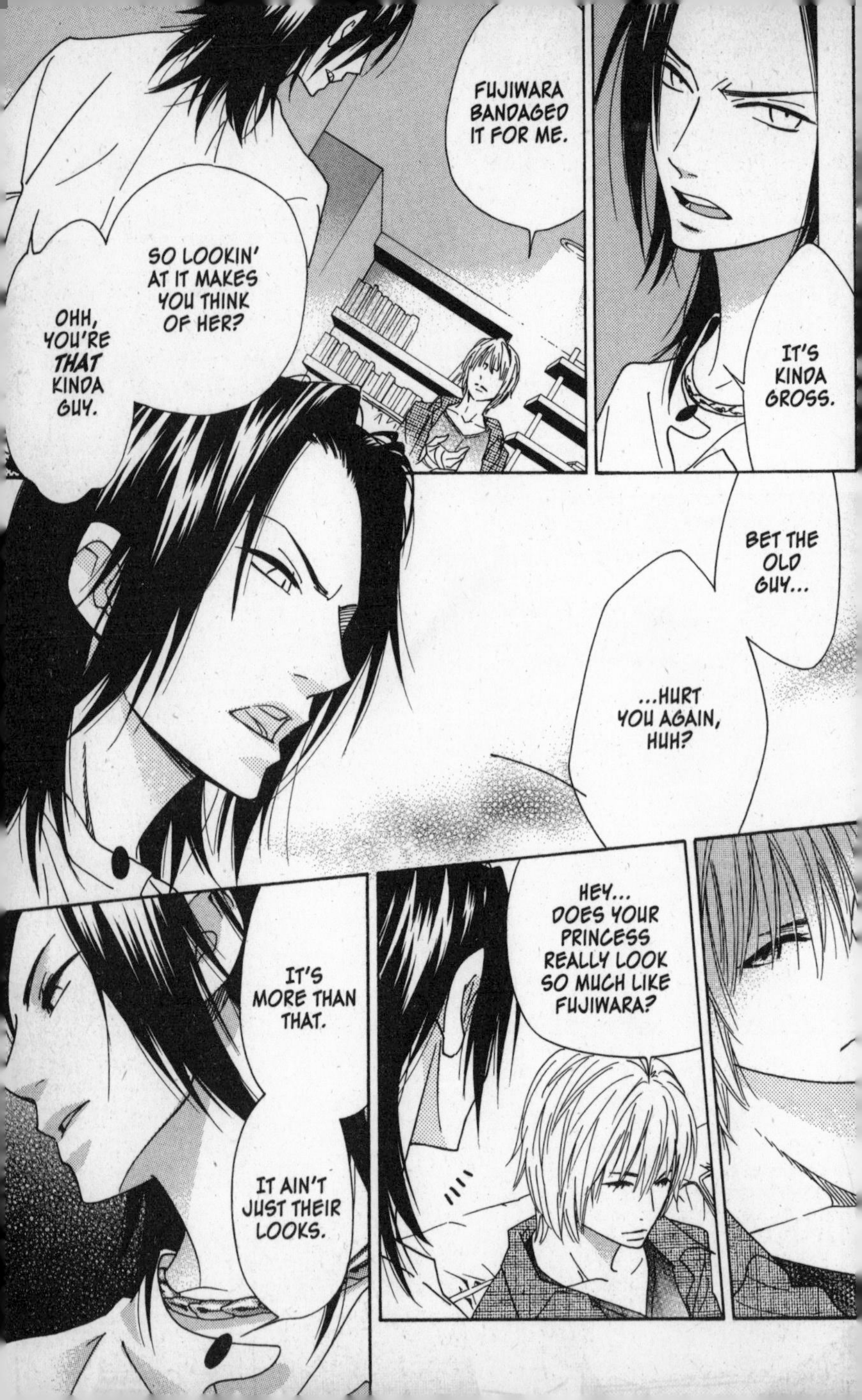
IT'S KINDA GROSS.
FUJIWARA BANDAGED IT FOR ME.
SO LOOKIN' AT IT MAKES YOU THINK OF HER?
OHH, YOU'RE *THAT* KINDA GUY.
BET THE OLD GUY...
...HURT YOU AGAIN, HUH?
HEY... DOES YOUR PRINCESS REALLY LOOK SO MUCH LIKE FUJIWARA?
IT'S MORE THAN THAT.
IT AIN'T JUST THEIR LOOKS.

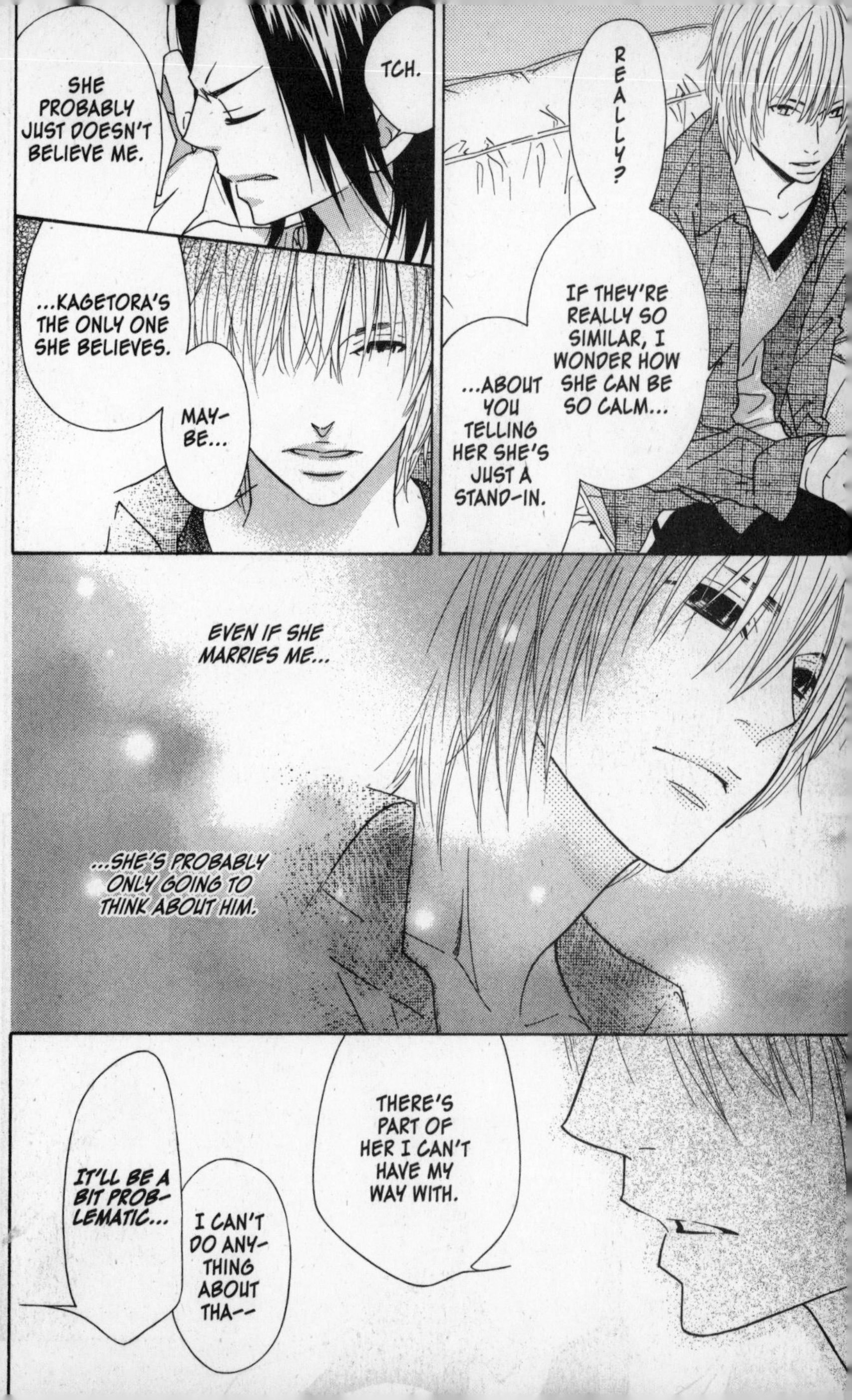
REALLY?
IF THEY'RE REALLY SO SIMILAR, I WONDER HOW SHE CAN BE SO CALM...
...ABOUT YOU TELLING HER SHE'S JUST A STAND-IN.
TCH.
SHE PROBABLY JUST DOESN'T BELIEVE ME.
...KAGETORA'S THE ONLY ONE SHE BELIEVES.
MAY-BE...
EVEN IF SHE MARRIES ME...
...SHE'S PROBABLY ONLY GOING TO THINK ABOUT HIM.
THERE'S PART OF HER I CAN'T HAVE MY WAY WITH.
IT'LL BE A BIT PROB-LEMATIC...
I CAN'T DO ANY-THING ABOUT THA--

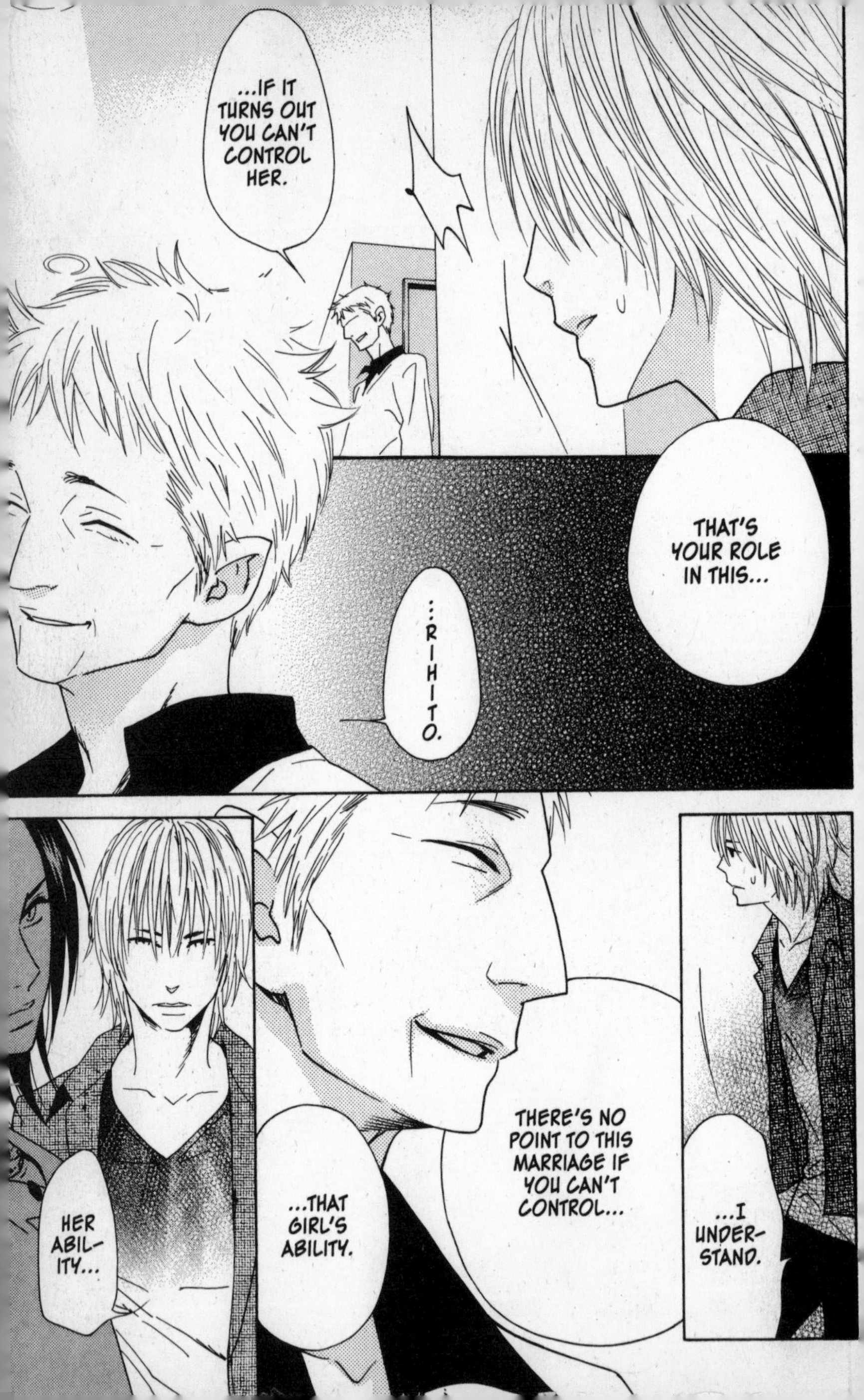
...IF IT TURNS OUT YOU CAN'T CONTROL HER.
THAT'S YOUR ROLE IN THIS...
...RIHITO.
...I UNDERSTAND.
THERE'S NO POINT TO THIS MARRIAGE IF YOU CAN'T CONTROL...
...THAT GIRL'S ABILITY.
HER ABILITY...

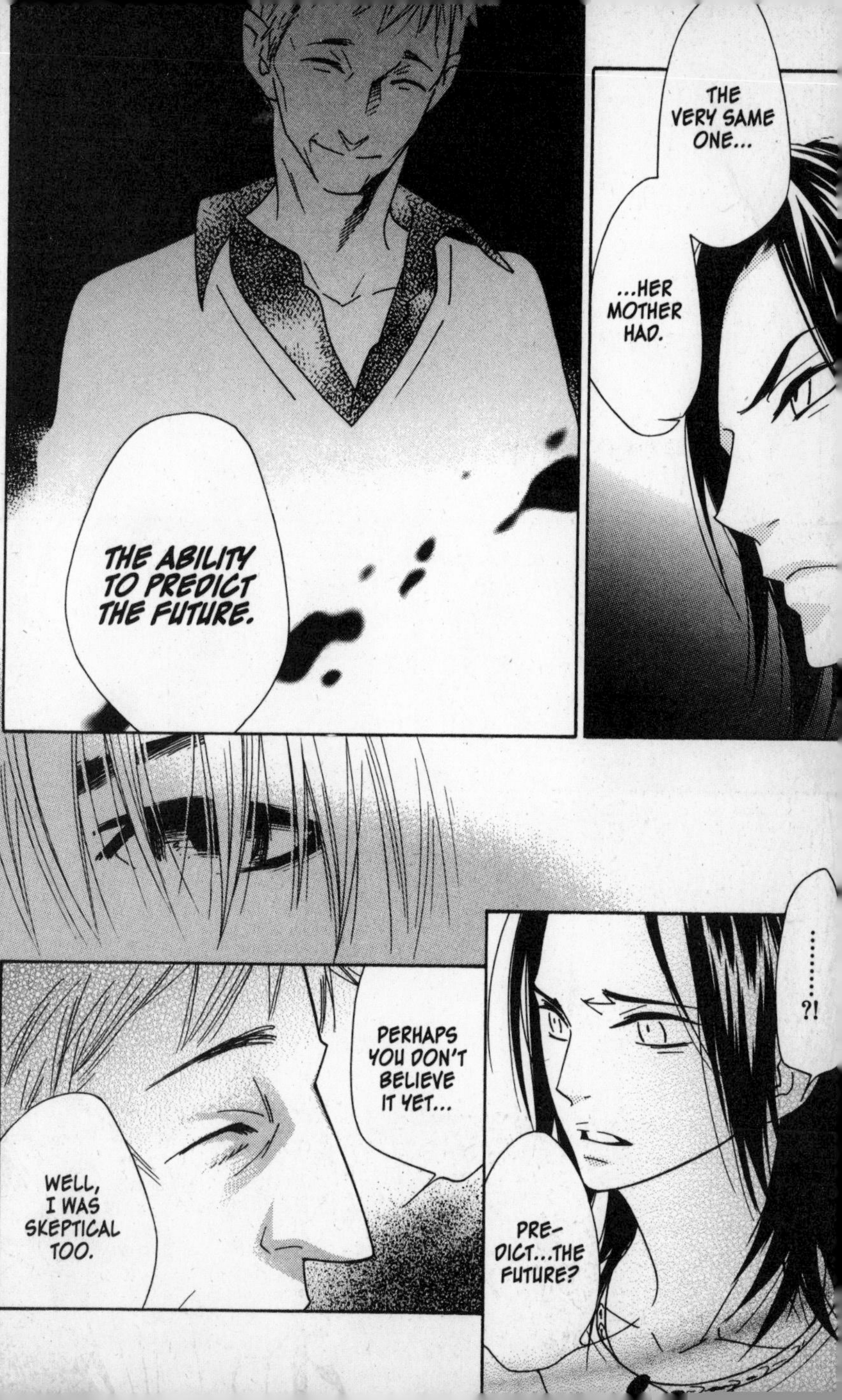
THE VERY SAME ONE...
...HER MOTHER HAD.
THE ABILITY TO PREDICT THE FUTURE.
......?!
PRE-DICT...THE FUTURE?
PERHAPS YOU DON'T BELIEVE IT YET...
WELL, I WAS SKEPTICAL TOO.

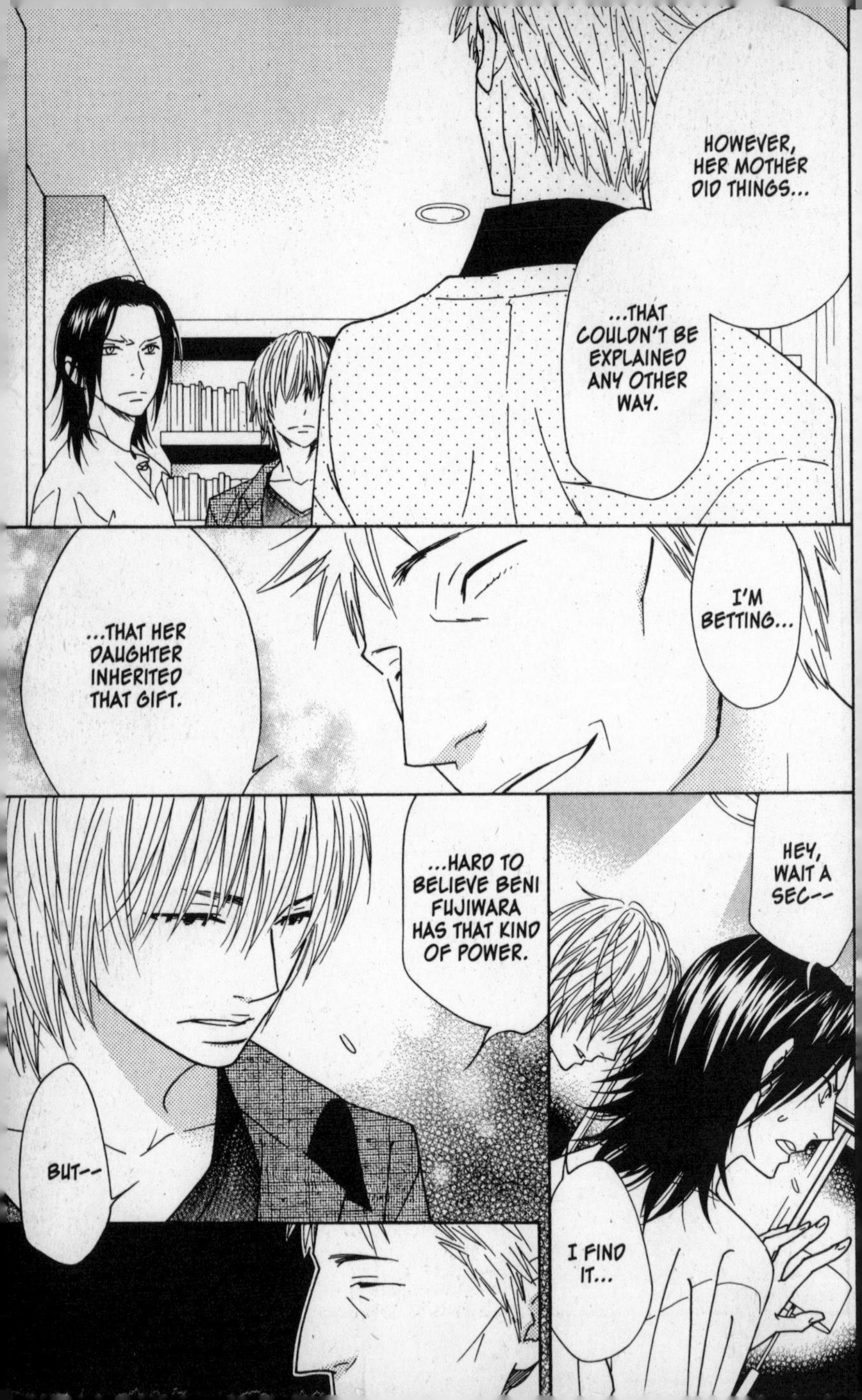
HOWEVER, HER MOTHER DID THINGS...
...THAT COULDN'T BE EXPLAINED ANY OTHER WAY.
I'M BETTING...
...THAT HER DAUGHTER INHERITED THAT GIFT.
HEY, WAIT A SEC--
I FIND IT...
...HARD TO BELIEVE BENI FUJIWARA HAS THAT KIND OF POWER.
BUT--

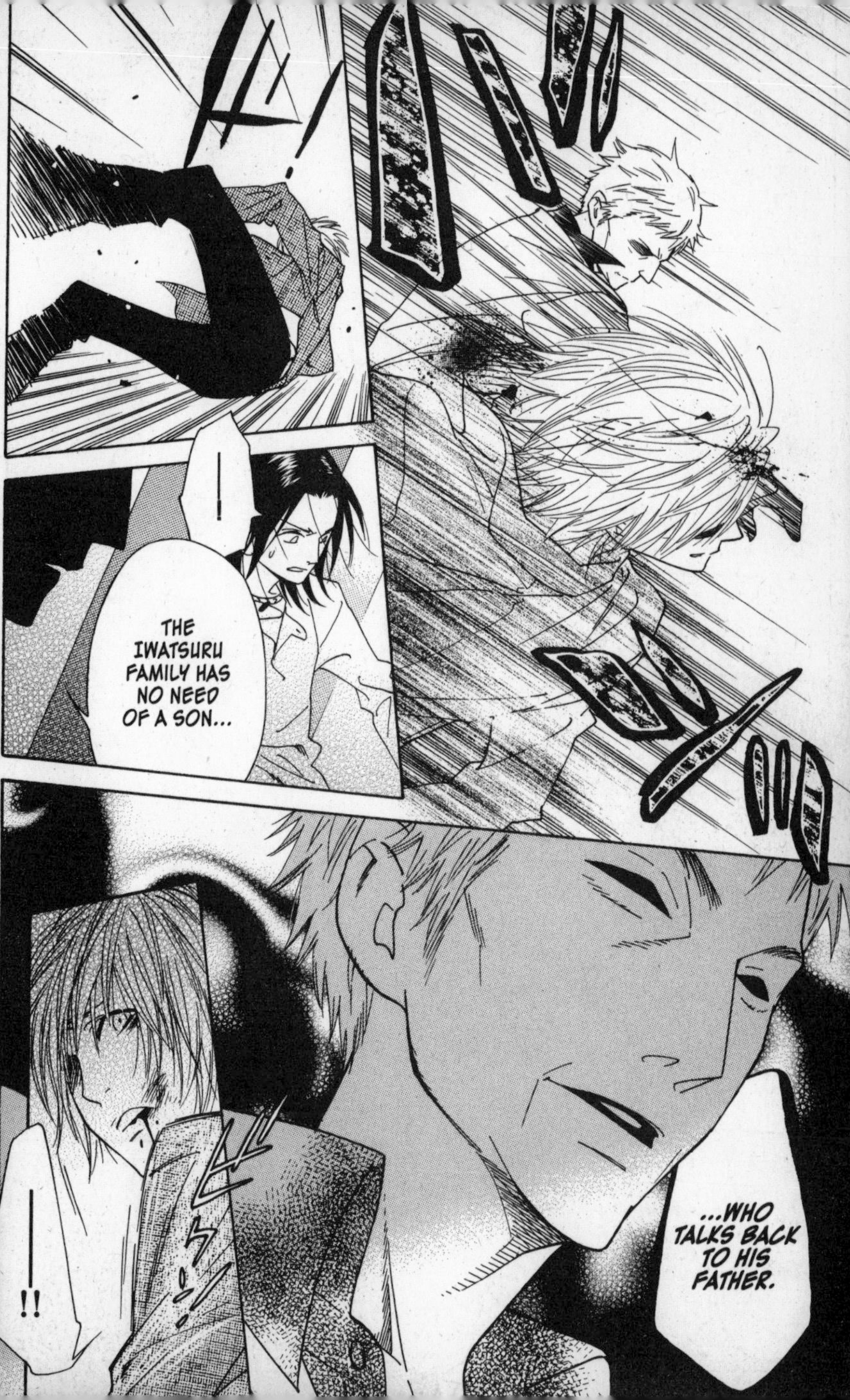

!
!
THE IWATSURU FAMILY HAS NO NEED OF A SON...
...WHO TALKS BACK TO HIS FATHER.
!!

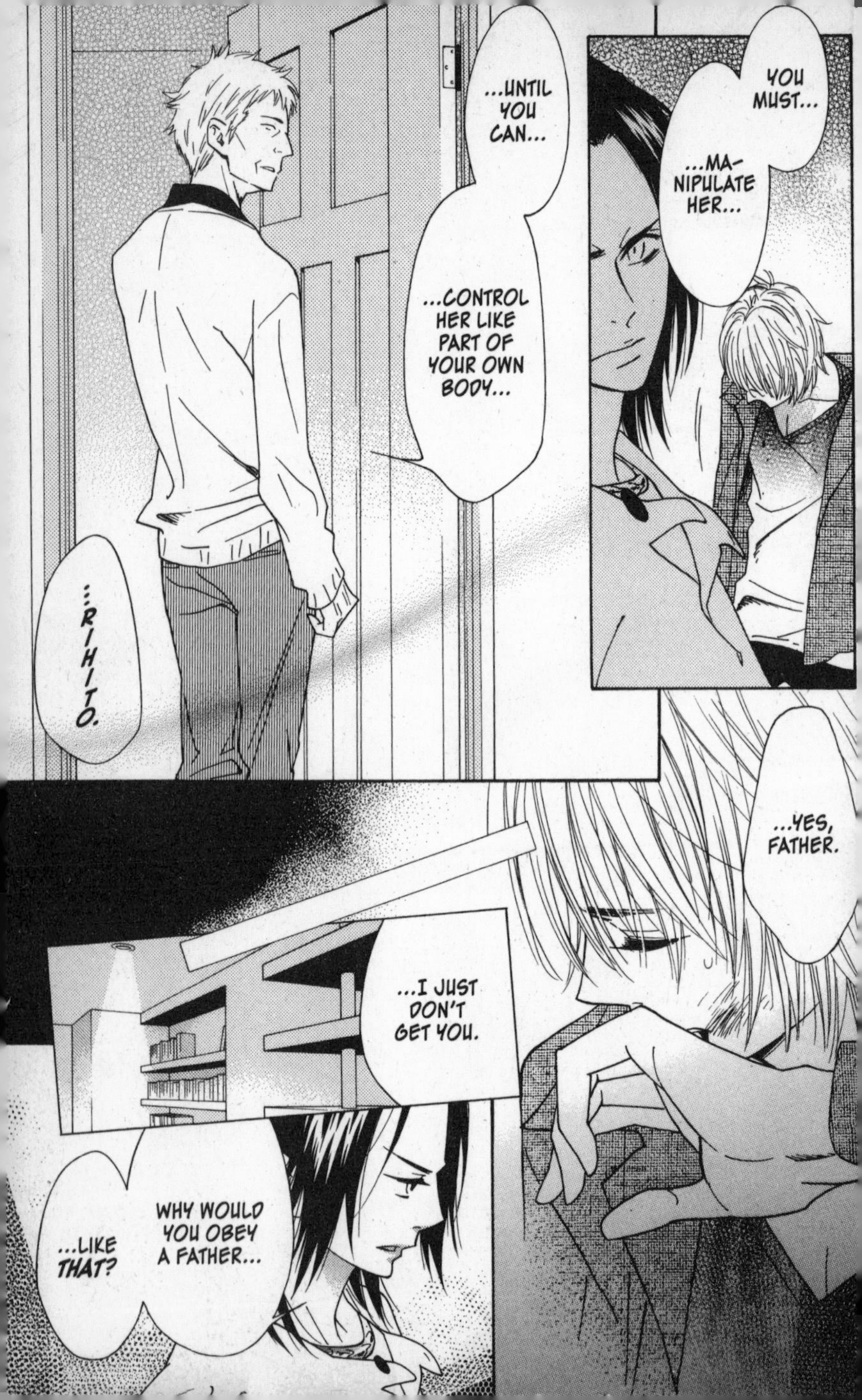
YOU MUST...
...MA-NIPULATE HER...
...UNTIL YOU CAN...
...CONTROL HER LIKE PART OF YOUR OWN BODY...
...RIHITO.
...YES, FATHER.
...I JUST DON'T GET YOU.
WHY WOULD YOU OBEY A FATHER...
...LIKE *THAT*?

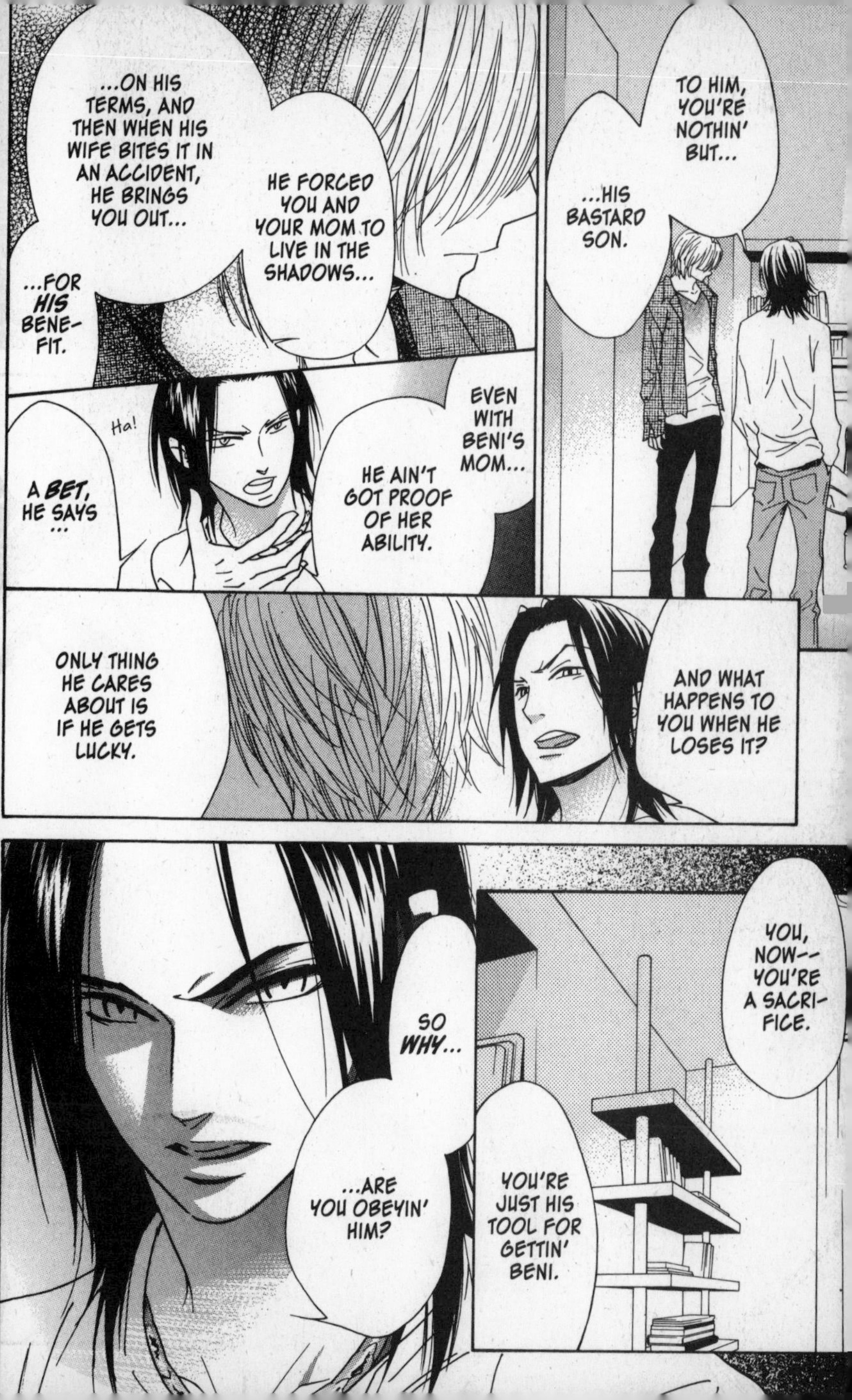
TO HIM, YOU'RE NOTHIN' BUT...
...HIS BASTARD SON.
HE FORCED YOU AND YOUR MOM TO LIVE IN THE SHADOWS...
...ON HIS TERMS, AND THEN WHEN HIS WIFE BITES IT IN AN ACCIDENT, HE BRINGS YOU OUT...
...FOR *HIS* BENE-FIT.
EVEN WITH BENI'S MOM...
HE AIN'T GOT PROOF OF HER ABILITY.
Ha!
A *BET*, HE SAYS ...
AND WHAT HAPPENS TO YOU WHEN HE LOSES IT?
ONLY THING HE CARES ABOUT IS IF HE GETS LUCKY.
YOU, NOW-- YOU'RE A SACRI-FICE.
YOU'RE JUST HIS TOOL FOR GETTIN' BENI.
SO *WHY*...
...ARE YOU OBEYIN' HIM?

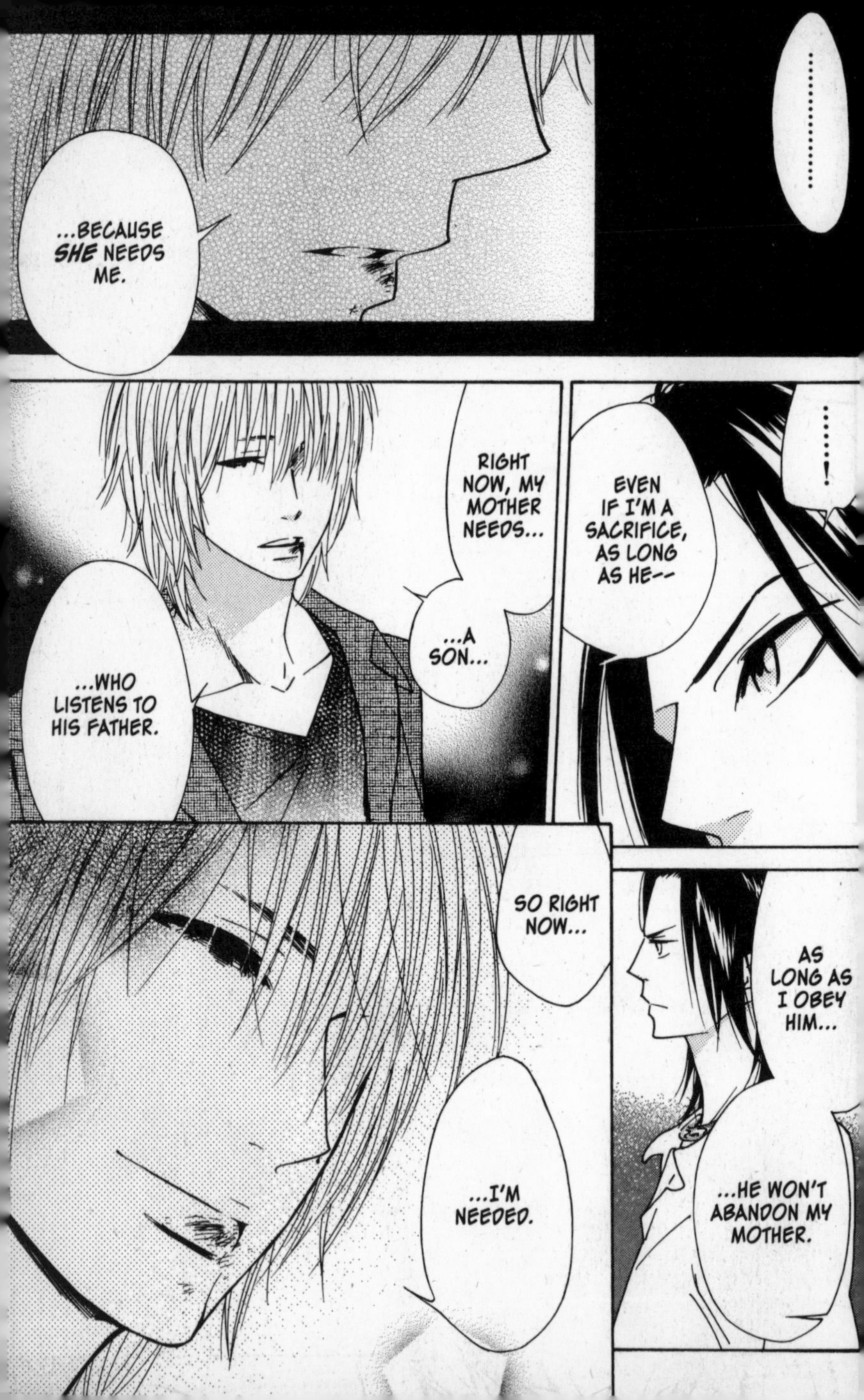
......
...BECAUSE SHE NEEDS ME.
......!
EVEN IF I'M A SACRIFICE, AS LONG AS HE--
RIGHT NOW, MY MOTHER NEEDS...
...A SON...
...WHO LISTENS TO HIS FATHER.
AS LONG AS I OBEY HIM...
...HE WON'T ABANDON MY MOTHER.
SO RIGHT NOW...
...I'M NEEDED.

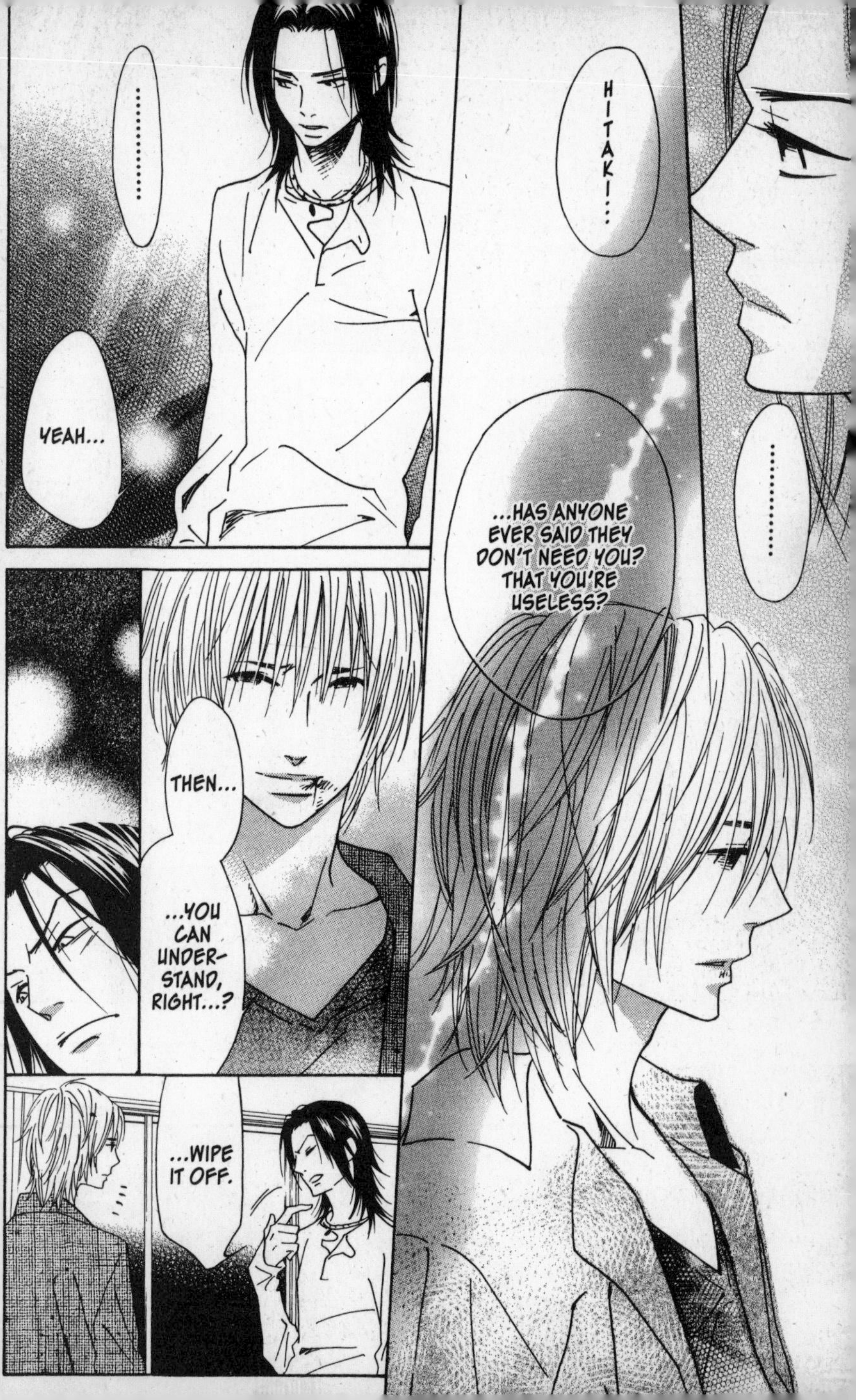

HITAKI...
......
...HAS ANYONE EVER SAID THEY DON'T NEED YOU? THAT YOU'RE USELESS?
......
YEAH...
THEN...
...YOU CAN UNDER-STAND, RIGHT...?
...WIPE IT OFF.
...

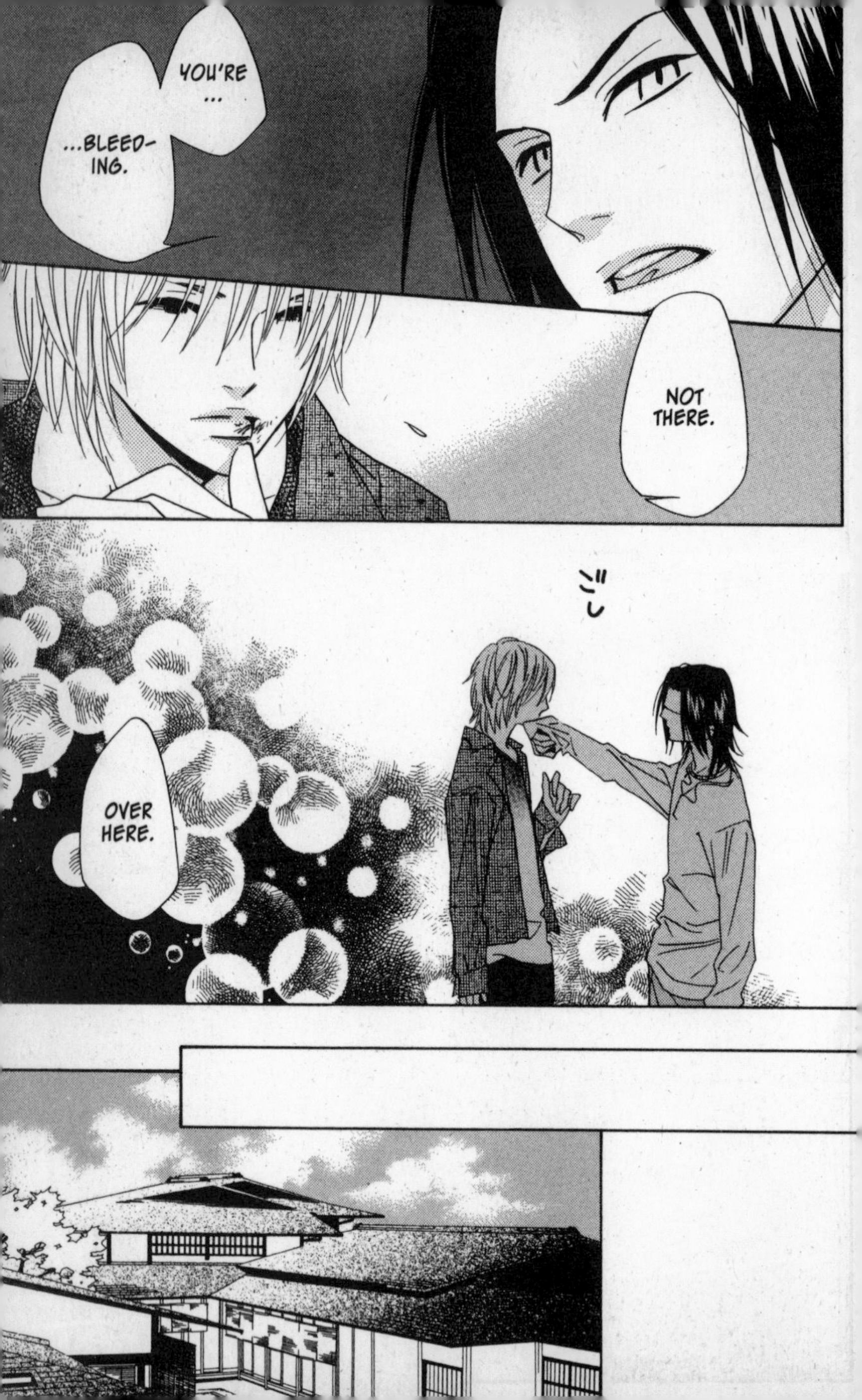
YOU'RE ... ...BLEED-ING.
NOT THERE.
ごし
OVER HERE.

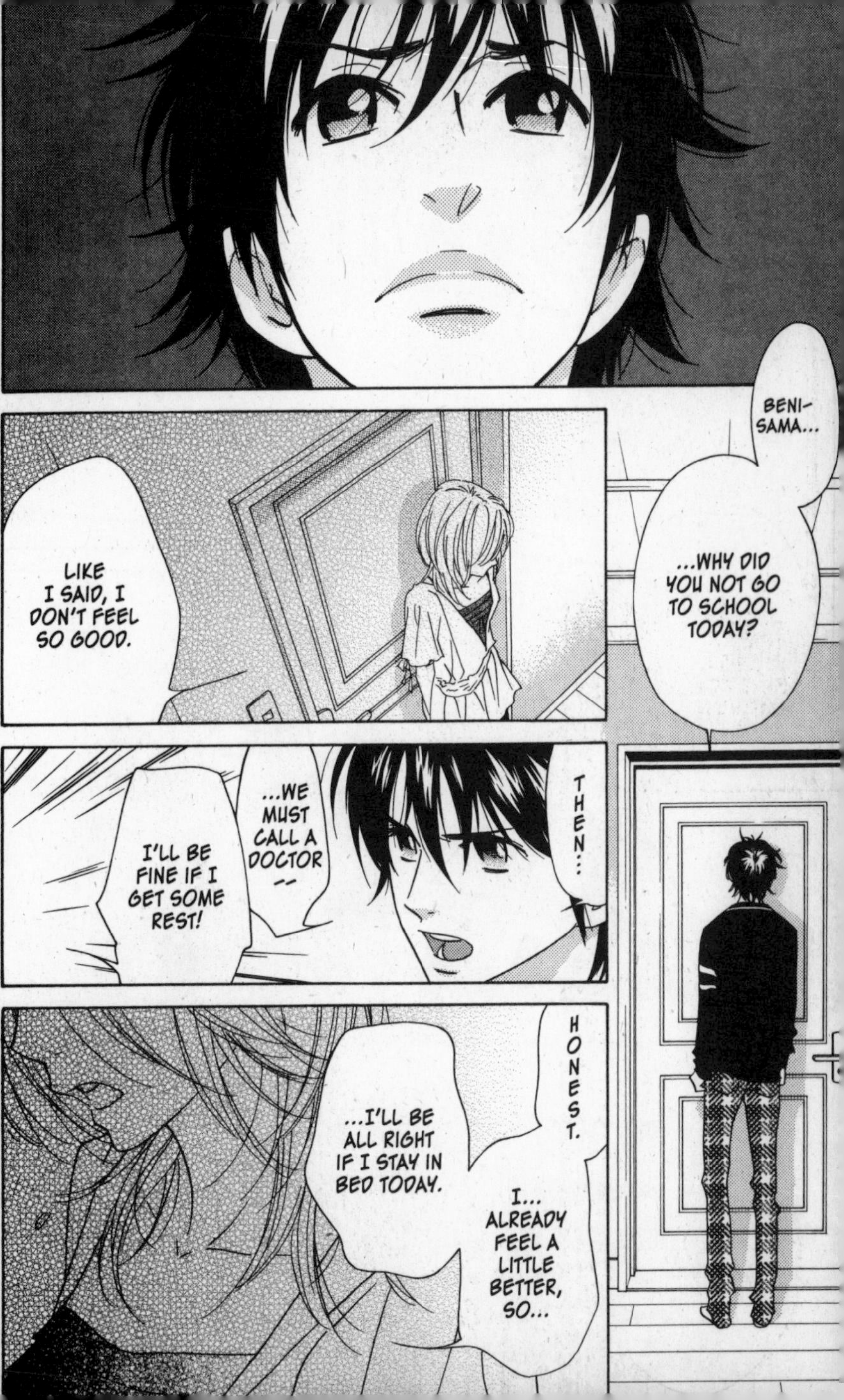
BENI-SAMA...
...WHY DID YOU NOT GO TO SCHOOL TODAY?
LIKE I SAID, I DON'T FEEL SO GOOD.
THEN...
...WE MUST CALL A DOCTOR --
I'LL BE FINE IF I GET SOME REST!
HONEST.
...I'LL BE ALL RIGHT IF I STAY IN BED TODAY.
I... ALREADY FEEL A LITTLE BETTER, SO...

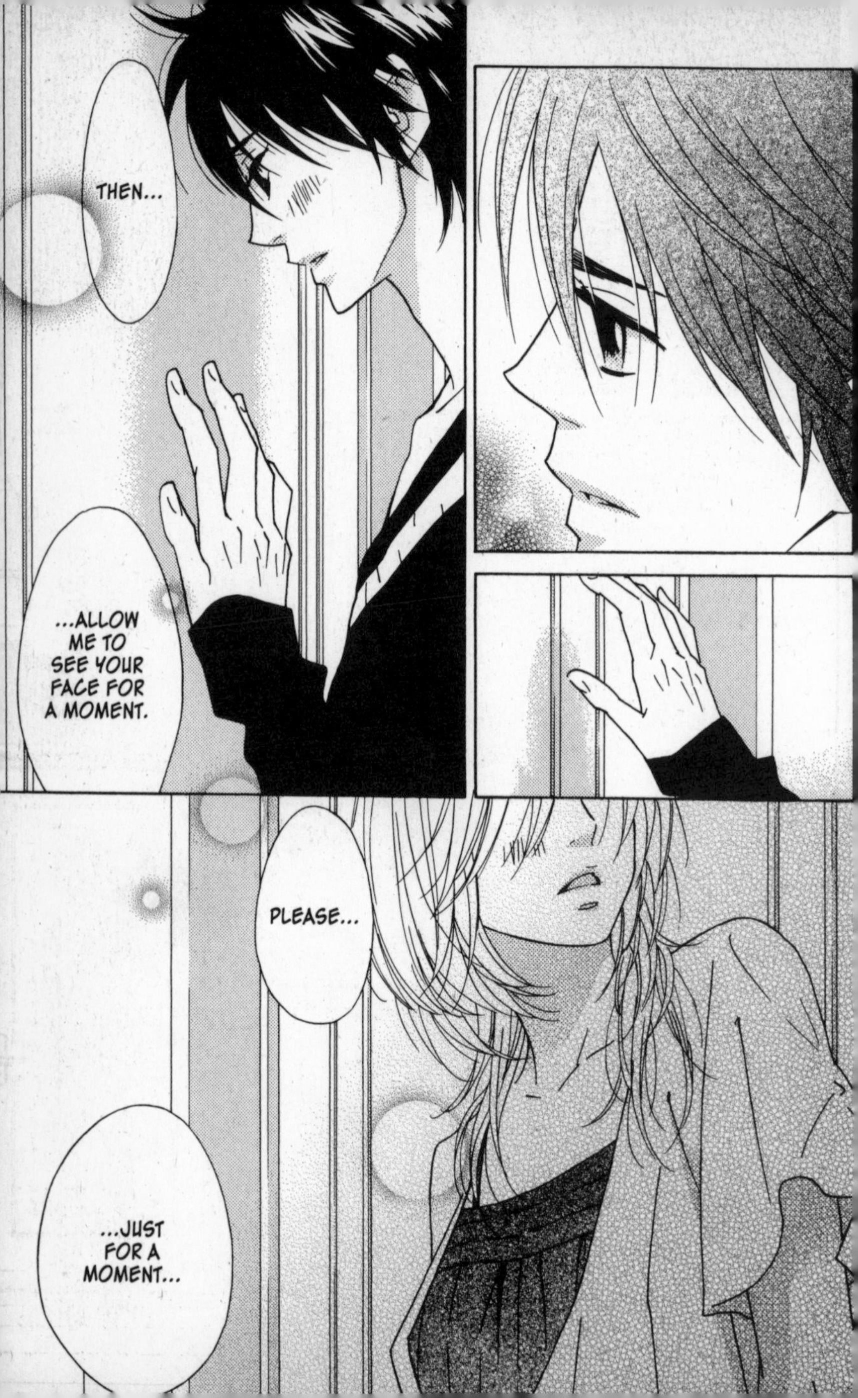
THEN...
...ALLOW ME TO SEE YOUR FACE FOR A MOMENT.
PLEASE...
...JUST FOR A MOMENT...

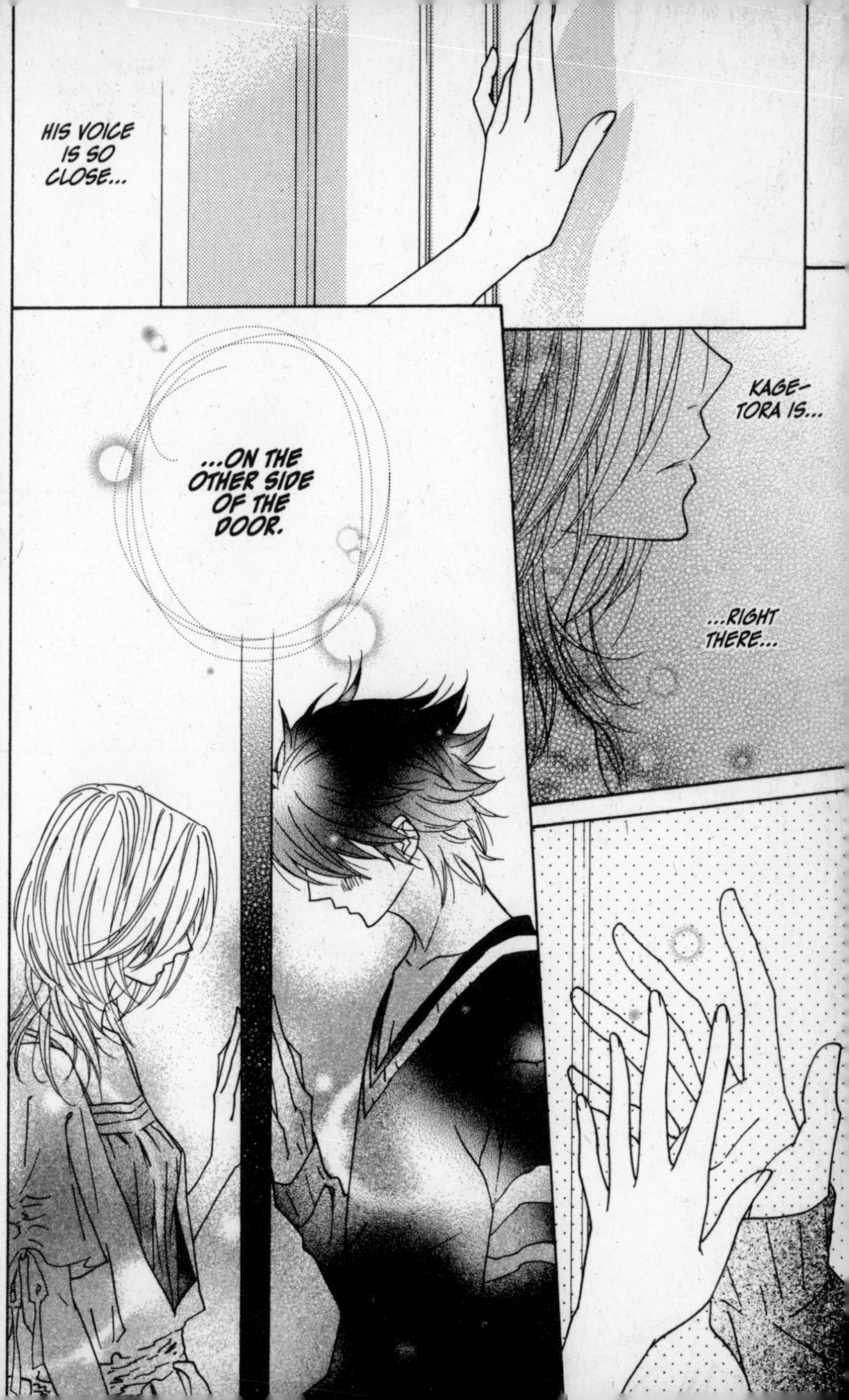
HIS VOICE IS SO CLOSE...
KAGE-TORA IS...
...RIGHT THERE...
...ON THE OTHER SIDE OF THE DOOR.

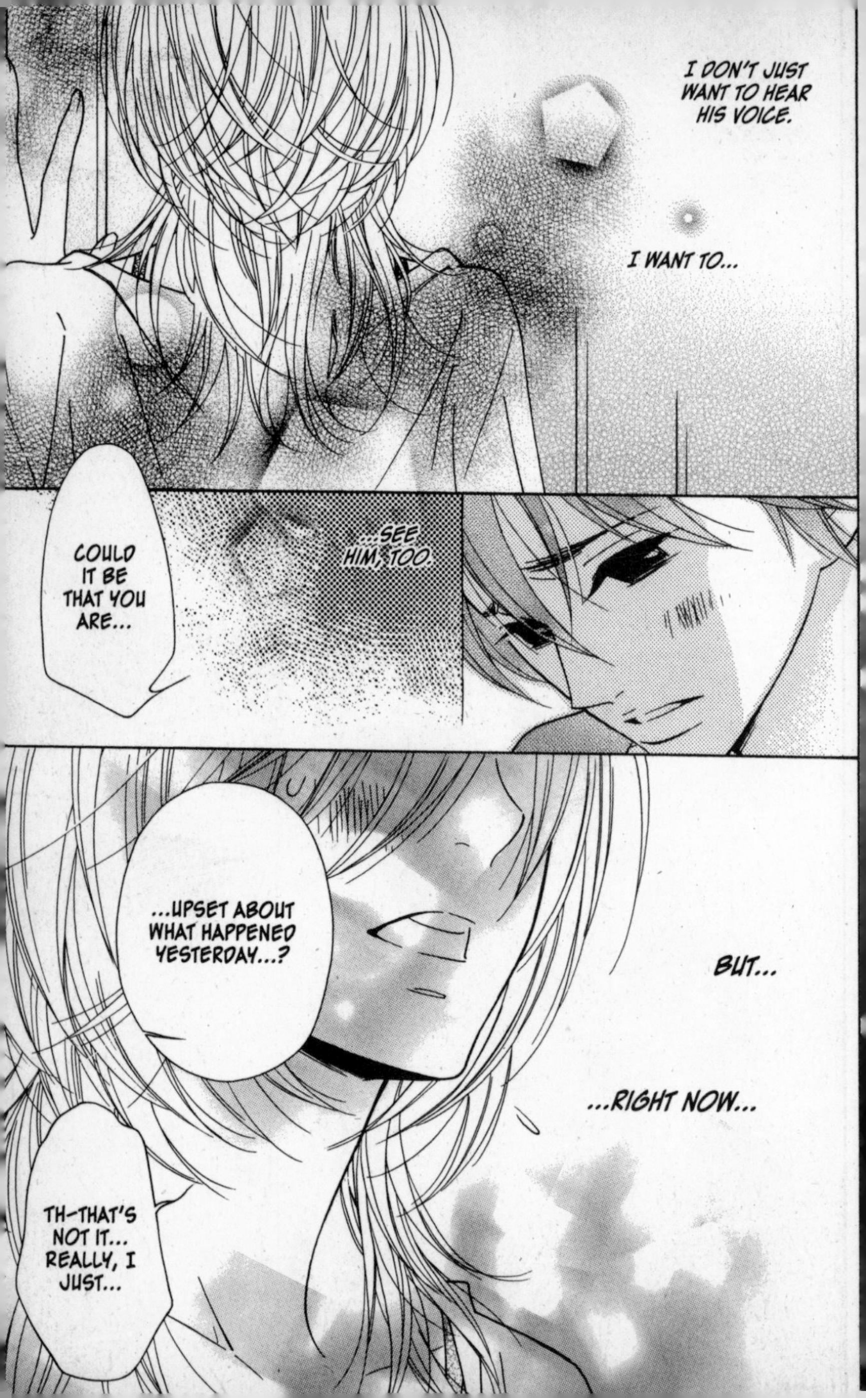
I DON'T JUST WANT TO HEAR HIS VOICE.
I WANT TO...
...SEE HIM, TOO.
COULD IT BE THAT YOU ARE...
...UPSET ABOUT WHAT HAPPENED YESTERDAY...?
BUT...
...RIGHT NOW...
TH-THAT'S NOT IT... REALLY, I JUST...

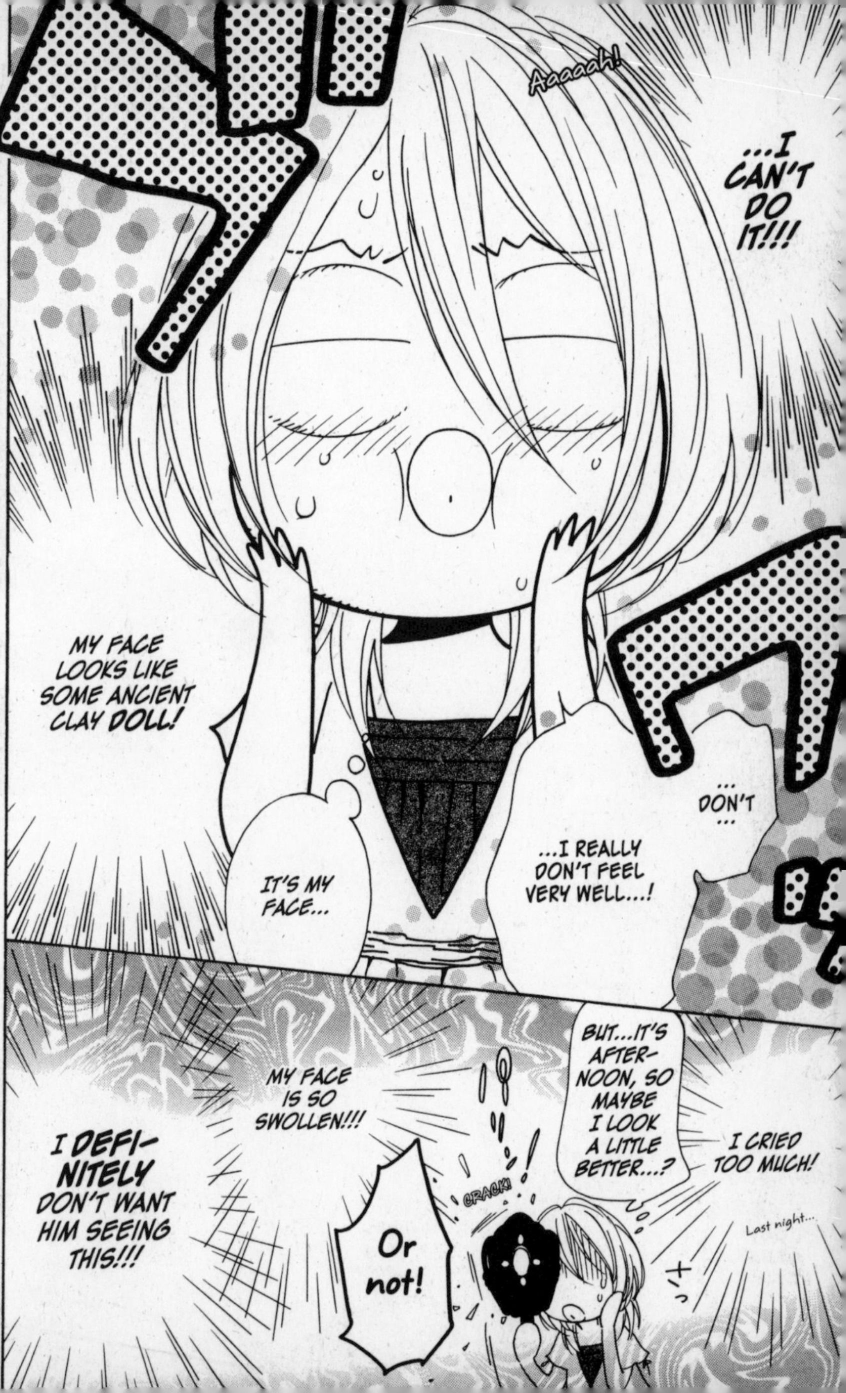
Aaaaah!
...I CAN'T DO IT!!!
MY FACE LOOKS LIKE SOME ANCIENT CLAY DOLL!
... DON'T ...
...I REALLY DON'T FEEL VERY WELL...!
IT'S MY FACE...
I CRIED TOO MUCH!
Last night...
BUT...IT'S AFTER-NOON, SO MAYBE I LOOK A LITTLE BETTER...?
CRACK!
MY FACE IS SO SWOLLEN!!!
Or not!
I DEFI-NITELY DON'T WANT HIM SEEING THIS!!!

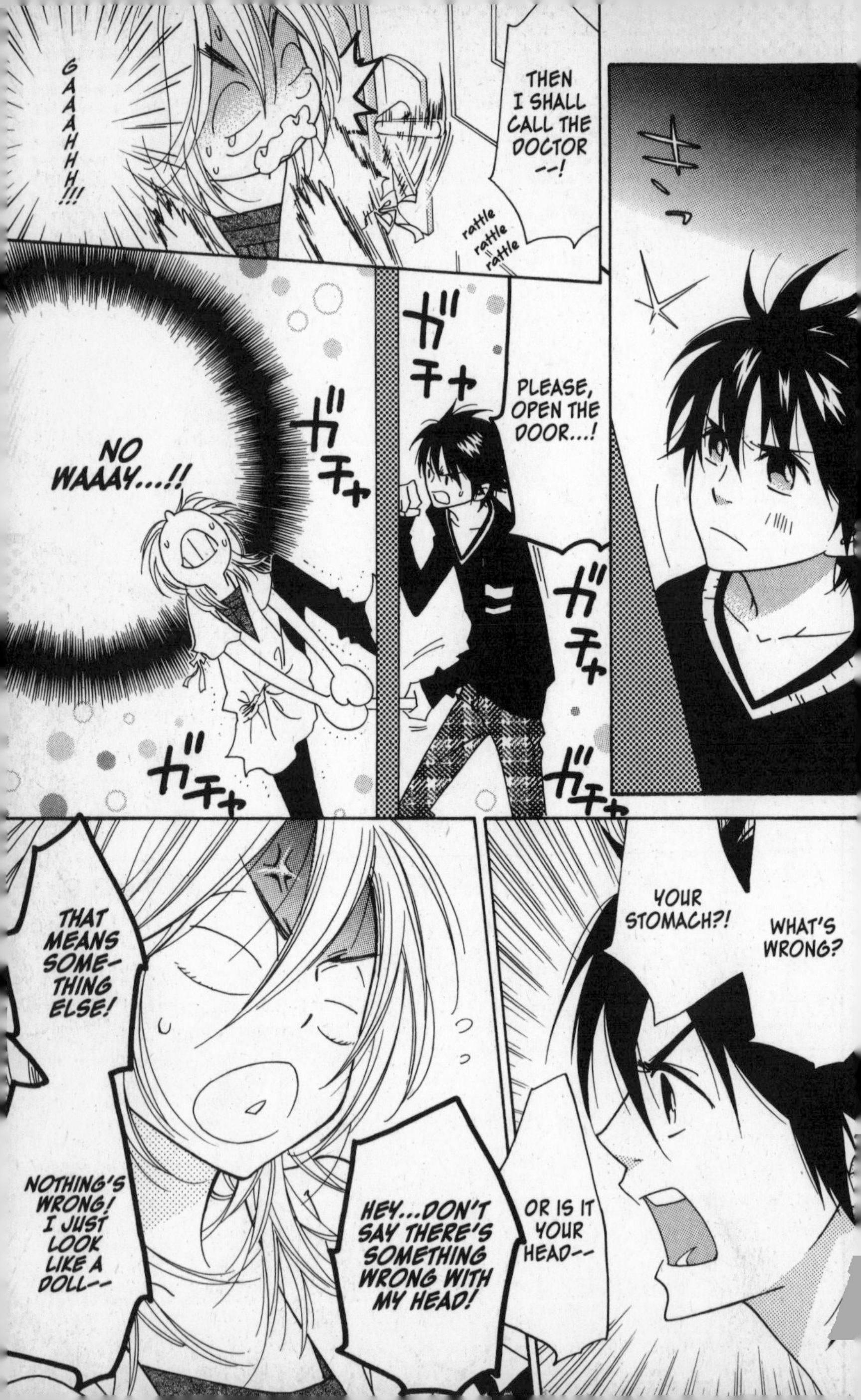
ギッ
THEN I SHALL CALL THE DOCTOR--!
rattle rattle rattle
GAAAAHHH!!!
ガチャ
PLEASE, OPEN THE DOOR...!
ガチャ
ガチャ
ガチャ
NO WAAAY...!!
ガチャ
WHAT'S WRONG?
YOUR STOMACH?!
OR IS IT YOUR HEAD--
HEY...DON'T SAY THERE'S SOMETHING WRONG WITH MY HEAD!
NOTHING'S WRONG! I JUST LOOK LIKE A DOLL--
THAT MEANS SOMETHING ELSE!

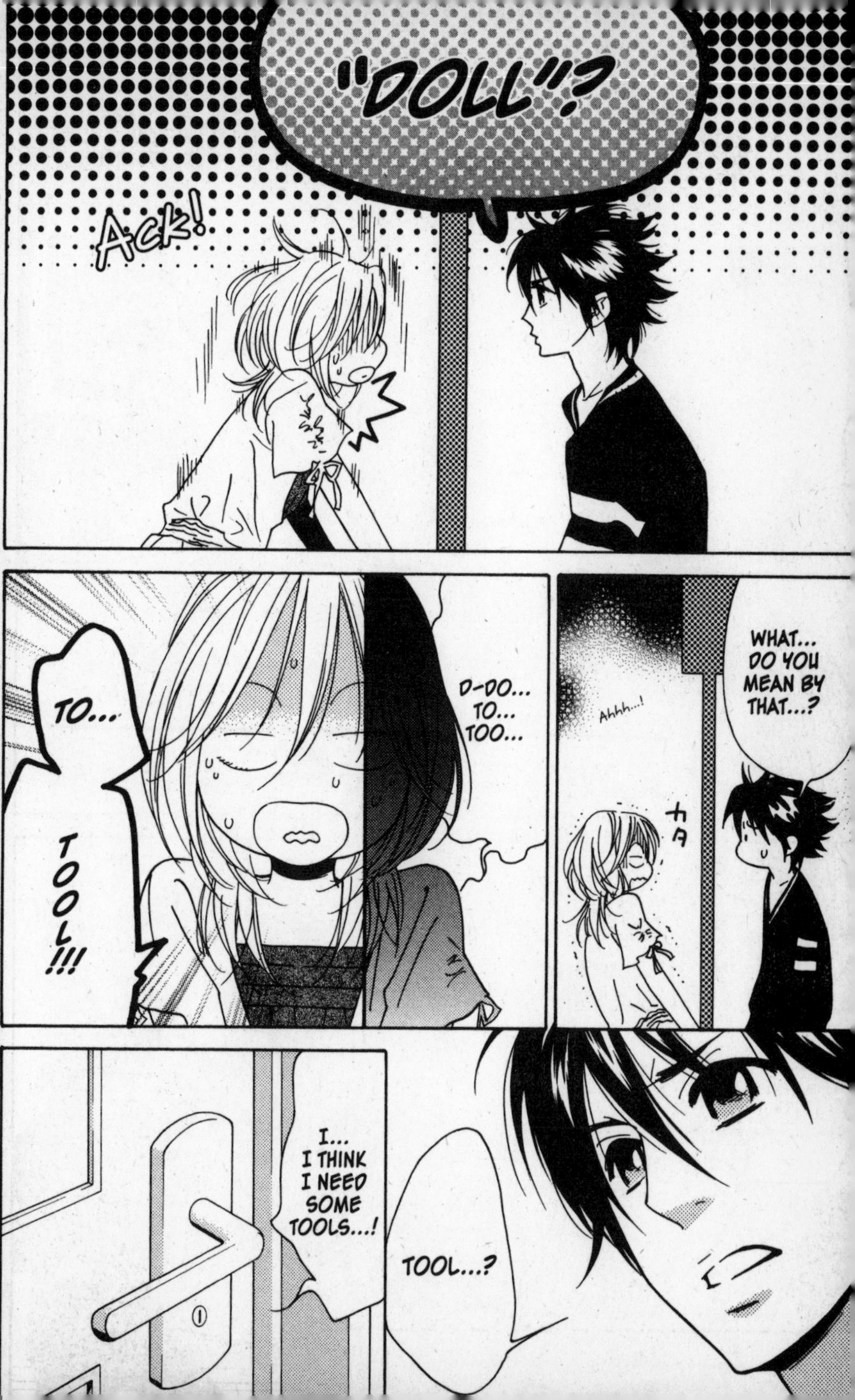
"DOLL"?
Ack!
WHAT... DO YOU MEAN BY THAT...?
Ahhh...!
カァ
D-DO... TO... TOO...
TO...
TOOOL!!!
TOOL...?
I... I THINK I NEED SOME TOOLS...!

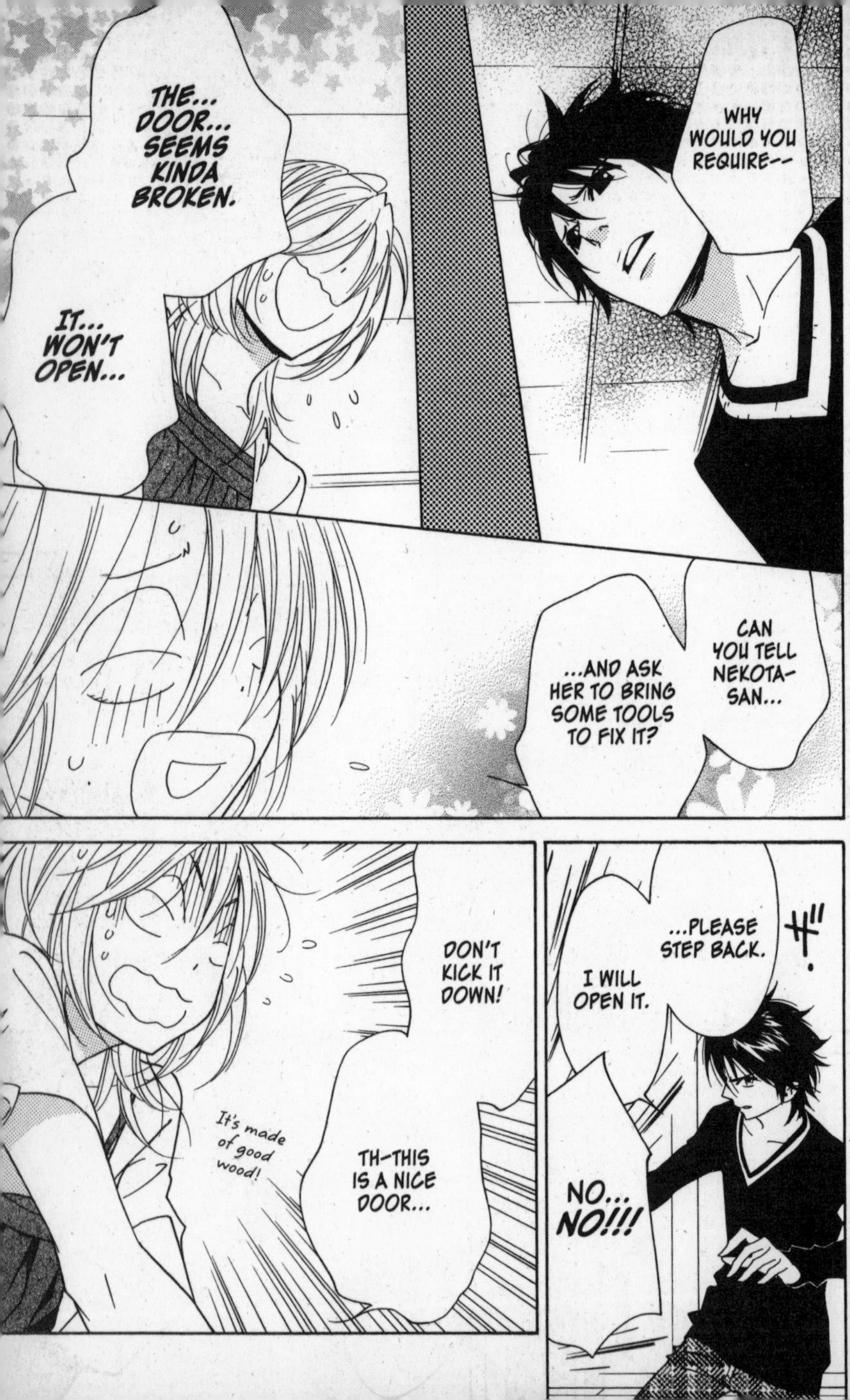
WHY WOULD YOU REQUIRE--
THE... DOOR... SEEMS KINDA BROKEN.
IT... WON'T OPEN...
CAN YOU TELL NEKOTA-SAN...
...AND ASK HER TO BRING SOME TOOLS TO FIX IT?
...PLEASE STEP BACK.
I WILL OPEN IT.
NO... NO!!!
DON'T KICK IT DOWN!
TH-THIS IS A NICE DOOR...
It's made of good wood!

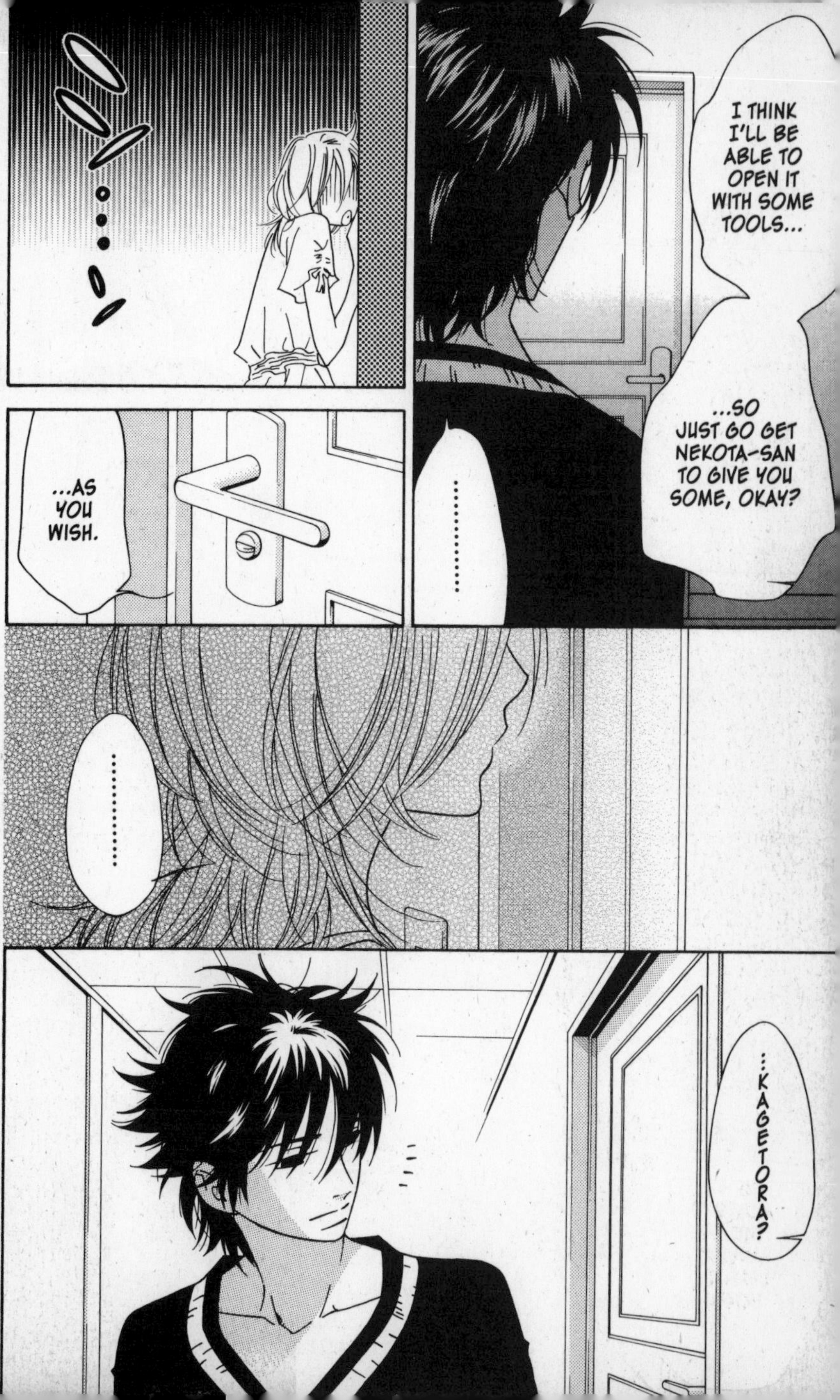

I THINK I'LL BE ABLE TO OPEN IT WITH SOME TOOLS...
...SO JUST GO GET NEKOTA-SAN TO GIVE YOU SOME, OKAY?
......
...AS YOU WISH.
......
...KAGETORA?

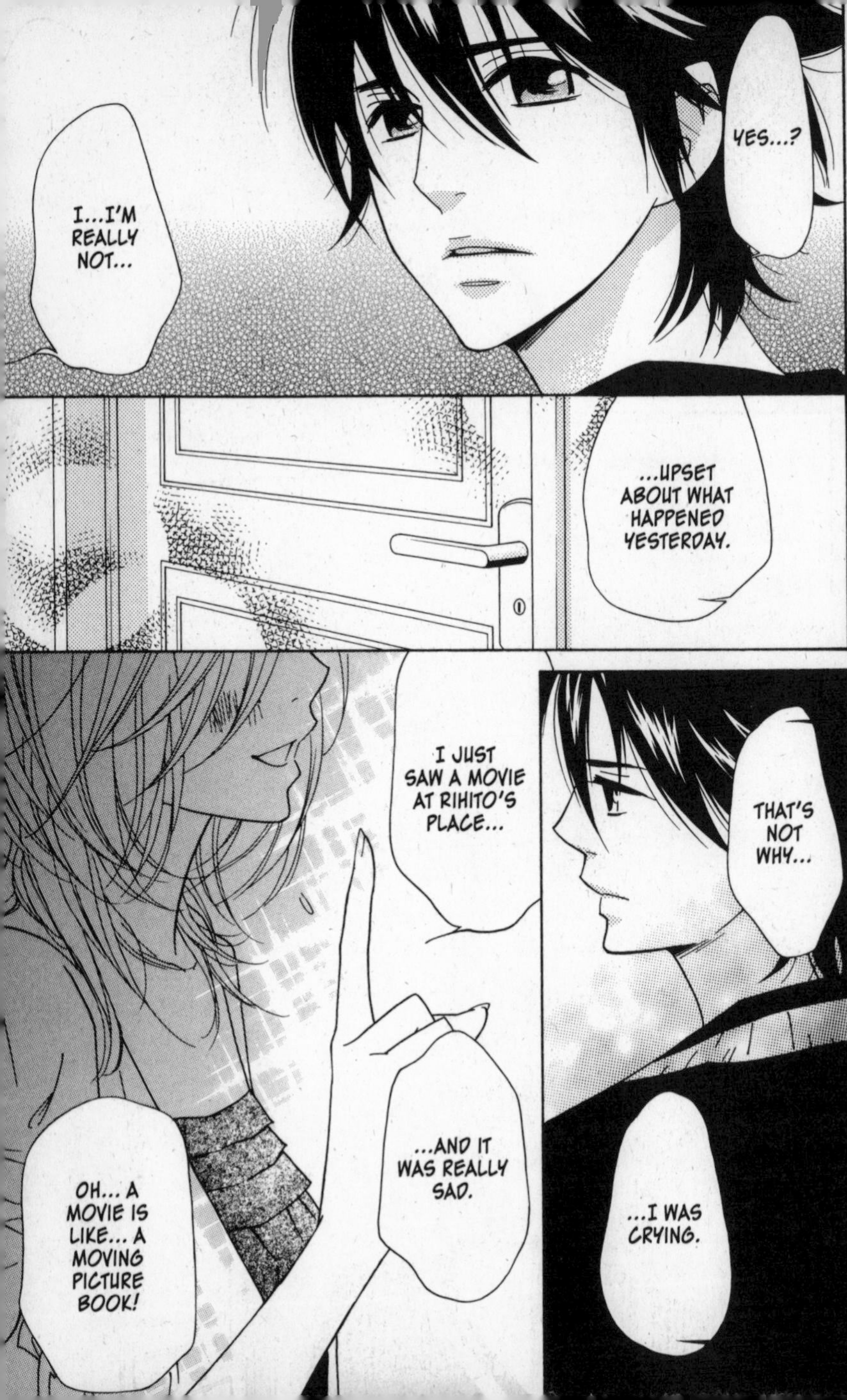
YES...?
I...I'M REALLY NOT...
...UPSET ABOUT WHAT HAPPENED YESTERDAY.
THAT'S NOT WHY...
...I WAS CRYING.
I JUST SAW A MOVIE AT RIHITO'S PLACE...
...AND IT WAS REALLY SAD.
OH... A MOVIE IS LIKE... A MOVING PICTURE BOOK!

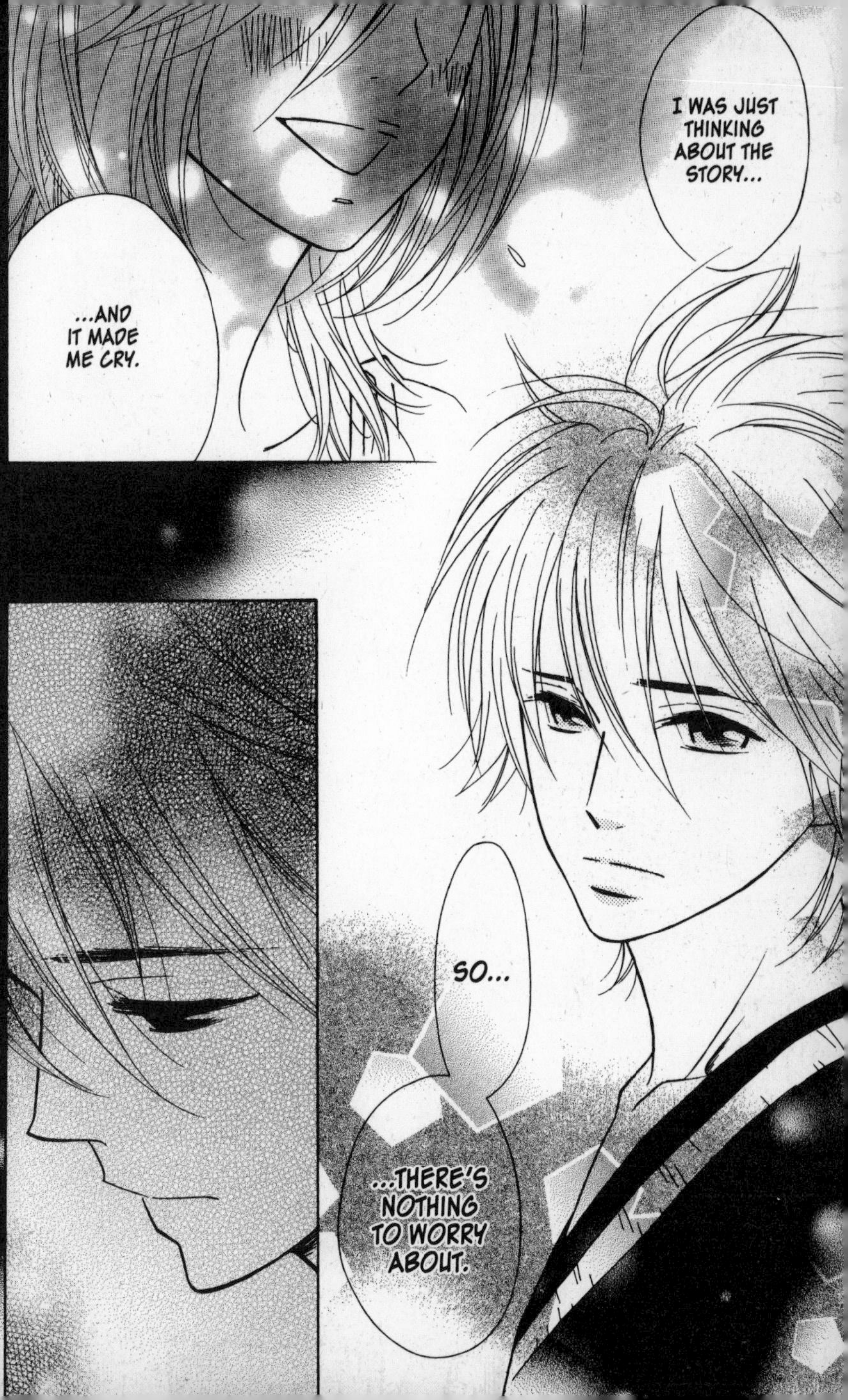
I WAS JUST THINKING ABOUT THE STORY...
...AND IT MADE ME CRY.
SO...
...THERE'S NOTHING TO WORRY ABOUT.

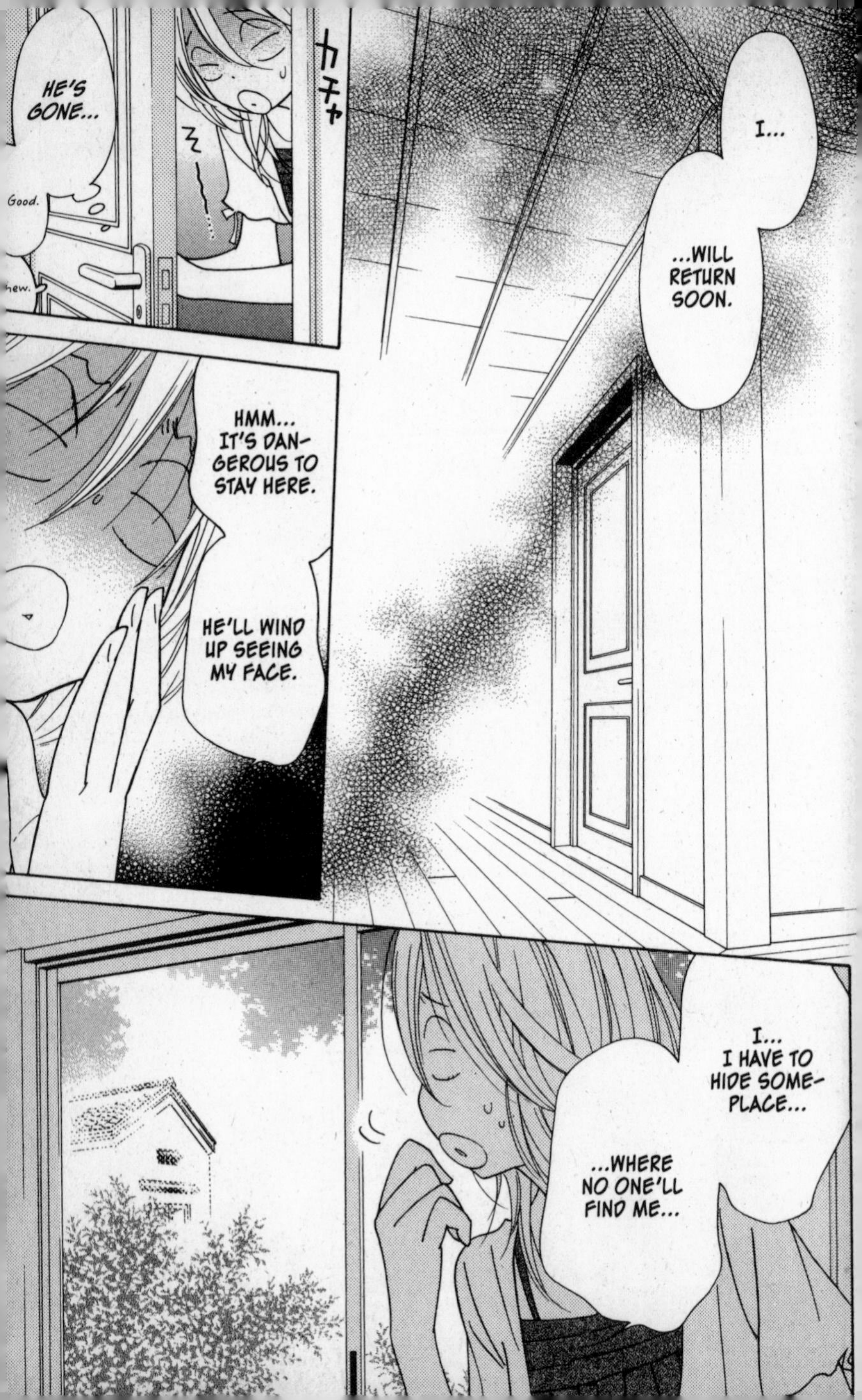
I...
...WILL RETURN SOON.
カチャ
HE'S GONE...
Good.
hew.
HMM... IT'S DAN-GEROUS TO STAY HERE.
HE'LL WIND UP SEEING MY FACE.
I... I HAVE TO HIDE SOME-PLACE...
...WHERE NO ONE'LL FIND ME...

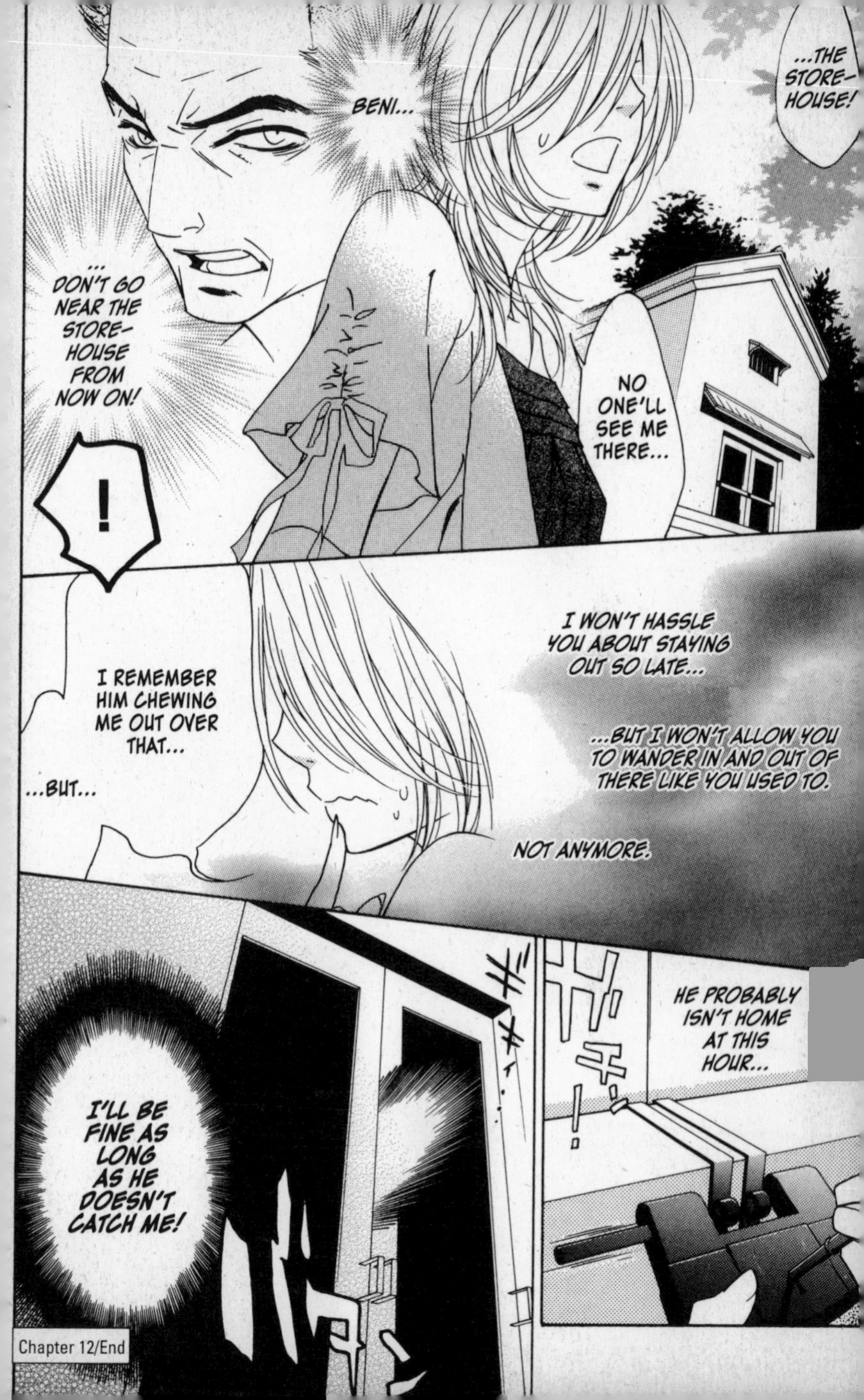
...THE STORE-HOUSE!
BENI...
NO ONE'LL SEE ME THERE...
... DON'T GO NEAR THE STORE-HOUSE FROM NOW ON!
!
I WON'T HASSLE YOU ABOUT STAYING OUT SO LATE...
...BUT I WON'T ALLOW YOU TO WANDER IN AND OUT OF THERE LIKE YOU USED TO.
NOT ANYMORE.
I REMEMBER HIM CHEWING ME OUT OVER THAT...
...BUT...
HE PROBABLY ISN'T HOME AT THIS HOUR...
I'LL BE FINE AS LONG AS HE DOESN'T CATCH ME!

Chapter 12/End

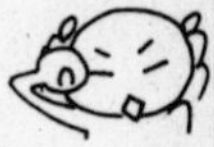

Now I'll address some of the questions you asked! Here we go!

● Profile

Born on August 24. Virgo.
Blood type: O.

Height: 167 cm.

Currently living in Wakayama Prefecture.

My hobbies are watching movies and traveling.

I haven't been able to do this recently.

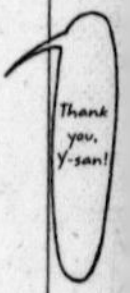
Thank you, Y-san!

● Favorite Games

I was abstaining from gaming for a while, but then a fan sent me Sengoku BASARA and now I'm getting addicted again. I even bought a Nintendo DS so I could play Tokimeki Memory Girls Side!

● Favorite Movies

There are too many to list here, but these are the ones that popped into my head: Spider-Man, Corpse Bride, Magnolia, Cider House Rules, Napoleon Dynamite...and others.

● Favorite Actors

Actors who make me want to watch every single movie they're in are...Jack Black, Philip Seymour Hoffman and Steve Buscemi. For Japanese actors, Yuu Aoi-chan and Karina-chan. They're both really cute.

● Favorite Music

This is diverse too... I love Oasis, Gorillaz, Nirvana, Sambomaster, Bump of Chicken, Asian Kung-Fu Generation, Mayumi Kojima and many others. I have eclectic taste.

● Favorite Country (?)

My list of favorite places I've already visited includes Maldives, Hawaii, Hong Kong, Paris and Bali. Places that I'd like to visit include Turkey, Italy, Tahiti and Canada, among others.

↖ Continued

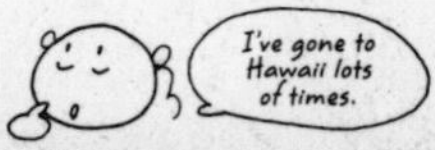
I've gone to Hawaii lots of times.

● About Drawing

I've liked drawing ever since I was a child. I think I started separating pictures into frames and drawing manga in late elementary school. I made my manga debut when I was 18.

● About Coloring

I color using a PC, with an application called Painter. If it's analog, I use Copic markers.

● About the Characters

I'm attached to all of the characters, so I don't have any I love most or hate, but...there are characters who are easier or harder to draw. Drawing Hitaki is very easy. It's relatively easy to draw the kind of characters who clearly show their emotions on their faces. By contrast, Rihito is harder to draw because he doesn't really show a lot of emotion, and I often redraw my drafts several times. I pay the most attention when I draw Kagetora and Beni. After all, they're the main characters!

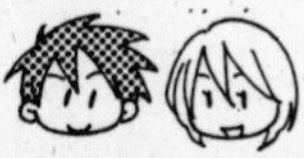

I'll stop here for now. If you have any more questions, please let me know! I'll be waiting for your comments and whatnot.♡

● Contact address ●

TOKYOPOP Inc.
Attn: Shoko Conami
5900 Wilshire Blvd.
Suite 2000
Los Angeles, CA
90036

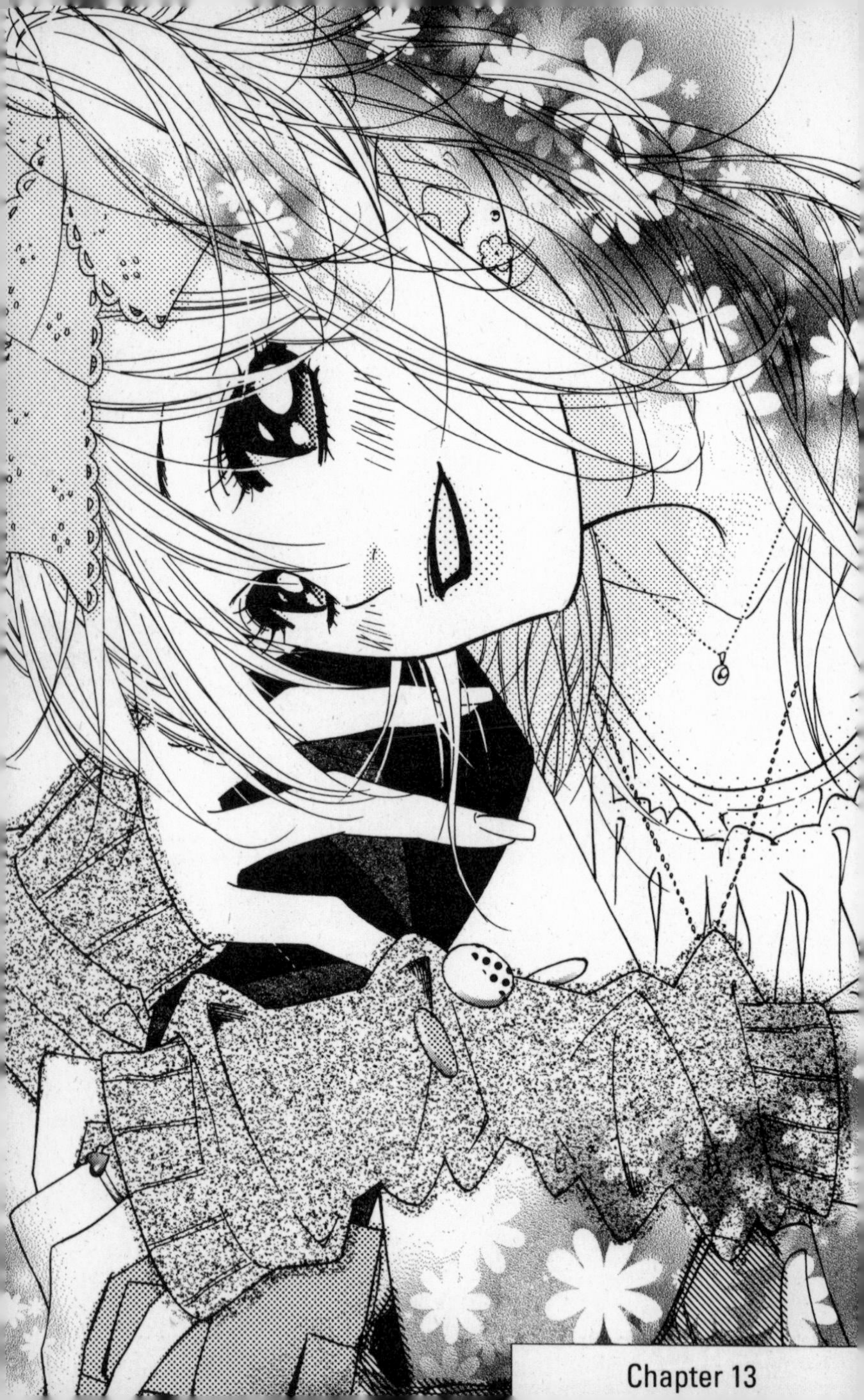

Chapter 13

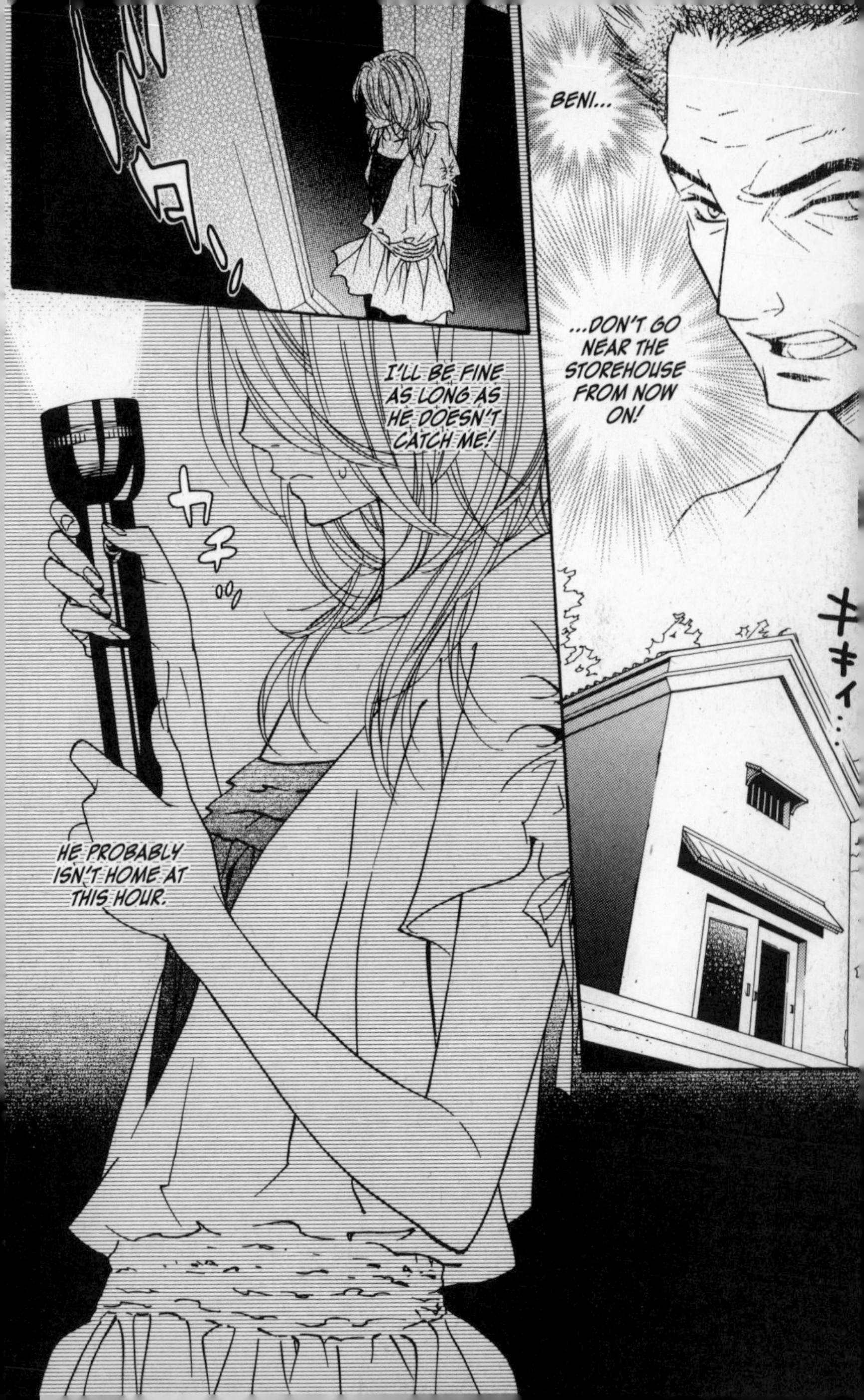
BENI...
...DON'T GO NEAR THE STOREHOUSE FROM NOW ON!
キキイ…
I'LL BE FINE AS LONG AS HE DOESN'T CATCH ME!
カチ
HE PROBABLY ISN'T HOME AT THIS HOUR.

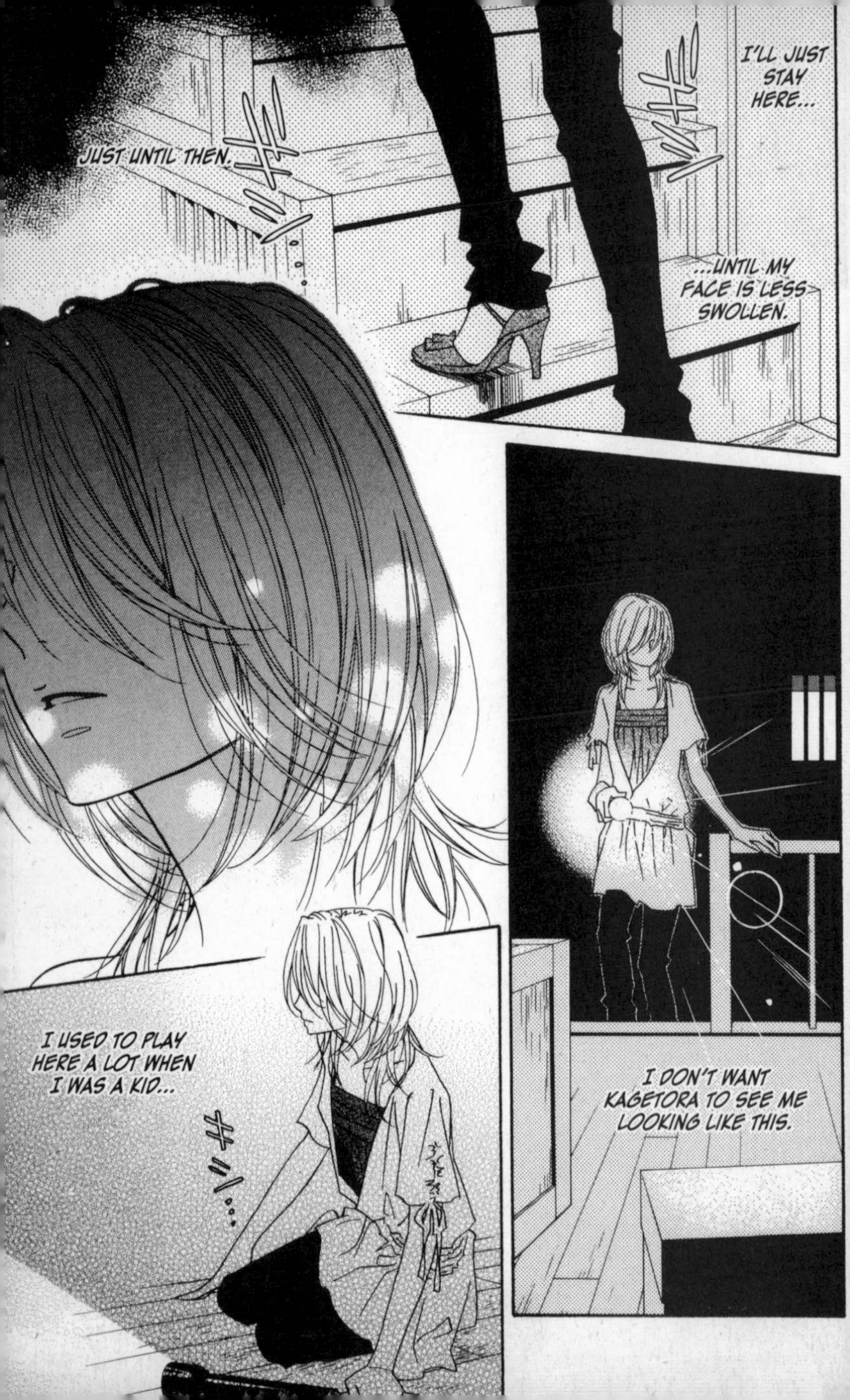
I'LL JUST STAY HERE...
...UNTIL MY FACE IS LESS SWOLLEN.
JUST UNTIL THEN.
I DON'T WANT KAGETORA TO SEE ME LOOKING LIKE THIS.
I USED TO PLAY HERE A LOT WHEN I WAS A KID...

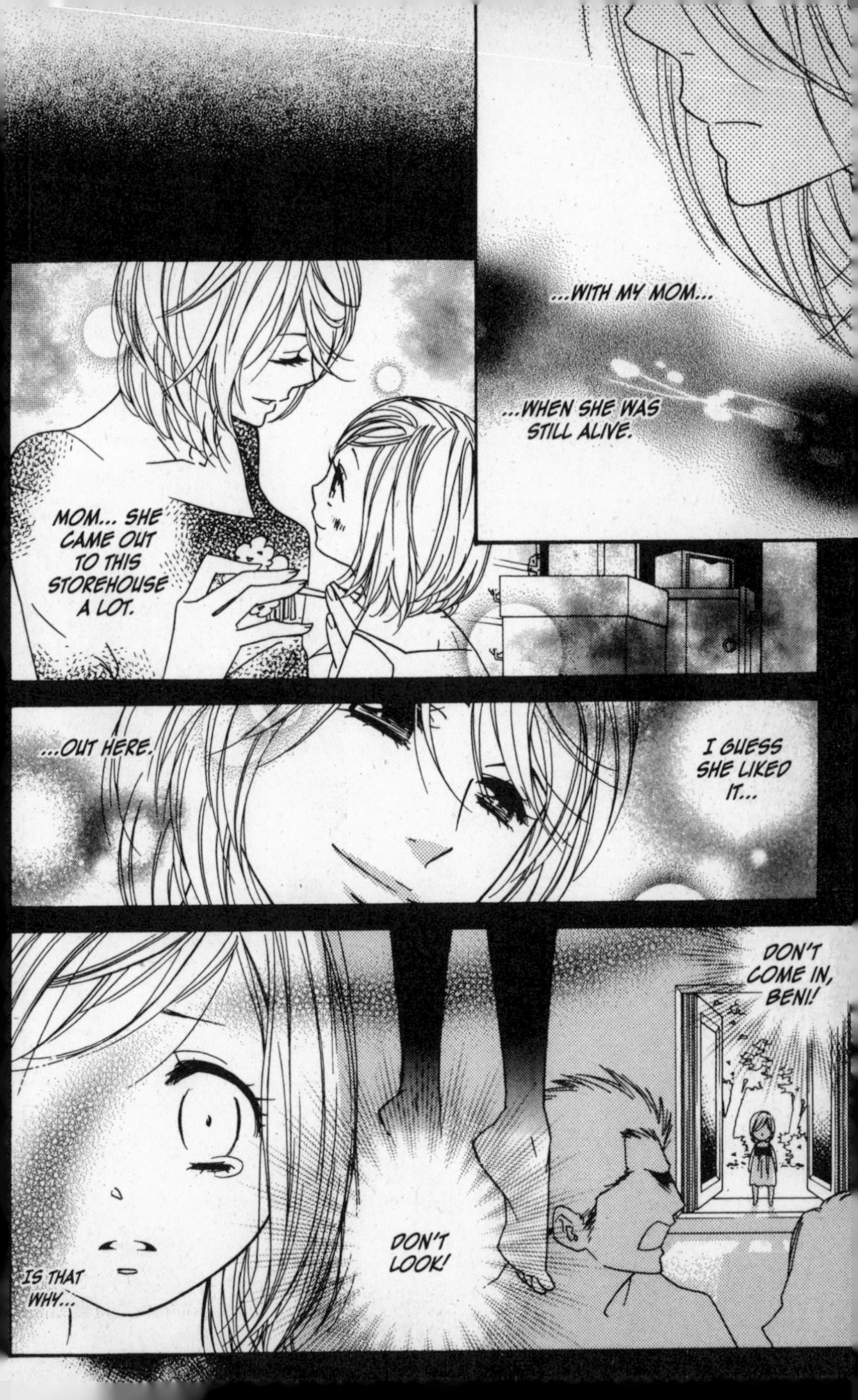
...WITH MY MOM...
...WHEN SHE WAS STILL ALIVE.
MOM... SHE CAME OUT TO THIS STOREHOUSE A LOT.
I GUESS SHE LIKED IT...
...OUT HERE.
DON'T COME IN, BENI!
DON'T LOOK!
IS THAT WHY...

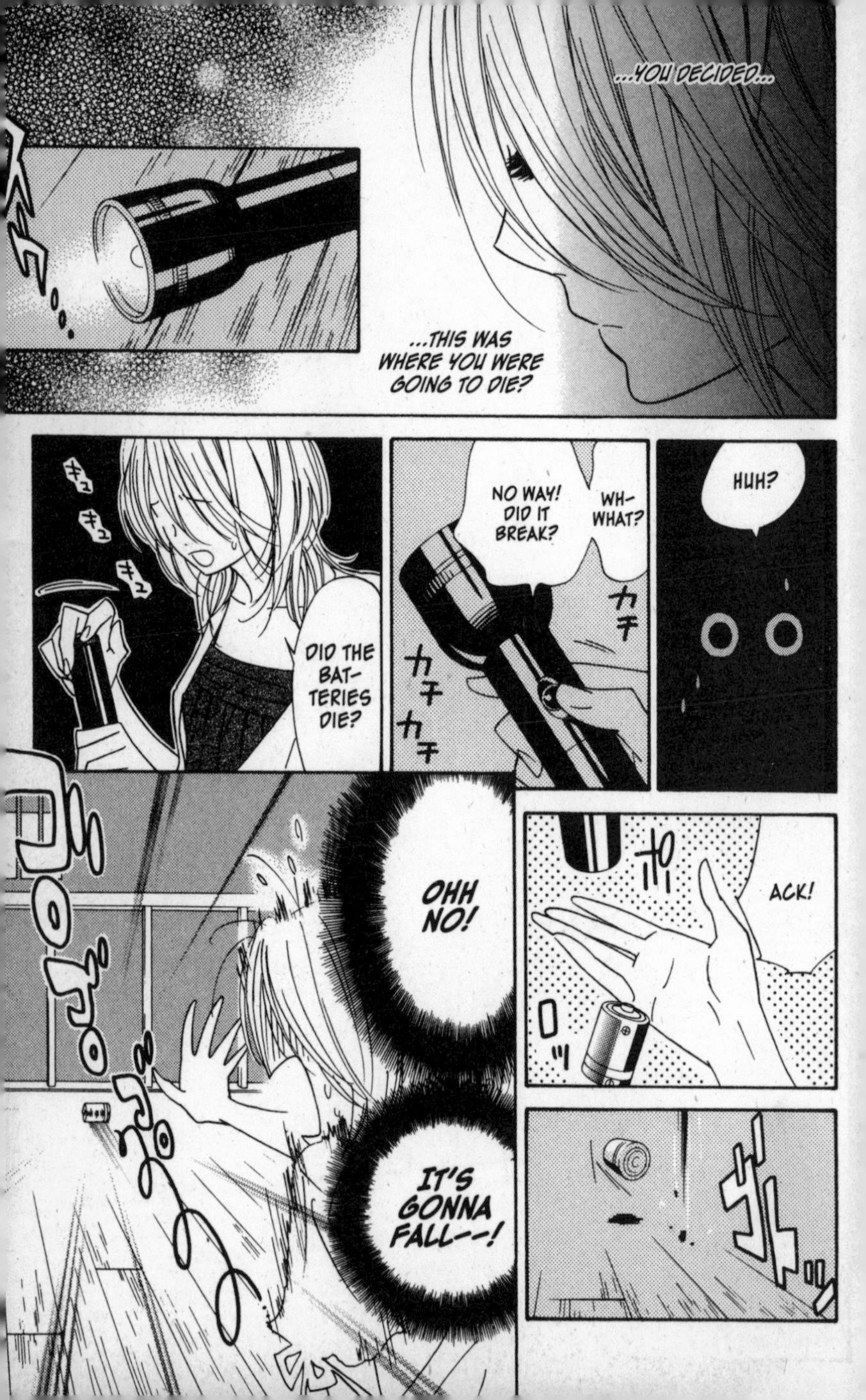
...YOU DECIDED...
...THIS WAS WHERE YOU WERE GOING TO DIE?
HUH?
WH-WHAT?
NO WAY! DID IT BREAK?
DID THE BAT-TERIES DIE?
ACK!
OHH NO!
IT'S GONNA FALL--!

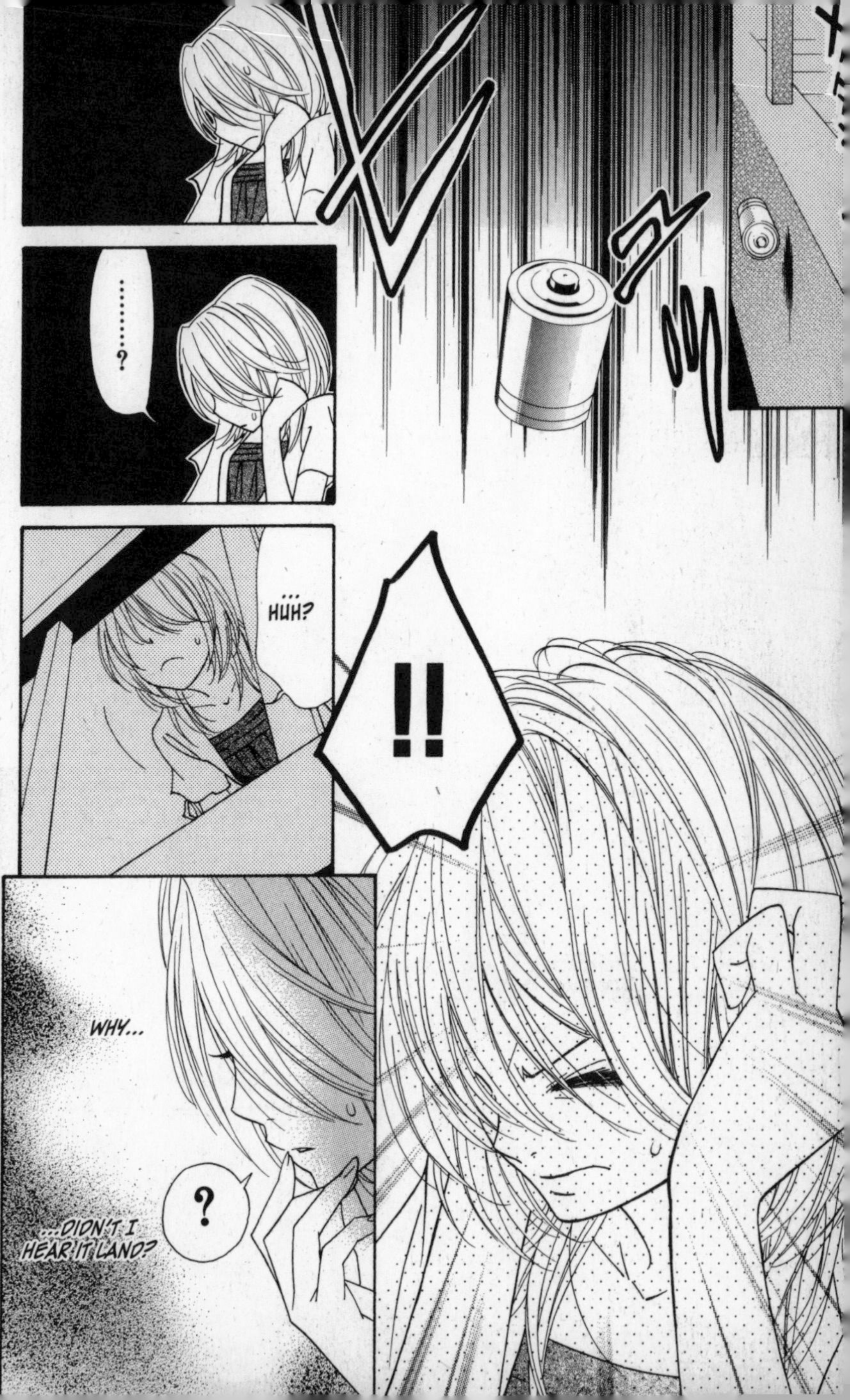

......?
HUH?
!!
WHY...
?
...DIDN'T I HEAR IT LAND?

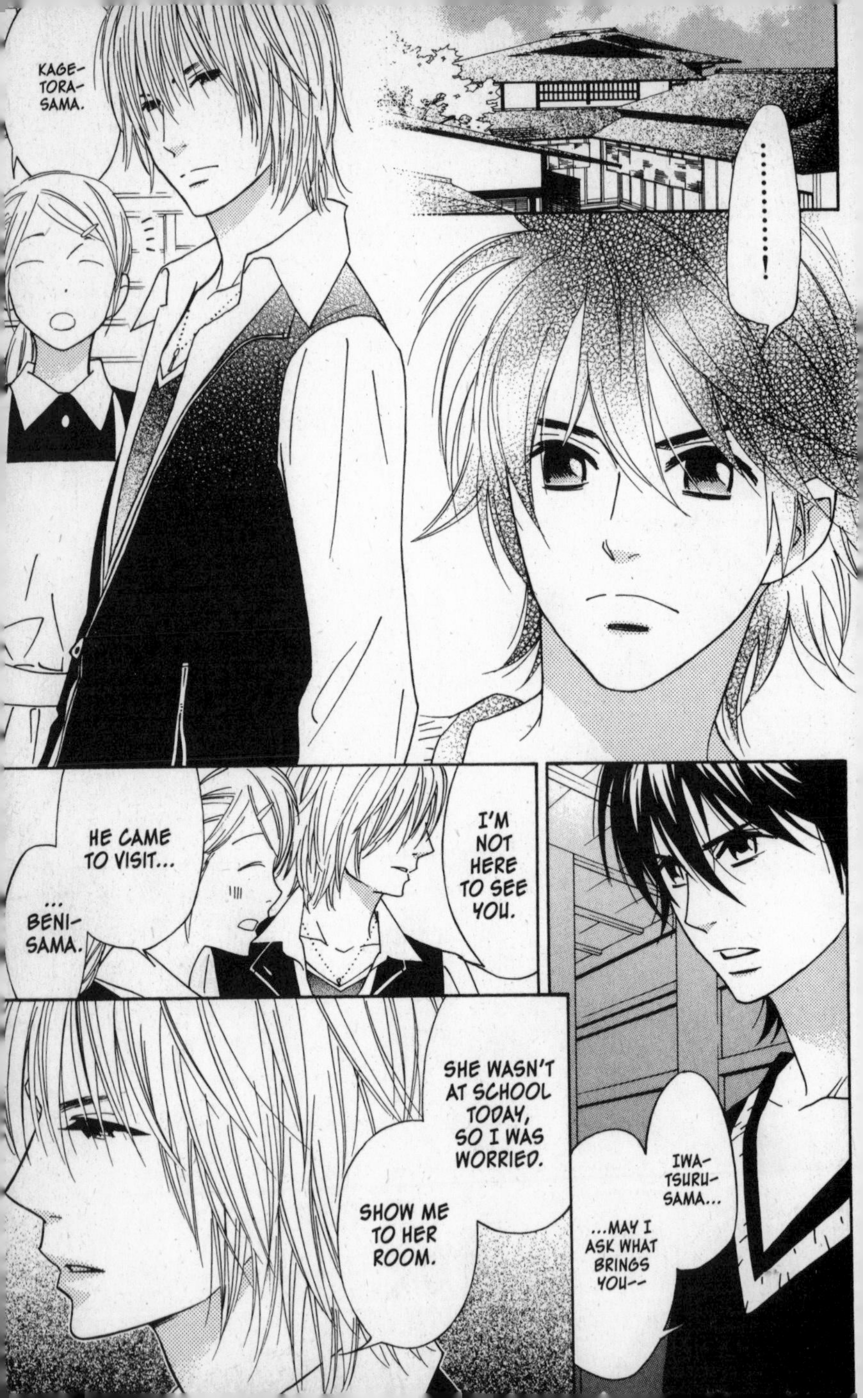
......!
KAGE-TORA-SAMA.
IWA-TSURU-SAMA...
...MAY I ASK WHAT BRINGS YOU--
I'M NOT HERE TO SEE YOU.
HE CAME TO VISIT...
...BENI-SAMA.
SHE WASN'T AT SCHOOL TODAY, SO I WAS WORRIED.
SHOW ME TO HER ROOM.

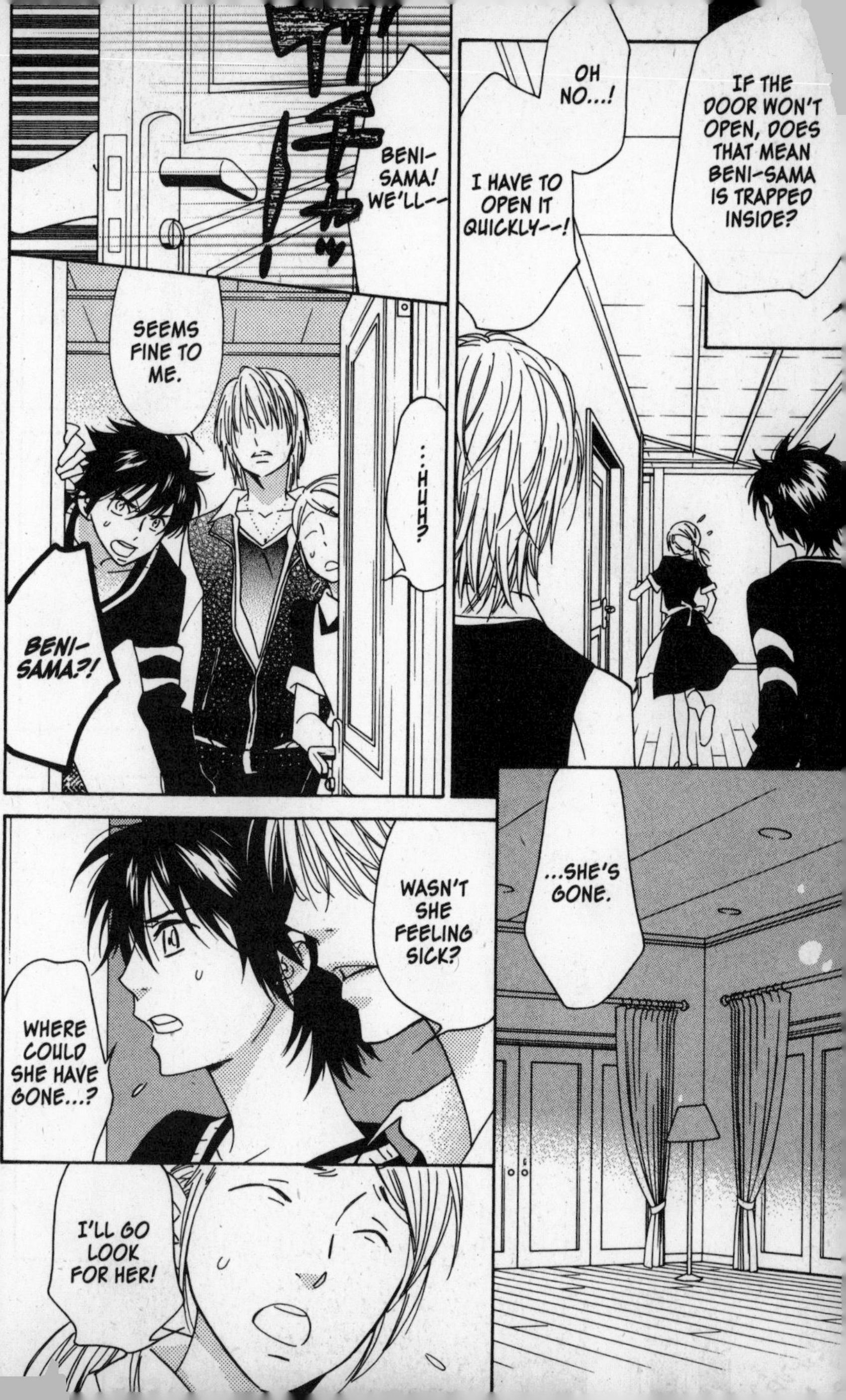
IF THE DOOR WON'T OPEN, DOES THAT MEAN BENI-SAMA IS TRAPPED INSIDE?
OH NO...!
I HAVE TO OPEN IT QUICKLY--!
BENI-SAMA! WE'LL--
...HUH?
SEEMS FINE TO ME.
BENI-SAMA?!
...SHE'S GONE.
WASN'T SHE FEELING SICK?
WHERE COULD SHE HAVE GONE...?
I'LL GO LOOK FOR HER!

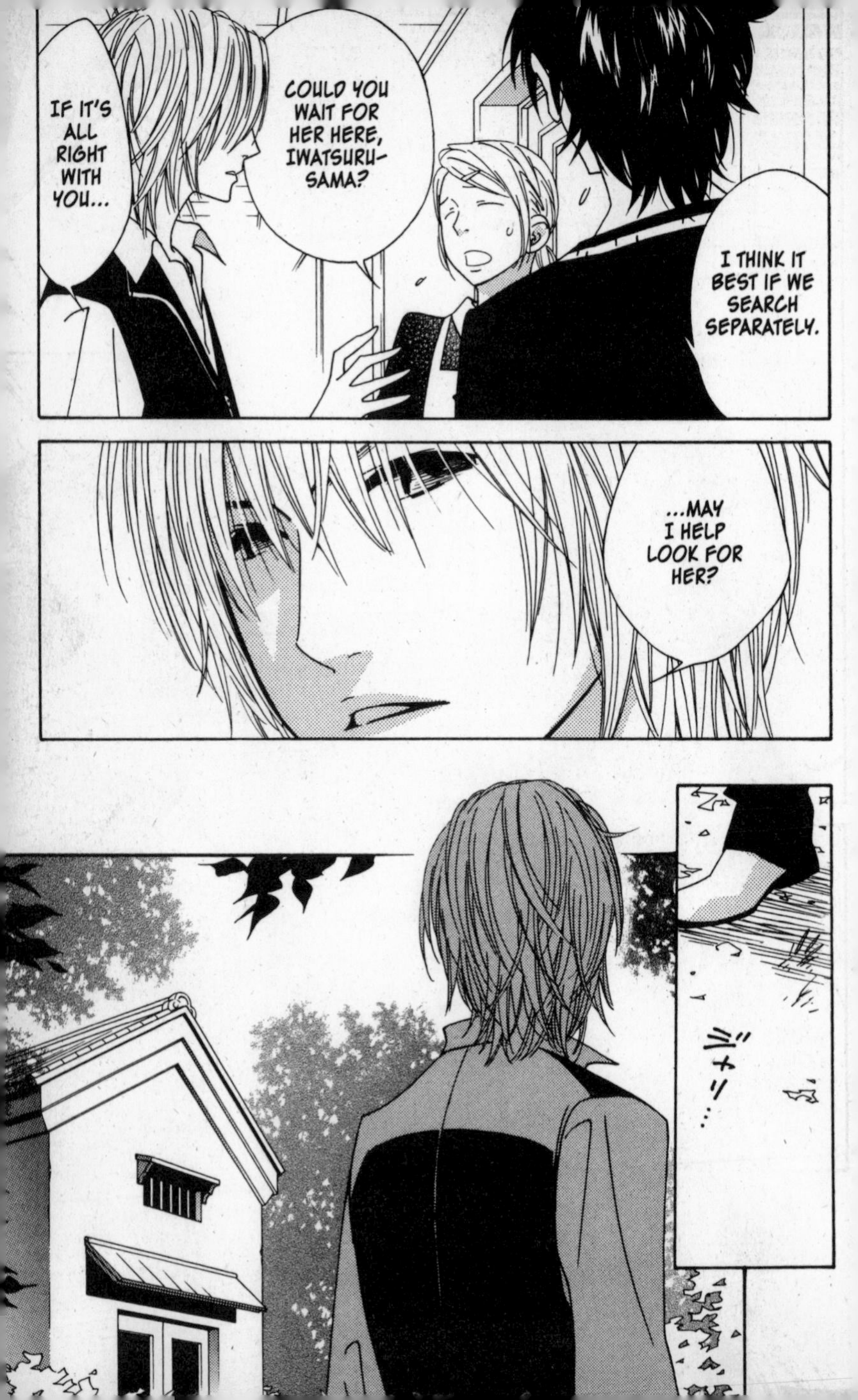
I THINK IT BEST IF WE SEARCH SEPARATELY.
COULD YOU WAIT FOR HER HERE, IWATSURU-SAMA?
IF IT'S ALL RIGHT WITH YOU...
...MAY I HELP LOOK FOR HER?
ジャリ…

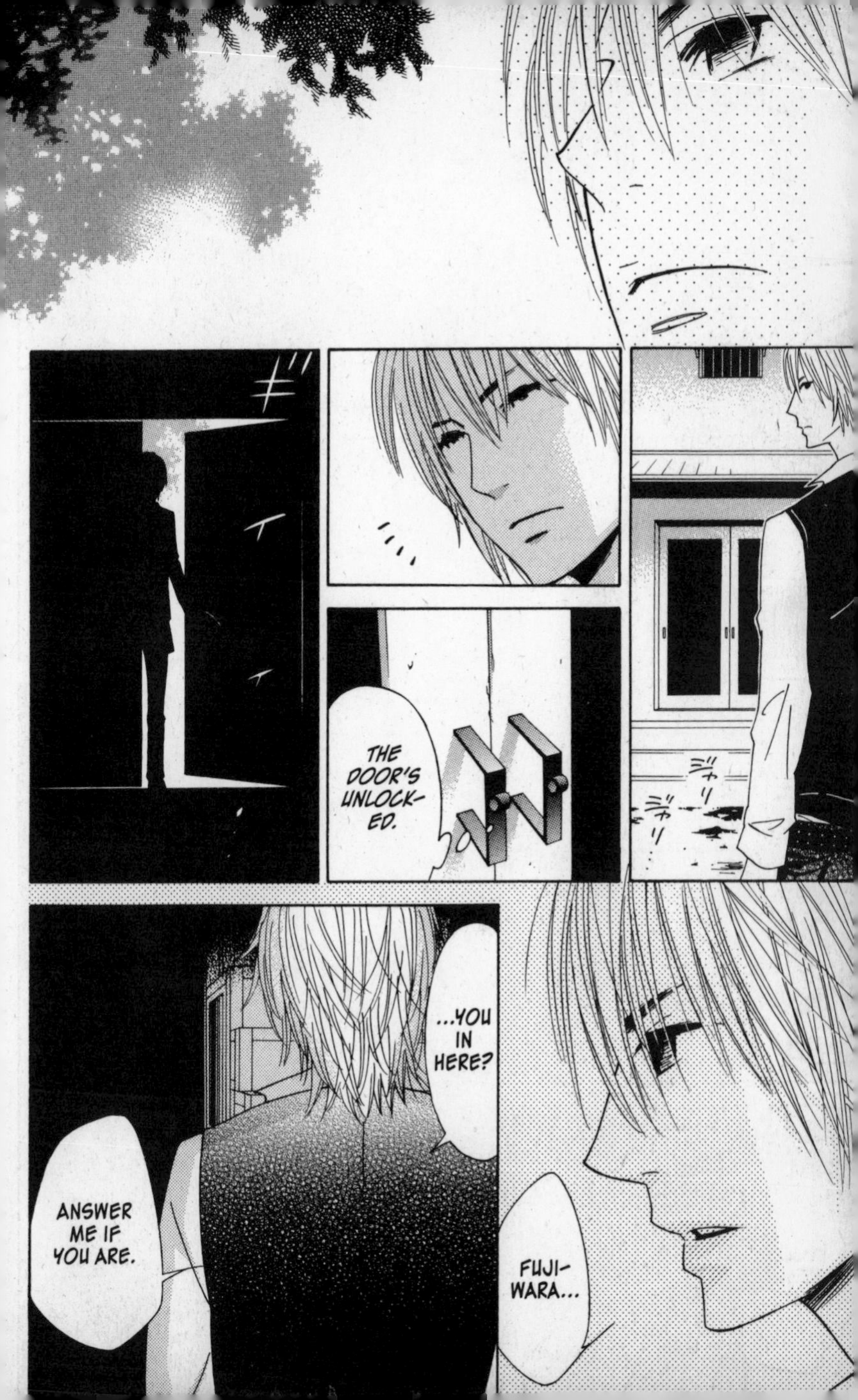
ジャリ
ジャリ
THE DOOR'S UNLOCK-ED.
FUJI-WARA...
...YOU IN HERE?
ANSWER ME IF YOU ARE.

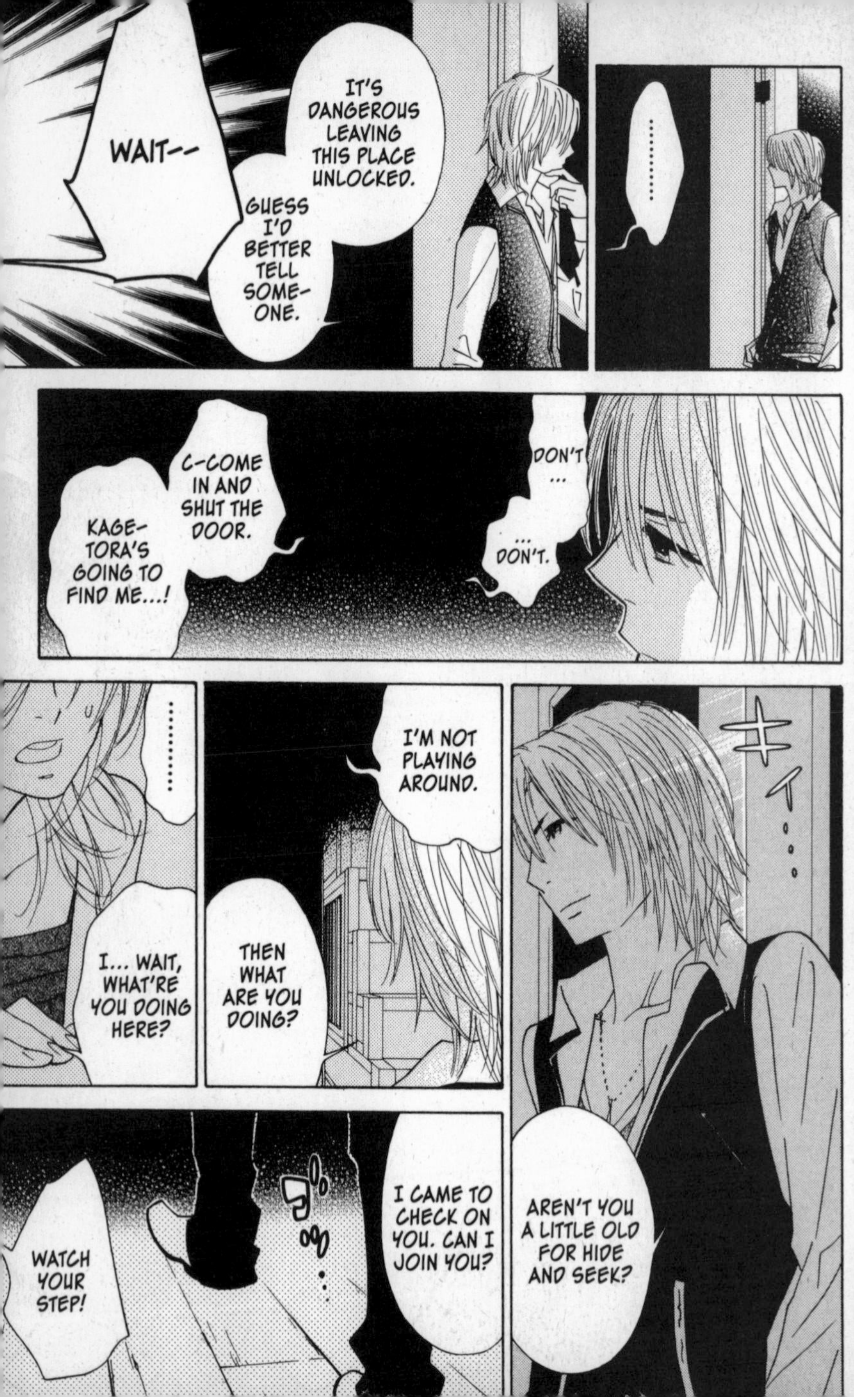
......
IT'S DANGEROUS LEAVING THIS PLACE UNLOCKED.
GUESS I'D BETTER TELL SOME-ONE.
WAIT--
DON'T ...
... DON'T.
C-COME IN AND SHUT THE DOOR.
KAGE-TORA'S GOING TO FIND ME...!
キィ...
AREN'T YOU A LITTLE OLD FOR HIDE AND SEEK?
I'M NOT PLAYING AROUND.
THEN WHAT ARE YOU DOING?
......
I... WAIT, WHAT'RE YOU DOING HERE?
I CAME TO CHECK ON YOU. CAN I JOIN YOU?
WATCH YOUR STEP!

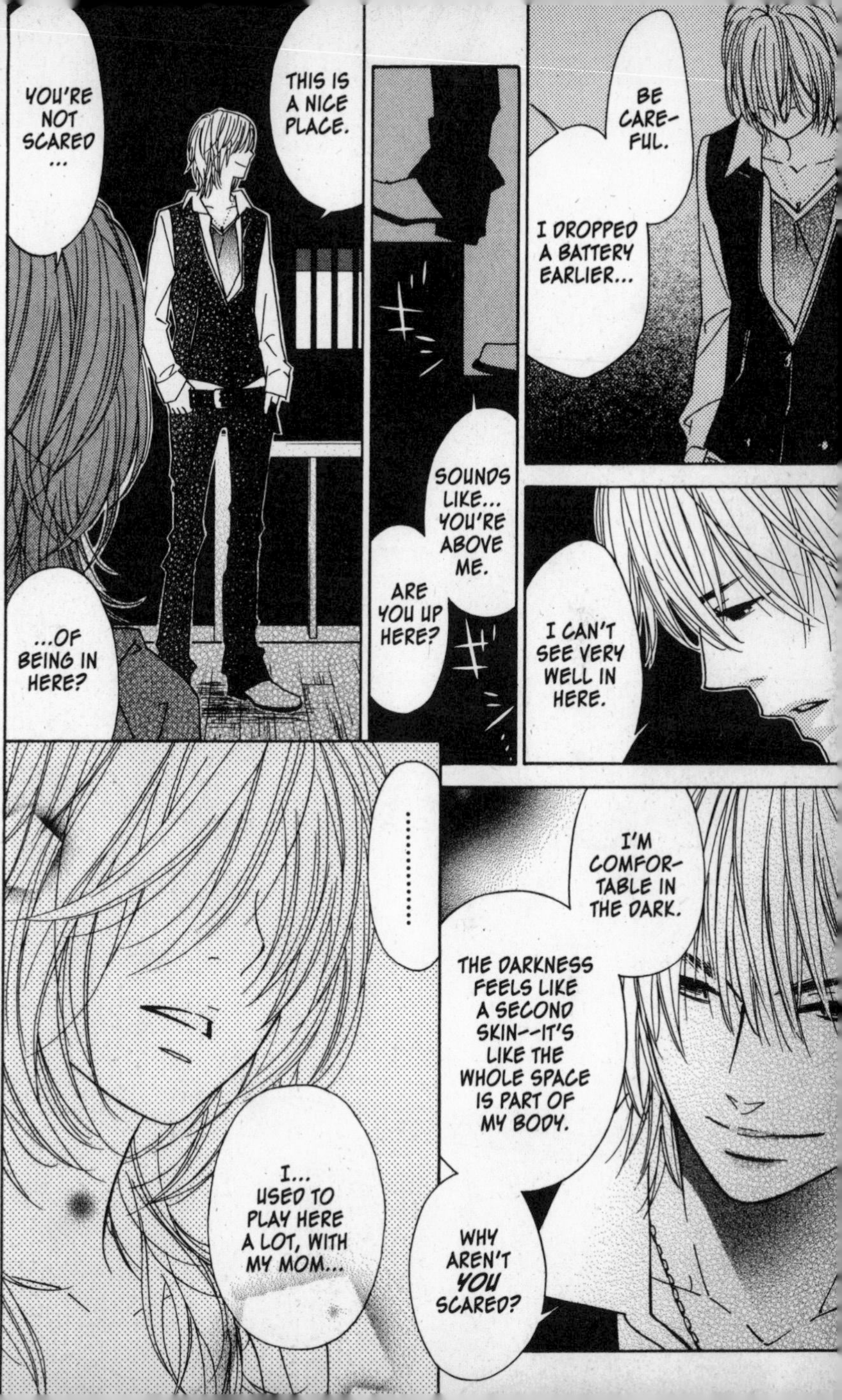
BE CAREFUL.
I DROPPED A BATTERY EARLIER...
I CAN'T SEE VERY WELL IN HERE.
SOUNDS LIKE... YOU'RE ABOVE ME.
ARE YOU UP HERE?
THIS IS A NICE PLACE.
YOU'RE NOT SCARED...
...OF BEING IN HERE?
I'M COMFORTABLE IN THE DARK.
THE DARKNESS FEELS LIKE A SECOND SKIN--IT'S LIKE THE WHOLE SPACE IS PART OF MY BODY.
WHY AREN'T *YOU* SCARED?
......
I... USED TO PLAY HERE A LOT, WITH MY MOM...

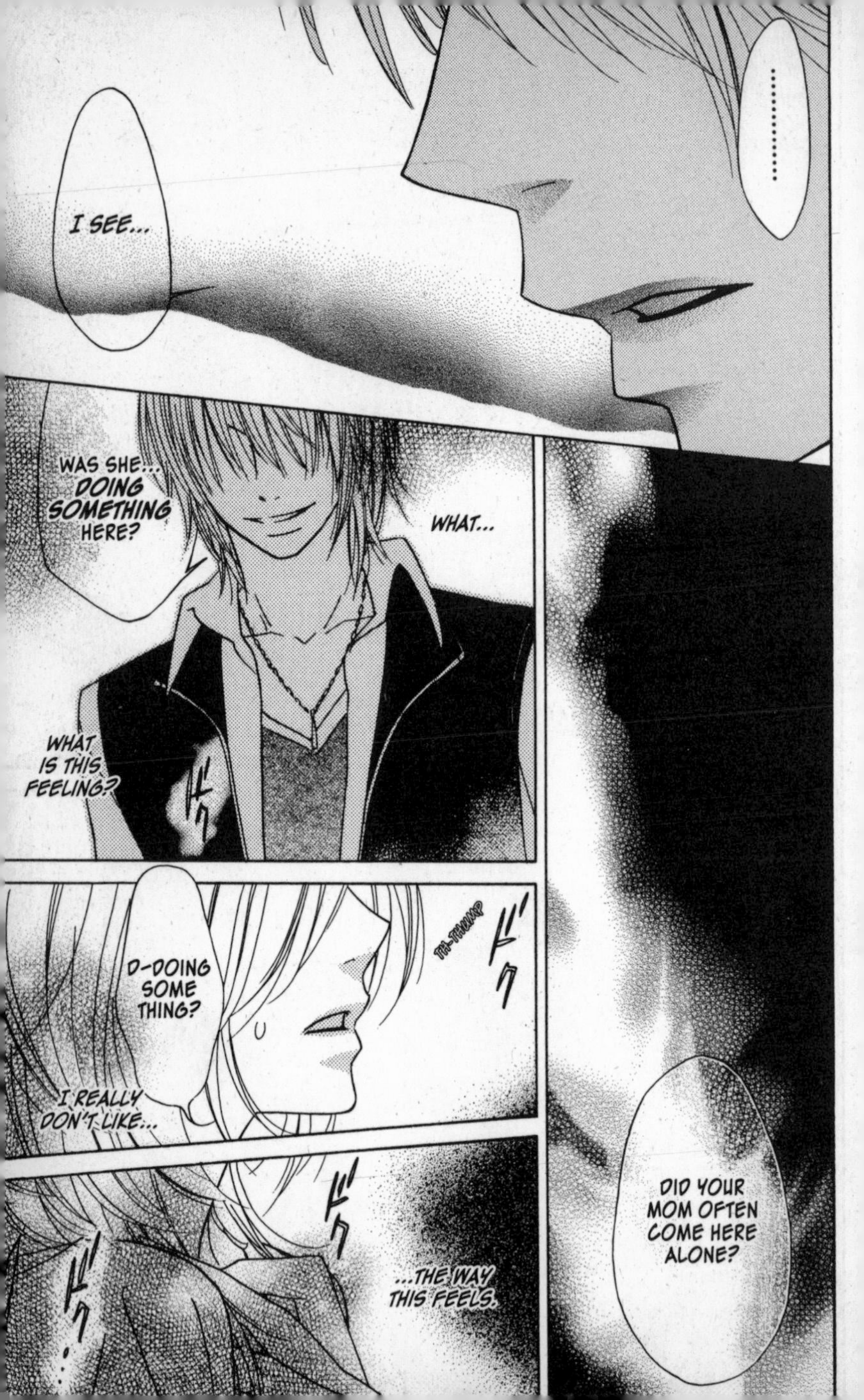
......
I SEE...
DID YOUR MOM OFTEN COME HERE ALONE?
WAS SHE... DOING SOMETHING HERE?
WHAT...
WHAT IS THIS FEELING?
TH-THUMP
D-DOING SOME THING?
I REALLY DON'T LIKE...
...THE WAY THIS FEELS.

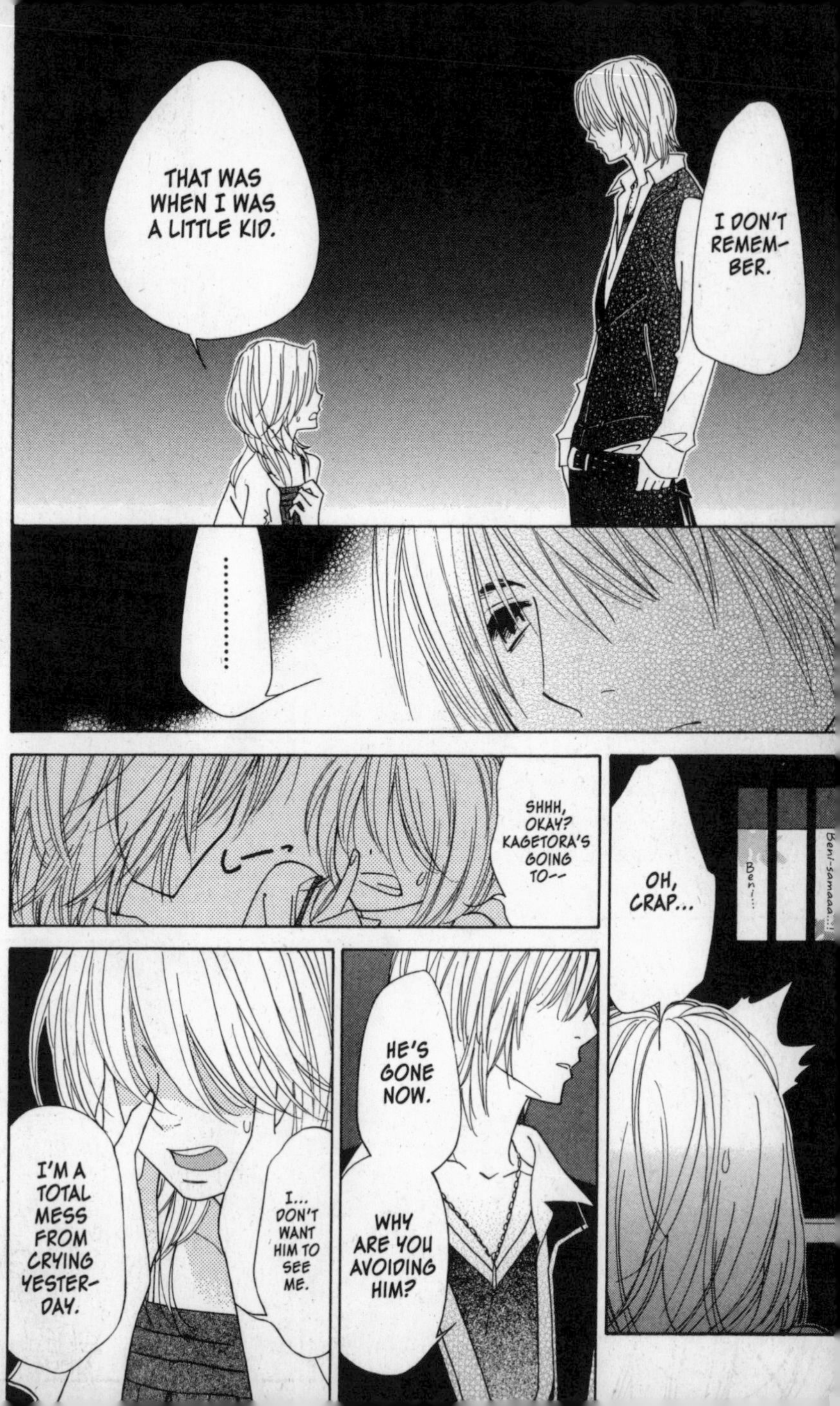
I DON'T REMEMBER.
THAT WAS WHEN I WAS A LITTLE KID.
......
Beni-samaaa...!
Beni...
OH, CRAP...
SHHH, OKAY? KAGETORA'S GOING TO--
HE'S GONE NOW.
WHY ARE YOU AVOIDING HIM?
I... DON'T WANT HIM TO SEE ME.
I'M A TOTAL MESS FROM CRYING YESTERDAY.

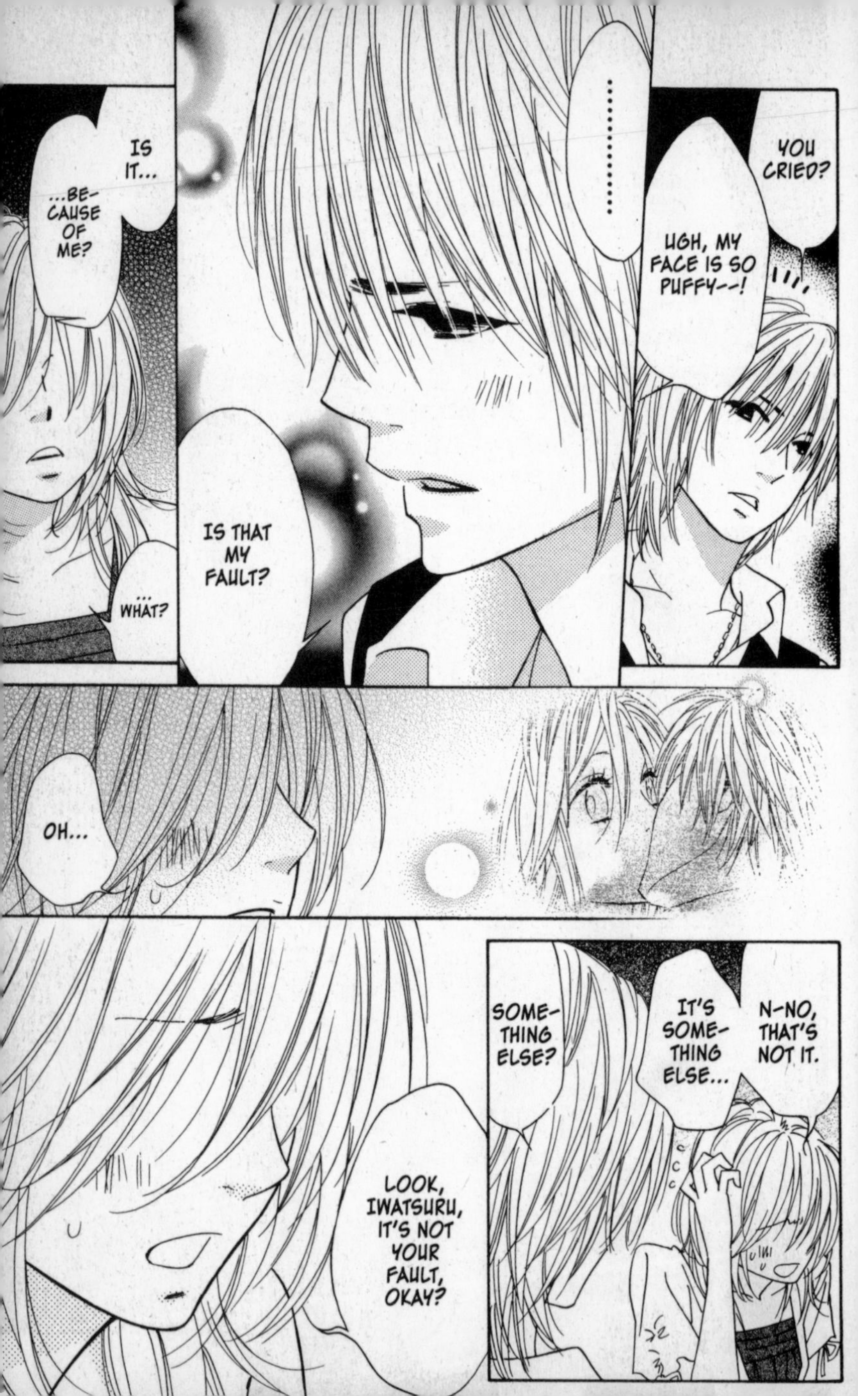
YOU CRIED?
UGH, MY FACE IS SO PUFFY--!
......
IS THAT MY FAULT?
...WHAT?
IS IT...
...BE-CAUSE OF ME?
OH...
N-NO, THAT'S NOT IT.
IT'S SOME-THING ELSE...
SOME-THING ELSE?
LOOK, IWATSURU, IT'S NOT YOUR FAULT, OKAY?

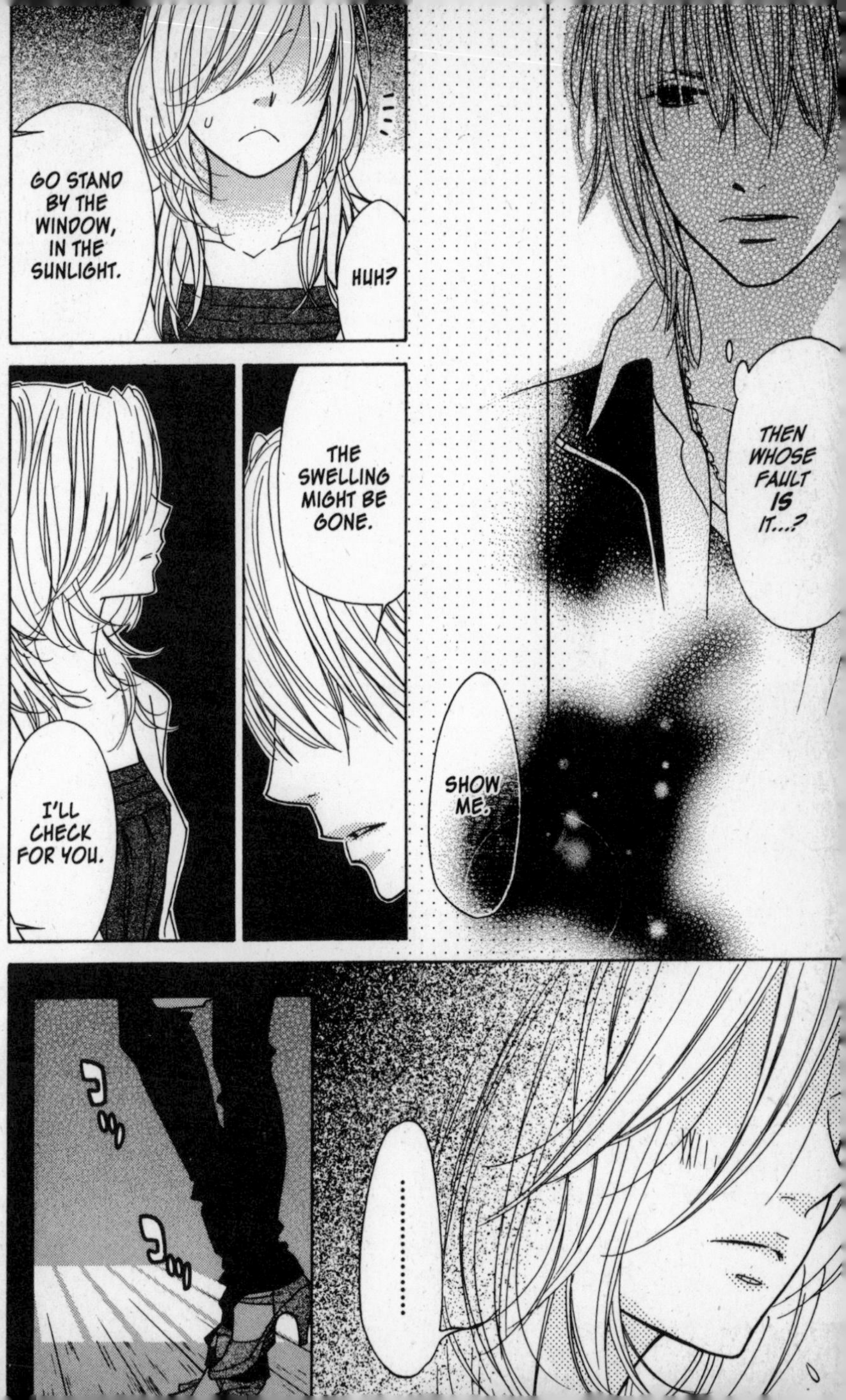
THEN WHOSE FAULT IS IT...?
SHOW ME.
GO STAND BY THE WINDOW, IN THE SUNLIGHT.
HUH?
THE SWELLING MIGHT BE GONE.
I'LL CHECK FOR YOU.
......

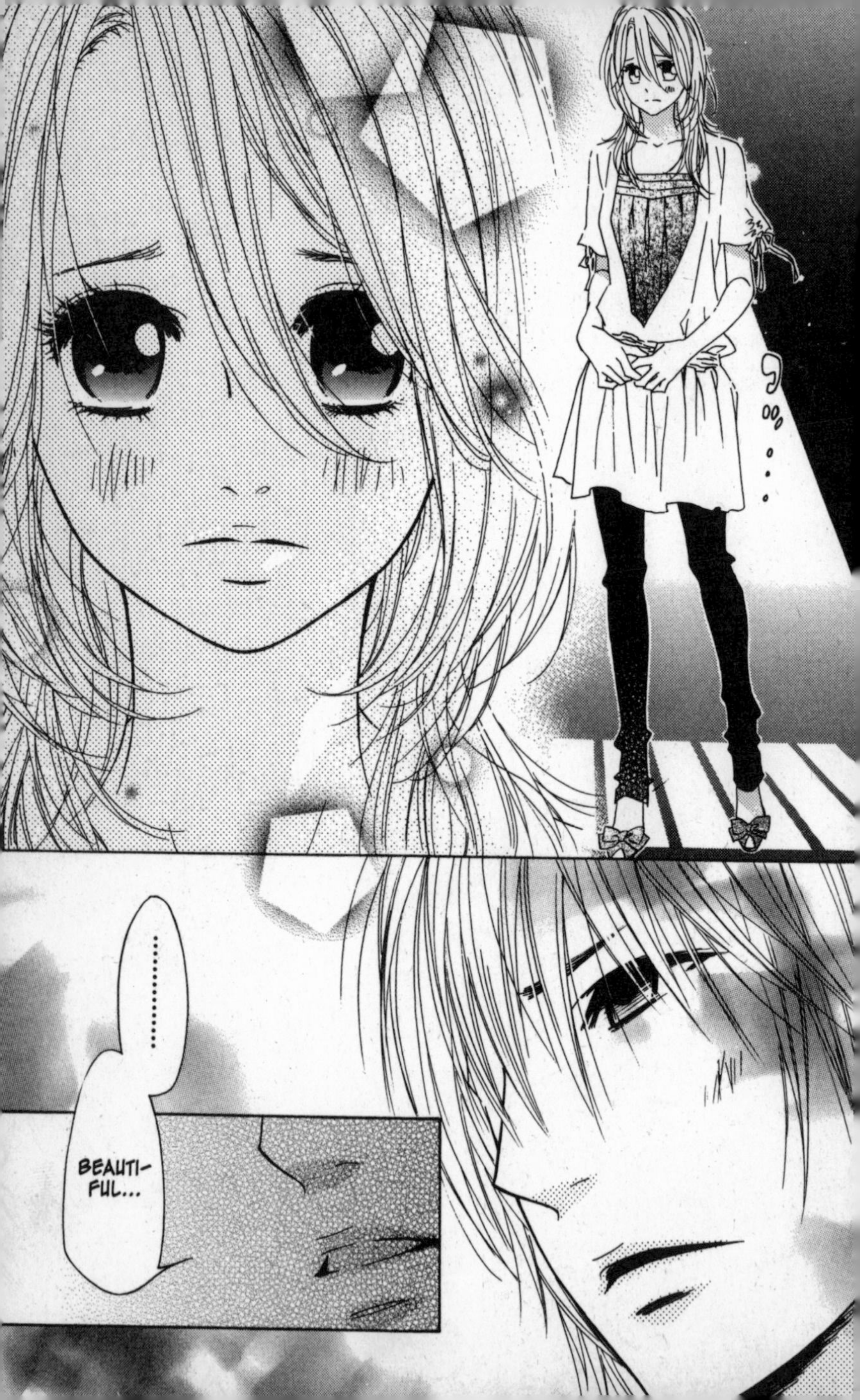
....
BEAUTI-FUL...

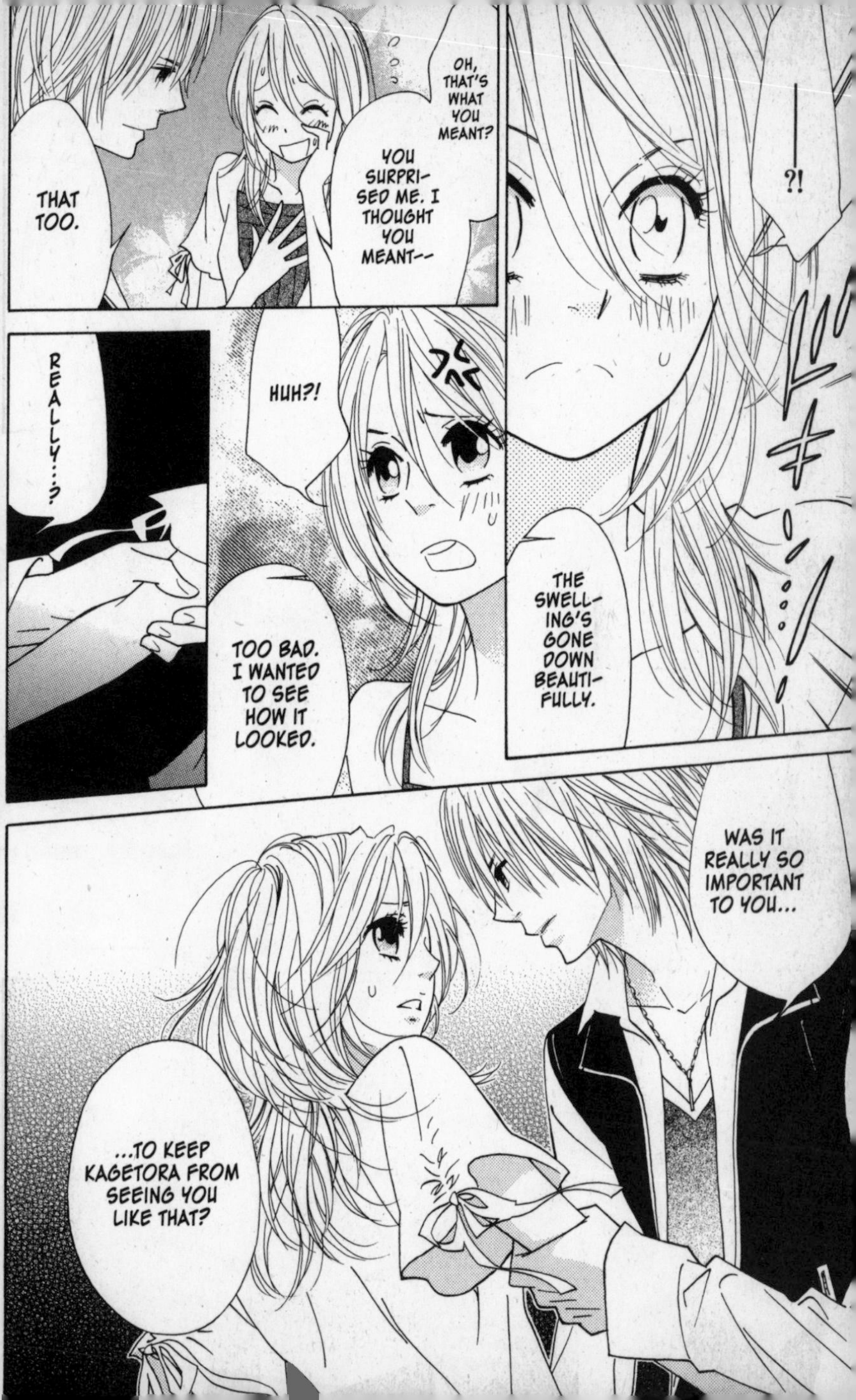
?!
THE SWELLING'S GONE DOWN BEAUTIFULLY.
OH, THAT'S WHAT YOU MEANT?
YOU SURPRISED ME. I THOUGHT YOU MEANT--
THAT TOO.
HUH?!
TOO BAD. I WANTED TO SEE HOW IT LOOKED.
REALLY...?
WAS IT REALLY SO IMPORTANT TO YOU...
...TO KEEP KAGETORA FROM SEEING YOU LIKE THAT?

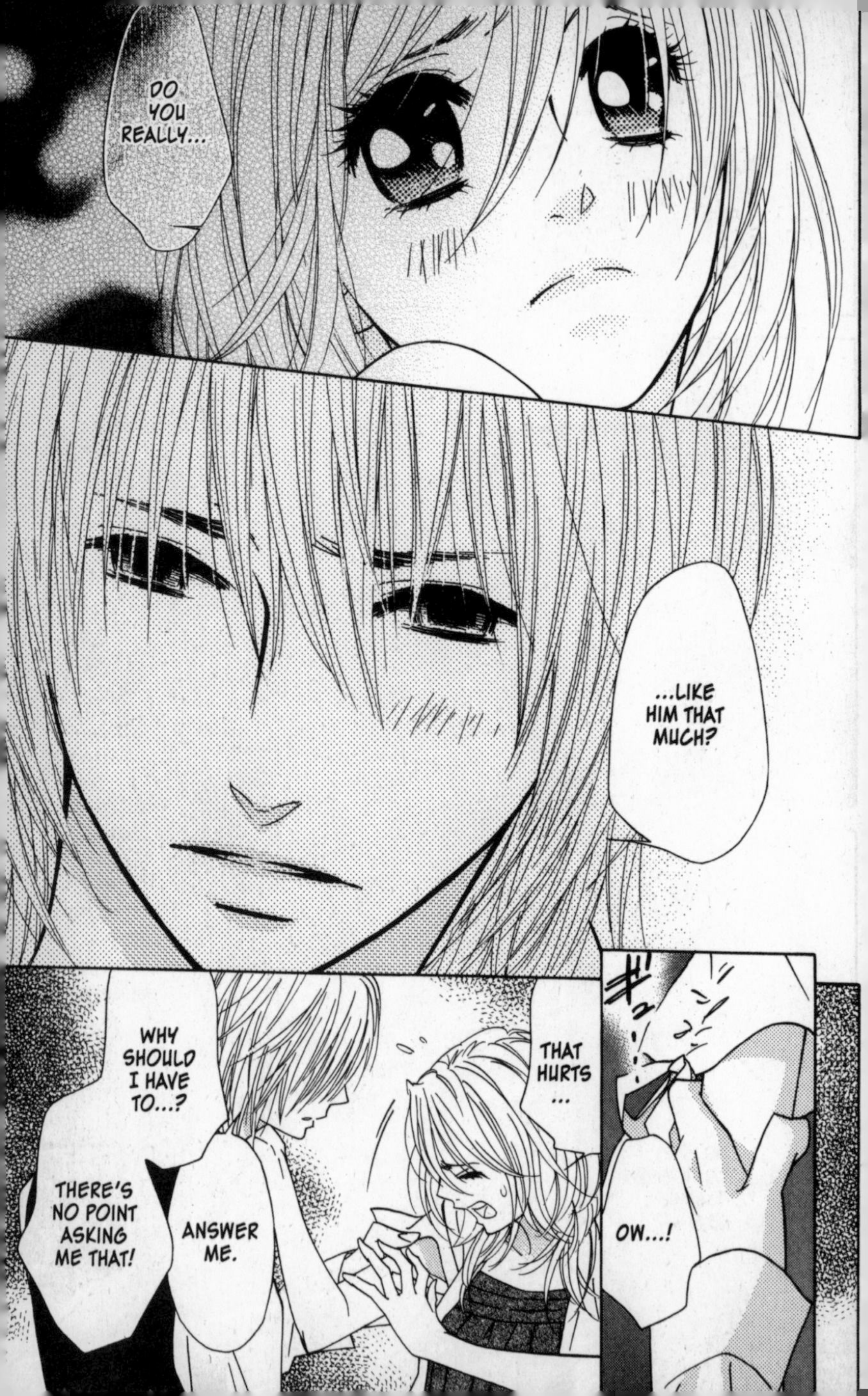
DO YOU REALLY...
...LIKE HIM THAT MUCH?
ギュ
OW...!
THAT HURTS...
WHY SHOULD I HAVE TO...?
ANSWER ME.
THERE'S NO POINT ASKING ME THAT!

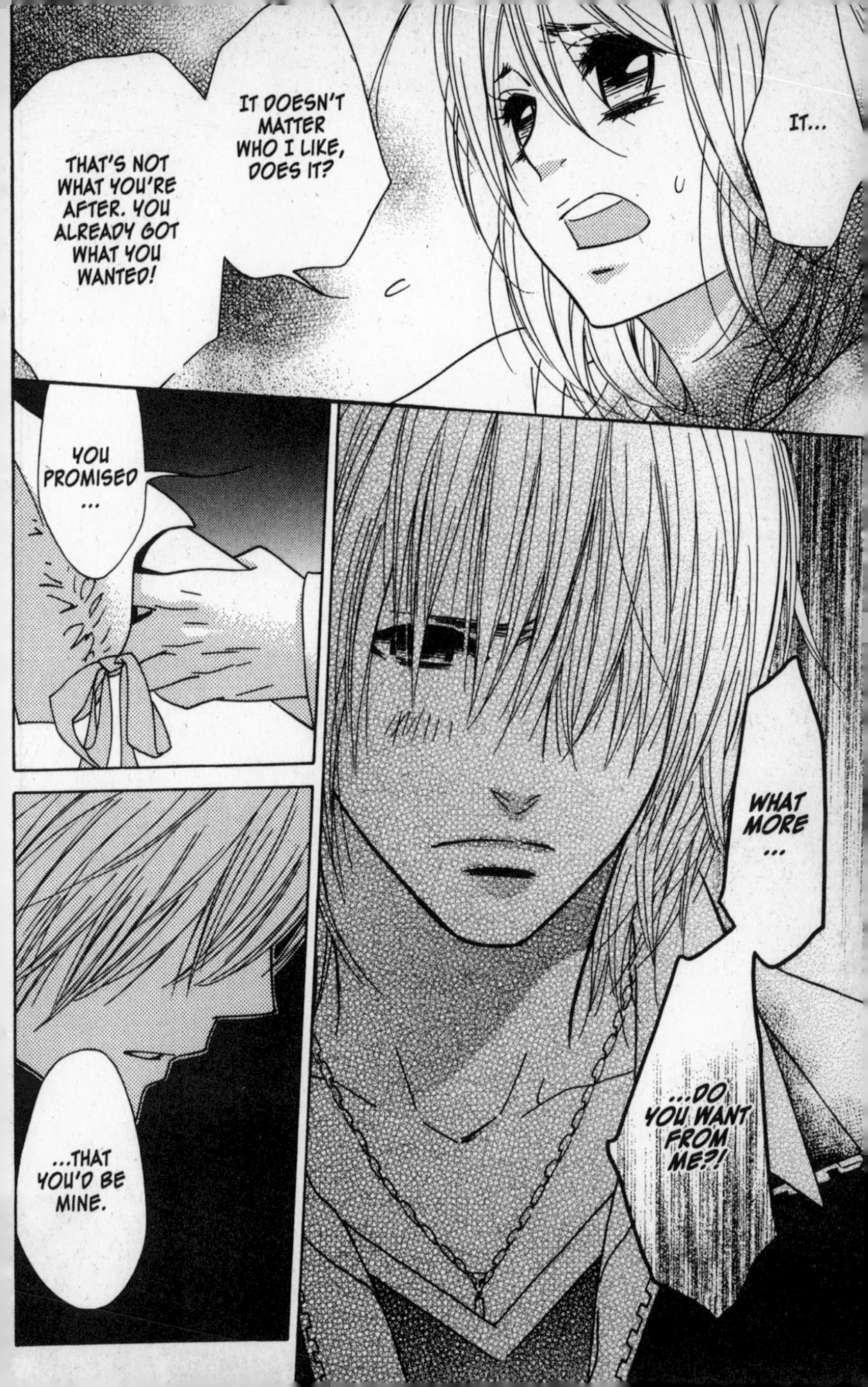
IT...
IT DOESN'T MATTER WHO I LIKE, DOES IT?
THAT'S NOT WHAT YOU'RE AFTER. YOU ALREADY GOT WHAT YOU WANTED!
WHAT MORE...
...DO YOU WANT FROM ME?!
YOU PROMISED...
...THAT YOU'D BE MINE.

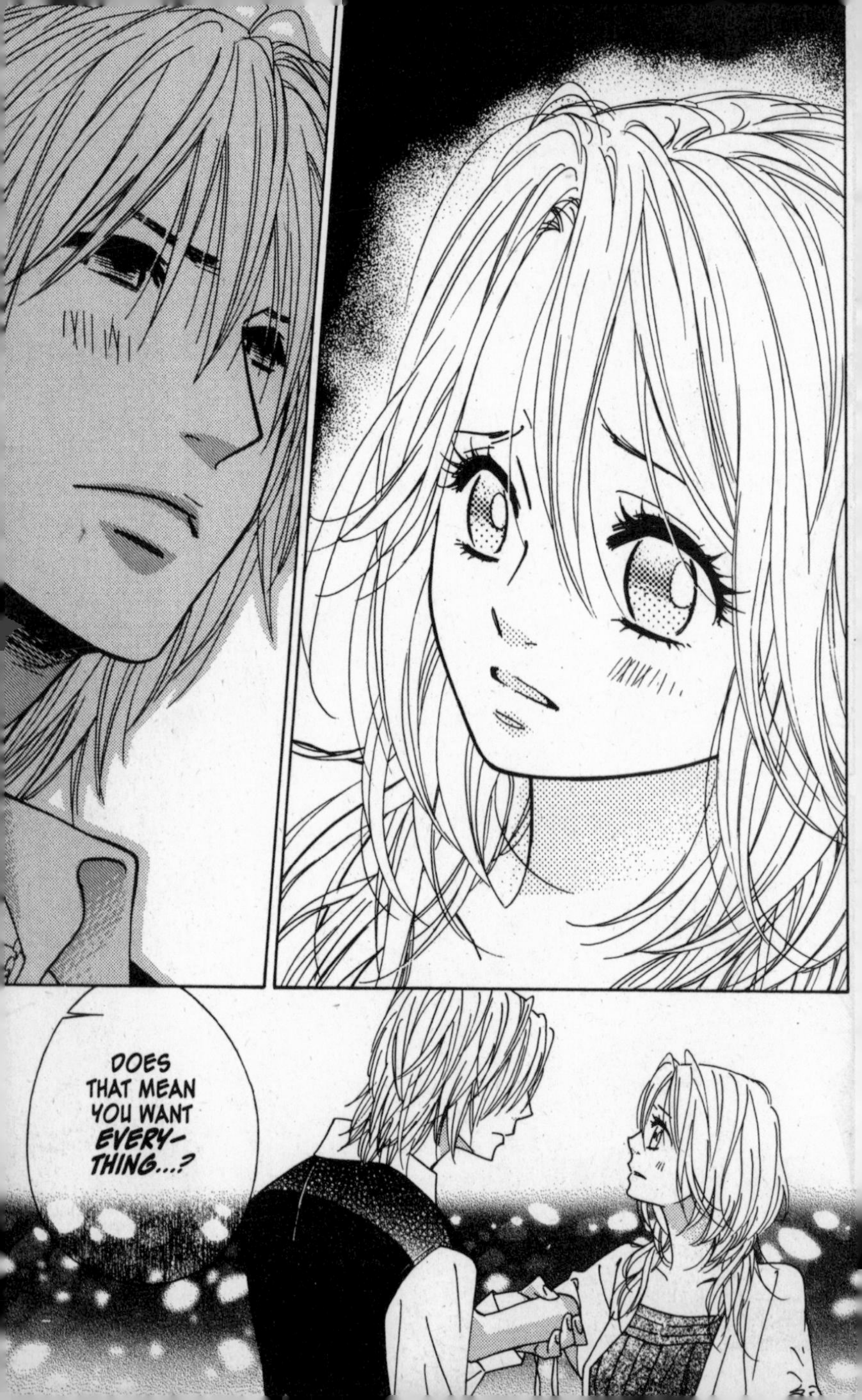
DOES THAT MEAN YOU WANT EVERY-THING...?

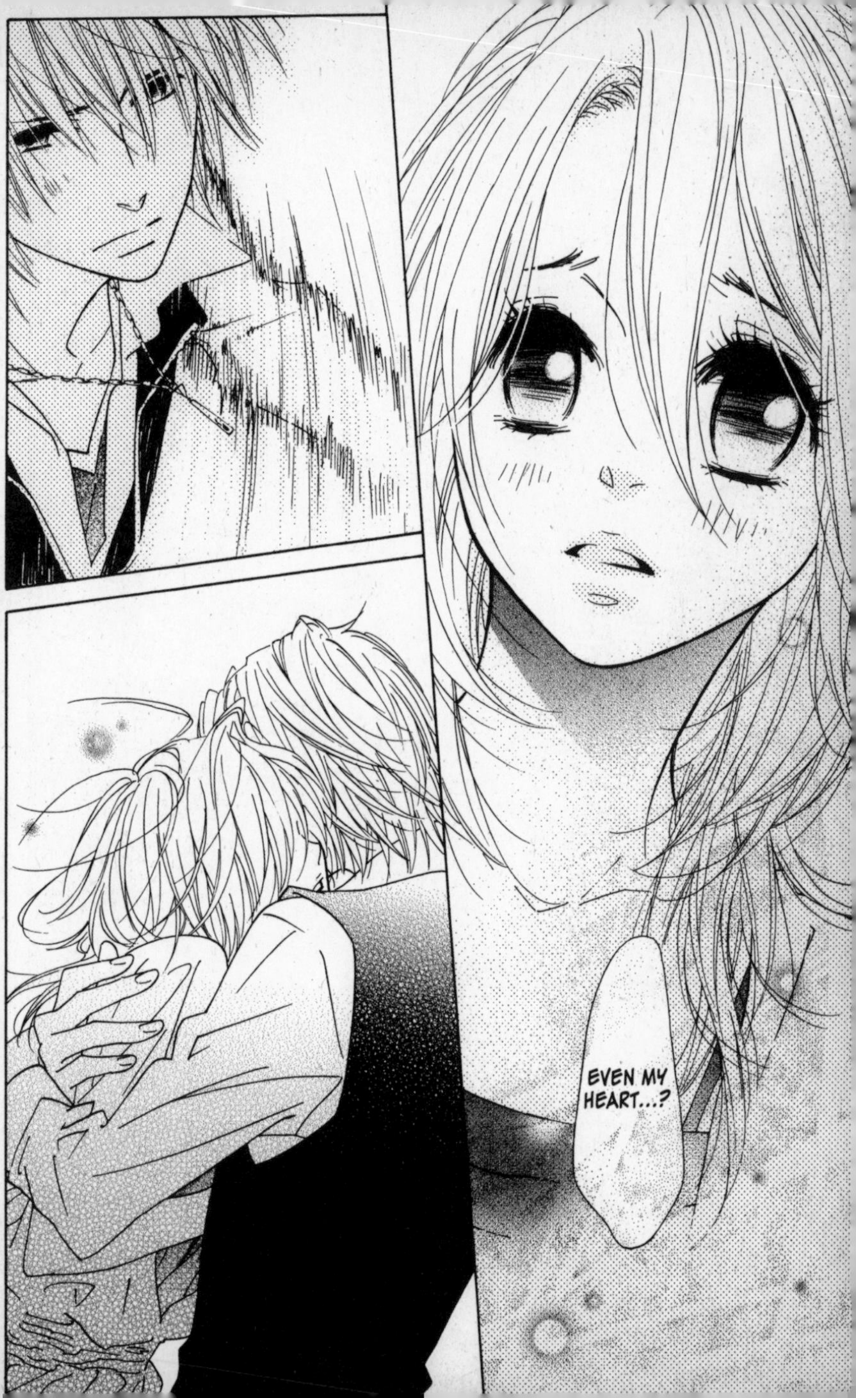
EVEN MY HEART...?

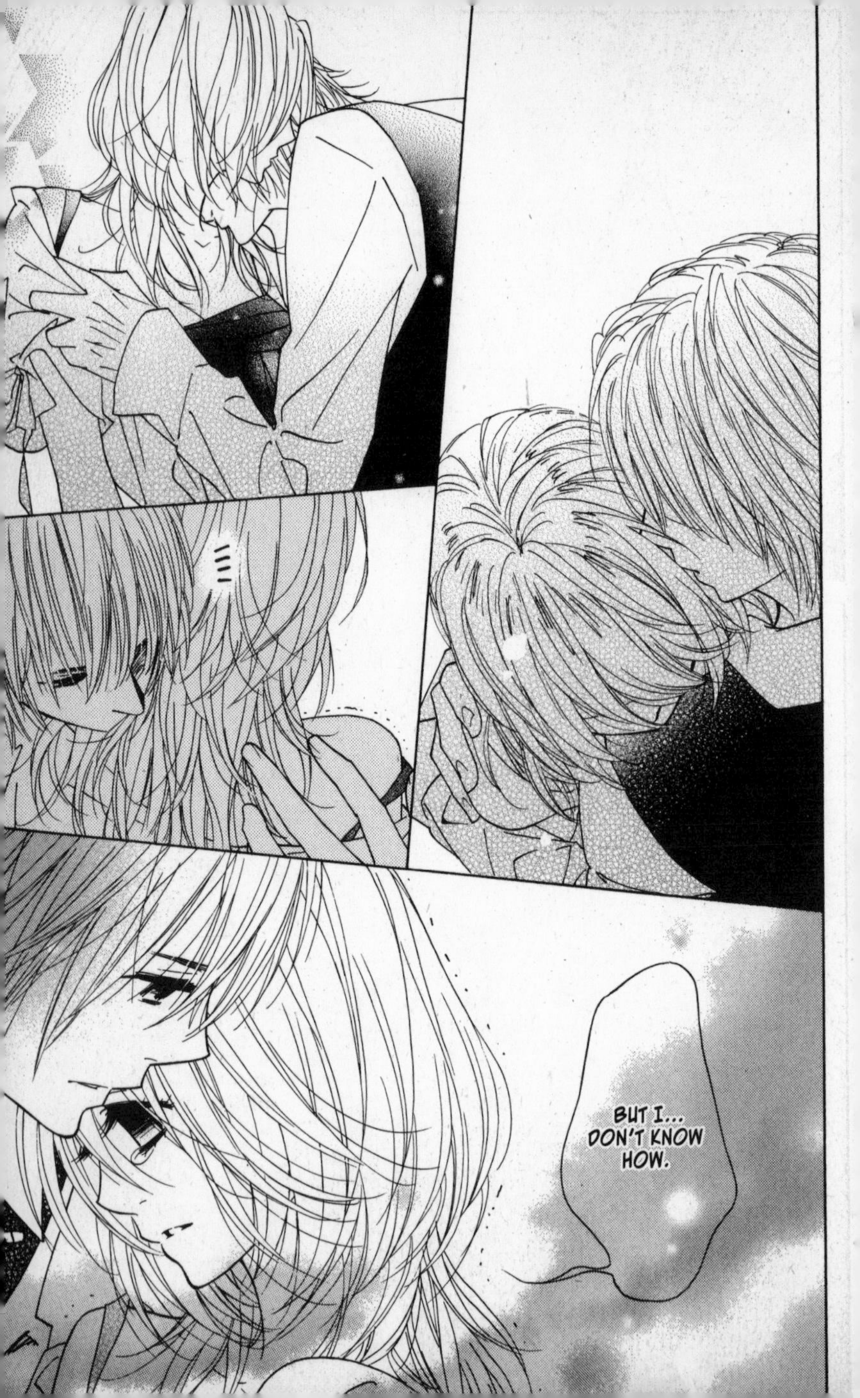
BUT I...
DON'T KNOW
HOW.

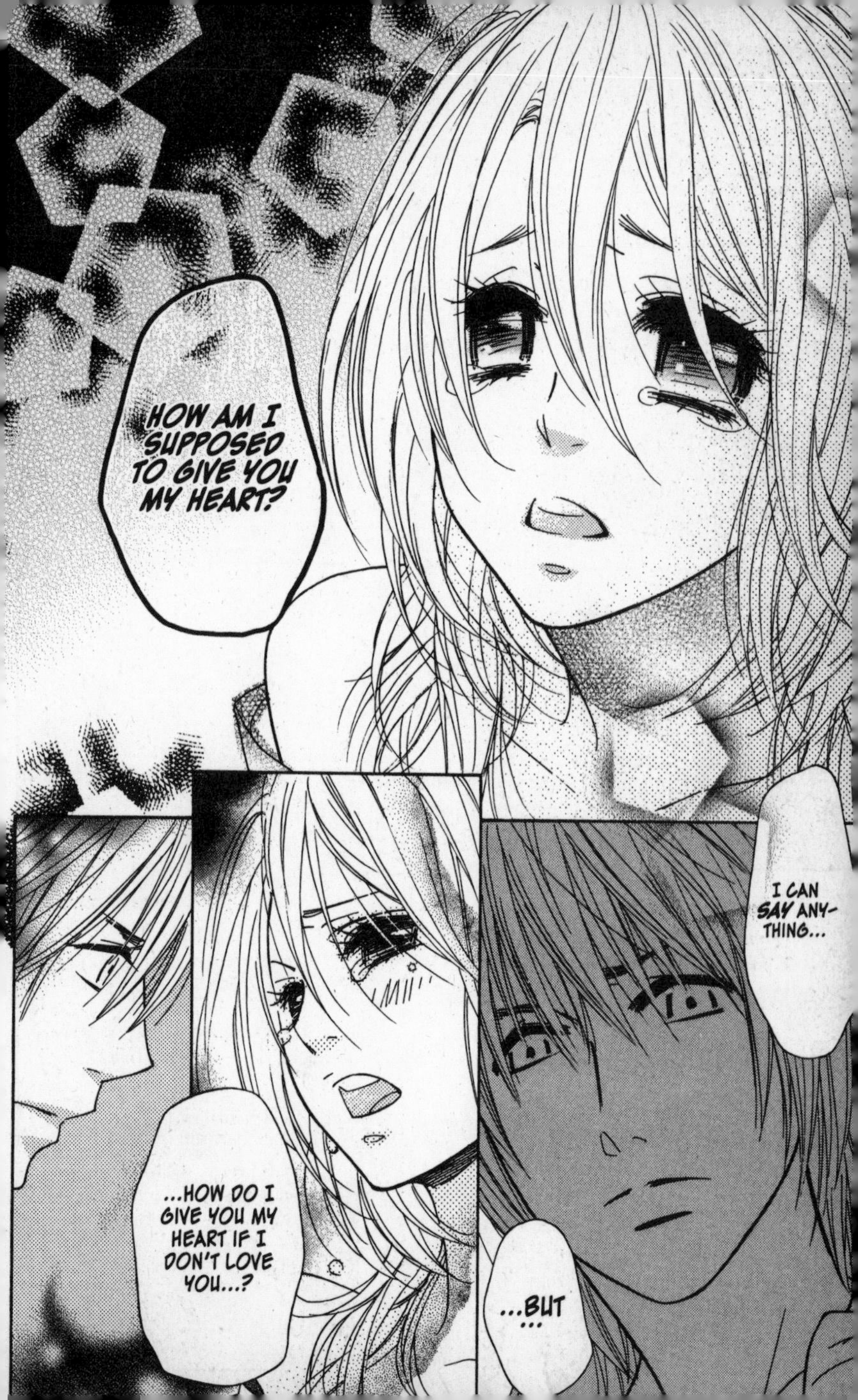
HOW AM I SUPPOSED TO GIVE YOU MY HEART?
I CAN SAY ANYTHING...
...BUT...
...HOW DO I GIVE YOU MY HEART IF I DON'T LOVE YOU...?

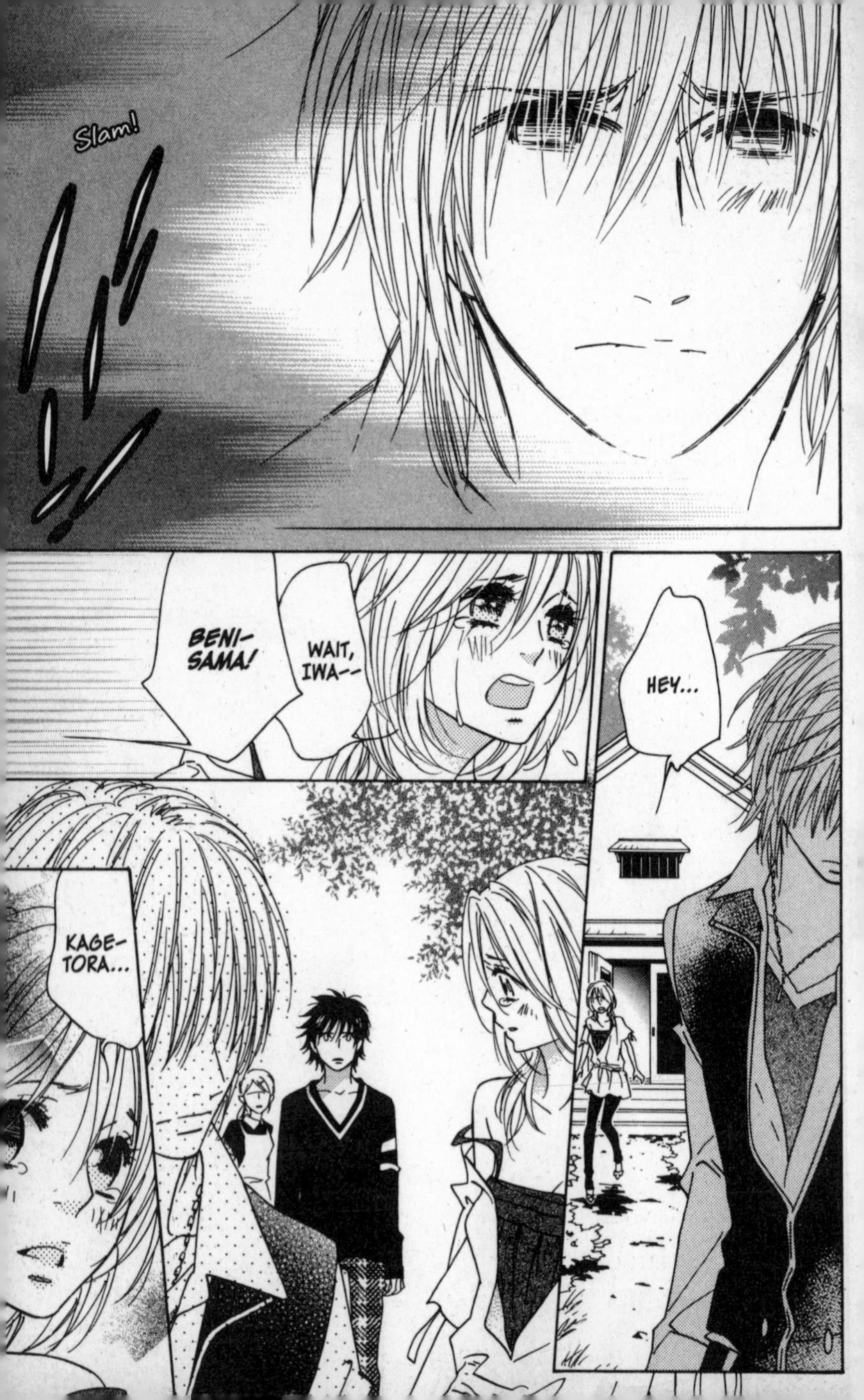
Slam!
HEY...
WAIT, IWA--
BENI-SAMA!
KAGE-TORA...

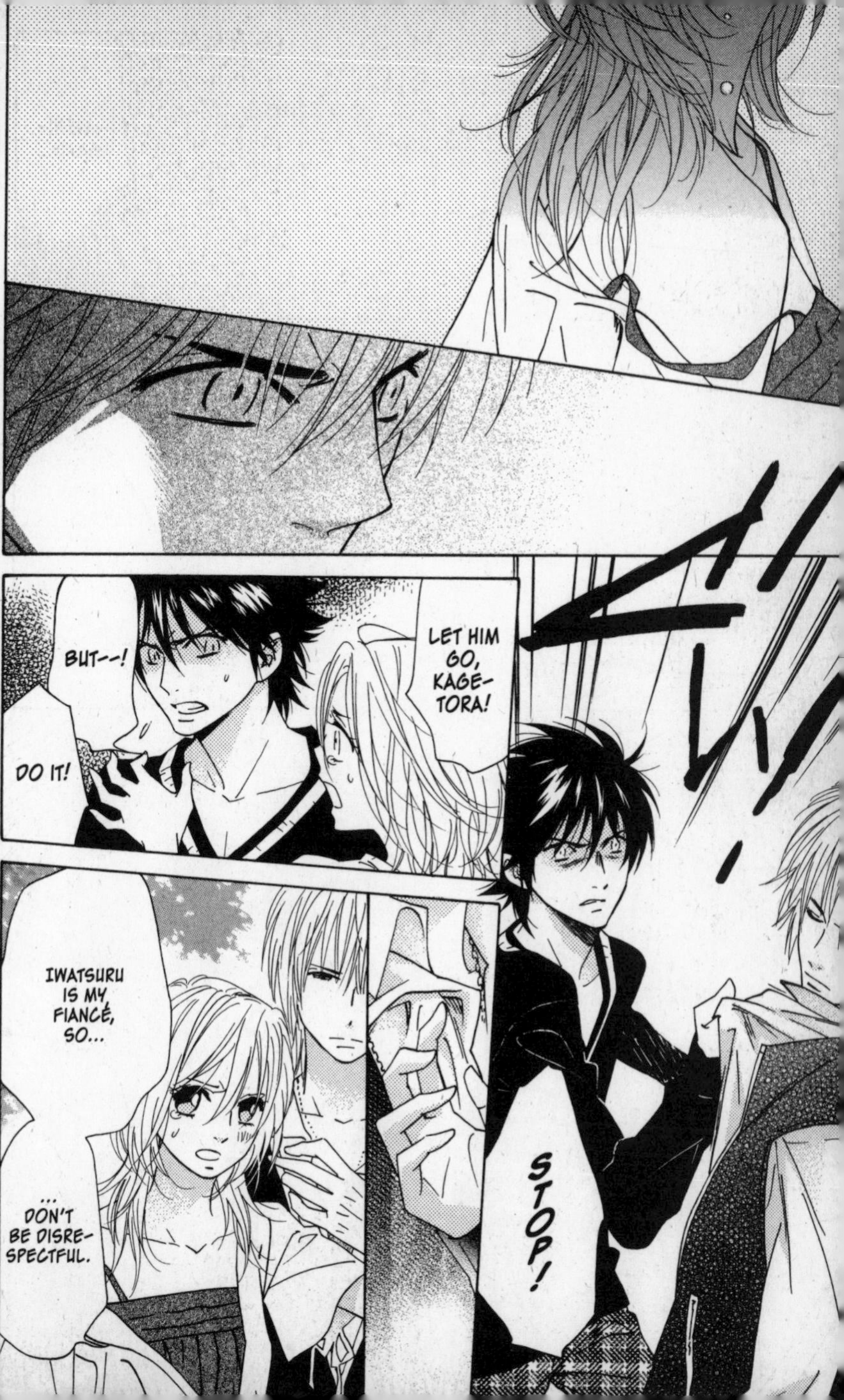
STOP!
LET HIM GO, KAGE-TORA!
BUT--!
DO IT!
IWATSURU IS MY FIANCÉ, SO...
... DON'T BE DISRE-SPECTFUL.

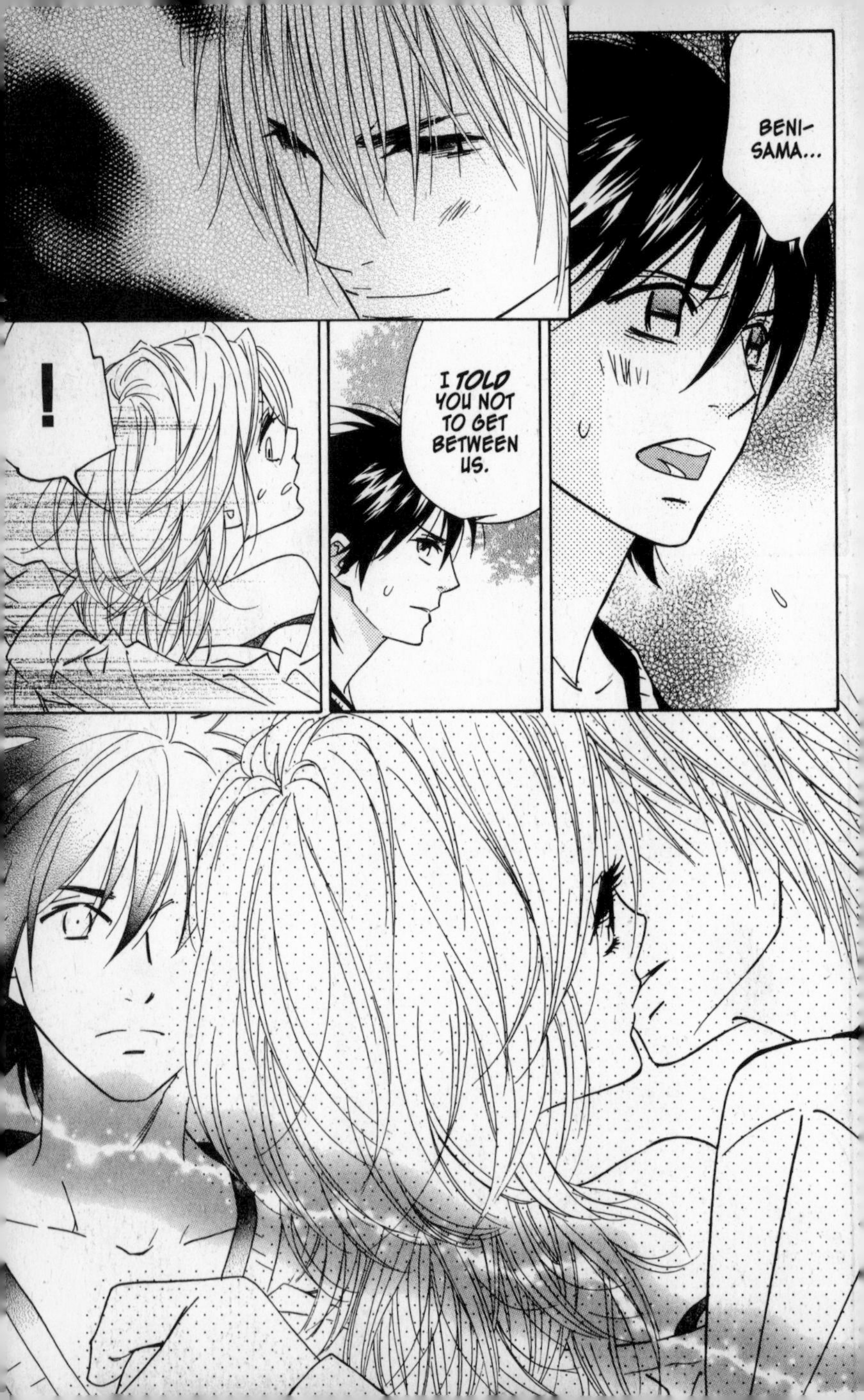
BENI-SAMA...
I TOLD YOU NOT TO GET BETWEEN US.
!

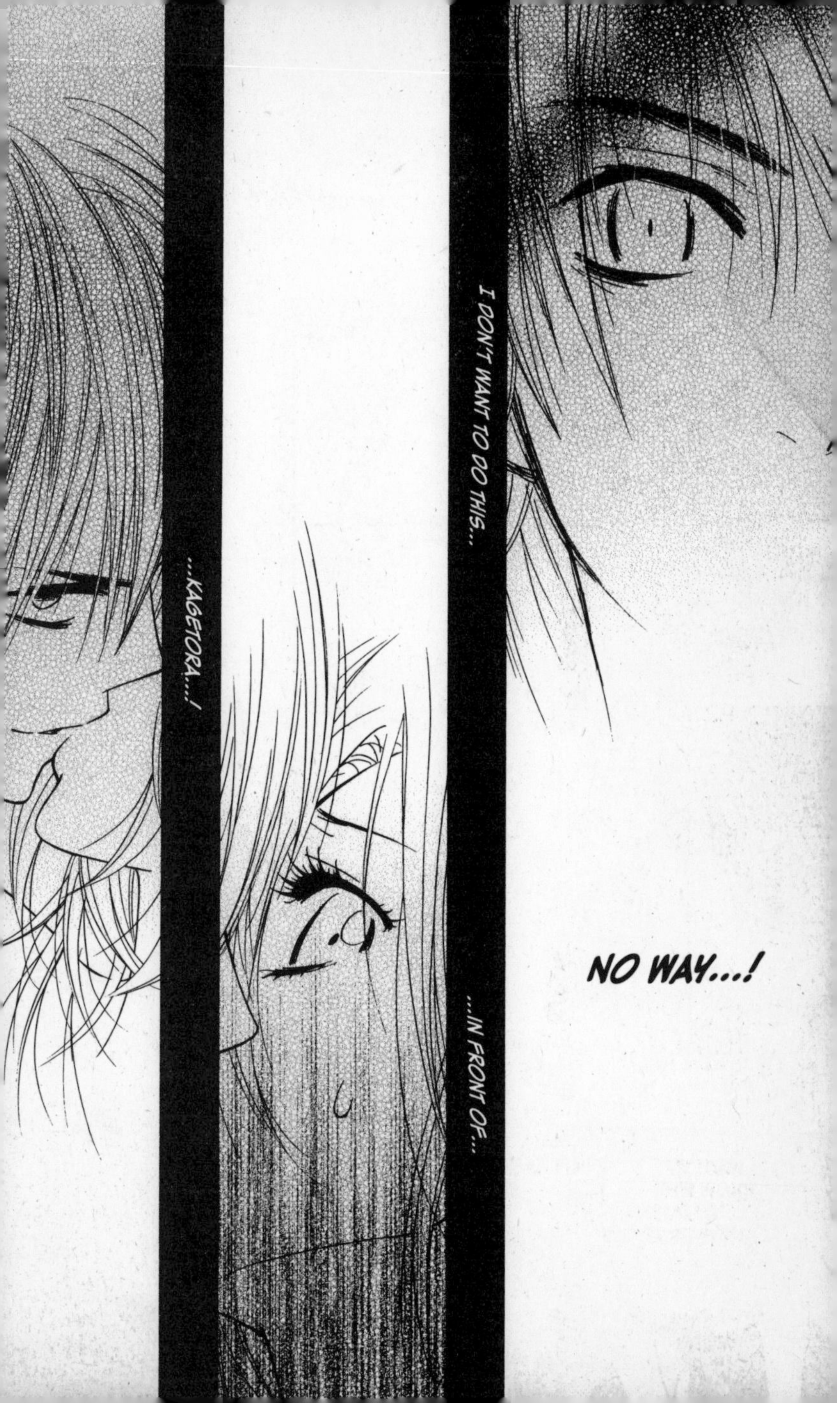
NO WAY...!
I DON'T WANT TO DO THIS...
...IN FRONT OF...
...KAGETORA...!

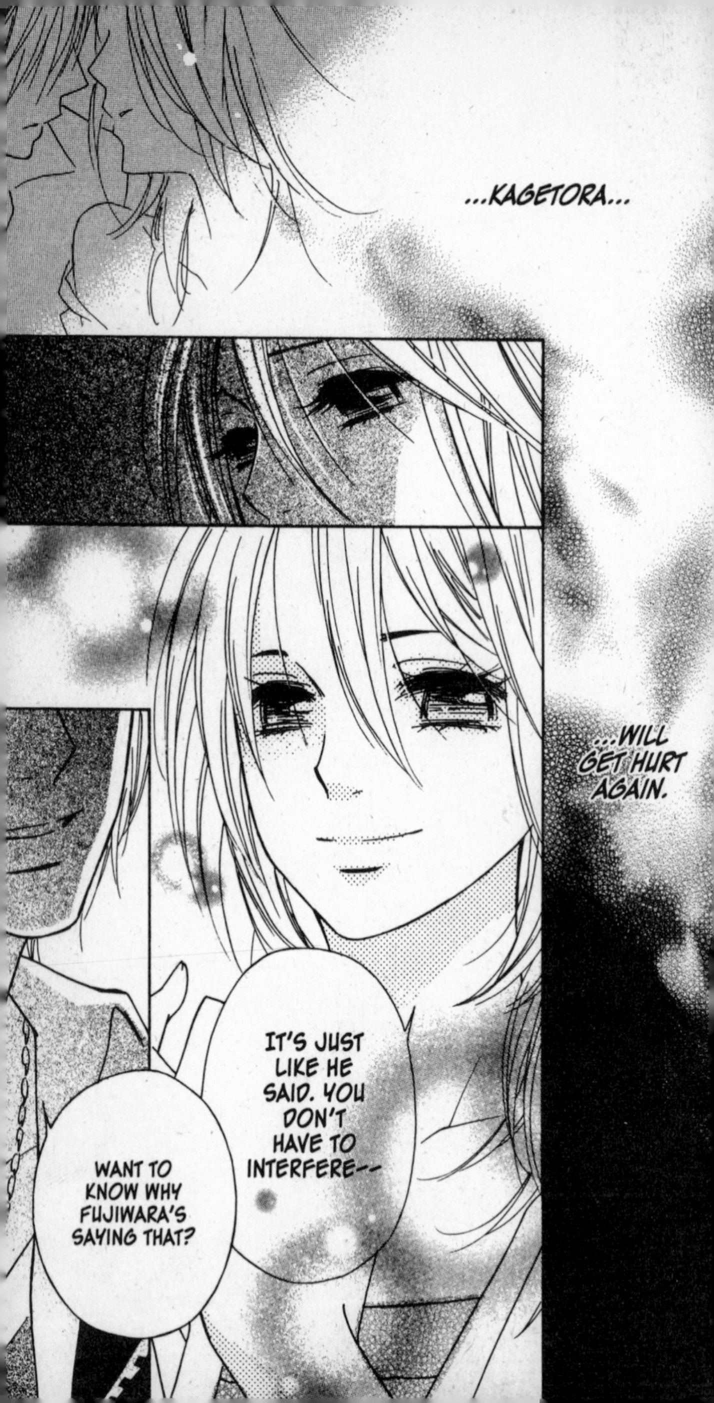
...KAGETORA...
...WILL GET HURT AGAIN.
IT'S JUST LIKE HE SAID. YOU DON'T HAVE TO INTERFERE--
WANT TO KNOW WHY FUJIWARA'S SAYING THAT?

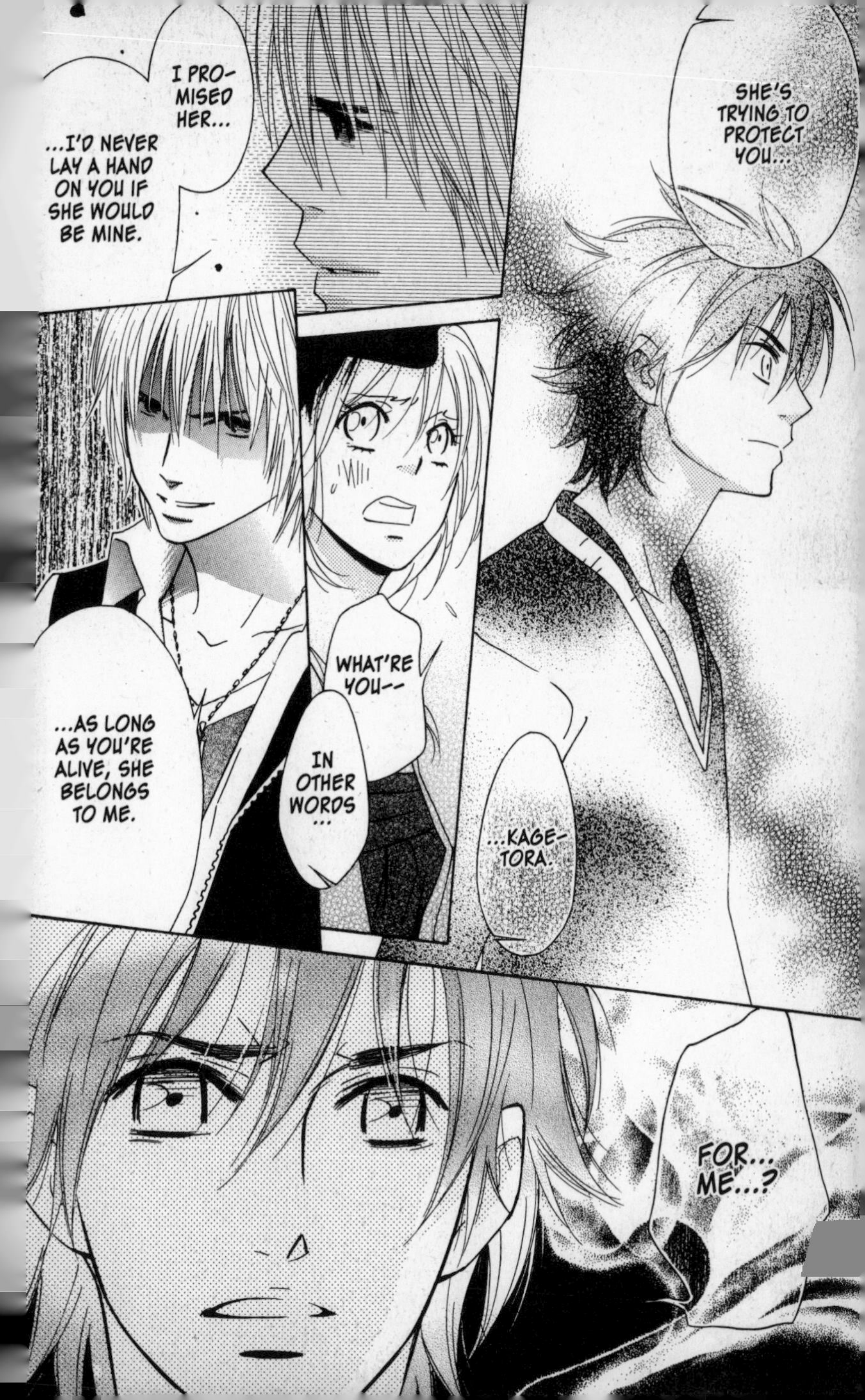
SHE'S TRYING TO PROTECT YOU...
...KAGE-TORA.
I PRO-MISED HER...
...I'D NEVER LAY A HAND ON YOU IF SHE WOULD BE MINE.
WHAT'RE YOU--
IN OTHER WORDS...
...AS LONG AS YOU'RE ALIVE, SHE BELONGS TO ME.
FOR... ME...?

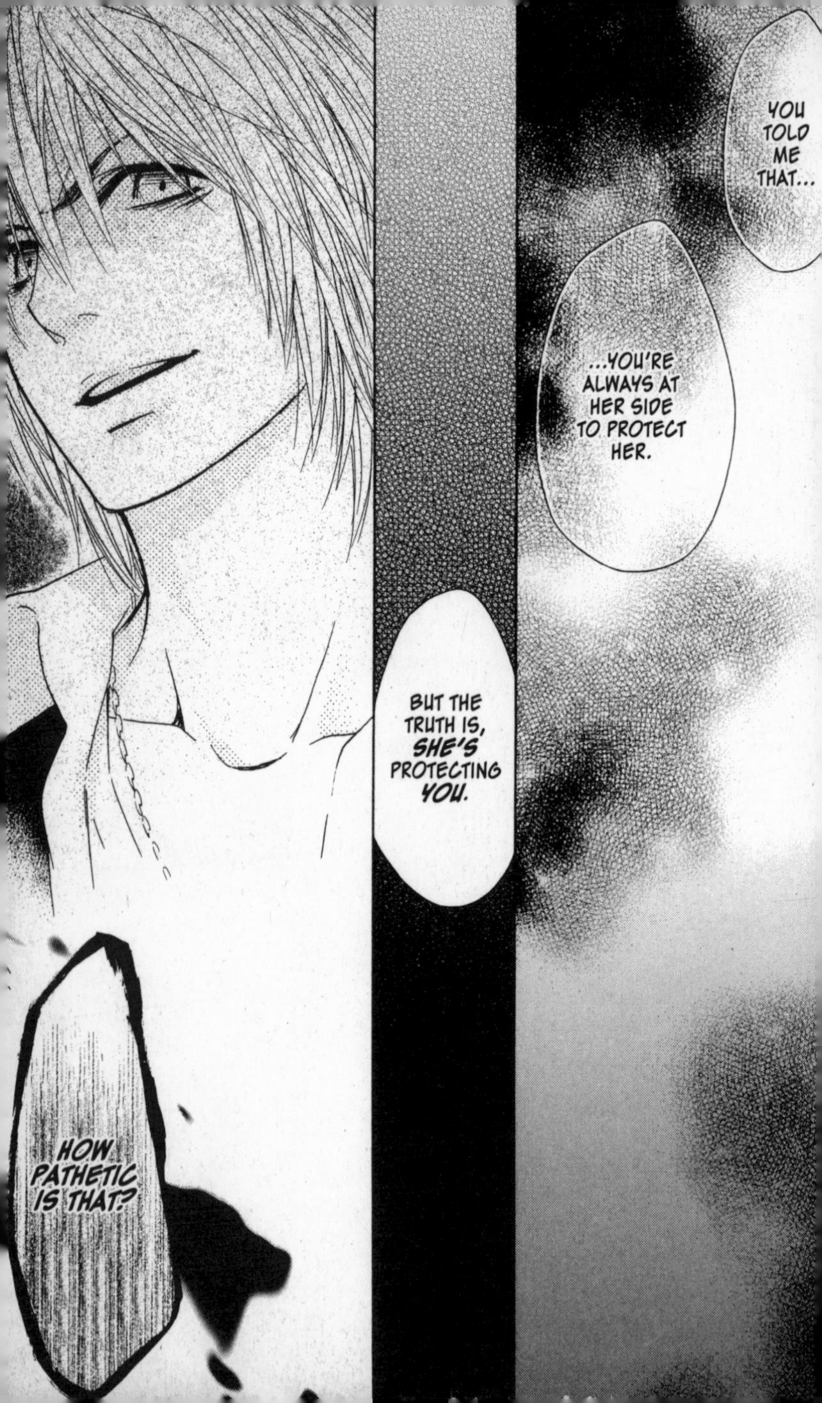
YOU TOLD ME THAT...
...YOU'RE ALWAYS AT HER SIDE TO PROTECT HER.
BUT THE TRUTH IS, *SHE'S* PROTECTING *YOU.*
HOW PATHETIC IS THAT?

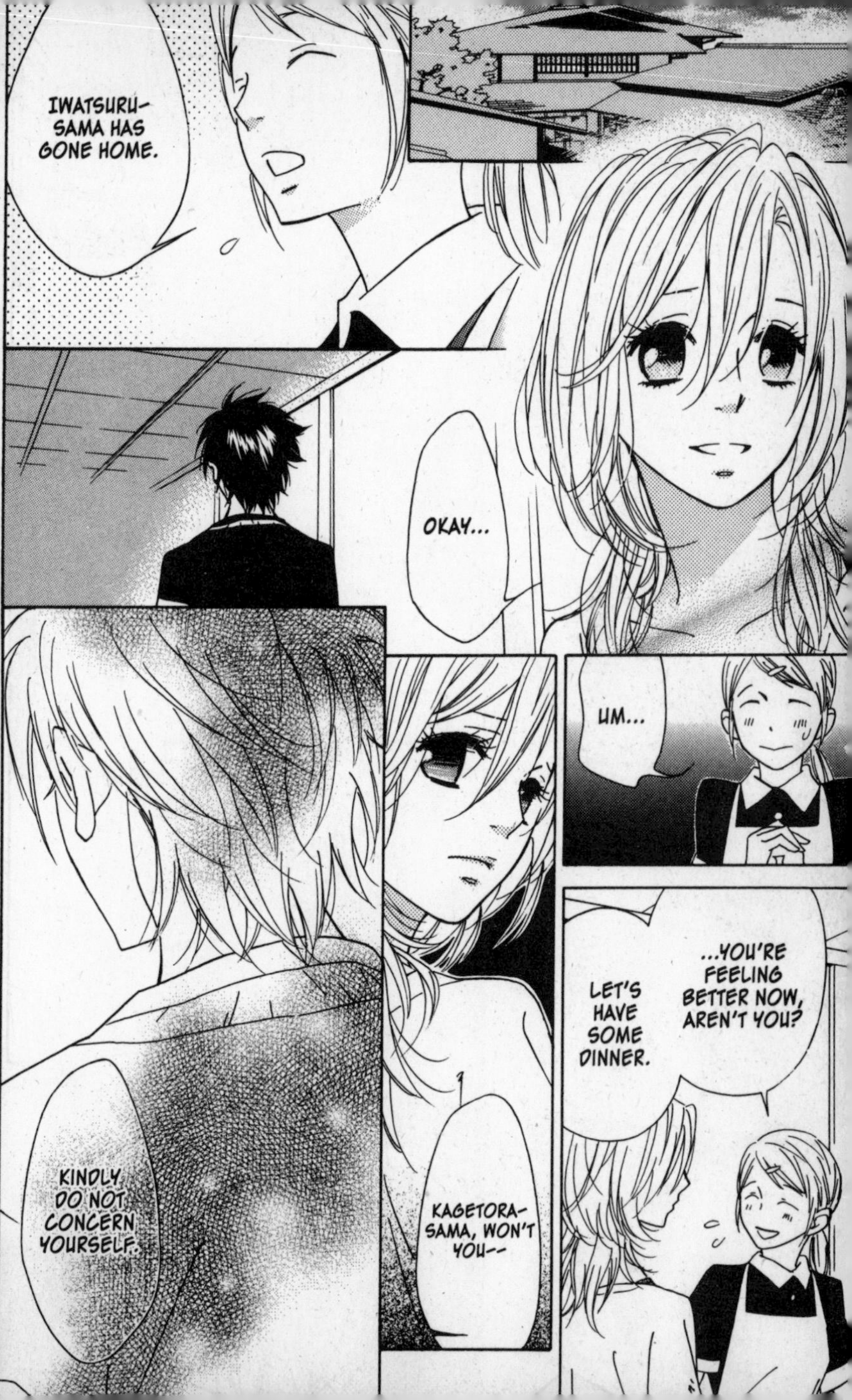
IWATSURU-SAMA HAS GONE HOME.
OKAY...
UM...
...YOU'RE FEELING BETTER NOW, AREN'T YOU?
LET'S HAVE SOME DINNER.
KAGETORA-SAMA, WON'T YOU--
KINDLY DO NOT CONCERN YOURSELF.

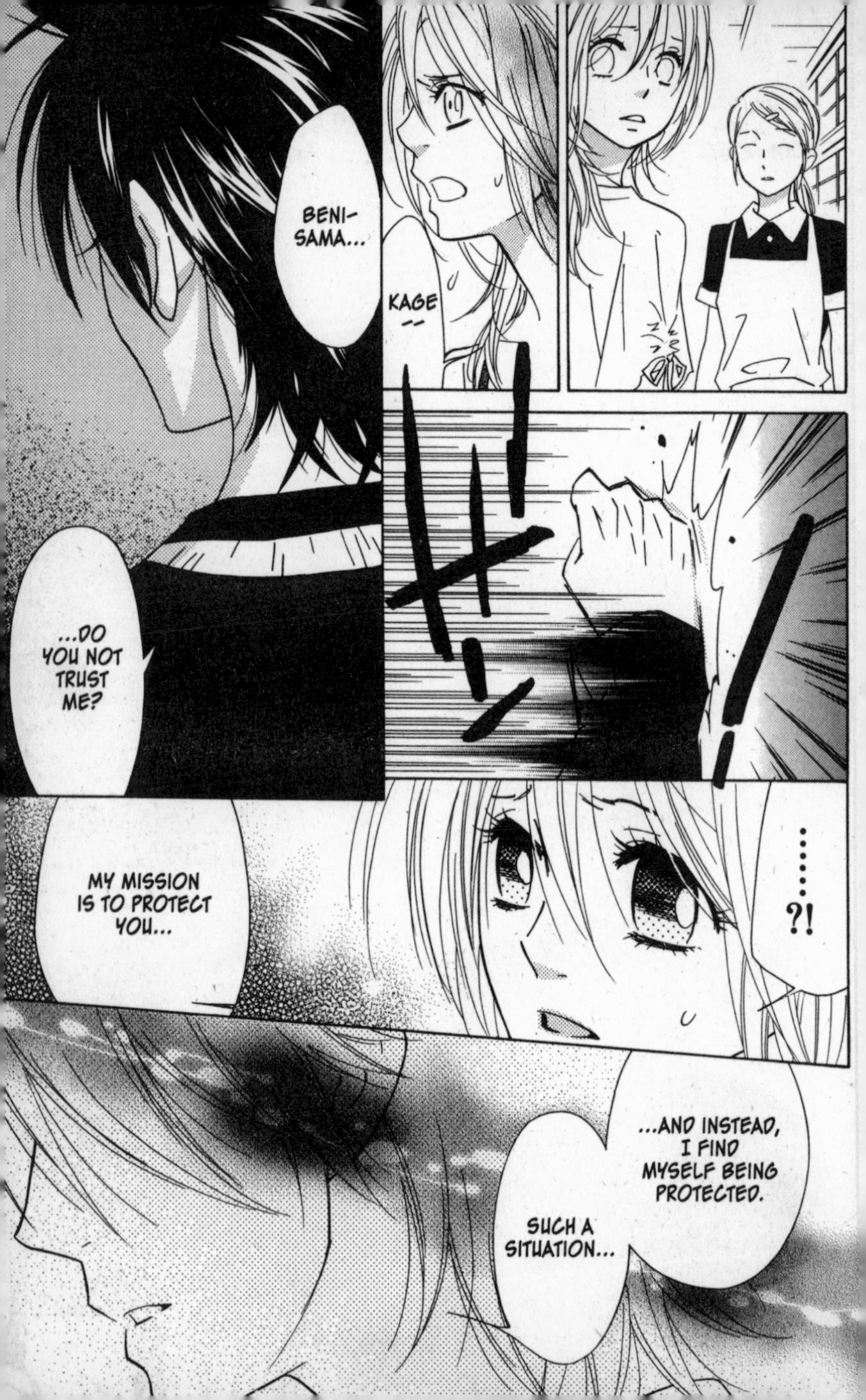
KAGE--
BENI-SAMA...
...DO YOU NOT TRUST ME?
......?!
MY MISSION IS TO PROTECT YOU...
...AND INSTEAD, I FIND MYSELF BEING PROTECTED.
SUCH A SITUATION...

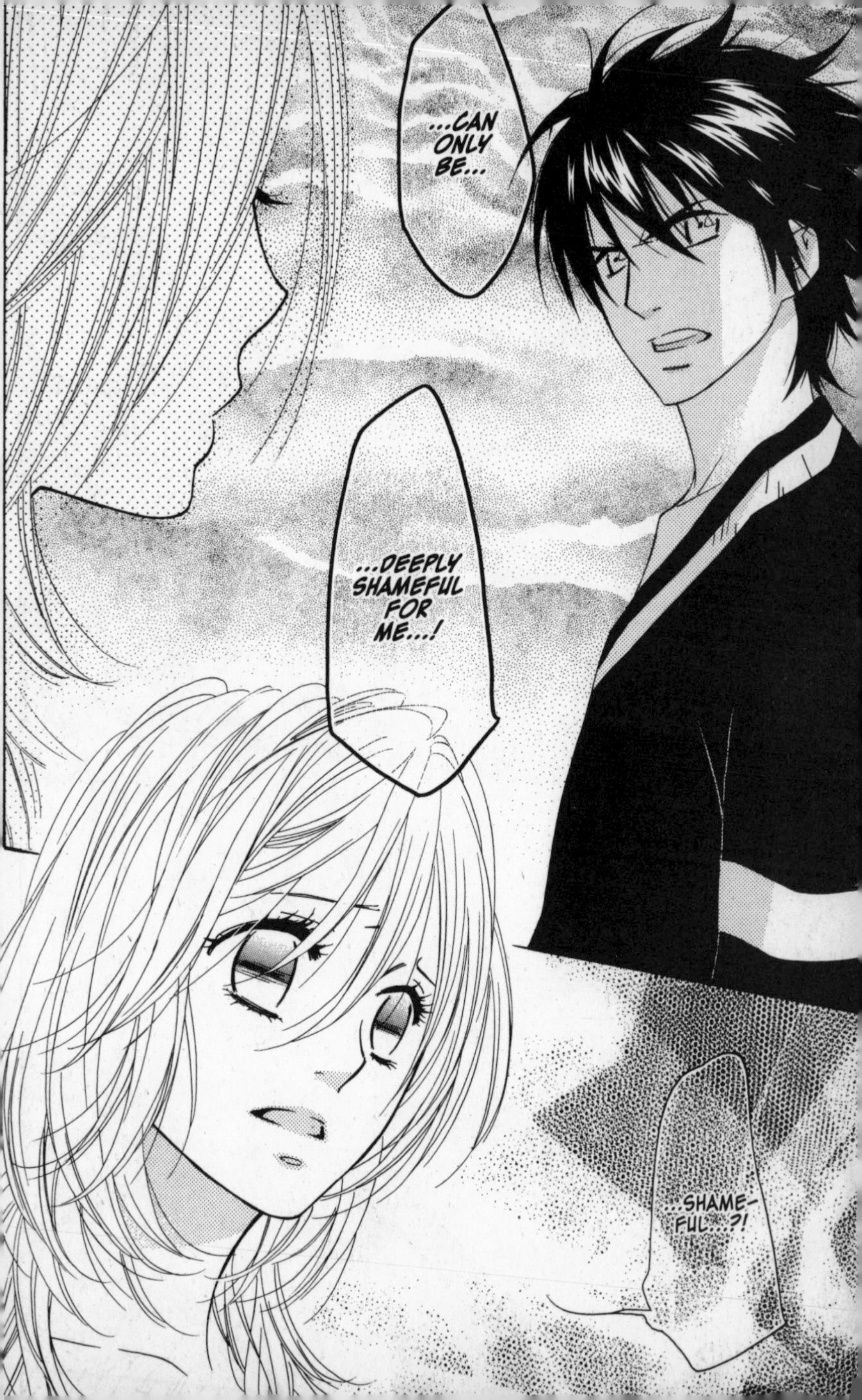
...CAN ONLY BE...
...DEEPLY SHAMEFUL FOR ME...!
...SHAME-FUL...?!

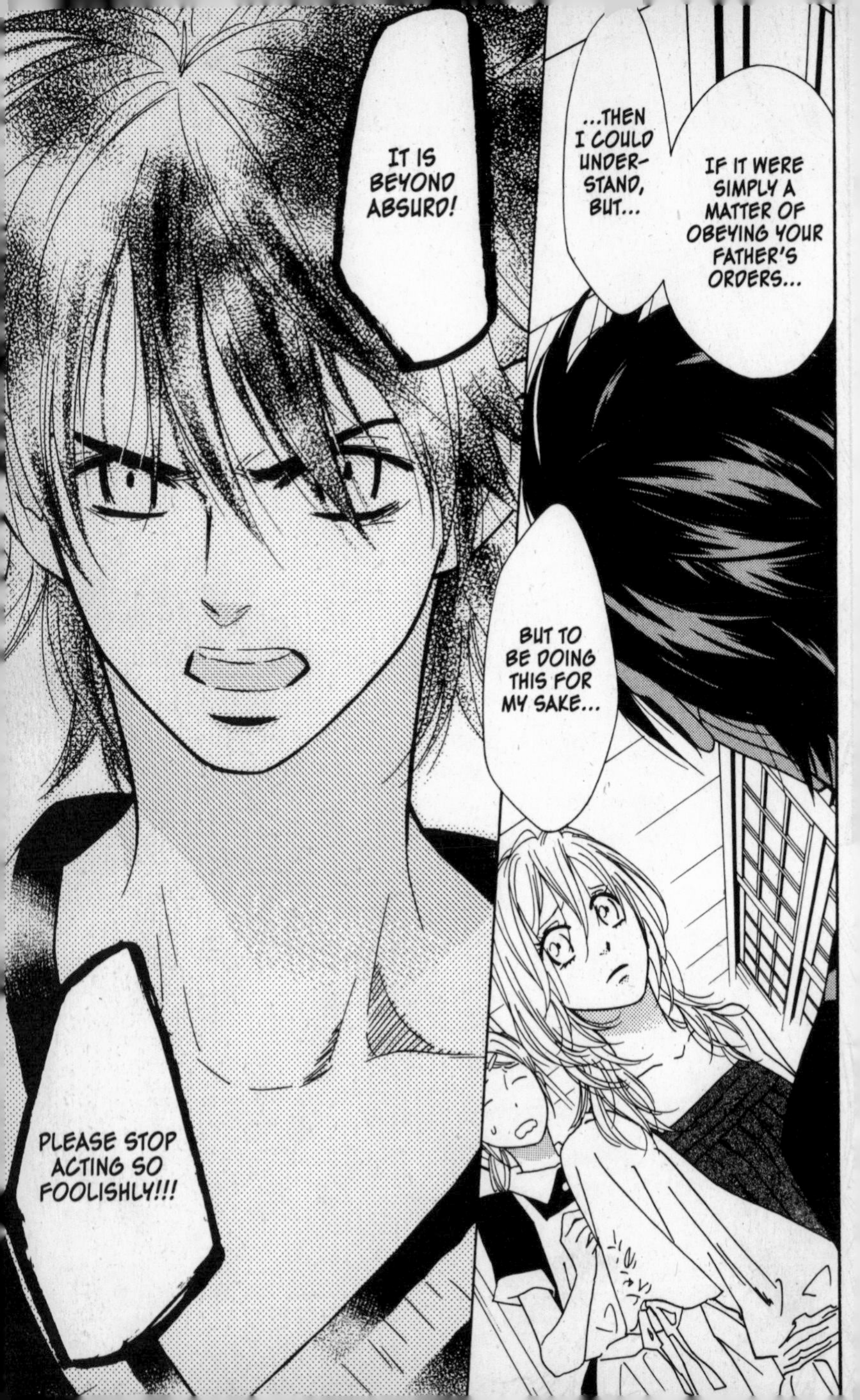
IF IT WERE SIMPLY A MATTER OF OBEYING YOUR FATHER'S ORDERS...
...THEN I COULD UNDER-STAND, BUT...
BUT TO BE DOING THIS FOR MY SAKE...
IT IS BEYOND ABSURD!
PLEASE STOP ACTING SO FOOLISHLY!!!

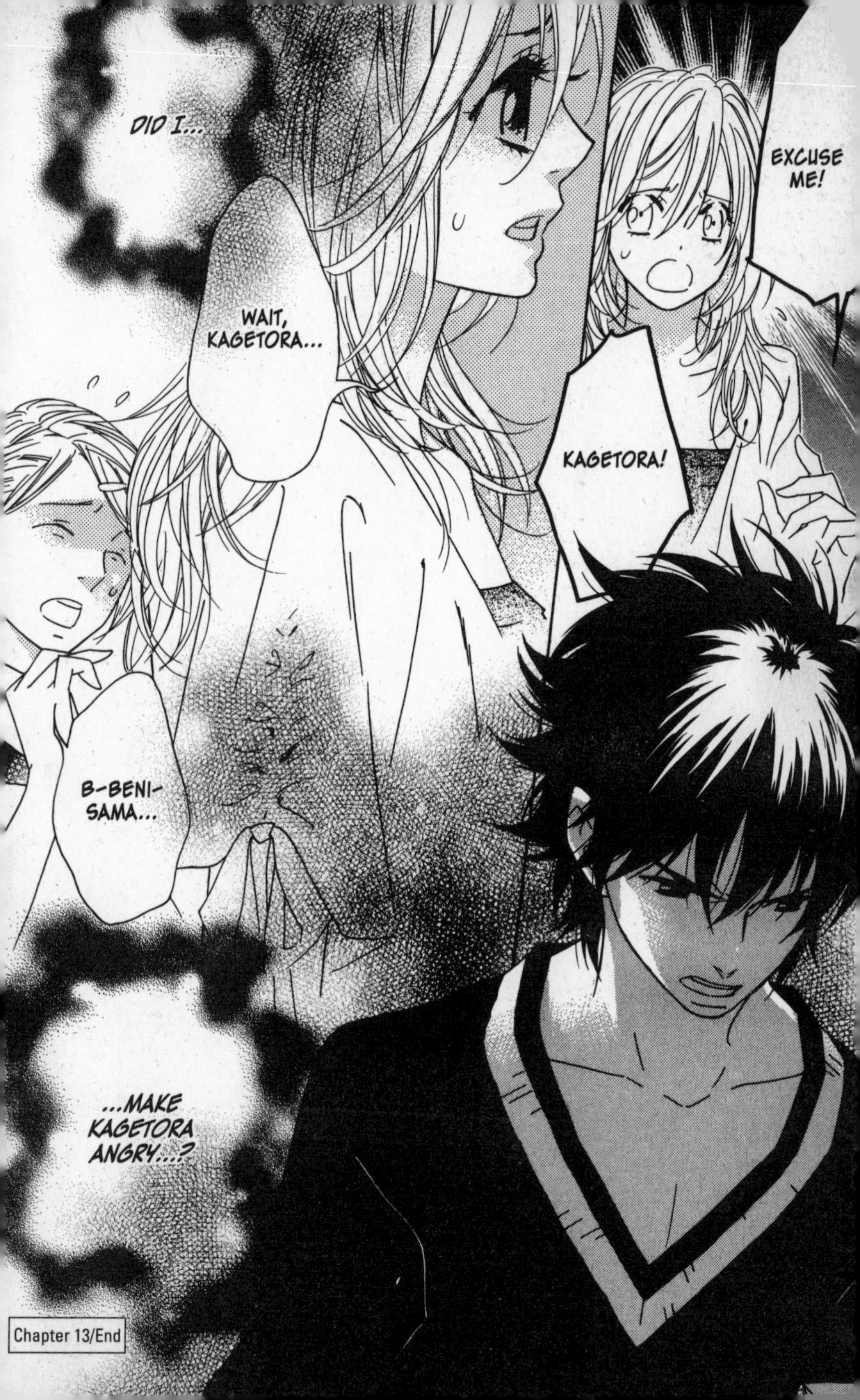
EXCUSE ME!
KAGETORA!
DID I...
WAIT, KAGETORA...
B-BENI-SAMA...
...MAKE KAGETORA ANGRY...?
Chapter 13/End

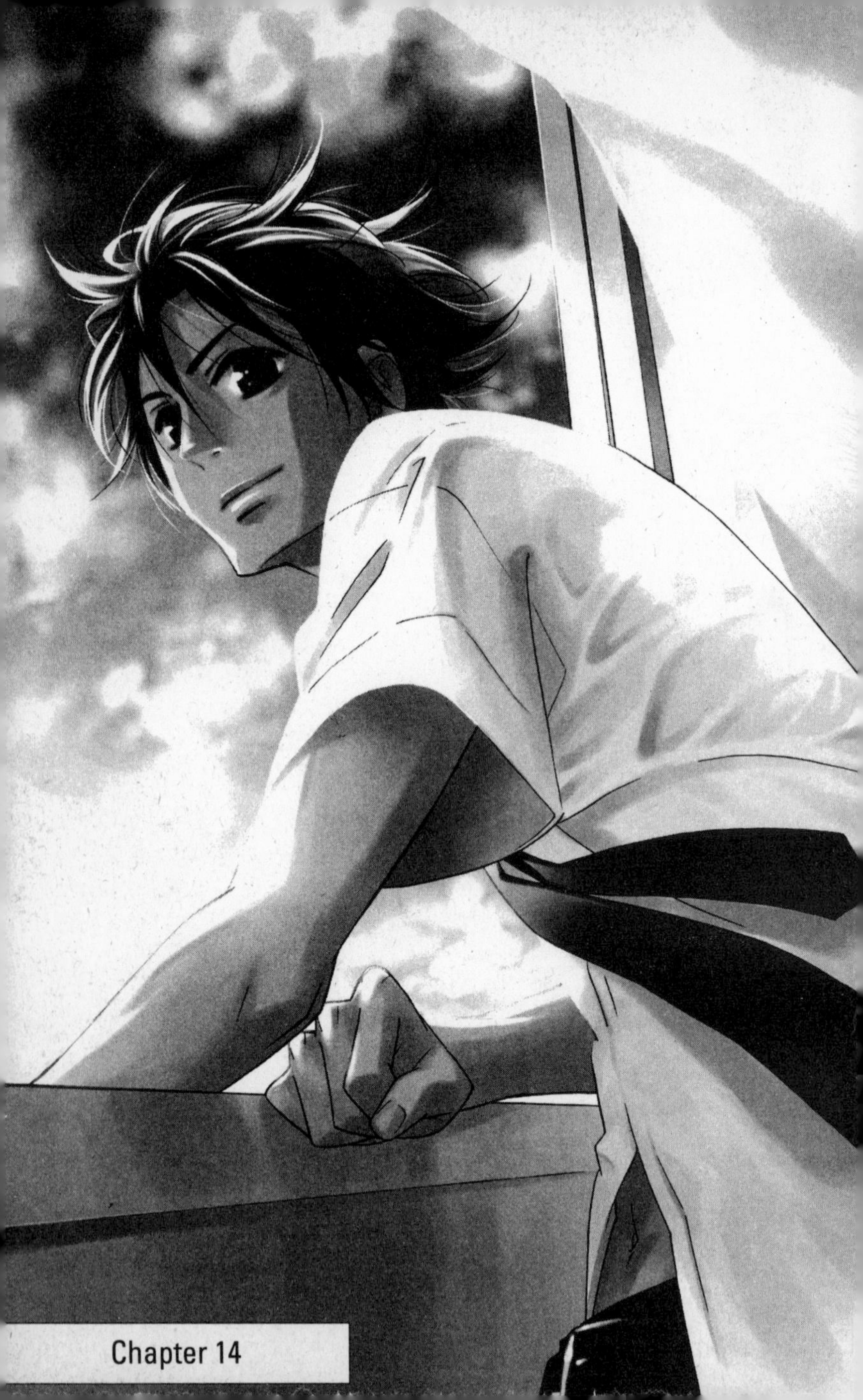

Chapter 14

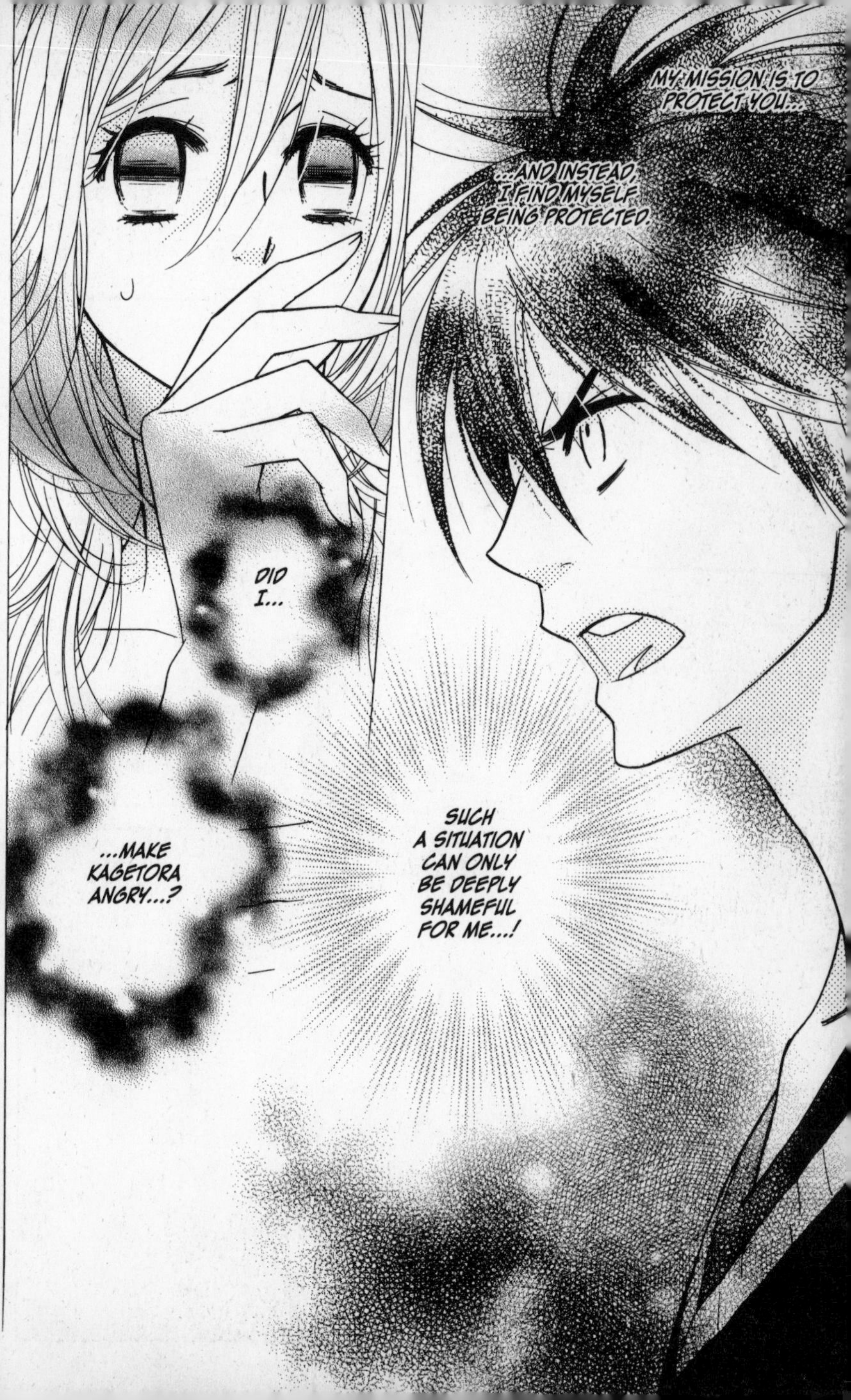
MY MISSION IS TO PROTECT YOU...
...AND INSTEAD, I FIND MYSELF BEING PROTECTED.
DID I...
SUCH A SITUATION CAN ONLY BE DEEPLY SHAMEFUL FOR ME...!
...MAKE KAGETORA ANGRY...?

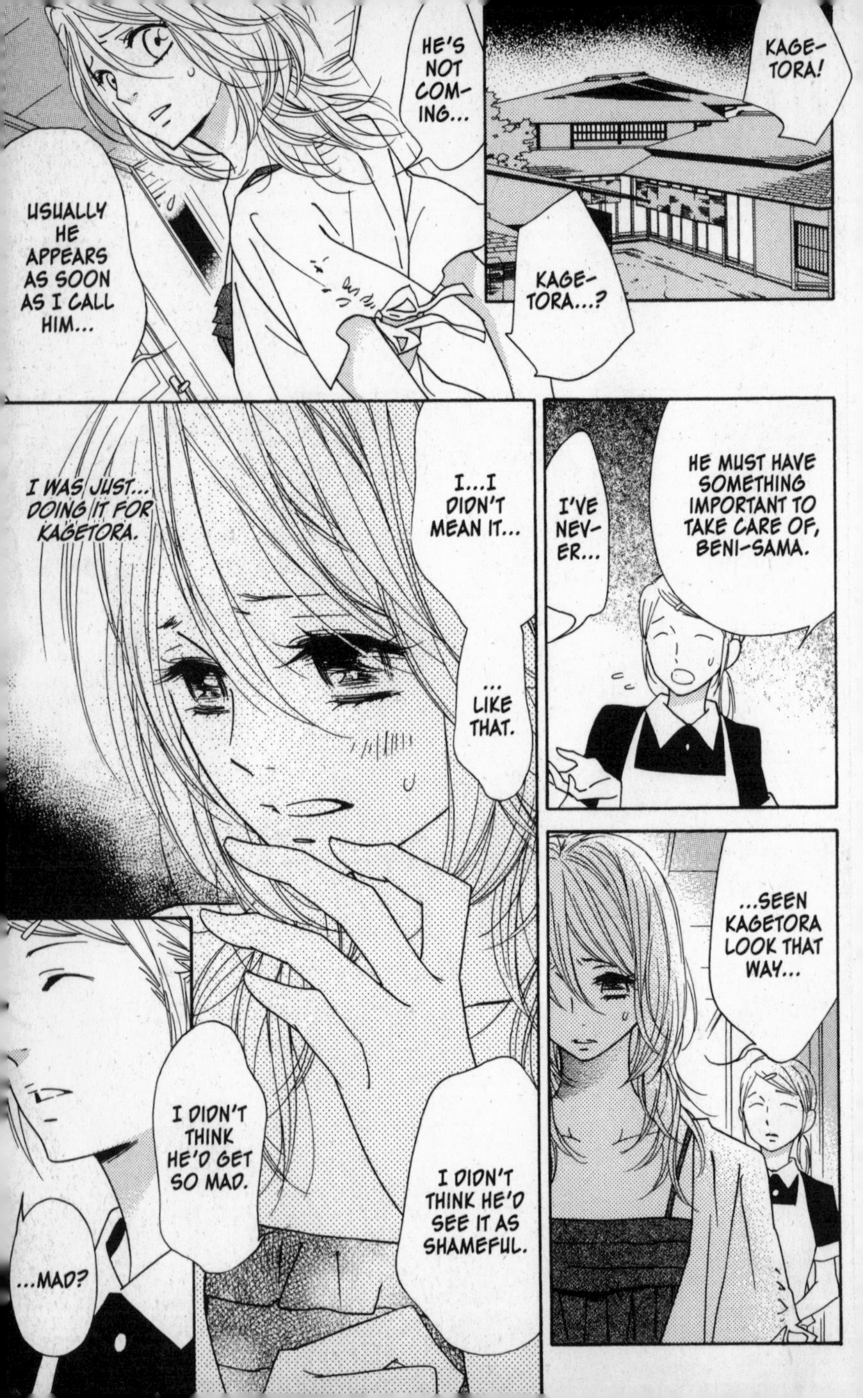
KAGE-TORA!
KAGE-TORA...?
HE'S NOT COMING...
USUALLY HE APPEARS AS SOON AS I CALL HIM...
HE MUST HAVE SOMETHING IMPORTANT TO TAKE CARE OF, BENI-SAMA.
I'VE NEVER...
I...I DIDN'T MEAN IT...
...LIKE THAT.
I WAS JUST... DOING IT FOR KAGETORA.
...SEEN KAGETORA LOOK THAT WAY...
I DIDN'T THINK HE'D SEE IT AS SHAMEFUL.
I DIDN'T THINK HE'D GET SO MAD.
...MAD?

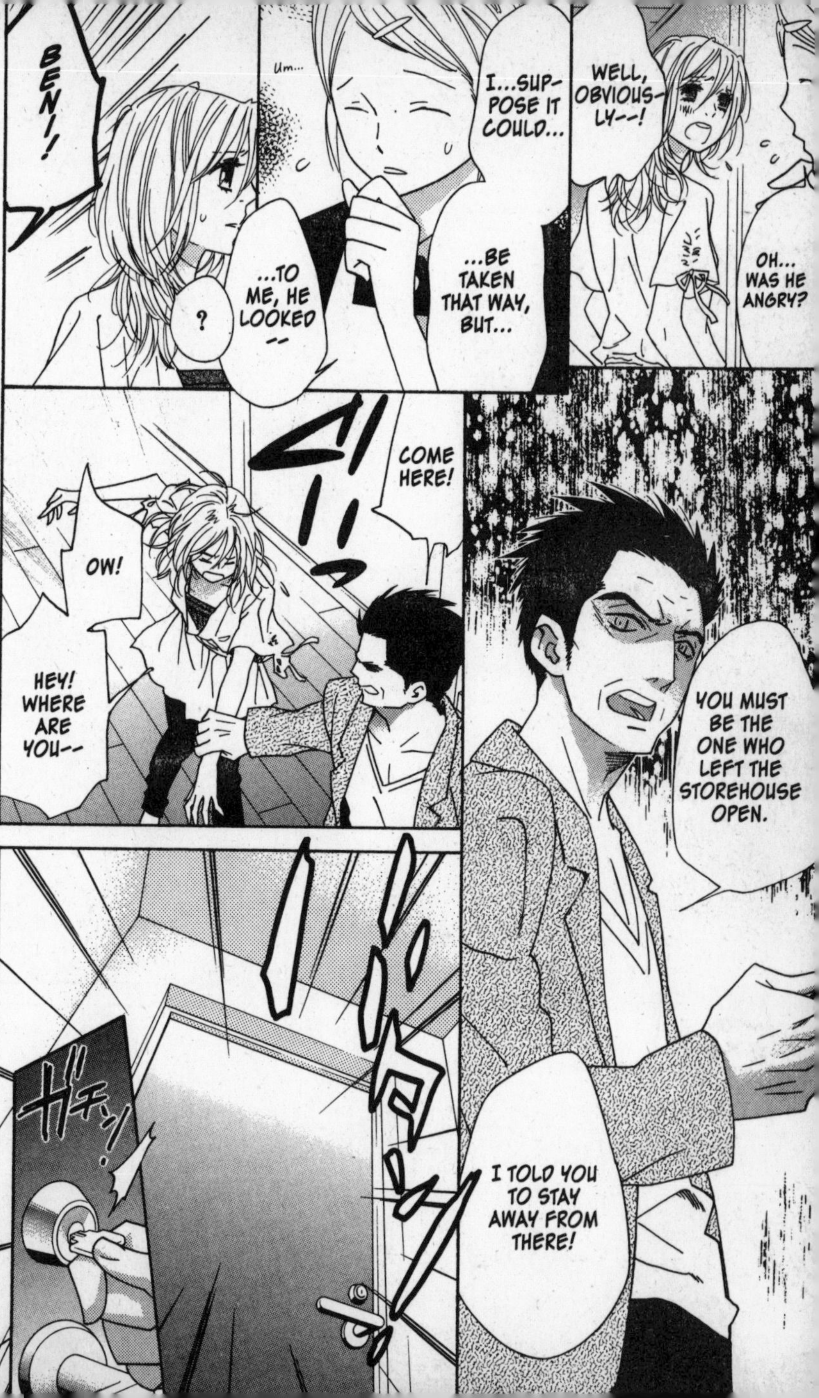
OH... WAS HE ANGRY?
WELL, OBVIOUSLY--!
I...SUPPOSE IT COULD...
...BE TAKEN THAT WAY, BUT...
Um...
...TO ME, HE LOOKED --
BENI!
?
YOU MUST BE THE ONE WHO LEFT THE STOREHOUSE OPEN.
I TOLD YOU TO STAY AWAY FROM THERE!
COME HERE!
OW!
HEY! WHERE ARE YOU--
ガチン!

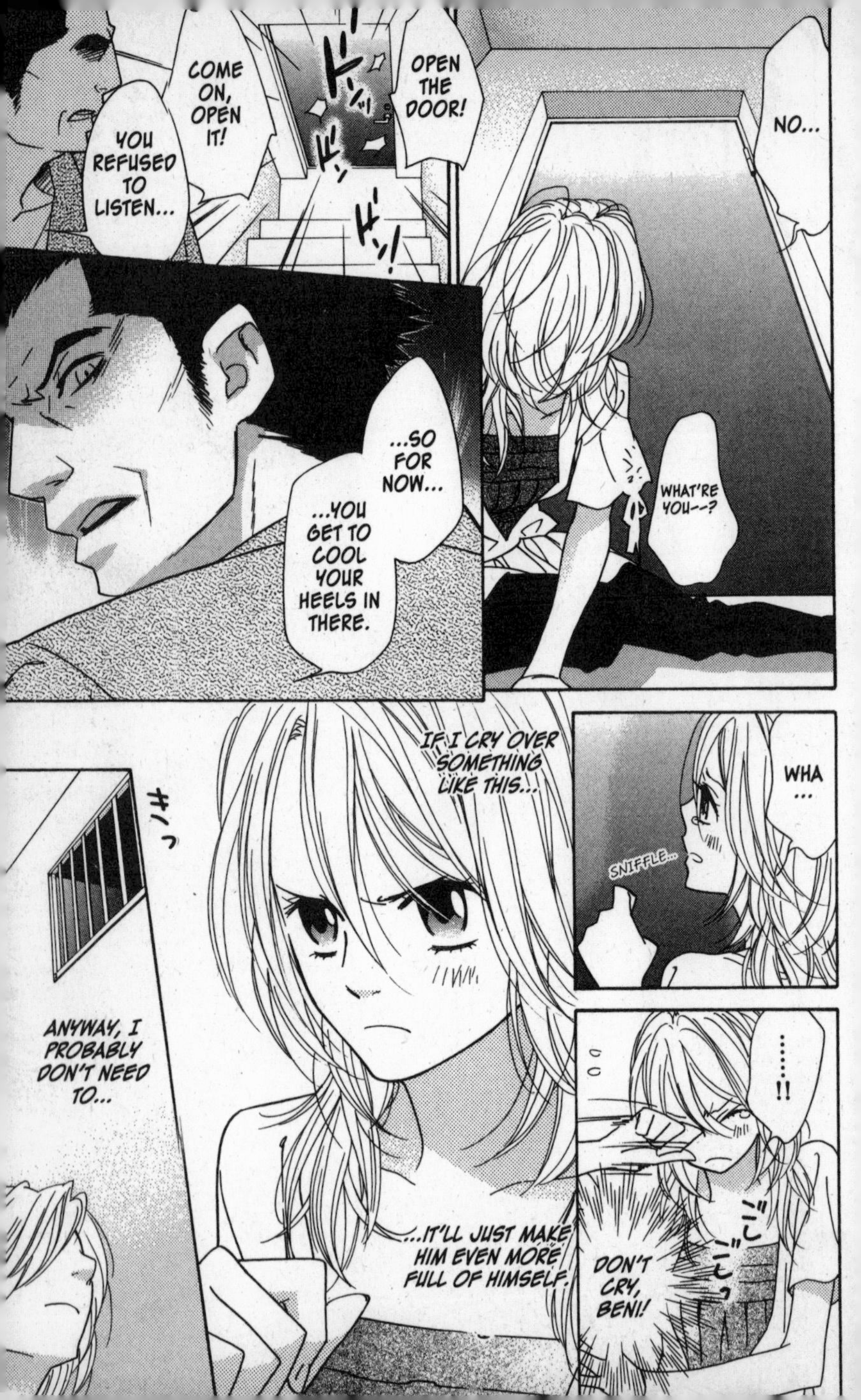
NO...
WHAT'RE YOU--?
OPEN THE DOOR!
COME ON, OPEN IT!
ドッ ドッ ドッ!
YOU REFUSED TO LISTEN...
...SO FOR NOW...
...YOU GET TO COOL YOUR HEELS IN THERE.
WHA ...
SNIFFLE...
......!!
ごしごしっ
DON'T CRY, BENI!
IF I CRY OVER SOMETHING LIKE THIS...
...IT'LL JUST MAKE HIM EVEN MORE FULL OF HIMSELF.
キッ
ANYWAY, I PROBABLY DON'T NEED TO...

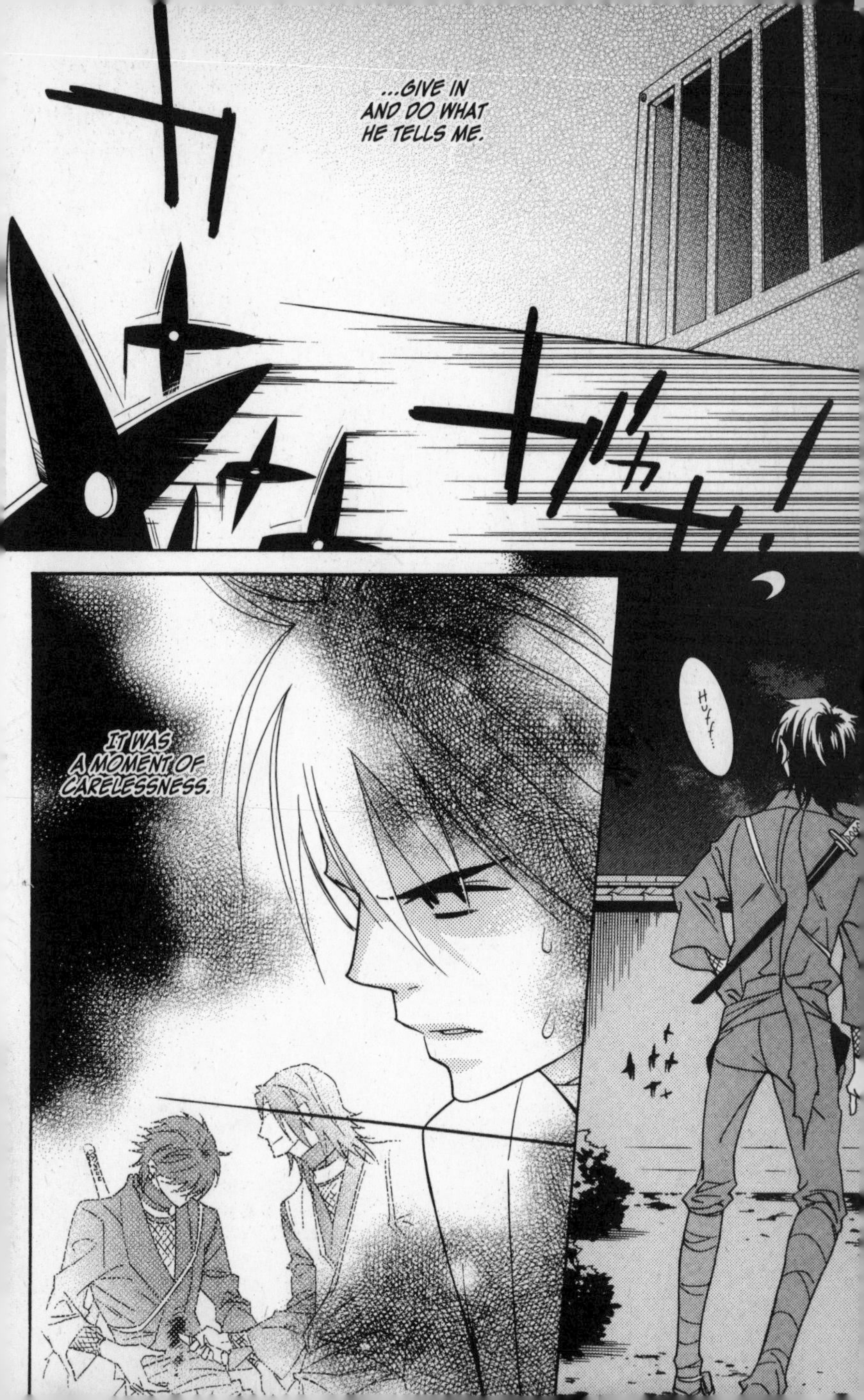
...GIVE IN
AND DO WHAT
HE TELLS ME.
HUFF...
IT WAS
A MOMENT OF
CARELESSNESS.

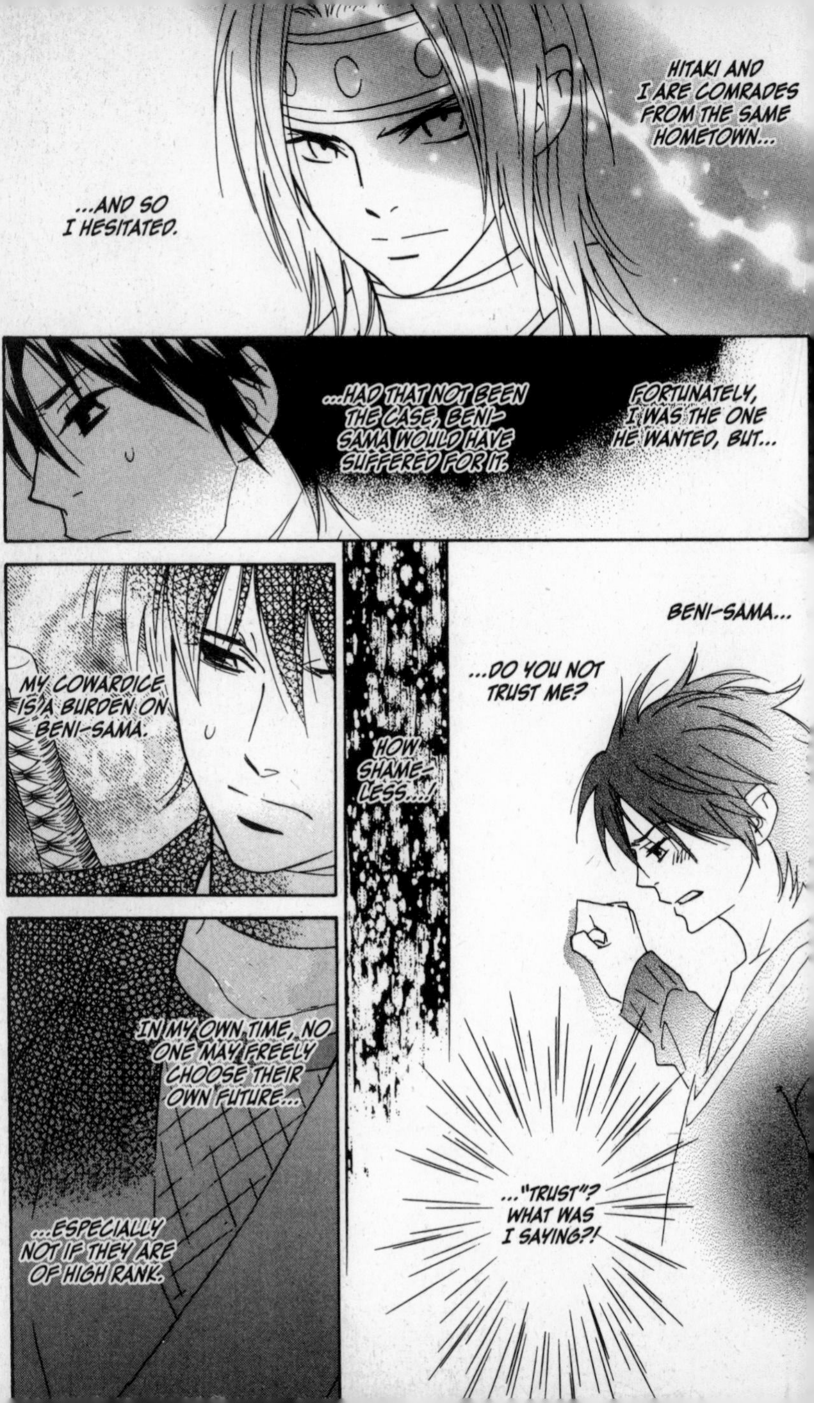
HITAKI AND I ARE COMRADES FROM THE SAME HOMETOWN...
...AND SO I HESITATED.
FORTUNATELY, I WAS THE ONE HE WANTED, BUT...
...HAD THAT NOT BEEN THE CASE, BENI-SAMA WOULD HAVE SUFFERED FOR IT.
BENI-SAMA...
...DO YOU NOT TRUST ME?
..."TRUST"? WHAT WAS I SAYING?!
HOW SHAME-LESS...!
MY COWARDICE IS A BURDEN ON BENI-SAMA.
IN MY OWN TIME, NO ONE MAY FREELY CHOOSE THEIR OWN FUTURE...
...ESPECIALLY NOT IF THEY ARE OF HIGH RANK.

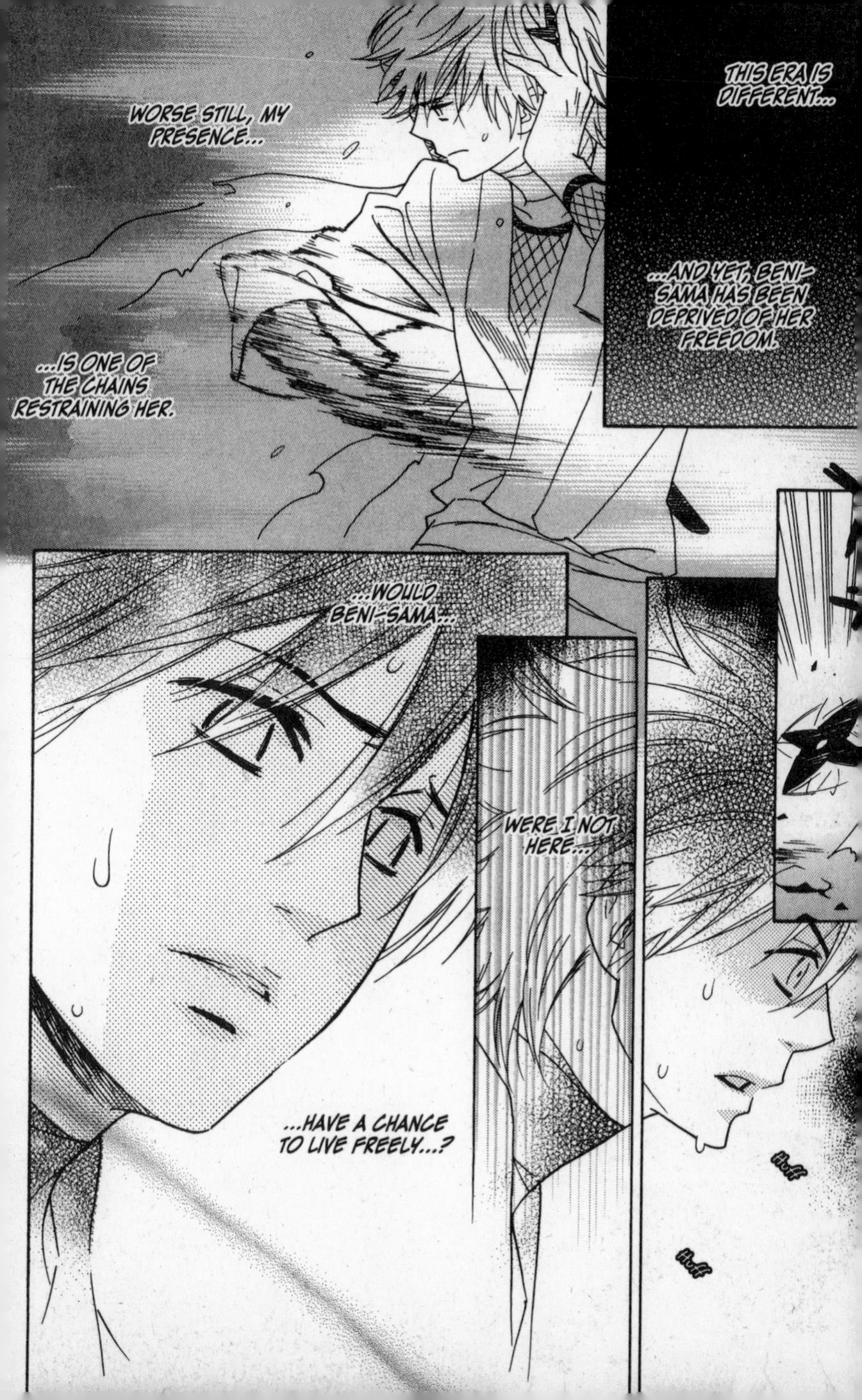
THIS ERA IS DIFFERENT...
...AND YET, BENI-SAMA HAS BEEN DEPRIVED OF HER FREEDOM.
WORSE STILL, MY PRESENCE...
...IS ONE OF THE CHAINS RESTRAINING HER.
Huff
Huff
WERE I NOT HERE...
...WOULD BENI-SAMA...
...HAVE A CHANCE TO LIVE FREELY...?

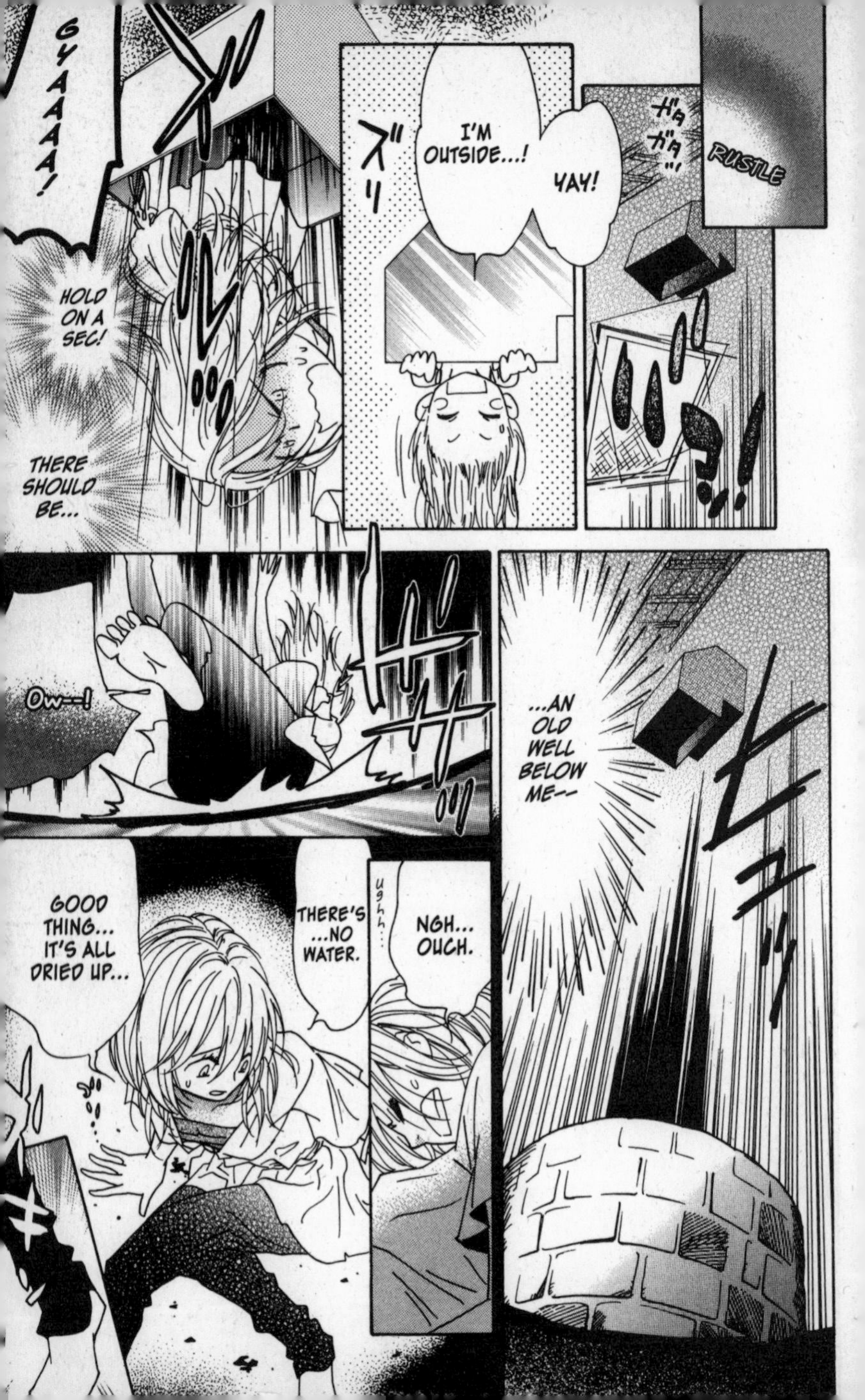
RUSTLE
I'M OUTSIDE...!
YAY!
GYAAAAA!
HOLD ON A SEC!
THERE SHOULD BE...
...AN OLD WELL BELOW ME--
Ow--!
NGH... OUCH.
Ughh...
THERE'S ...NO WATER.
GOOD THING... IT'S ALL DRIED UP...

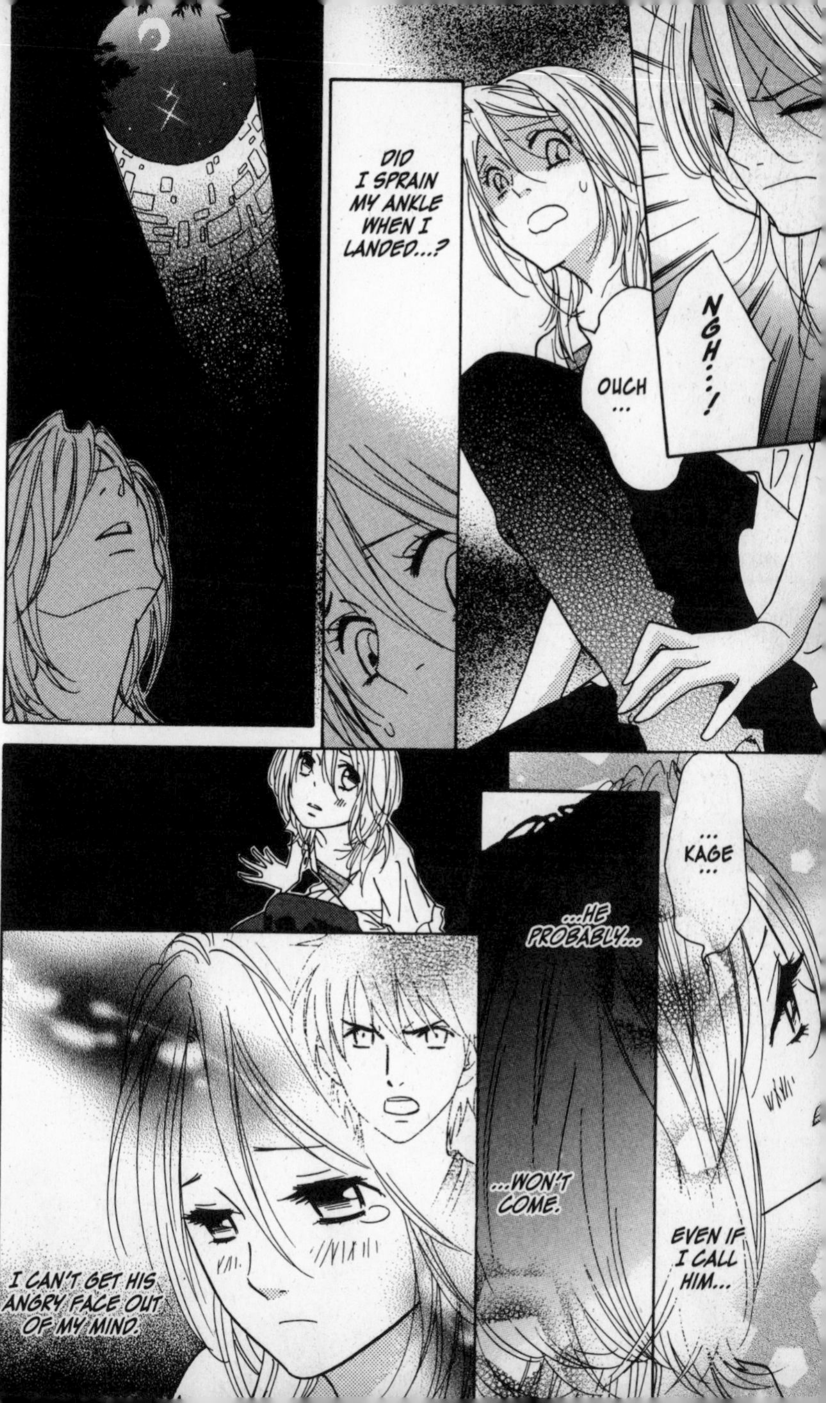
NGH...!
OUCH...
DID I SPRAIN MY ANKLE WHEN I LANDED...?
...KAGE...
EVEN IF I CALL HIM...
...HE PROBABLY...
...WON'T COME.
I CAN'T GET HIS ANGRY FACE OUT OF MY MIND.

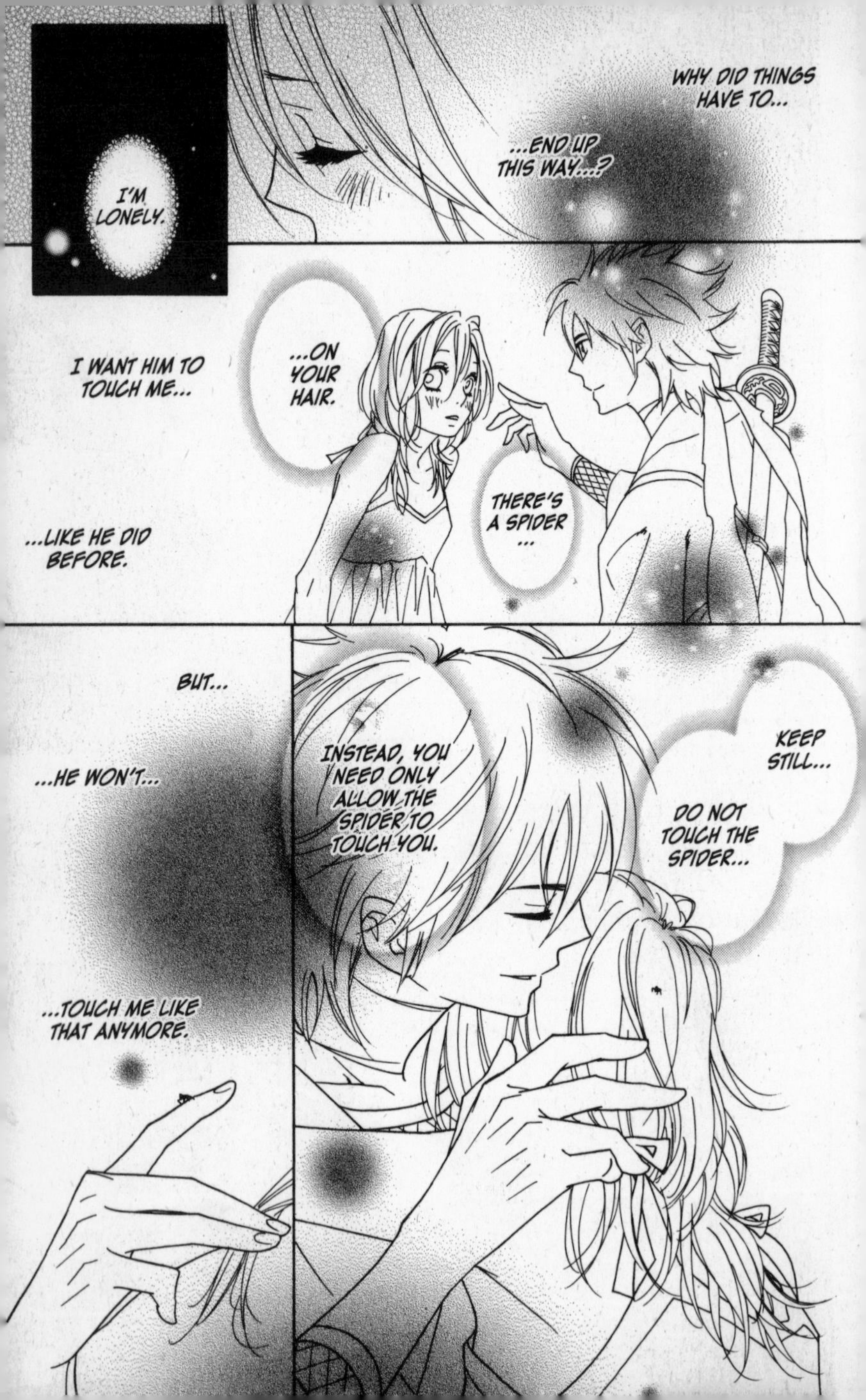
WHY DID THINGS HAVE TO...
...END UP THIS WAY...?
I'M LONELY.
THERE'S A SPIDER ...
...ON YOUR HAIR.
I WANT HIM TO TOUCH ME...
...LIKE HE DID BEFORE.
KEEP STILL...
DO NOT TOUCH THE SPIDER...
INSTEAD, YOU NEED ONLY ALLOW THE SPIDER TO TOUCH YOU.
BUT...
...HE WON'T...
...TOUCH ME LIKE THAT ANYMORE.

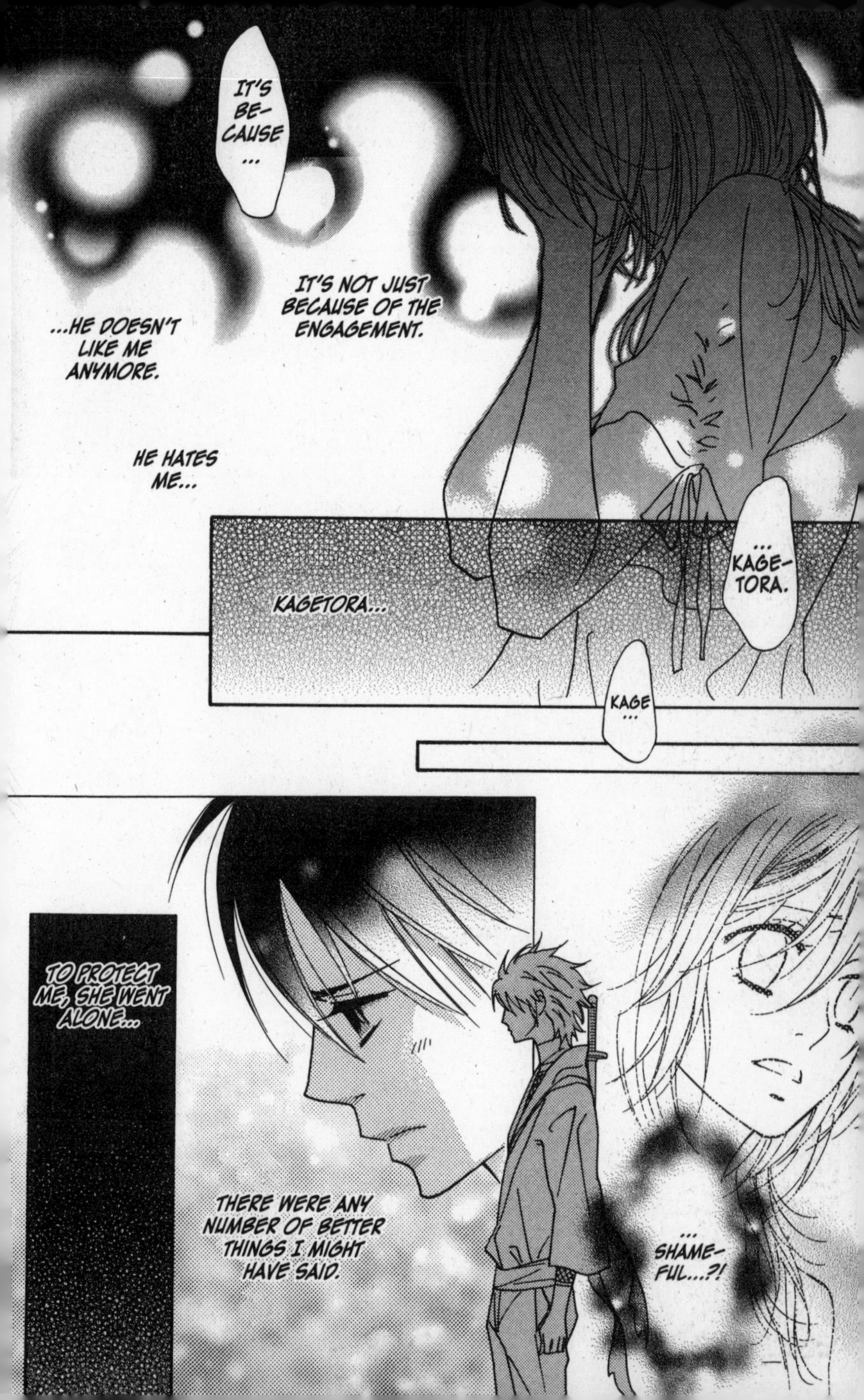
IT'S BE-CAUSE...
IT'S NOT JUST BECAUSE OF THE ENGAGEMENT.
...HE DOESN'T LIKE ME ANYMORE.
HE HATES ME...
...KAGE-TORA.
KAGETORA...
KAGE...
...SHAME-FUL...?!
TO PROTECT ME, SHE WENT ALONE...
THERE WERE ANY NUMBER OF BETTER THINGS I MIGHT HAVE SAID.

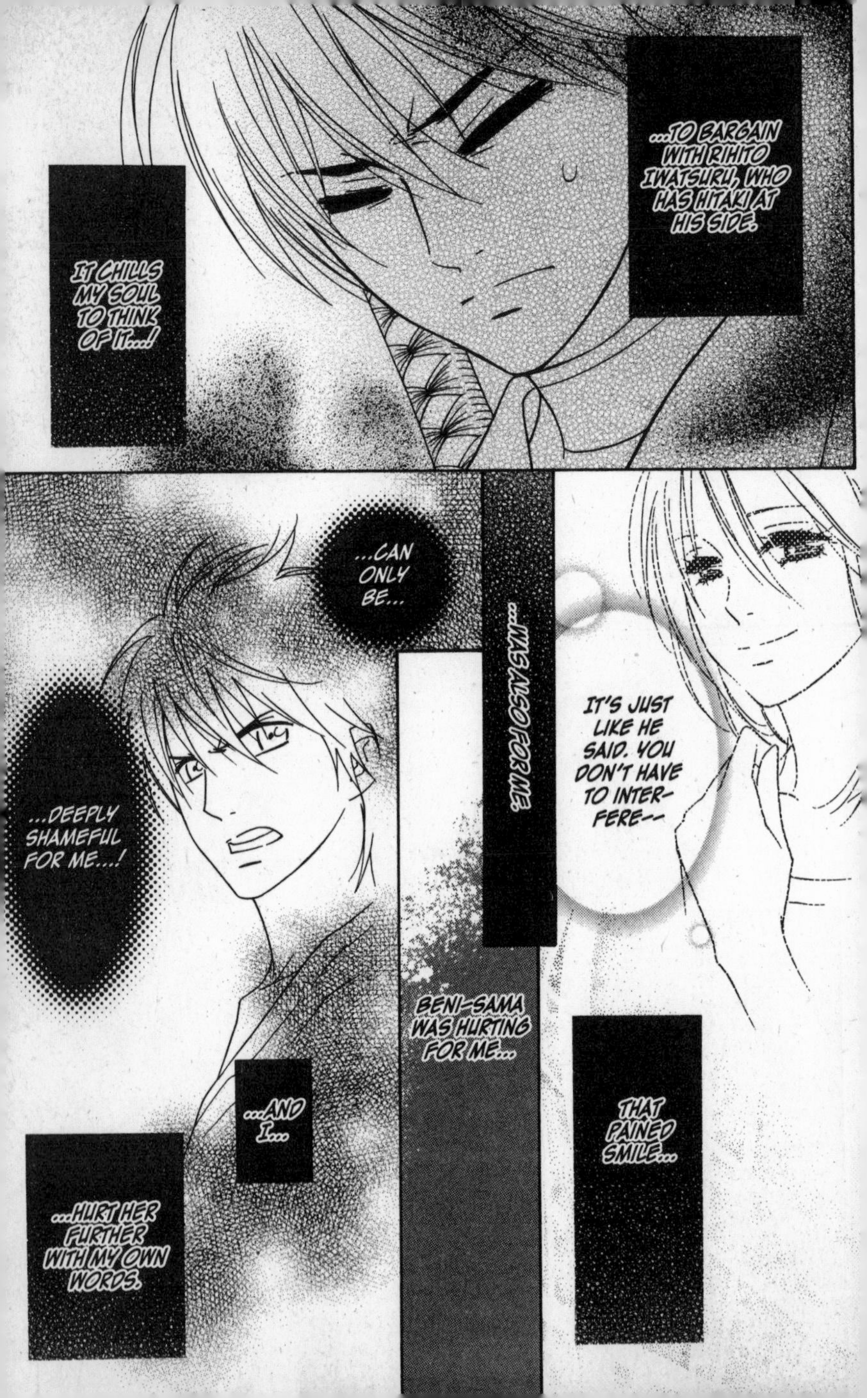
...TO BARGAIN WITH RIHITO IWATSURU, WHO HAS HITAKI AT HIS SIDE.
IT CHILLS MY SOUL TO THINK OF IT...!
IT'S JUST LIKE HE SAID. YOU DON'T HAVE TO INTER-FERE--
THAT PAINED SMILE...
...WAS ALSO FOR ME.
BENI-SAMA WAS HURTING FOR ME...
...AND I...
...HURT HER FURTHER WITH MY OWN WORDS.
...CAN ONLY BE...
...DEEPLY SHAMEFUL FOR ME...!

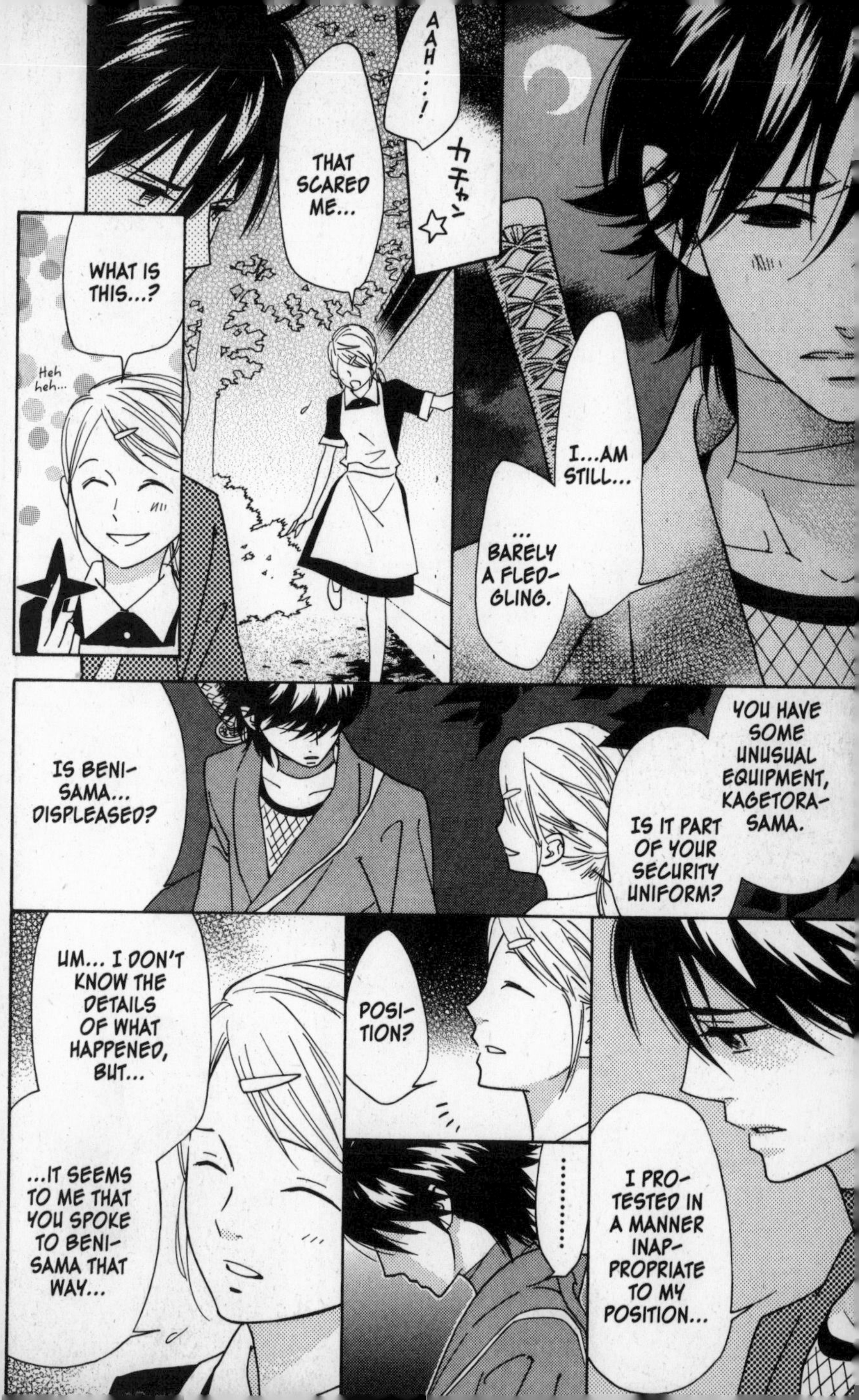
I...AM STILL...
...BARELY A FLEDGLING.
AAH...!
カチャン☆
THAT SCARED ME...
WHAT IS THIS...?
Heh heh...
YOU HAVE SOME UNUSUAL EQUIPMENT, KAGETORA-SAMA.
IS IT PART OF YOUR SECURITY UNIFORM?
IS BENI-SAMA... DISPLEASED?
I PROTESTED IN A MANNER INAPPROPRIATE TO MY POSITION...
POSITION?
......
UM... I DON'T KNOW THE DETAILS OF WHAT HAPPENED, BUT...
...IT SEEMS TO ME THAT YOU SPOKE TO BENI-SAMA THAT WAY...

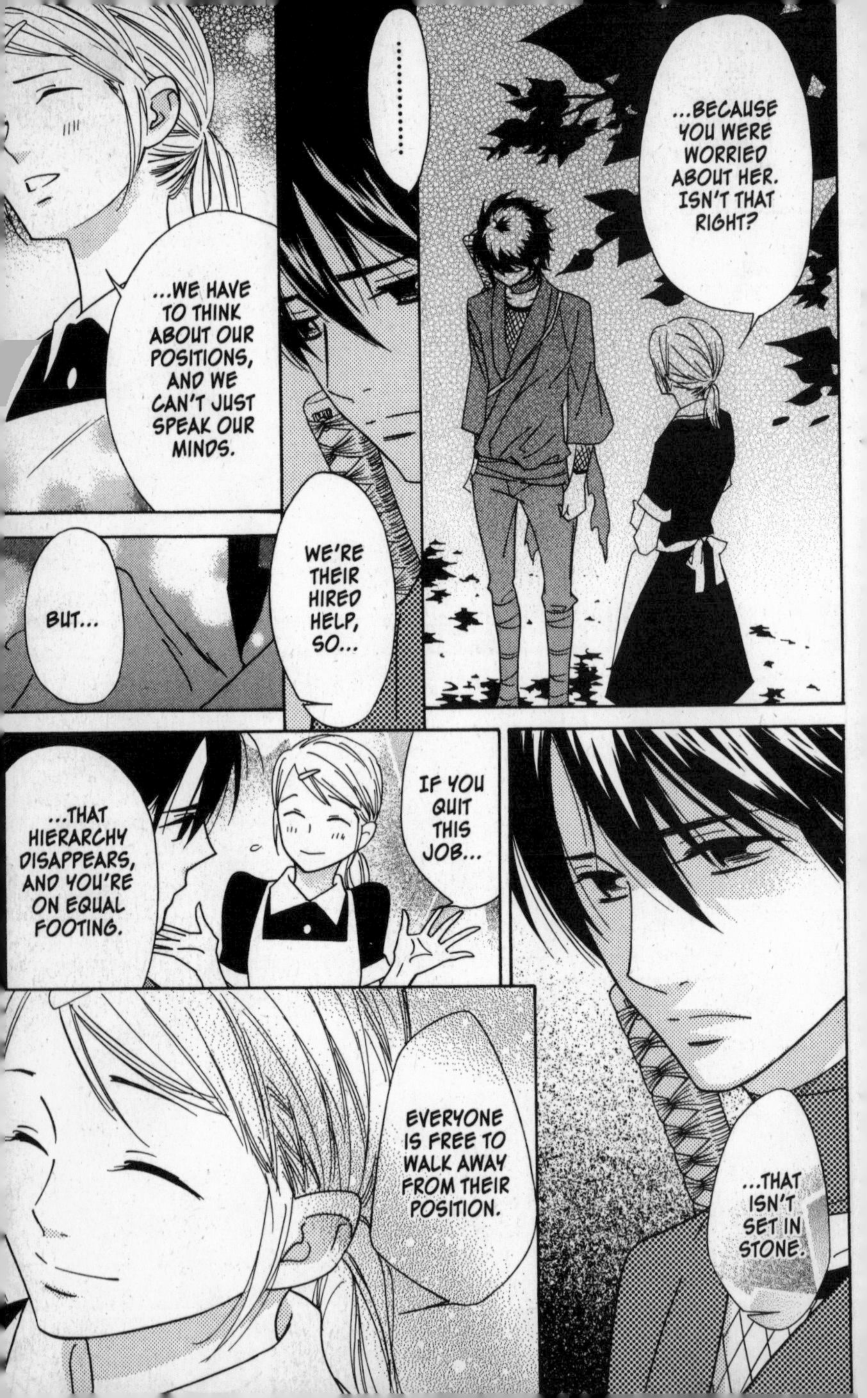
...BECAUSE YOU WERE WORRIED ABOUT HER. ISN'T THAT RIGHT?
......
WE'RE THEIR HIRED HELP, SO...
...WE HAVE TO THINK ABOUT OUR POSITIONS, AND WE CAN'T JUST SPEAK OUR MINDS.
BUT...
IF YOU QUIT THIS JOB...
...THAT HIERARCHY DISAPPEARS, AND YOU'RE ON EQUAL FOOTING.
EVERYONE IS FREE TO WALK AWAY FROM THEIR POSITION.
...THAT ISN'T SET IN STONE.

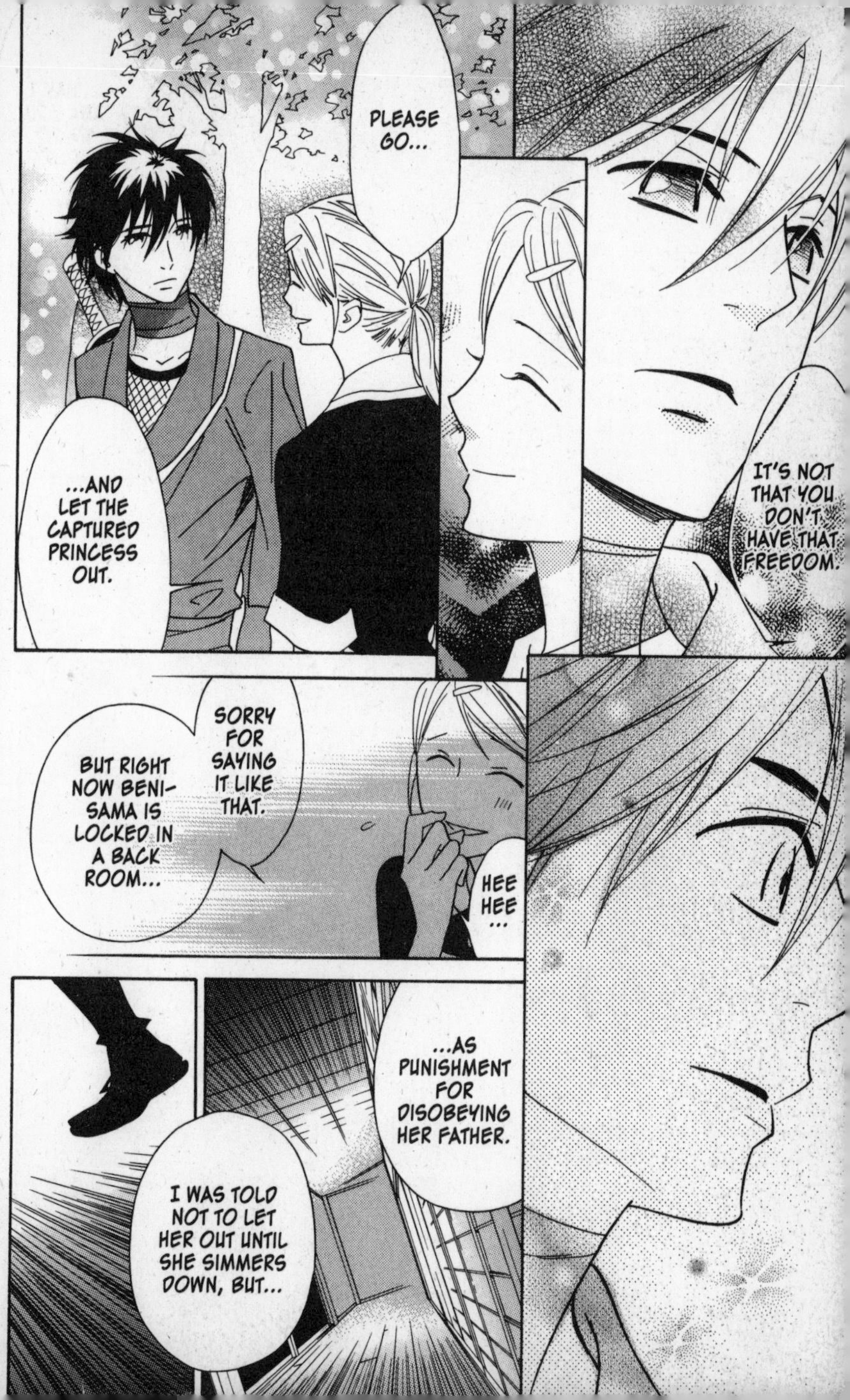
IT'S NOT THAT YOU DON'T HAVE THAT FREEDOM.
PLEASE GO...
...AND LET THE CAPTURED PRINCESS OUT.
SORRY FOR SAYING IT LIKE THAT.
HEE HEE...
BUT RIGHT NOW BENI-SAMA IS LOCKED IN A BACK ROOM...
...AS PUNISHMENT FOR DISOBEYING HER FATHER.
I WAS TOLD NOT TO LET HER OUT UNTIL SHE SIMMERS DOWN, BUT...

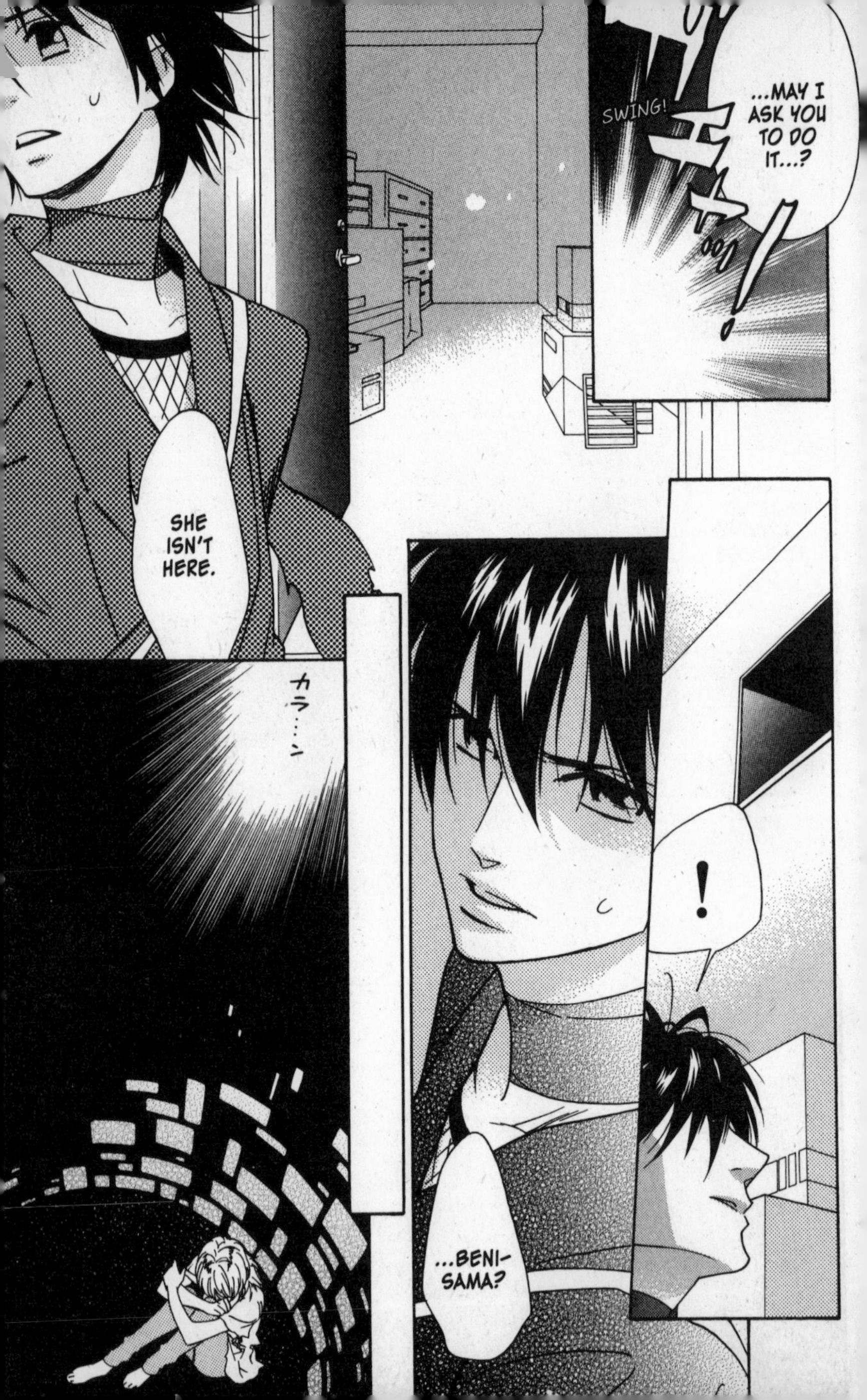
SWING!
...MAY I ASK YOU TO DO IT...?
SHE ISN'T HERE.
!
...BENI-SAMA?
カラ…ン

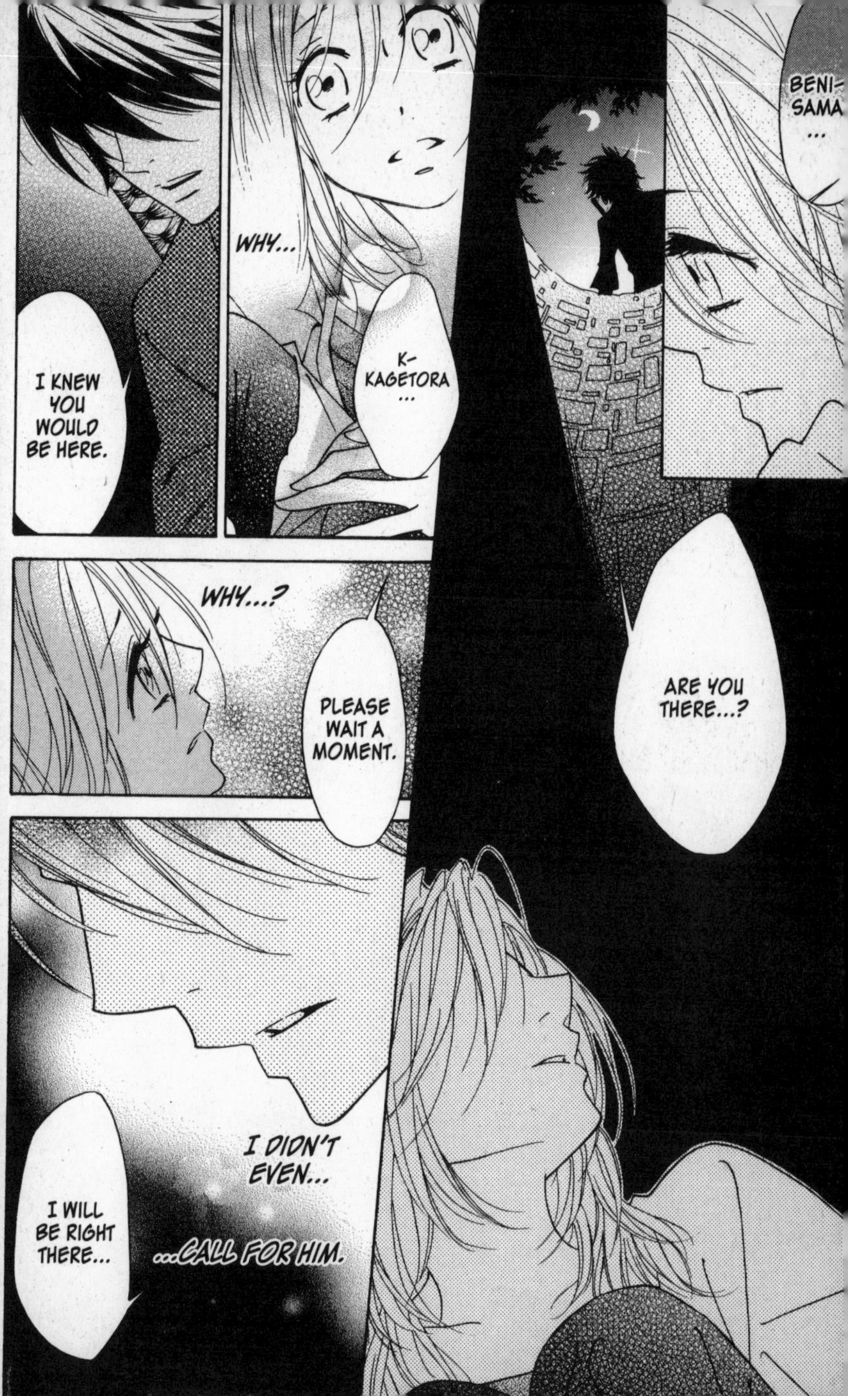
BENI-SAMA...
ARE YOU THERE...?
WHY...
K-KAGETORA...
I KNEW YOU WOULD BE HERE.
WHY...?
PLEASE WAIT A MOMENT.
I DIDN'T EVEN...
...CALL FOR HIM.
I WILL BE RIGHT THERE...

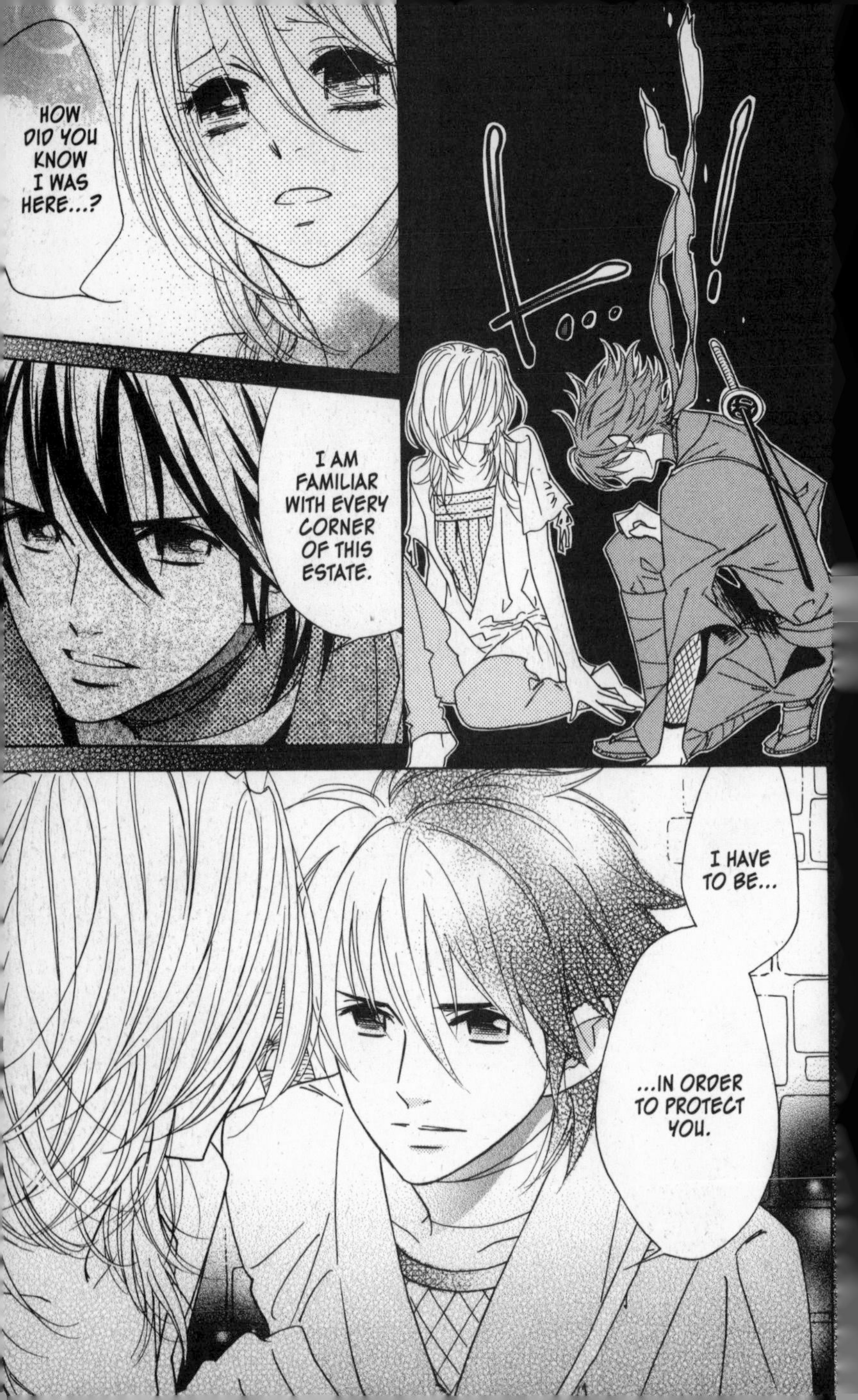
HOW DID YOU KNOW I WAS HERE...?
I AM FAMILIAR WITH EVERY CORNER OF THIS ESTATE.
I HAVE TO BE...
...IN ORDER TO PROTECT YOU.

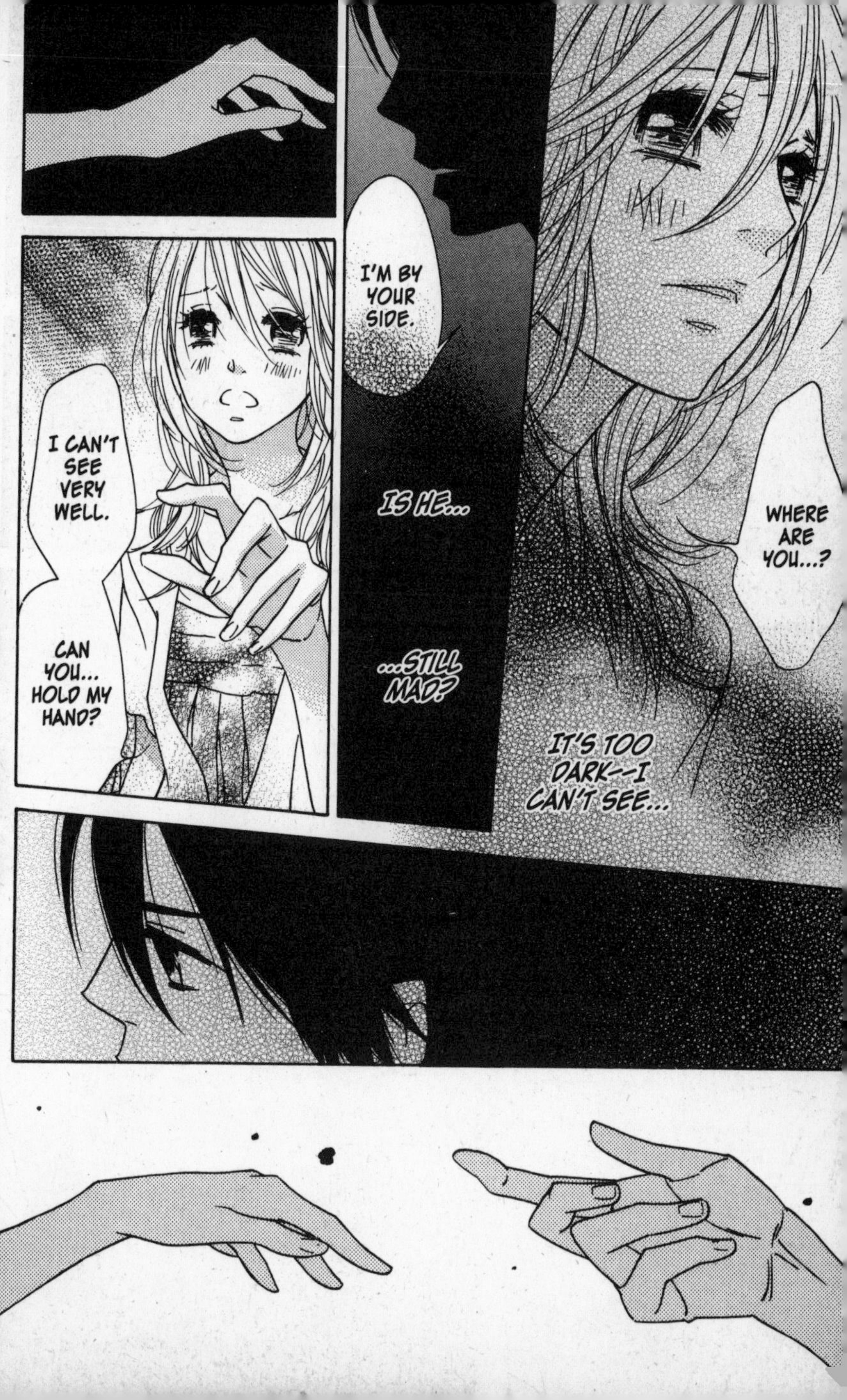
WHERE ARE YOU...?
IT'S TOO DARK--I CAN'T SEE...
I'M BY YOUR SIDE.
IS HE...
...STILL MAD?
I CAN'T SEE VERY WELL.
CAN YOU... HOLD MY HAND?

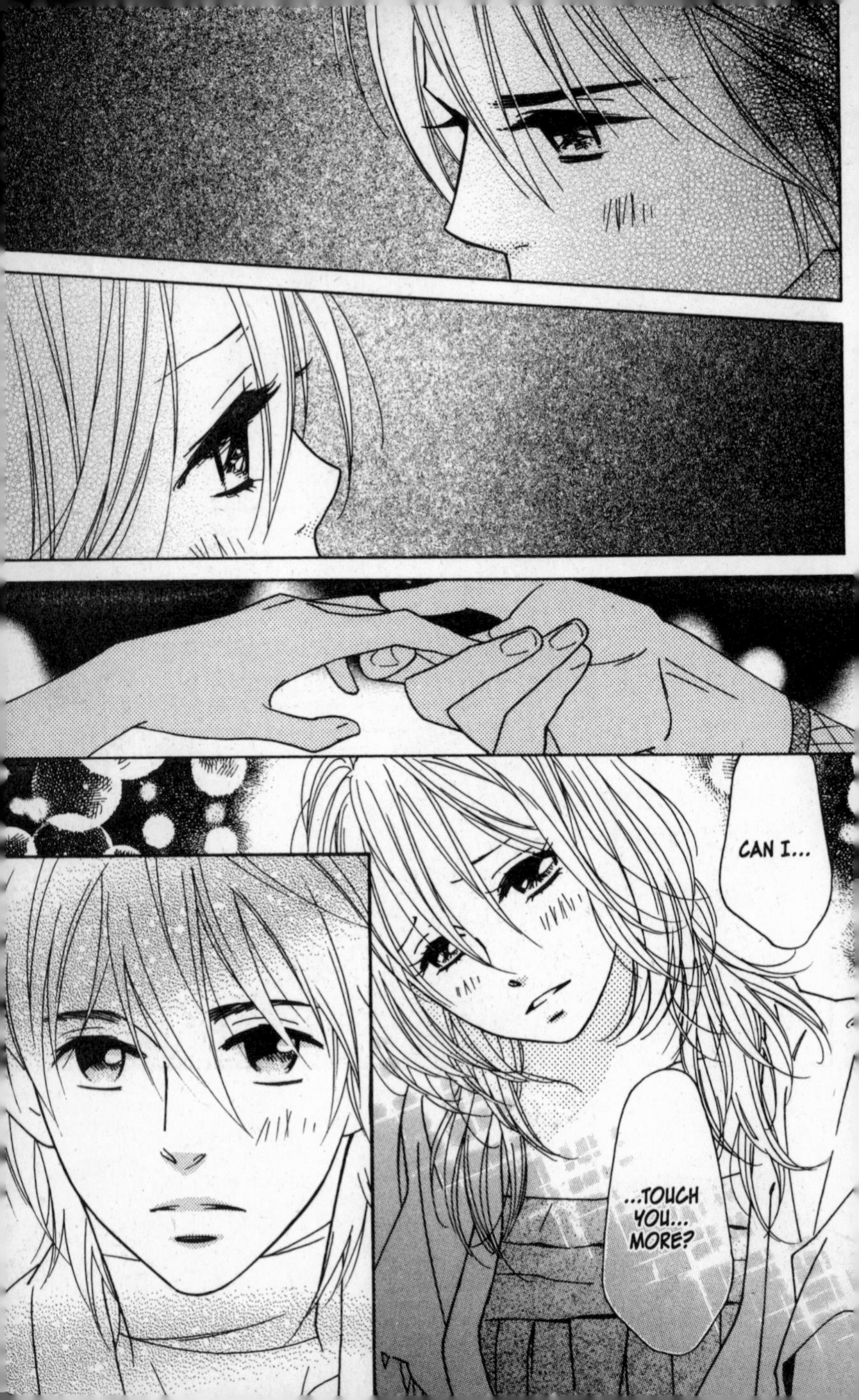
CAN I...
...TOUCH YOU... MORE?

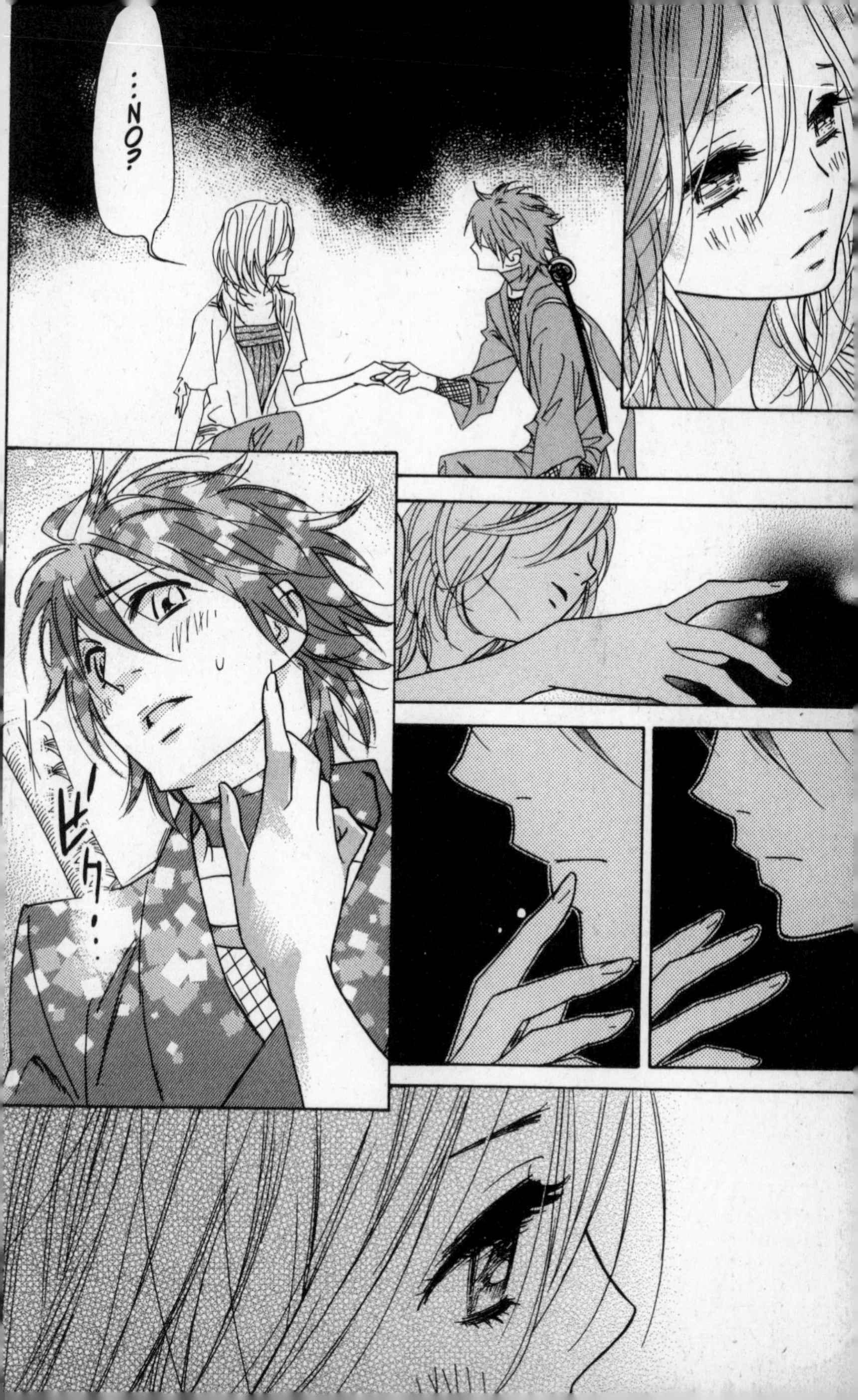
...NO?
ビクッ...

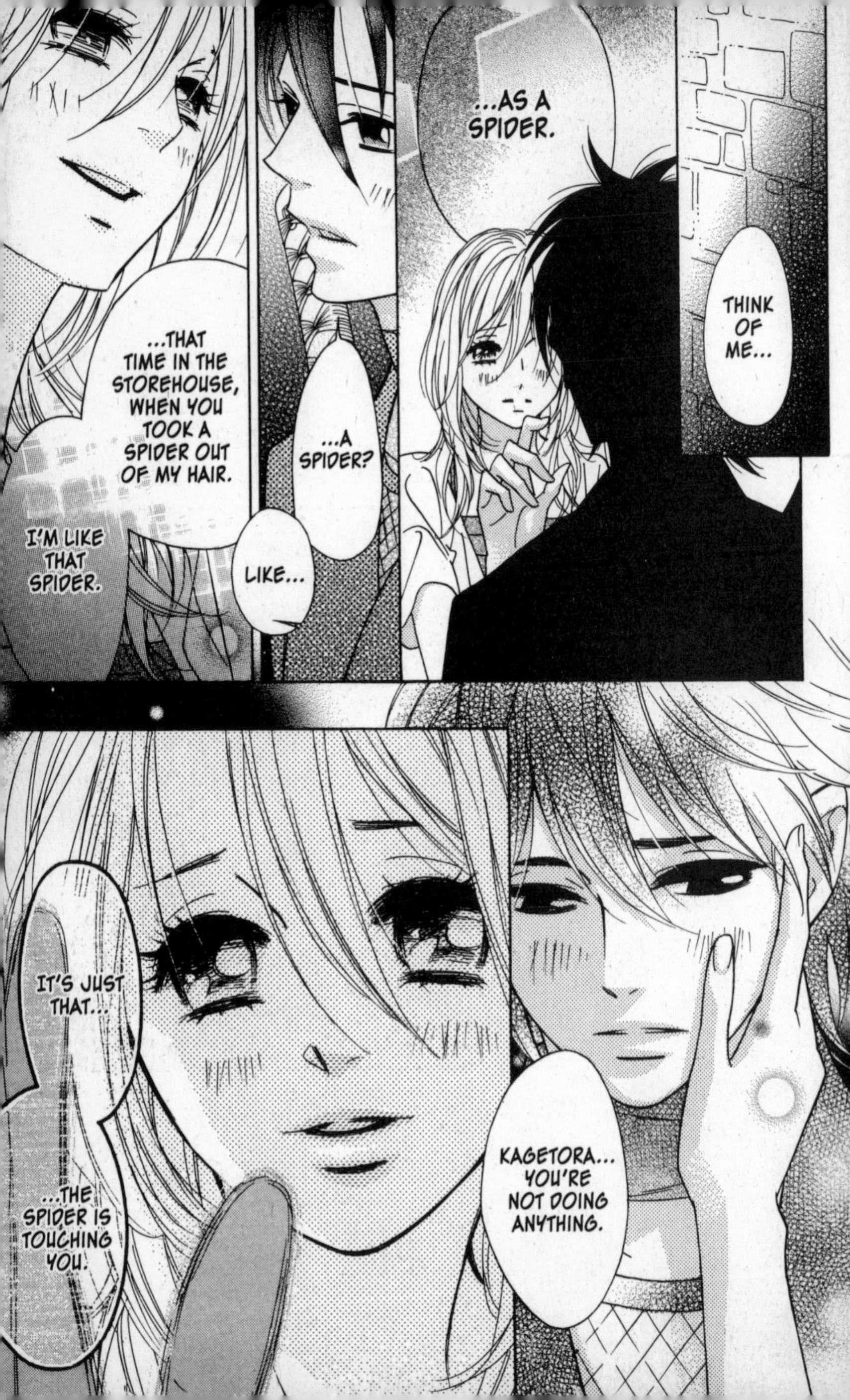
THINK OF ME...
...AS A SPIDER.
...A SPIDER?
LIKE...
...THAT TIME IN THE STOREHOUSE, WHEN YOU TOOK A SPIDER OUT OF MY HAIR.
I'M LIKE THAT SPIDER.
KAGETORA... YOU'RE NOT DOING ANYTHING.
IT'S JUST THAT...
...THE SPIDER IS TOUCHING YOU.

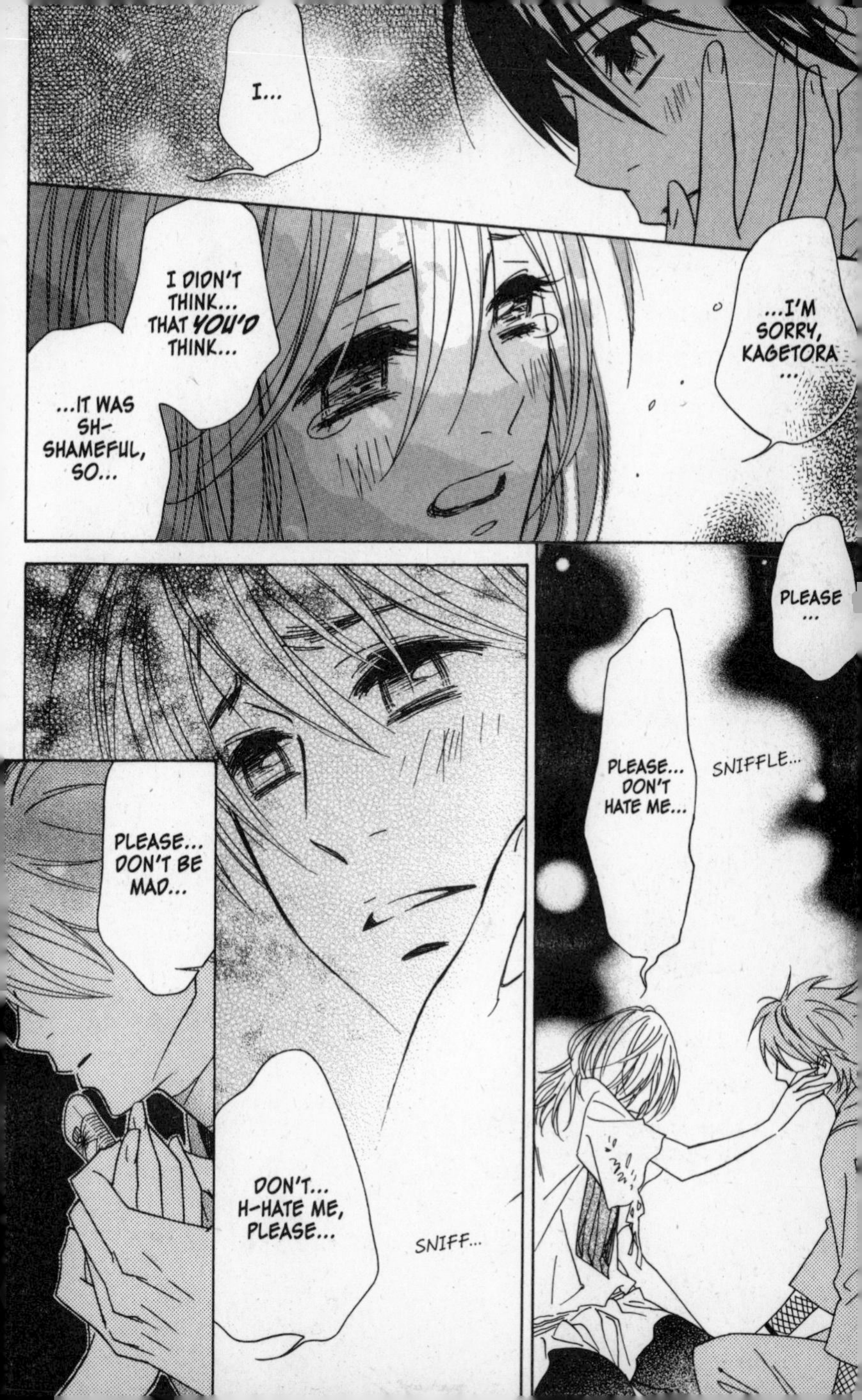
I...
...I'M SORRY, KAGETORA...
I DIDN'T THINK... THAT YOU'D THINK...
...IT WAS SH-SHAMEFUL, SO...
PLEASE...
PLEASE... DON'T HATE ME...
SNIFFLE...
PLEASE... DON'T BE MAD...
DON'T... H-HATE ME, PLEASE...
SNIFF...

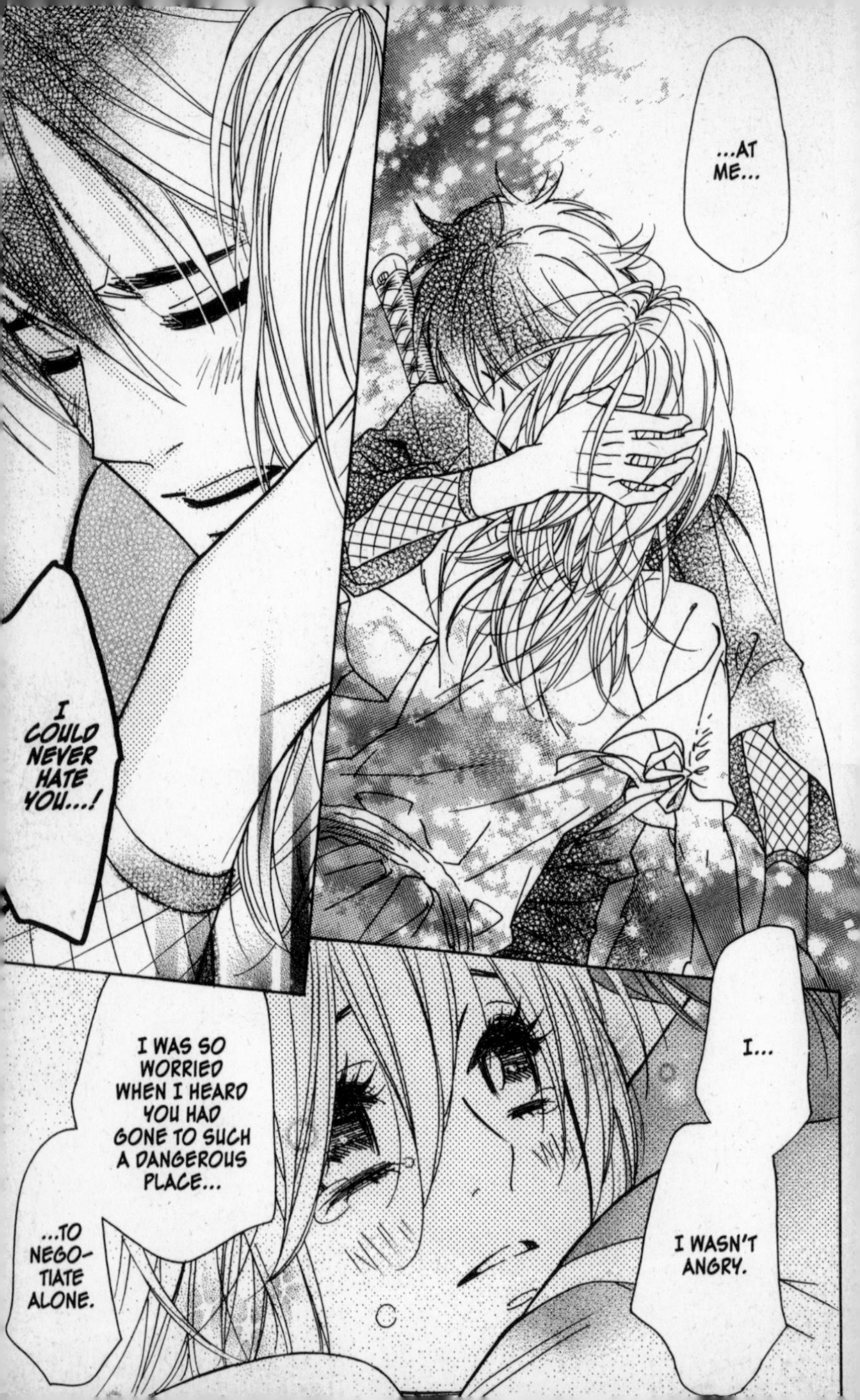
...AT ME...
I COULD NEVER HATE YOU...!
I...
I WASN'T ANGRY.
I WAS SO WORRIED WHEN I HEARD YOU HAD GONE TO SUCH A DANGEROUS PLACE...
...TO NEGO-TIATE ALONE.

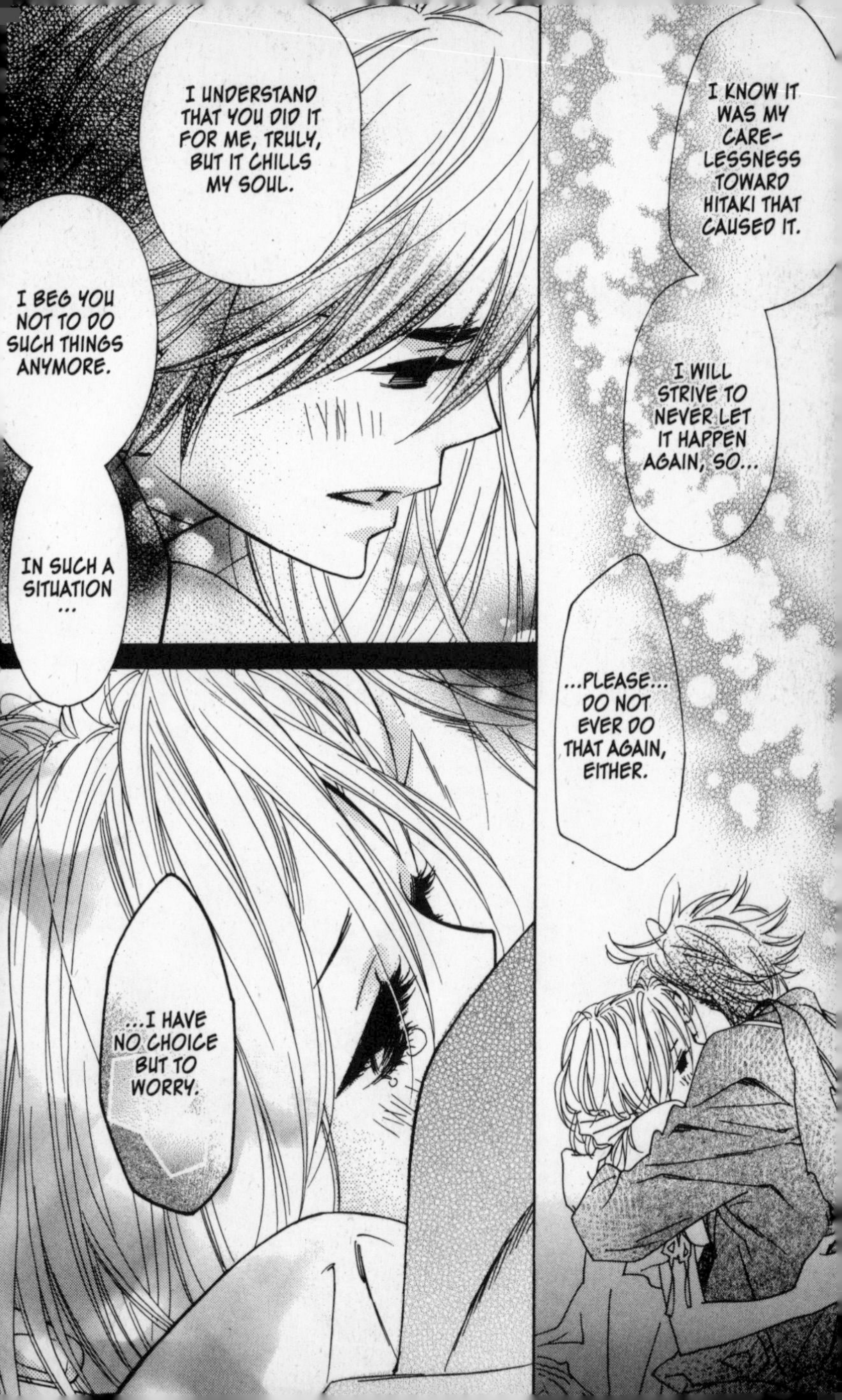
I KNOW IT WAS MY CARE-LESSNESS TOWARD HITAKI THAT CAUSED IT.
I WILL STRIVE TO NEVER LET IT HAPPEN AGAIN, SO...
...PLEASE... DO NOT EVER DO THAT AGAIN, EITHER.
I UNDERSTAND THAT YOU DID IT FOR ME, TRULY, BUT IT CHILLS MY SOUL.
I BEG YOU NOT TO DO SUCH THINGS ANYMORE.
IN SUCH A SITUATION ...
...I HAVE NO CHOICE BUT TO WORRY.

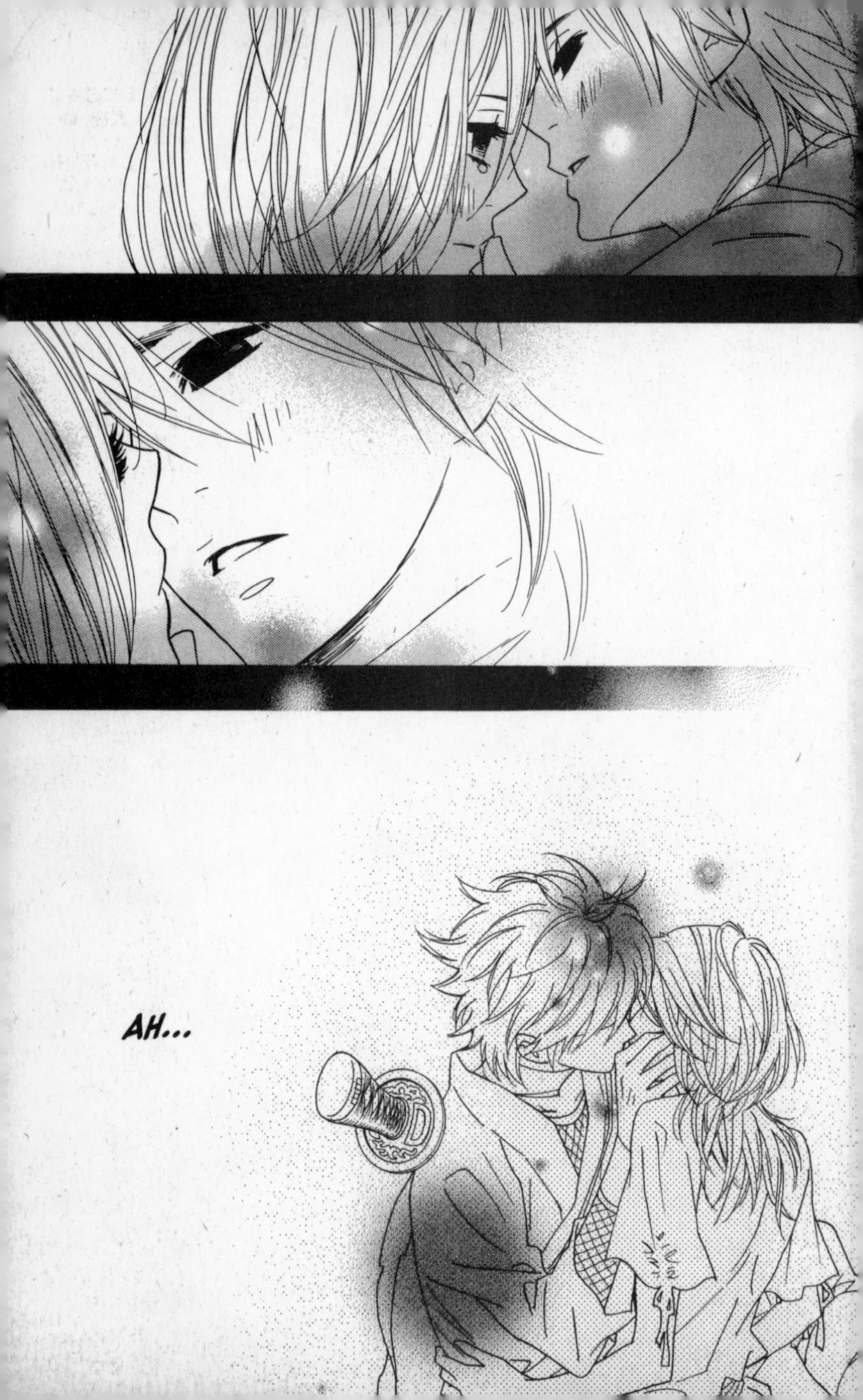
AH...

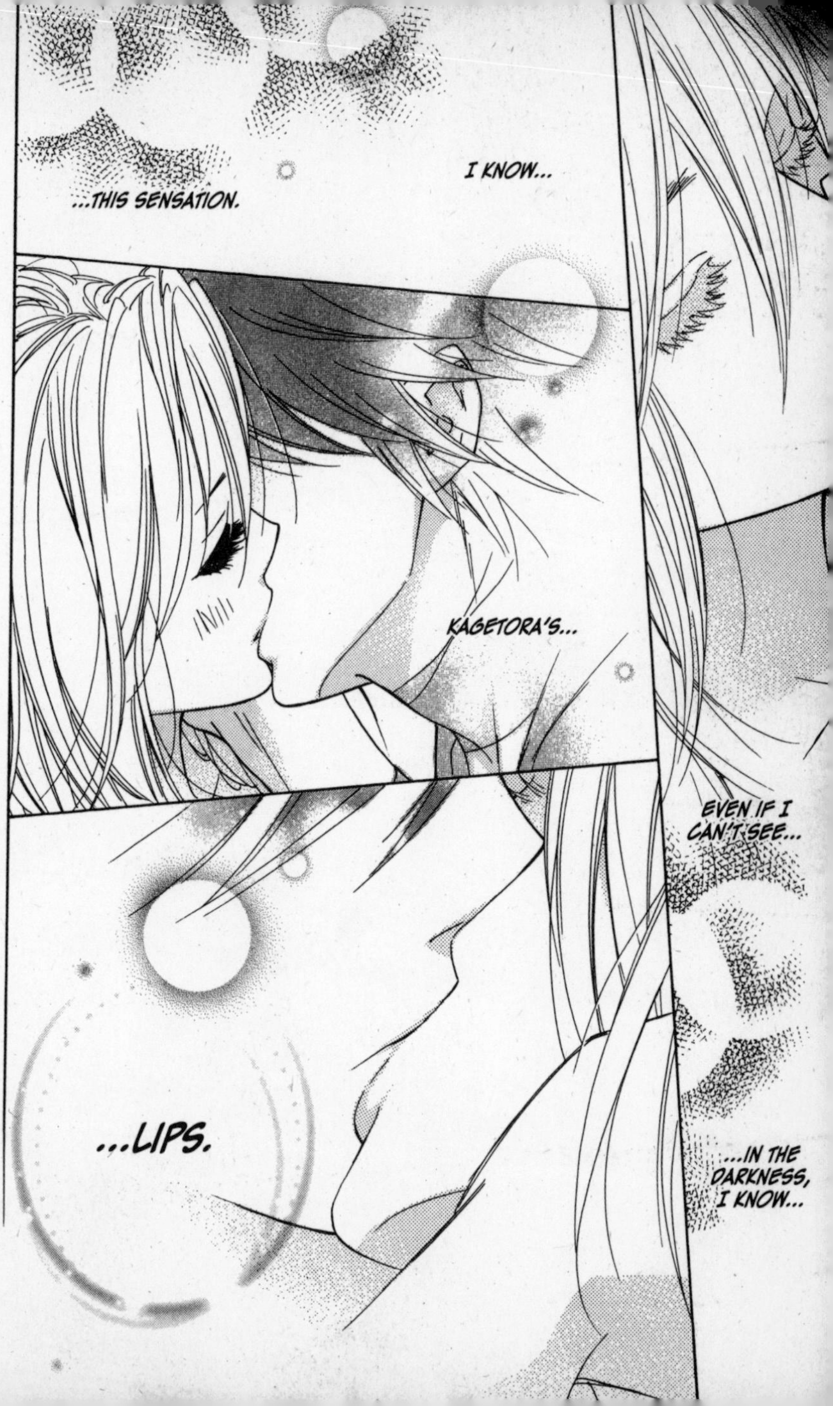
EVEN IF I CAN'T SEE...
...IN THE DARKNESS, I KNOW...
I KNOW...
...THIS SENSATION.
KAGETORA'S...
...LIPS.

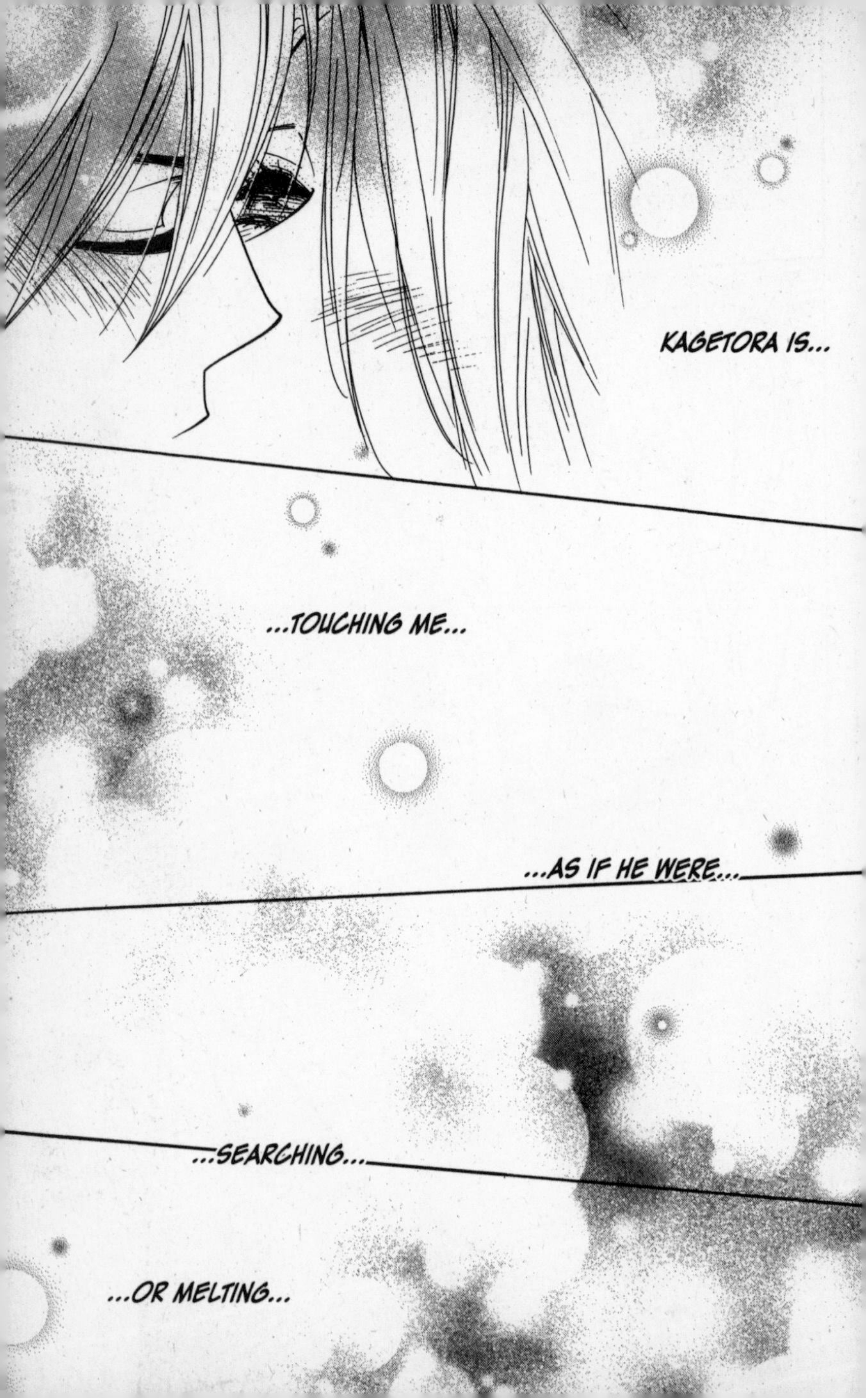
KAGETORA IS...
...TOUCHING ME...
...AS IF HE WERE...
...SEARCHING...
...OR MELTING...

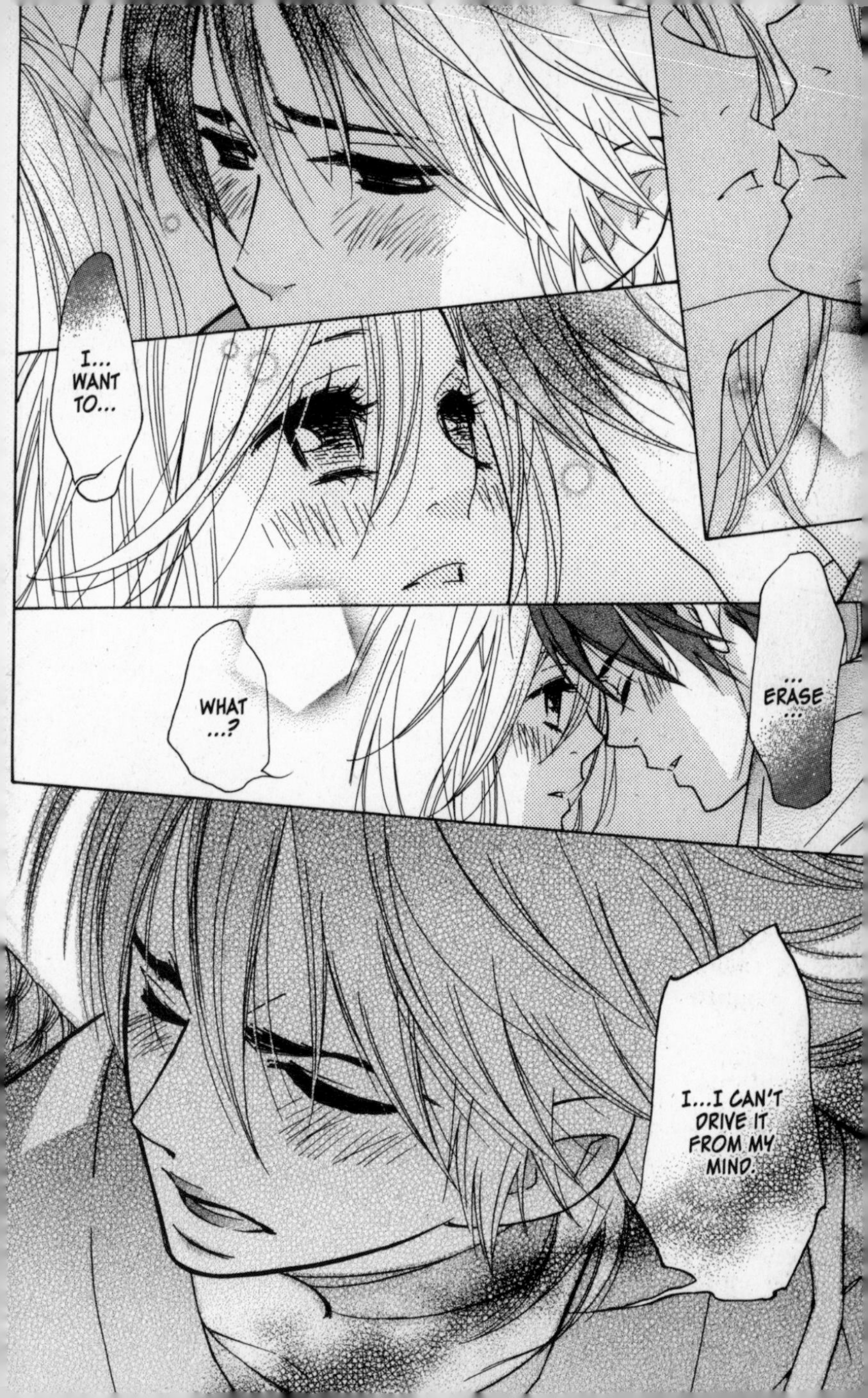
I... WANT TO...
...ERASE...
WHAT ...?
I...I CAN'T DRIVE IT FROM MY MIND.

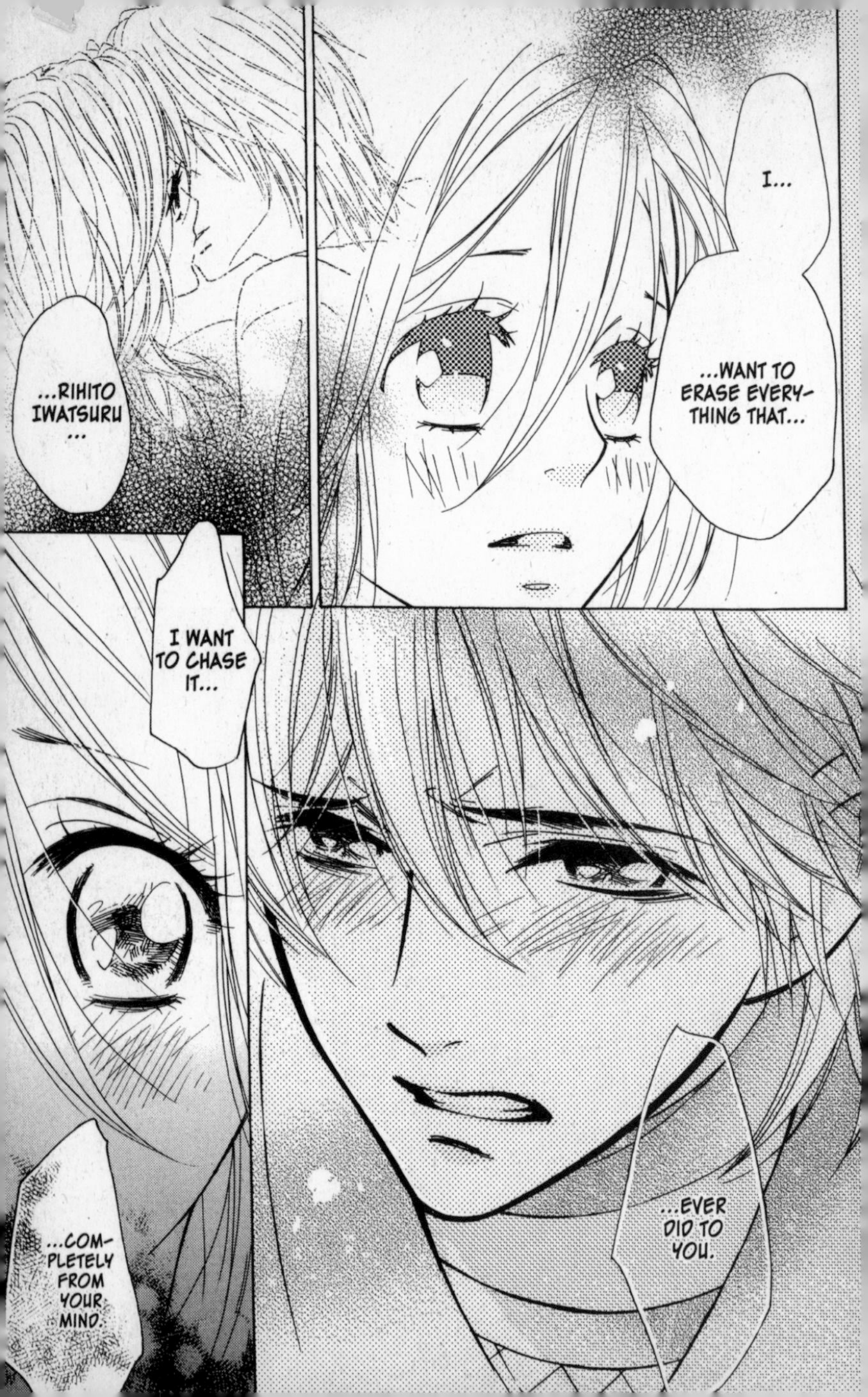
I...
...WANT TO ERASE EVERY-THING THAT...
...RIHITO IWATSURU ...
...EVER DID TO YOU.
I WANT TO CHASE IT...
...COM-PLETELY FROM YOUR MIND.

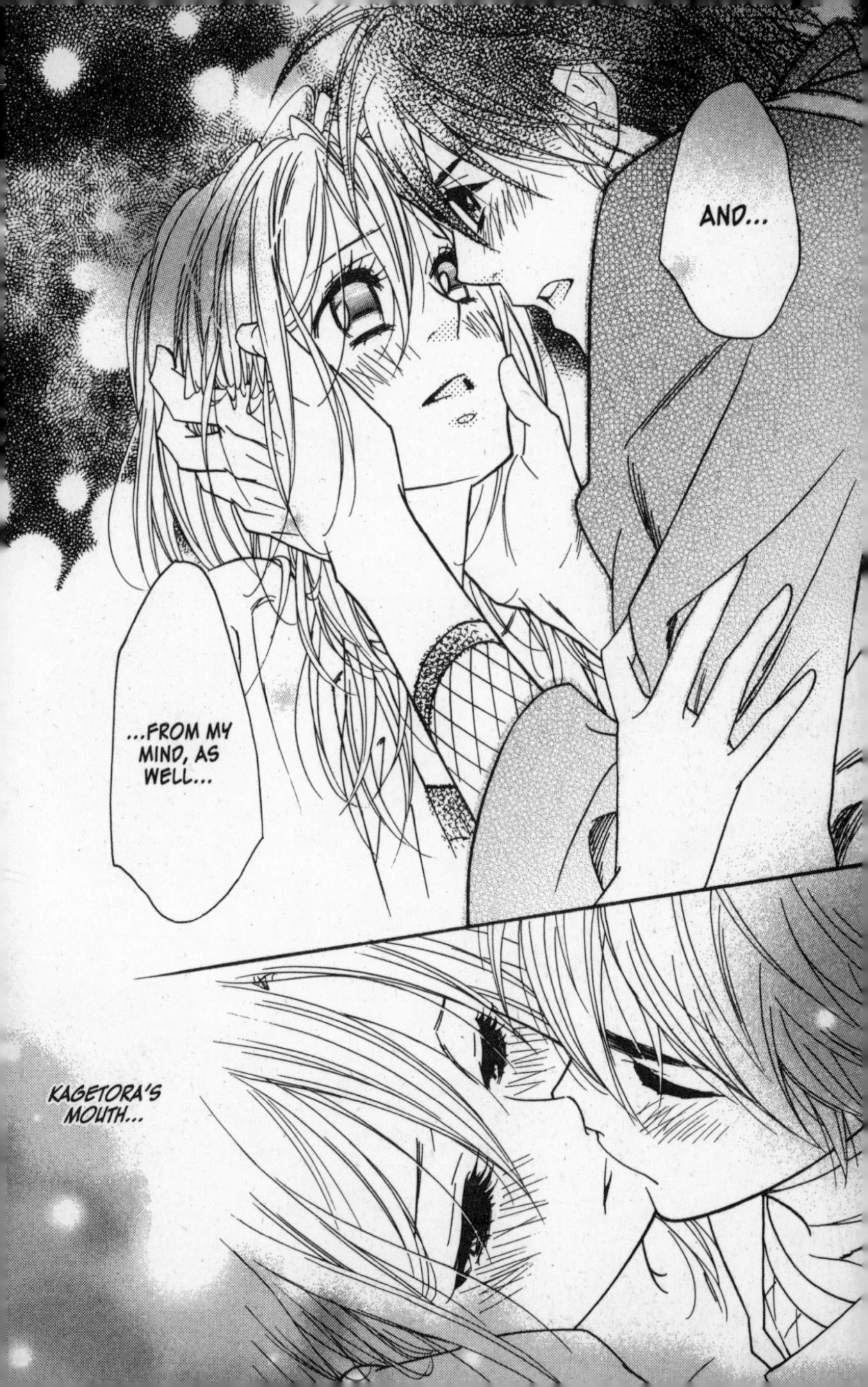
AND...
...FROM MY MIND, AS WELL...
KAGETORA'S MOUTH...

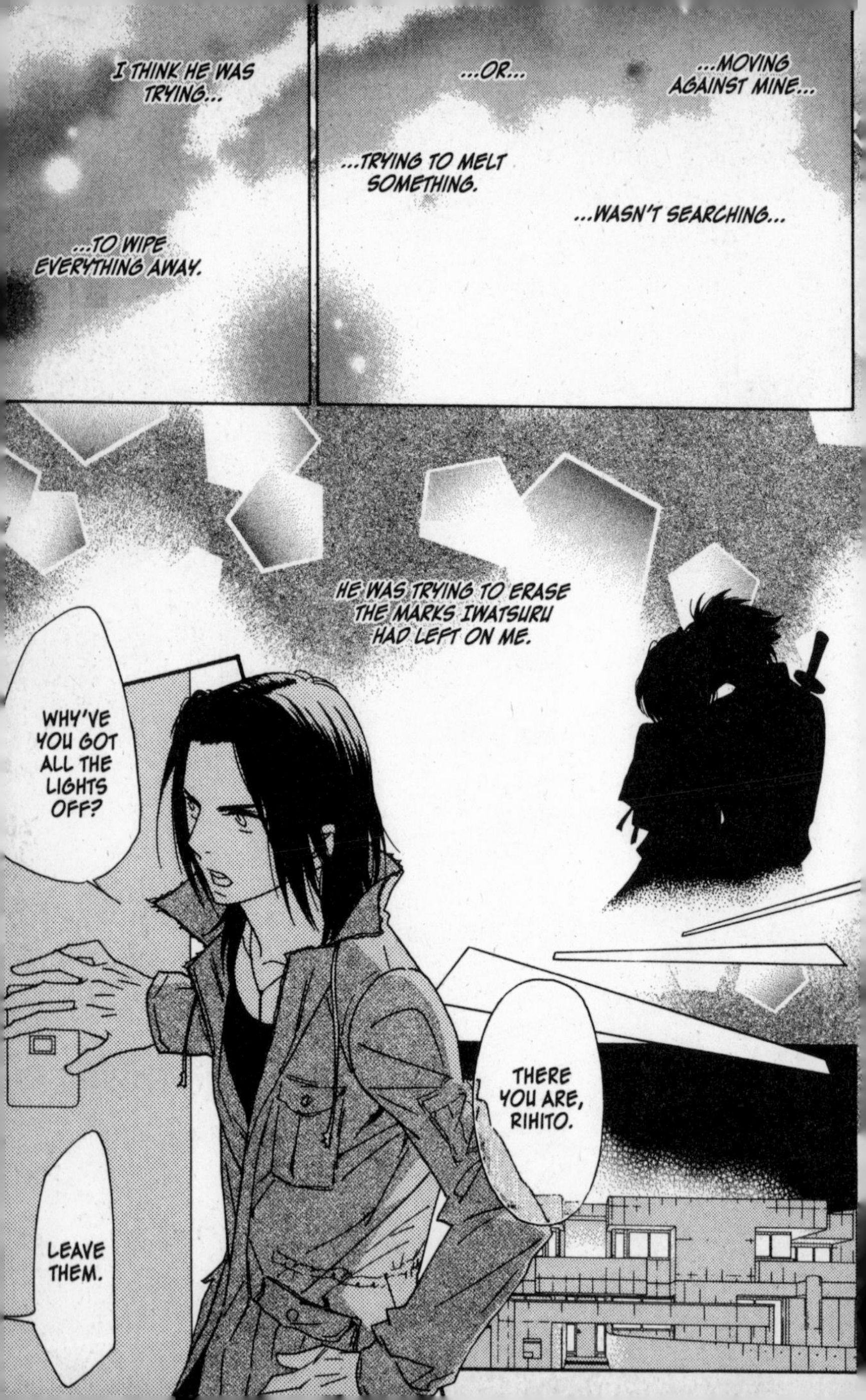
...MOVING AGAINST MINE...
...OR...
...WASN'T SEARCHING...
...TRYING TO MELT SOMETHING.
I THINK HE WAS TRYING...
...TO WIPE EVERYTHING AWAY.
HE WAS TRYING TO ERASE THE MARKS IWATSURU HAD LEFT ON ME.
THERE YOU ARE, RIHITO.
WHY'VE YOU GOT ALL THE LIGHTS OFF?
LEAVE THEM.

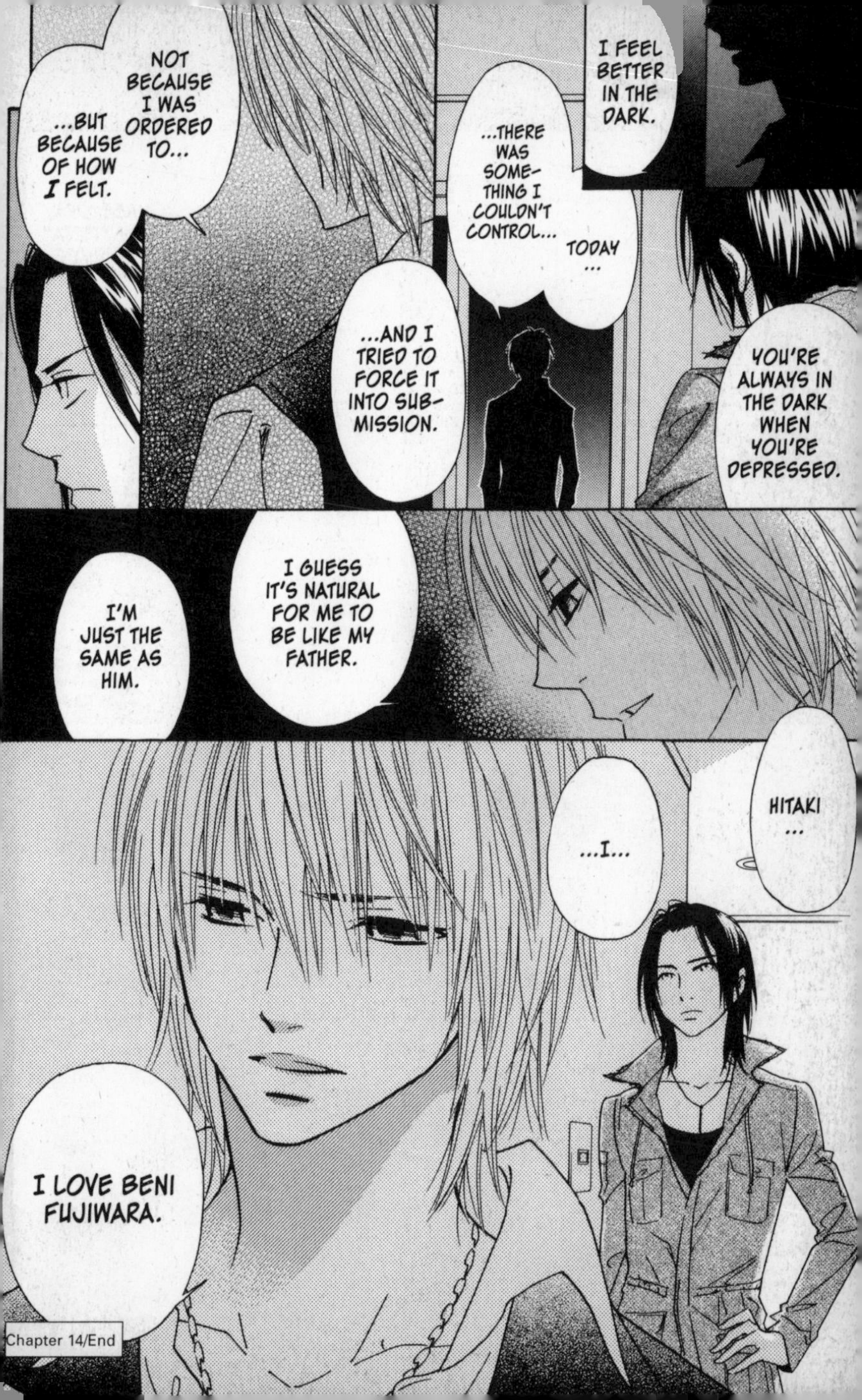
I FEEL BETTER IN THE DARK.
YOU'RE ALWAYS IN THE DARK WHEN YOU'RE DEPRESSED.
TODAY...
...THERE WAS SOMETHING I COULDN'T CONTROL...
...AND I TRIED TO FORCE IT INTO SUBMISSION.
NOT BECAUSE I WAS ORDERED TO...
...BUT BECAUSE OF HOW *I* FELT.
I GUESS IT'S NATURAL FOR ME TO BE LIKE MY FATHER.
I'M JUST THE SAME AS HIM.
HITAKI...
...I...
I LOVE BENI FUJIWARA.
Chapter 14/End

Bonus Manga! •Kagetora-kun the Ninja!•

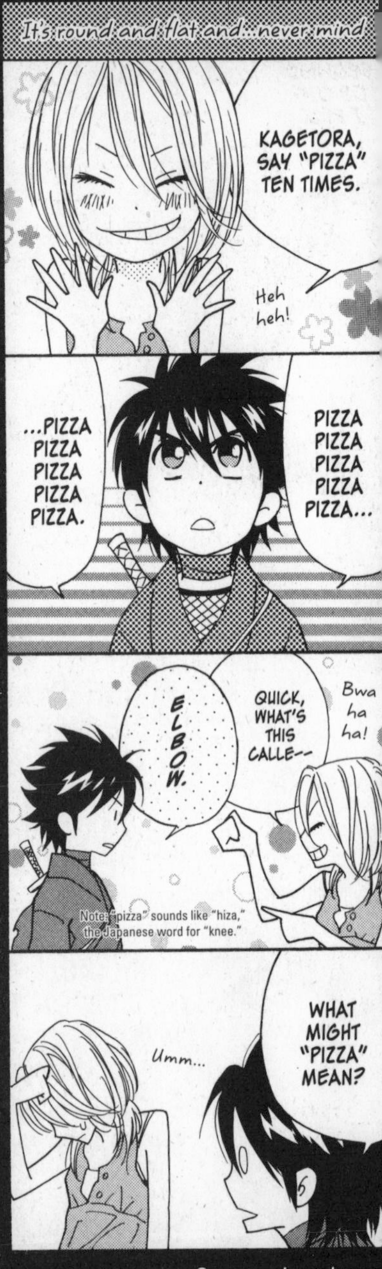
It's round and flat and... never mind
KAGETORA, SAY "PIZZA" TEN TIMES.
Heh heh!
PIZZA PIZZA PIZZA PIZZA PIZZA...
...PIZZA PIZZA PIZZA PIZZA PIZZA.
Bwa ha ha!
QUICK, WHAT'S THIS CALLE--
ELBOW.
Note: "pizza" sounds like "hiza," the Japanese word for "knee."
WHAT MIGHT "PIZZA" MEAN?
Umm...

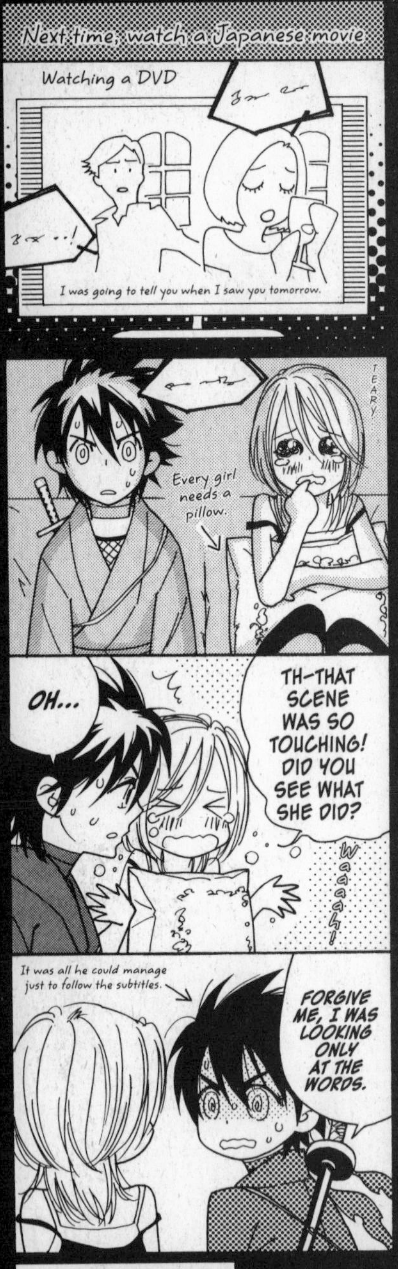
Next time, watch a Japanese movie
Watching a DVD
I was going to tell you when I saw you tomorrow.
TEARY
Every girl needs a pillow.
TH-THAT SCENE WAS SO TOUCHING! DID YOU SEE WHAT SHE DID?
OH...
Waaaaah!
FORGIVE ME, I WAS LOOKING ONLY AT THE WORDS.
It was all he could manage just to follow the subtitles.

Shinobi Life vol. 3/End

See you in volume 4

In the next volume of

HITAKI AND IWATSURU TEAM UP TO
GO AFTER BENI AGAIN, PROMPTING KAGETORA
TO MAKE A MAJOR DECISION--HE REFUSES
TO TAKE BENI'S FATHER'S ORDERS, AND
INSTEAD SWEARS THAT HIS ONLY LOYALTY
IS TO BENI HERSELF. WHEN HER FATHER IS
PREDICTABLY OUTRAGED, KAGETORA AND BENI
FLEE FROM THE FUJIWARA HOUSEHOLD. BUT
IT SEEMS UNLIKELY THAT THEY CAN REMAIN
SAFE AND HIDDEN TOGETHER FOR LONG,
ESPECIALLY WHEN IT IS REVEALED THAT BENI'S
FATHER MAY KNOW A LOT MORE ABOUT
THE TIME-SLIPPING INCIDENTS
THAN ANYONE IMAGINED...

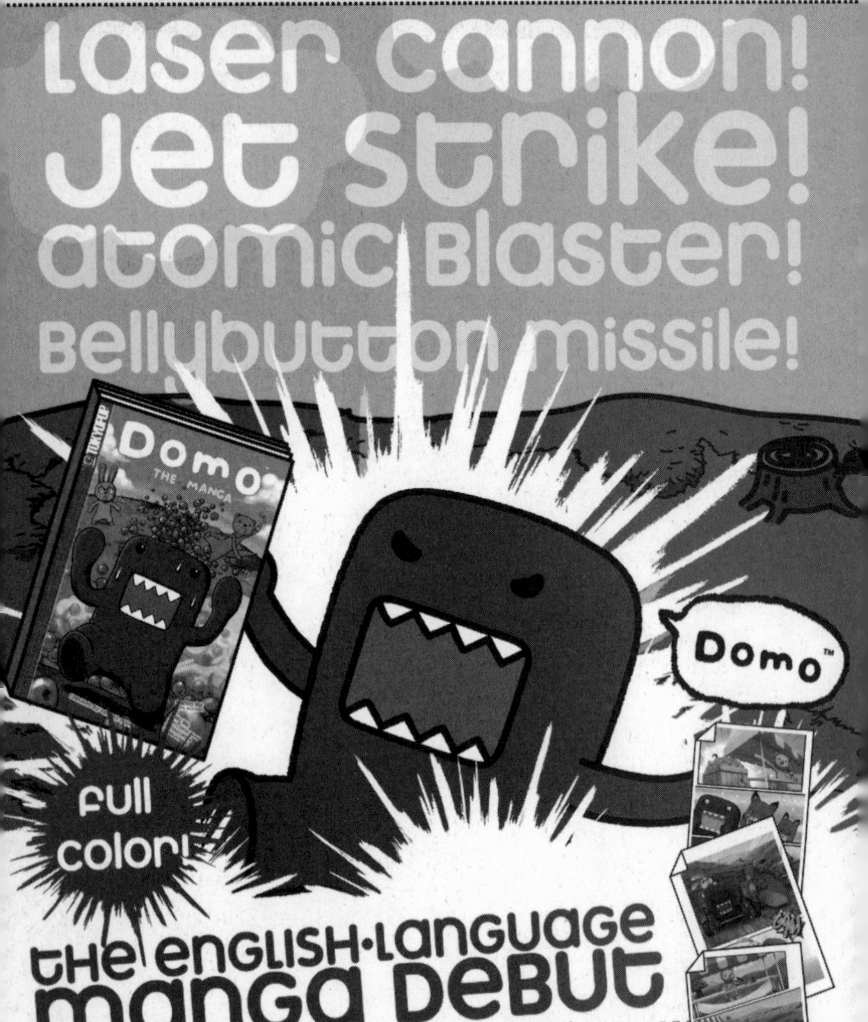
Laser Cannon!
Jet Strike!
Atomic Blaster!
Bellybutton Missile!
TOKYOPOP
Domo
THE MANGA
Domo™
full color!
The English-Language Manga Debut
of the world-famous Domo!
Invading stores everywhere!
PREVIEWS, CONTESTS, AND MORE AT WWW.TOKYOPOP.COM/DOMO_MANGA
DOMO © NHK-TYO 1998-2009. DOMO ANIMATION © DOMO PRODUCTION COMMITTEE. ALL RIGHTS RESERVED. WWW.DOMONATION.COM

STOP!

This is the back of the book.
You wouldn't want to spoil a great ending!

This book is printed "manga-style," in the authentic Japanese right-to-left format. Since none of the artwork has been flipped or altered, readers get to experience the story just as the creator intended. You've been asking for it, so TOKYOPOP® delivered: authentic, hot-off-the-press, and far more fun!

DIRECTIONS

If this is your first time reading manga-style, here's a quick guide to help you understand how it works.

It's easy... just start in the top right panel and follow the numbers. Have fun, and look for more 100% authentic manga from TOKYOPOP®!